T0299070

Lifting Productivity in Singapore's Retail and Food Services Sectors

The Role of Technology, Manpower and Marketing

Lifting Productivity in Singapore's Retail and Food Services Sectors

The Role of Technology, Manpower and Marketing

Mun Heng TOH
National University of Singapore, Singapore

W **World Scientific**

NEW JERSEY · LONDON · SINGAPORE · BEIJING · SHANGHAI · HONG KONG · TAIPEI · CHENNAI · TOKYO

Published by

World Scientific Publishing Co. Pte. Ltd.

5 Toh Tuck Link, Singapore 596224

USA office: 27 Warren Street, Suite 401-402, Hackensack, NJ 07601

UK office: 57 Shelton Street, Covent Garden, London WC2H 9HE

Library of Congress Cataloging-in-Publication Data
Names: Toh, Mun Heng, author.
Title: Lifting productivity in Singapore's retail and food services sectors :
    the role of technology, manpower and marketing / Mun Heng Toh (NUS, Singapore).
Description: 1 Edition. | New Jersey : World Scientific, [2017] |
    Includes bibliographical references and index.
Identifiers: LCCN 2017045431 | ISBN 9789813228313
Subjects: LCSH: Retail trade--Singapore--Management. | Food service--Singapore--Management.
Classification: LCC HF5429.6.S55 T63 2017 | DDC 658.8/7--dc23
LC record available at https://lccn.loc.gov/2017045431

British Library Cataloguing-in-Publication Data
A catalogue record for this book is available from the British Library.

Copyright © 2018 by World Scientific Publishing Co. Pte. Ltd.

All rights reserved. This book, or parts thereof, may not be reproduced in any form or by any means, electronic or mechanical, including photocopying, recording or any information storage and retrieval system now known or to be invented, without written permission from the publisher.

For photocopying of material in this volume, please pay a copying fee through the Copyright Clearance Center, Inc., 222 Rosewood Drive, Danvers, MA 01923, USA. In this case permission to photocopy is not required from the publisher.

For any available supplementary material, please visit
http://www.worldscientific.com/worldscibooks/10.1142/10664#t=suppl

Desk Editor: Shreya Gopi

Typeset by Stallion Press
Email: enquiries@stallionpress.com

Printed in Singapore

Contents

About the Author

Dr Mun Heng Toh is an economics professor specializing in the quantitative evaluation and assessment of public policies and programs. He is currently lecturing at the Department of Strategy & Policy, NUS Business School.

Professor Toh is a member of the Expert Group tasked to study the feasibility and implementation of the ASEAN-China Free Trade Agreement in 2001, and also a member of the Expert Group in 2008 to evaluate the feasibility of the ASEAN+6 free trade agreement. He served as Lead Economist at the Ministry of Trade and Industry from 2003 to 2005.

He is the recipient of the National Trade Union Congress 'Friend of Labor' Award in 2008, and was also awarded the Public Service Star in 2009's National Day Award.

Professor Toh obtained his doctoral degree in Economics and Econometrics from the University of London, London School of Economics. His research interests and publications are in the areas of development strategies of emerging economies in the Asia Pacific, econometric modelling, input-output analysis, international trade and investment, human resource development, and productivity measurement. He has substantive experience as an economic consultant for many international organization, private enterprises and governmental agencies.

Professor Toh has co-authored and edited several titles including *The Economics of Education and Manpower Development: Issues and Policies in Singapore; Health Policies in Singapore; Economic Impact of the Withdrawal of the GSP on Singapore; Challenge and Response: Thirty Years of the Economic Development Board; Public Policies in Singapore: A Decade of Changes; ASEAN Growth Triangles; Principles of Economics; Competitiveness of the Singapore Economy; Production Networks and Industrial Clusters: Integrating Economies in Southeast Asia; and Productivity in Singapore's Retail and Food Services Sectors.*

Acknowledgements

The author is grateful to the Singapore Productivity Centre (SPC) for commissioning and funding the research studies. Special thanks go to Mr Michael Tan (CEO of SPC), Dr Woon Kin Chung (former CEO of SPC), Ms Loo Ya Lee (former Director, Planning & Corporate Development), Ms Lim Sui Lan (Manager, Planning & Corporate Development) and Ms Goh Ying Hua (Manager, Marketing & Events) for rendering significant assistance in conjunction with the research studies and the production of this publication.

I am grateful for the advice from fellow academics and colleagues, and the hard work of the research assistants in conducting field work and preparing many useful drafts and notes. They are Lee Shi Xuan (Chapter 1); Professor Ruth Tan, Pearl Tan Hui Lin and Toh Hong Hao (Chapter 2); Lee Shisan (Chapter 3); Ng Jia Le and Lee Xinghui (Chapter 4); Wu Minfei, Terence Ng, and Jasmine Tan (Chapter 5); Germaine Goh (Chapter 6); Loh Soh Leng and Ching Hayden (Chapter 7); Hoang Mai Lan, Huynh Thi Quynh Nhu, Radhika Swaminathan and Wu Minfei (Chapter 8); Jin Riu Chuian (Chapter 9) and Lu Si Hong (Chapter 10). Their contributions provided the inputs that were critical for the research studies. Their help has made a somewhat arduous task become interesting and refreshing.

The author would also like to express his gratitude to the companies and the consumers who participated in the various surveys and interviews conducted to support and facilitate the studies. In particular, thanks to NTUC management and staff for the generosity in sharing the information and experience in the operation self-service checkout machines, which contribute positively to the knowledge of productivity improvement in the retail industry in Singapore.

Finally, the author would like to thank Ms Sim Ann, Senior Minister of State, Ministry of Trade and Industry for contributing the Foreword which reminds us of the pertinent effort of the government via the Industry Transformation Program, to help companies in the retail and food services sector in their journey of productivity improvement and transformation.

Foreword

Eating and shopping are often described as Singaporeans' favourite pastimes. As with consumers worldwide, Singaporeans have readily taken to new trends that have disrupted the Food Services and Retail industries, such as online shopping.

These trends, along with our domestic constraints on manpower resources, have significantly changed the way our Food Services and Retail businesses operate. Many companies have realised that they must update themselves to remain relevant.

As part of the $4.5 billion Industry Transformation Programme introduced during Budget 2016, the Food Services and Retail Industry Transformation Maps (ITMs) have been implemented to help companies on this journey. Both ITMs chart out strategies for companies in each sector to innovate, raise productivity, internationalise, and develop human capital to catalyse growth and stay competitive.

Since the launch of the ITMs in September 2016, we have seen encouraging progress in reshaping both sectors. Many companies in the Food Services and Retail industries have taken ownership of their transformation journeys to hone their competitive edge. I have seen a good number of SMEs achieve laudable results in uplifting firm-level productivity by applying technology, optimising manpower, and going omni-channel.

For the individual company, embarking on this journey alone can be a daunting task. I therefore applaud the Singapore Productivity Centre in producing this book. It provides insights from empirical research into effective strategies, and highlights key areas and pitfalls to look out for when implementing productivity measures.

I encourage you, especially if you are an SME owner or manager in the Food Services or Retail industries, to study the findings captured in the 10 chapters. I hope they will serve as a useful guide for you in making informed decisions in building business capabilities, and in becoming more successful and productive.

Sim Ann
Senior Minister of State for Trade and Industry,
and Culture, Community and Youth

Preface

The Singapore Productivity Centre (SGPC) is a one-stop competency centre set up under the auspices of the Future Economy Council, previously known as the National Productivity Council. SGPC's mission is to drive productivity for sustained growth and competitiveness for enterprises in the services sector, starting with Food Services, Retail, and Hotel sectors.

To transform enterprises in these sectors, SGPC provides a comprehensive range of services and solutions, targeted to deliver tangible results. These include in-depth productivity and business consultancy, workshops and masterclasses and overseas study missions to learn best practices. SGPC is also a resource centre with research and publications of benchmarking studies, applied research and case studies.

Having assisted over 1,000 companies through its various initiatives, SGPC hopes to demystify the concept of productivity and innovation, thereby promoting a better understanding of its efforts to help transform enterprises to be future-proof and future-ready.

This publication, consisting of 10 chapters, serves to provide insights on Technology, Manpower and Marketing measures being rolled out to improve the productivity of small and medium enterprises (SMEs) in the Retail and Food Services sectors. Holistically, this book outlines key four-fold issues that are pertinent to productivity improvement in the retail and F&B sectors, requiring the buy-in of Business Owners, Customers and Employees. Collectively, Awareness, Manpower, Economies of Scale and Technology Anxiety, form the four-fold framework that needs to be addressed successfully to ensure sustainable productivity improvement over the long haul. Individually, each chapter deep-dives into specific measures being adopted and its effectiveness, providing policy recommendations and suggestions in refining the rollout of these measures.

The findings in this publication will be particularly useful and actionable for companies in the Retail and Food Services sectors seeking to implement various productivity improvement measures, especially SMEs. Policy-makers in these two sectors will also find the substantive content useful. Consultants, trainers and students with an interest in these sectors will also benefit from the insights put together in this book.

Dr Ahmad Mohd Magad
Chairman
Singapore Productivity Centre

Introduction

Continuous productivity improvement is essential for countries to stay on edge. While many countries have been growing at positive rates over the past few years, several are still grappling with ways to improve productivity. A recent study done by the Boston Consultancy Group and the National Association of Manufacturers indicated that while US manufacturers stated productivity improvement as a top priority, several manufacturers have not implemented any rigorous solutions to step up productivity, and have rather depended on traditional levers to steer improvement. As a result of this, the productivity growth has remained rather slow. The study further indicated that key reason for this is the lack of urgency when it comes to productivity improvement-related decisions. In the Singapore context, Deputy Prime Minister Tharman Shanmugaratnam recently noted that while there are several innovations being carried out by industry leaders, it takes a very long for these innovations to sink in to the operations of smaller companies, thereby warranting a need to speed up the learning process. All of these collectively indicate the need for enterprises to adopt a proactive approach and have a disciplined business plan for the execution of productivity improvement projects.

As such, the Singapore government has been continuously making efforts to improve productivity in the economy. This book is part of this effort, and it aims to familiarize enterprise owners, managers and other stakeholders about tools that enterprises could utilize in order to boost productivity. These tools range from the use of mobile applications to a more fundamental change in the mind-set to do business, like the implementation of Lean Philosophy. Furthermore, the book also provides a useful compilation of case studies of Singapore businesses that have incorporated these tools into their business, and their implementation stories. Hence, this book not just provides a primer to productivity-improvement tools, but is also relevant to the Singaporean business context.

Efforts to boost productivity are not new to the Singapore commercial scene. Singapore has been encouraging productivity-led growth since the 1970s. One of the earliest efforts includes the passing of the National Productivity Bill in 1972 in order to promote the National Productivity Centre under EDB to a full statutory board, the National Productivity Board. In as early as 1981, the government promoted a "total productivity approach" to inculcate productivity consciousness. Particularly with Singapore being a primarily foreign-investments and foreign-labor dependent economy, there has always been pressure to keep improving value-add per worker, such that more output could be generated with less input.

Since 2010, the government has introduced numerous measures on several fronts, including innovation-related incentives, tax benefits as well as wage- and manpower-related measures. Some of the key measures in this regard include: Initiatives for Industry-Wide Collaboration, Productivity and Innovation Credit, and Workfare Income Supplement. The initiative for industry-wide collaboration encourages several firms to share their productivity improvement stories with other enterprises as well as co-invest with much larger organizations, in projects that improve productivity. The Productivity and Innovation Credit (PIC) is a hallmark initiative that has encouraged several firms to implement productivity-enhancing investments in their operations. The PIC scheme allows enterprises to obtain a 400% tax credit whenever they make an investment which is related to R&D, automation and other productivity-enhancing activities.

The Workfare Income Supplement allows enterprises to retain older, low-wage employees, thereby reducing the need to employ new employees and retrain them.

As emphasized earlier, this book aims to provide readers with information about a wide variety of productivity-enhancing tools that are available in Singapore. The following paragraphs provide a brief overview of the different chapters.

Chapter 1 investigates the pervasiveness of the practice of lean management principles and concepts among enterprises in the F&B and retail sectors in Singapore. Results from the studies have reflected the lack of awareness on Lean Principle in business enterprises, as well as a lack of proper service and inventory management which ultimately affects the implementation of Lean. This chapter therefore elucidates means that managers can adopt to inculcate Lean thinking into the overall culture of the enterprise.

Chapter 2 examines the trend of Self-service Technology (SST) in the supermarket industry and investigates customers' sentiment toward the change, through the use of surveys, interviews as well as observational field studies. Furthermore, the 8M productivity framework is used to craft recommendations on how to encourage the use of SST. In particular, the focus is on the following five factors — Manpower, Message, Make, Method and Management.

Chapter 3 serves as an extension of Chapter 2, as it examines the application of SSTs to the food and beverage industry. An overall study of the pervasiveness of SST usage in the F&B sector indicates that there is still room to increase adoption of SSTs to improve productivity. This chapter indicates that restaurant owners should be extremely careful while choosing the type of SSTs and the technology platforms to be adopted. The suitability of a particular type of SST varies depending on the size and mode of operation.

RFID is touted to be a game changer by industry leaders as a result of the plethora of productivity benefits it brings along. Chapter 4 assesses the applicability of RFID technology in retail and F&B enterprises in Singapore. It was found that cost of infrastructure, lack of global standards and lack of awareness are key reasons for the lukewarm adoption. The chapter delves into possible policy suggestions of how Singapore SMEs[1] can use RFID technology to achieve a leaner supply chain and achieve sustainable increases in productivity.

Chapter 5 considers some of the major shared services practiced in Food and Beverage (F&B) service sector in Singapore and examines their role in productivity improvement. The chapter also examines the issues of government subsidies in encouraging use of these shared services. A total of four shared services have been covered in this paper: an internal shared services, Central Kitchen (CK) and three other industry shared services, Centralised Dishwashing Services, and Part-time Pool Program (PPP).

Chapter 6 seeks to examine the current development of 3D printing technology and provides some insights into the current local market through case studies. The results of this study show that more can be done to promote the growth and adoption of 3D printing technology among companies at this stage although the technology is still new and growing. Some key problems and challenge at present include the lack of industry standards, safety regulations and also the lack of cohesiveness in the industry.

Chapter 7 examines how M-commerce can be a strategy for retailers with physical stores to improve their revenue performance and profitability and ways to increase adoption of mobile commerce. This was done by interviewing both retailers and consumers to understand their concerns in M-commerce. With this, recommendations on how to improve M-commerce are crafted to aid in resolving challenges that arise from both consumers and retailers.

Prevailing issues in cash management that have not been recognized or addressed properly by companies. Chapter 8 analyses the effectiveness of cash management technologies and recommends different models which could be tailored to different types of retail and F&B businesses.

Chapter 9 aims to consolidate insights on how businesses utilize job redesign to ease manpower shortage and improve service standards. Primary research indicated that almost all of the SMEs which responded have implemented some form of flexible work arrangements and replaced repetitive tasks with automation, and these were mostly efforts which do not require much capital investment. The chapter concludes that embracing flexible work arrangements under job redesign is the way forward for Singapore SMEs in the retail and food services sectors.

In Chapter 10, the loyalty card situation in Singapore is analyzed. Case studies on the NTUC Plus! card and The Soup Spoon are developed as representative firms of the retail and F&B industries respectively. The main takeaway from the two case studies is the importance of the formation of a brand web and product loyalty. Policies employing Message, Management and Method of the 8M Framework are then presented for SMEs to adopt should they want to implement loyalty card programs or develop existing loyalty card program further.

Overall, it is hoped that the book will provide readers with a better perspective of the several tools and platforms that assist companies to enhance their productivity, and moreover, it is hoped that the book motivates business owners to incorporate some of these measures into their own businesses too.

Endnote

1. In Singapore, SMEs refer to enterprises with annual sales turnover of not more than S$100 million, or employment not more than 200 workers. They are further categorised based on their annual sales turnover. A micro-SME refers to firms with an annual sales turnover less than S$1million in annual revenue (Waytogo, 2014)

Chapter 1

The Use of Lean Management Principle and Practices for Productivity Improvement in the Retail and Food Services Sectors of Singapore

1. Introduction

Lean Principle was known to originate from the Japanese manufacturing industry. John Krafcik coined the term in his master's thesis, "Triumph of the Lean Production System", when he was doing his research at MIT Sloan School of Management in 1988.

Lean is a business-improvement initiative that best fits in the organizational culture of an enterprise (Sayer and Williams, 2010). In Lean management, you pursue the ideal state of value flow chain with minimal waste and maximal value. The logic of Lean management in an enterprise should be based on a philosophy of continuous improvement and the resilience to perfect all service processes (Oakland, 2014). The fundamental concept of Lean management in an enterprise follows the logic (Lean Enterprise Research Centre, 2015):

(a) *Deliver value from your customers' perspective:* This refers to delivering the value of a product from the end customers' perspective. In this way, waste processes that are non-value-added can be removed.

(b) *Identify and map the value stream:* The value stream encompasses all the service processes and activities included in the organization that were involved in the product or service delivery process. Once the first step of identifying customers' wants has been achieved, the next step is to examine what processes are needed for the delivery to be successful.

(c) *Eliminate waste (Muda in Japanese):* Physically mapping out a value stream renders the visualization of waste easier. And by eliminating these wastes, services or products can reach the customers smoothly.

(d) *Respond to customer pull:* Responding to customer pull refers to understanding the customers' demand on your service and creating a process to it. A Lean organization would produce when the customer wants the product or service at the right time, at the right amount.

(e) *Continuous improvements (Kaizen):* To inculcate Lean philosophy into the enterprise, one has to be resilient in terms of moving their enterprise toward a perfect value stream system free of waste.

Lean Principle is now believed to be applicable not only in the manufacturing industry, but also in the service industry. Lean Principle can be carried out through concept of standardizing work process to make the visualization of waste easier and developing the critical thinking skills of members in a team (Ross, 2013). Evident from the concept of Lean Principle, the applicability of the Principle can be ubiquitous in most other sectors.

In the current study, we intend to explore and evaluate the extent of Lean Principles being applied in on the Retail and Food

Services Sectors in Singapore. It is envisaged that through the implementation of Lean Principle, organizations would be able to create processes that require less resources, thereby achieving efficiency in terms of their strategy deployment, large batch processes and operation management (SMU, 2010). This study also aims to highlight the importance of Lean management as an effective business strategy for firms in both the Retail and Food Services Industry. Through successful case studies, it would demonstrate the positive effects of using Lean management within a firm.

The chapter is organized into five parts. In Section 2, a literature review has been conducted to further elucidate the features and principles of Lean Principle. Five main principles of Lean thinking will be explained, followed by the elaboration of a few Lean tools and how they can help an enterprise to transit to a Lean organization. In Section 3, the methodology of the research adopted is presented, followed by analysis of the interview and survey results gathered. In Section 4, we conclude the chapter with some possible recommendations and solutions to the problems identified in the analysis.

2. Literature Review

Lean Principle originated from the manufacturing industry, and therefore many may believe that its applicability is limited to the manufacturing industry. However, contrary to popular belief, Lean Principle has been able to transcend the productivity in sectors such as healthcare, banking and finance, airlines and public sectors in other countries (Damrath, 2012).

We begin the literature review with the discussion on the application of Lean concepts in a manufacturing setting to that of an enterprise in the service-oriented environment. Following that, we particularize the applicability of the Lean Principle to the Retail and Food Services sectors. We review how the use Lean tools can help to streamline daily operations and maximize the operating efficiency of a business.

2.1 *Lean principle in service*

There are five main principles of Lean thinking adopted in manufacturing activities that can be modified and made relevant to enterprises in the services sector. The five principles that an enterprise intend on embracing Lean philosophy in their business activities include (Damrath, 2012):

(1) *Value*: The value of the end product that will be delivered to the customers.
(2) *Value stream*: The value chain system of the service delivery process to be optimized.
(3) *Flow*: Value flow will be less visible due to the intangibility of the service procedures and delivery process.
(4) *Pull*: In a service environment it means to delivery service upon customers' demand, similar to Just-in-Time (JIT).
(5) *Perfection*: To achieve perfection through Kaizen, continuous improvements can be transferred to the service organization.

For the services industry, the adoption of the five principles originally developed for the manufacturing industries carries risk of misinterpretation of concepts. Hence, it is paramount for the enterprise to appreciate the five main principles and decipher the concepts with a focus for a service organization with caution (Bicheno, 2008).

It may be too generic to simply apply "Lean Management" to the whole organization. As identified by Dr. Chen, three of the main managerial domains of an enterprise that affects competitiveness are Inventory Management, Supply Chain Management and Service Management (Ming-Chuan University, 2015). To ensure a holistic analysis of competitiveness, "Leadership Management" has been added to the aforementioned three criteria. To incorporate the notion of Lean philosophy into business operations, Leadership Management will have to cover the intangible area of the business strategy. For example, Leadership Management entails the management of workers' emotions, morale and mentality. The notion of continuous improvement (*Kaizen*) and the emphasis on the mentality of "doing the right thing, right the first time, every time" requires close monitoring in order to ensure high productivity of employees (Mukherjee, 2006).

Inventory Management involves the monitoring and controlling of ordering, storage and use of items in the production line (Investopedia, 2015). It is one of the key managerial domains of a business to remain competitive. To be able to manage the inventory of an enterprise efficiently will allow a business to remain strategic (Russell and Taylor, 2006).

Supply Chain Management is the management of the flow of products from the time the customer orders the product to the time the product reaches the customer. It is the active management of supply chain activities to maximize customer value for a business to sustain competitive advantage (Handfield, 2011).

Service is a coherent and standardized set of processes that allow customers to value the end product. The purpose of Service Management is to reduce cost incurred by integrating products and services to maximize the value of supply chain (Business Dictionary, 2015). A more intensive utilization of technology will allow shorter service time and lower customers' turnover rate. The settings of an enterprise should allow services to be continuous and competent enough to meet the needs of the customers (University of California, 2015). The extent of lean practices in service through the various processes such as multifunctional teams, good service technology and standardized procedures will allow an enterprise to maximize profits at minimal cost.

As elaborated above, these factors (i.e. Leadership, Supply Chain, Inventory and Service Management) are indispensable for a competitive, strategic and productive business enterprise (Russell and Taylor, 2006). The incorporation of Lean management can be spearheaded through these four managerial domains. Through these channels, the concept, implementation and effectiveness of Lean Management can better understood and appreciated.

2.1.1. *Lean wastes in service*

The concept of Lean wastes in service sectors is analogous to that in manufacturing environments. To be on the right path of engaging lean philosophy, the enterprise has to rigorously recognize the correct types of waste relevant to a service environment (Damrath, 2012).

(1) *Duplication*: Re-entering of data and repeating details that were not done well the first time (Arfmann and Federico, 2014).
(2) *Defects*: Service that does not conform to customers' needs (such as imperfect items) (Damrath, 2012).
(3) *Delay*: Customers waiting for service delivery (Arfmann and Federico, 2014).
(4) *Lost opportunity to win customers*: Poor service quality due to unfriendliness (Arfmann and Federico, 2014).
(5) *Motion*: Poor layout and planning in terms of service delivery processes or Value Stream Mapping (VSM), which results in unnecessary work done (Damrath, 2012).
(6) *Inventories*: Any work process that is in excess of what is needed for the customer, pending request and queues (Tepsich, 2010).
(7) *Errors in the service transaction*: Including product damage in product–service bundle (Arfmann and Federico, 2014).

The aforementioned seven service wastes are an evolution from the traditional wastes as seen in the manufacturing environment. We consider the wastes in a service organization on those resources that are untapped or overproduced due to ineffective planning for their value stream system.

2.2 *Application of Lean within the retail industry*

Within the retail industry, Lean retail is a modern operating strategy that focuses on maximum efficiency and the elimination of waste (Lukic, 2012). It first requires modern Lean thinking in the business model, which would then gradually inculcate into the Lean organizational culture overall.

The above provides the transition of thinking in traditional business models to the current Lean retail thinking. This approach allows the owner to exhibit values of a Lean leader through a continuous improvement mindset, to effectively utilize resources to

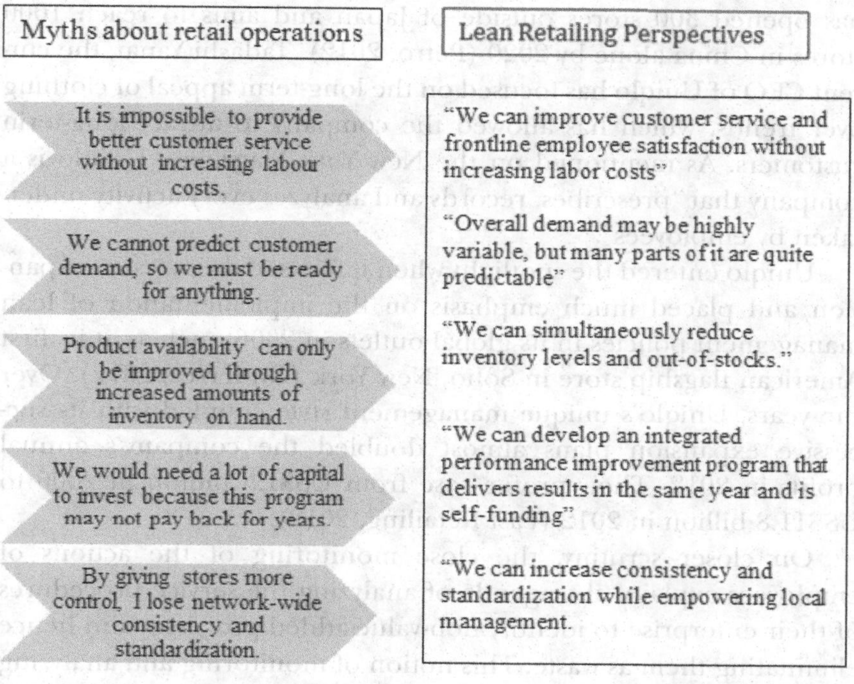

Myths about retail operations	Lean Retailing Perspectives
It is impossible to provide better customer service without increasing labour costs.	"We can improve customer service and frontline employee satisfaction without increasing labor costs"
We cannot predict customer demand, so we must be ready for anything.	"Overall demand may be highly variable, but many parts of it are quite predictable"
Product availability can only be improved through increased amounts of inventory on hand.	"We can simultaneously reduce inventory levels and out-of-stocks."
We would need a lot of capital to invest because this program may not pay back for years.	"We can develop an integrated performance improvement program that delivers results in the same year and is self-funding"
By giving stores more control, I lose network-wide consistency and standardization.	"We can increase consistency and standardization while empowering local management.

Figure 1: Lean Retailing: Myths about Retail Operations vs. Lean Retail Thinking

Source: Lean Retailing: Achieving Breakthroughs in Store Profitability. McKinsey & Company.

meet organizational goals and to promote a culture of improvement within the organization.

As the core idea behind Lean retail is the elimination of waste, it focuses on improving operational efficiency (Lukic, 2012). This involves techniques such as simplifying the design of work and the use of a demand-pull to stimulate stock replenishment within the business. It also focuses on removing bottlenecks such as delivery time, quality control etc. throughout the supply chain. Furthermore, Lean retail also focuses on an Effective Consumer Response (ECR) strategy, which aims to retrieve data on consumer demand. This is because retailers need to match inventory movement with consumer demand to reduce waste.

Uniqlo, founded by Tadashi Yanai, Japan's richest man, is a company well known for its Lean production and management. Uniqlo has opened 300 stores outside of Japan and aims to reach 1000 stores in China alone by 2020 (Petro, 2012). Tadashi Yanai, the current CEO of Uniqlo has focused on the long-term appeal of clothing over trends, which has allowed the company to attract long-term customers. As mentioned on the New York Magazine, Uniqlo is a company that "prescribes, records and analyzes every activity undertaken by employees".

Uniqlo entered the spotlight when it focused on overseas expansion and placed much emphasis on the implementation of lean management policies in its global outlets in 2006, such as at its first American flagship store in Soho, New York (Gutierrez, 2012). Over the years, Uniqlo's unique management style coupled with its successive expansion plans almost doubled the company's annual profits in 2012. Their profits rose from US$1.5 billion in 2006 to US$11.8 billion in 2012 (Fast Retailing, 2012).

On closer scrutiny, the close monitoring of the actions of employees explains the agenda of analyzing the service procedures of their enterprise to identify non-value-added processes and hence eliminating them as waste. This notion of monitoring and analyzing allows us to see the inextricable link with the lean tool, VSM. VSM proposed the elimination of non-value-added processes in the supply chain, to increase productivity and efficiency (Raisanen, 2013), linking quite closely to how Uniqlo has implemented Lean practices into its business model.

Apart from VSM, Uniqlo has also applied several strategies within Lean retail, as mentioned above. Its business model is to market basic, stylish items in an affordable manner, and it invests heavily in training of staff. Uniqlo's management also focuses primarily on tools such as the Lean philosophy and *Kaizen*. The management focuses less on a hierarchical system and often encourages employees to suggest ways for continuous improvement. The agenda of a flat power structure and transparent management is to drive the enterprise, on a whole scale level, to embrace *Kaizen* (New York Magazine, 2009). It is evident that Uniqlo has modernized its business model by adapting to a Lean thinking and a Lean organizational culture, by having a mindset of continuous improvement.

2.3 *Application of Lean within the F&B industry*

Back in 2009, the iconic coffee chain Starbucks adopted the Lean transformation in an attempt to improve business profits after the financial crisis. Howard Schultz, the CEO of Starbucks, wanted to transform the Starbucks experience and streamline operations to make it cost effective (Bloomberg, 2008). Part of this transformation included improving the management of the company to support customer-focused initiatives, in line with the Lean Principle of focusing on effectively delivering value to your customer. Customer-focused initiatives also included better in-store visuals and better training and tools for its workers (Bloomberg, 2008).

To improve the Starbucks experience, store managers had to analyze how the baristas move and where ingredients are located, in order to reduce queue lengths. Furthermore, as part of the lean practice, stores have implemented color coding of items to identify them more efficiently, and this has helped to smoothen the coffee making process. Consequently, the smoother coffee making process allows the same number of baristas to produce a higher amount of coffee. For example, in one of the stores at Oregon, the store manager was asked to make coffee and alter the arrangement of the items at the same time. It managed to reduce the preparation time by 36%, from 25 seconds to 16 seconds. The store, which boasts to hold the fastest coffee-making timing in town, was astounded by the time reduction to prepare a drink after the adjustments. The store also experienced a 10% increase in transaction rate with the reduced preparation time (WSJ, 2009). Another store in Chicago implemented color coding of items to reduce the preparation time of coffee. With reduced waiting time, the store also received positive feedback, having an increase in customer satisfaction scores from 56% to 76% (WSJ, 2009).

In other words, productivity has increased ever since the implementation of the new methods. From the Lean perspective, the practices of labeling and the relocation of items are part of the effort to reduce waste due to "motion". As mentioned above, the waste (i.e. motion) is due to the poor layout and planning of service processes.

By embracing such a Lean approach toward their service procedures, not only can the store reduce waste on "motion" but also reduce waste on "delay" and "errors in service transaction". This approach has allowed better quality products, less waiting time and a less crowded cafe. Evidently, with the reduced waiting time, the store also had received an increase in the customer satisfaction scores.

Such observation and analysis of the value stream in the service procedure, in this case of coffee making, has successfully eliminated waste on motion and managed to boost the stores transactions and, in turn, store revenue (WSJ, 2009). This productivity improvement has allowed Starbucks to cut costs to a better-than-expected profit in the third quarter of the year. Starbucks has successfully reduced costs by $175 million in the quarter, way above the expected $150 million in the US (WSJ, 2009).

Another factor worth mentioning about Starbucks is the resilient mentality continuous improvement, Kaizen. Mr. Heydon, the company's vice president of lean thinking, has mentioned on the Wall Street Journal that his enterprise is on a never-ending quest to get to perfection. In conjunction with the receptiveness of other Starbucks outlets, these phenomena have reflected the strong cultural organization of the enterprise in terms of the alignment to Lean philosophy. This top-down approach of encouraging the adoption of Lean philosophy has made Starbucks one of the few F&B enterprises that have successfully embraced Lean Principle.

2.4 *Lean tools*

There are many different sets of lean tools to help enterprises to incorporate lean thinking and principle into their field of interest. A few examples are 5S', *Kanban* demand-pull system, VSM and Total Quality Management (TQM) (see Figure 2). Given the range of Lean tools, it is essential for enterprises to first detect the problem that is hindering their productivity, and then choose the right tool from the vast array of tools which will help them incorporate lean thinking.

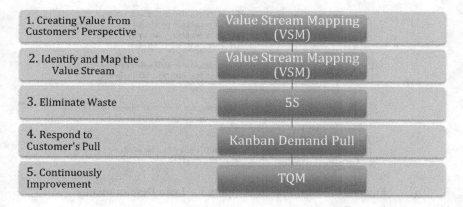

1. Creating Value from Customers' Perspective	Value Stream Mapping (VSM)
2. Identify and Map the Value Stream	Value Stream Mapping (VSM)
3. Eliminate Waste	5S
4. Respond to Customer's Pull	Kanban Demand Pull
5. Continuously Improvement	TQM

Figure 2:   Four Main Lean Tools: VSM, 5S, TQM, *Kanban*

Source: Author's compilation.

Intuitively, to be able to successfully implement Lean, it would be necessary to embrace the five principle of Lean as mentioned above. And Lean Tools, as the name goes, are tools that are indispensable for an enterprise/business to apply and achieve the above five fundamental principle of Lean. As shown above in Figure 1, each tool that will be discussed in the following section carries a significant role as a stepping-stone for enterprise to achieve Lean successfully.

(a) Value Stream Mapping (VSM)

To be able to take on the first step (i.e. Principles 1 and 2) to embrace Lean management in their organization, it is vital for the enterprise to understand the role of the tool, VSM (see Figure 3). VSM involves the visualization of intangible and tangible operating procedures and service delivery processes to make errors conspicuous for easier elimination of waste. As an initial step, the value stream based on the business' current state is drawn. Steps with no value-add can hence be removed from the value stream to cut down on waste as mentioned above.

Value stream can also be a communication tool, a business planning tool and a tool to manage your change process (Rother and

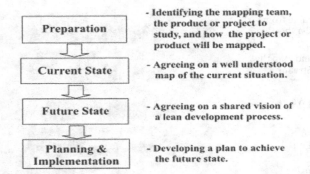

Figure 3:   Value Stream Mapping for Lean Development

Source: Author's compilation.

Shook, 2007). The initial step will always be drafting out the current value stream to develop and improve into a future state. VSM involves a cross-functional team of employees and is led by a value stream manager. The team will then use Lean concept to revamp the current value stream and improve its performance to create a plan for the implementation of the new process (Locher, 2008).

The implementation of the VSM system in the enterprise will allow people to graphically visualize most if not all of the services processes and streamline their daily business operations. As the non-value-added processes have been identified, steps can be taken to get rid of excess *Muda* (waste), thereby improving productivity through the smoother and organized flow of processes. More importantly, VSM allows the enterprise to be able to value processes from customers' value perspective and identify the value map stream (i.e. Principles 1 and 2).

(b) Five S (5S) (Sort, Straighten, Shine, Standardize and Sustain)

After graphically mapping out the value flows of all processes, the next step is to reorganize the disarrays amongst the service procedures to sieve out the non-value-added (i.e. eliminating waste). 5S tool of Lean Principle is a method of creating a clean and orderly workplace that exposes waste and abnormalities so that they could be eradicated easily (GembaAcademy, 2009) (see Figure 4).

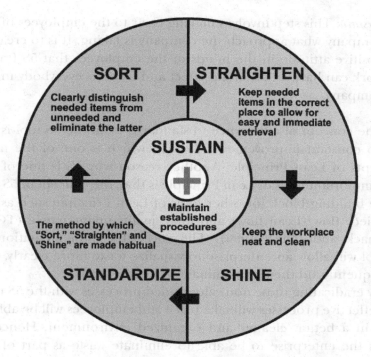

Figure 4: 5S: Sort, Straighten, Shine, Standardize and Sustain

Source: http://bestmachineshop.com/advantages/5s-leanmfg/.

1. *Sort:* Sort is to get rid of the things that one doesn't need or use (i.e. non-value add) from the remaining items which are useful (i.e. value-adds). Hoarding and cluttering will only lead to disorganization and a less productive work environment.

2. *Straighten:* After the *Sort* process, one will have to straighten the useful things (i.e. value-add) up in an orderly fashion. When items are being neatly sorted out, missing items and faulty tools can be replaced in time before they are needed.

3. *Sweep/Shine:* The main principle behind the Sweep/Shine Step is to clean and inspect. As a gesture beyond just cleaning, one will clean and identify the source of dirt. Dirt and grime is sometimes the vital source of low productivity in machines and devices.

4. *Standardize:* Standardizing things using templates such as checklists will improve one's vision of abnormalities. When abnormalities are spotted, it is easy to get rid of them.

5. *Sustain*: This step involves making clear to the employees of the company what approach the company is taking. It is to create a positive attitude in the minds of the employees that 5S framework can have a bottom-up effect and involves everybody in the company.

The concept of adherence to standards from the 5S tool is the key to constant improvement (*Kaizen*), which is one of the main concepts of Lean Principle. Another reason why 5S is one of the most important tools of Lean Principle is that, the concept of 5S acts as the building block for other tools of Lean Principle such as the one-piece flow (Lean flow) and total quality maintenance (TQM) (Womack and Jones, 1996). The successful implementation of 5S tool will allow an enterprise to visualize waste more clearly, and consequently aid them to eliminate waste efficiently.

By eradicating these non-value-added processes with the 5S tool, only effective processes will take place and employees will be able to work in a better, cleaner and organized environment. Hence, it allows the enterprise to be able to eliminate waste as part of the effort to achieve the third principle of Lean management. Consequently, with the possible successful implementation of Lean management, productivity of the enterprise will be upgraded via the creation of value and the eradication of waste in the service processes (Tetteh and Uzochukwu, 2015).

(c) *Kanban* Demand Pull

When the value flow of most, if not all, processes have been sorted out and reorganized, the subsequent key step is to engage the enterprise in a "customer demand-pull system" (see Figure 5). This step is critical in preventing further accumulation of *Muda* within the enterprise and to validate the viability of the preceding few Lean fundamentals. *Kanban* (Signal in Japanese) system is important in creating a demand-pull culture not only in the manufacturing sector but also in a service environment in terms of the principle of Lean philosophy. The upstream operation of an enterprise should be fed with a JIT effort from the lower stream (customers' demand) to ensure smooth flow of operations.

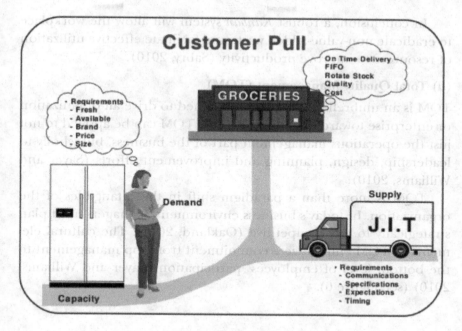

Figure 5:   *Kanban* Demand-Pull System

Source: http://www.slideshare.net/dgrossu/kanban-pull-system-presentation.

There are six rules to ensure a properly setup *Kanban* system in the workplace. Customers (downstream processes) will demand from the supplier or retailer (upstream). Supplier will supply downstream in the exact amount and sequence specified by *Kanban*. At any stage of the process, *Kanban* will disallow any defects and wrong amount of goods to be passed on to the next stage.

Furthermore, *Kanban* is a technique that signals replenishment (Gilliam *et al.*, 2005). The successful implementation of *Kanban* will allow an enterprise to specifically determine the quantity, part numbers and description of the items passed down to the next value stream. In short, *Kanban* allows the enterprise to be able to utilize realized customer demand quantities to supply them with the right amount of goods, at the right time, with the right goods. Evidently, *Kanban* will aid in fulfilling the fourth fundamental idea of Lean management, which is to respond to your customers' pull.

In conclusion, a robust *Kanban* system will allow the workplace to eradicate non-value-added waste and facilitate effective utilization of resources to improve productivity (Sabry, 2010).

(d) Total Quality Management (TQM)

TQM is an umbrella strategy tool designed to drive an organization or enterprise toward quality excellence. TQM can be applied to not just the operations management part of the business, but wholly to leadership, design, planning and improvement efforts (Sayer and Williams, 2010).

TQM is more than a paradigm shift in the intangibles of the organization. In today's business environment, managers must plan strategically to stay competitive (Oakland, 2014). The cultural elements of TQM emphasize a commitment from top management to the bottom level of employees' participation (Sayer and Williams, 2010) (see Figure 6).

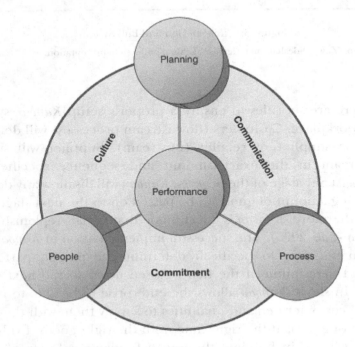

Figure 6:   TQM and Operational Excellence

Source: ET&C: http://www.endeavourtraining.org/2014/11/06/synergism-within-business/.

The implementation of the TQM framework requires a balanced approach through systems. The successful implementation of TQM requires the enterprise to leverage on self-assessment tools such as process analysis and benchmarking to better visualize room for improvement and people development, in order to spearhead the enterprise (Oakland, 2014).

Overall, TQM is a technique that allows enterprises to embrace a bottom-up revamp in terms of the cultural organization of an enterprise. It should be taken as a philosophy to transform an organization in terms of its growth, mindset of people and hence productivity (Mukherjee, 2006). With TQM, the enterprise would be aligned to a positive strong cultural organization of continuous improvement. This technique allows the enterprise to attain the fifth fundamental of Lean management, *Kaizen,* where continuous improvement is assimilated in the organization's culture.

There may be many more Lean tools out there which serve various other purposes. At the very least, the abovementioned four Lean tools should be able to cover the five fundamentals of Lean management mentioned in the Introduction. These tools should set a strong foundation for any enterprise to harness more of the other Lean tools to continue building up the ideology of Lean philosophy within their organization. Given the importance of the use of the multiple Lean tools to achieve successful Lean management, the four tools mentioned above can serve to kick-off Lean implementation (Mann, 2015).

2.5 *Applicability of Lean principle in the service industry*

The payoffs of embracing Lean Principle in the service industry have been as substantial or even more than that of the manufacturing industry (Hanna, 2007). Lean Principle and tools are a great fit even for service processes that tend to have long cycle time or complex variables (Ross, 2013).

The transformation of inputs such as manpower, materials and machineries requires efficient inventory management and supply chain management in order to generate profits. Effective operations management is indispensable to run a productive and lucrative business (Boyer and Verma, 2010). The ubiquity of the Lean Principle on the operations of businesses reflects the possible implementation in many industries. In the following section, the applicability of Lean management in a variety of other sectors has been elaborated.

(a) Healthcare

Womack and Jones have proposed in their book *Lean Thinking* that Lean Principle can be applicable to the healthcare sector. Patients would be viewed similar to customers in the service industry (Womack and Jones, 1996).

Inefficiencies from the manufacturing perspective such as waiting periods, delays and errors can also be found in the healthcare sector. Problems such as these could be remedied with the engagement of lean philosophy in the organization. (Collins and Muthusamy, 2007). According to a US survey study, US healthcare organizations reported that the application of Lean service has indeed upgraded productivity and cost effectiveness and reduced delay and waiting times (Jones and Mitchell, 2006).

(b) Education

In the education sector, Lean Principle can be applied to administrative issues at schools or universities. In many publications, the TQM approach has been transferred to education institutions (Damrath, 2012). Furthermore, Emiliani has inferred from his research that even educational processes, in both the teaching and administrative aspects, can be improved through the application of *Kaizen* (Emiliani, 2005).

Furthermore, according to Dahlgaard and Osteraard (2000), with students seen as customers, the crux of Lean Principle (Six Sigma and seven types of waste), can be applied to a university education.

(c) Banking and Finance Industry

In the banking and finance industry, there are case studies documenting how credit institutes have used Lean philosophy in their offices (Damrath, 2012). Banks in Europe have improved their service delivery with the use of IT systems which are lean supported

(Batiz-Lazo and Wood, 2001). As a result, the company's operations were able to significantly cut costs related to double work and labor, thereby turning the tables around for their business (Swank, 2003).

(d) Airline Industry

Lastly, there are practical case studies that reflect the positive improvement in service deliveries through the engagement of Lean in the airline industry as well (Damrath, 2012). According to Greenwood *et al.* (2002), an airline company has successfully improved customer satisfaction through the application of Lean.

With the substantiation that the Lean Principle is applicable to different industries that were first thought to be insignificant, it has been made clear that the Lean Principle is certainly not limited to the manufacturing environment, but is applicable to a variety of sectors.

3. Methodology

The research methodology adopted is similar to the one of an evidence-based study. In this study, a total of 30 SMEs, 10 from the Retail industry and 20 from the F&B industry, were interviewed and analyzed to examine the extent of the use of Lean Principle and the possible hindrances keeping them from being lean. We consider the hypothesis that Lean management is an effective business tool and strategy for enterprises in both the Retail and Food Services sectors to raise their productivity and revenue performance. Using the method of case studies and interviews, we would be able to evaluate the efficacies and positive effects of using Lean management as well as to identify the difficulties and barriers faced by enterprises in their implementation of Lean management.

Business enterprises were interviewed and their feedback was calibrated according to the score sheet given in the appendix. For instance, based on the extent of inventory management, the interviewer will provide enterprises with a grade based on the score sheet. The score sheet would ensure fairness and consistency throughout the grading of different firms, thereby reducing any subjective bias.

The score sheet is also prepared based on the level and extent of Lean management being exercised in each of the four management domains: Supply Chain Management, Service Management, Inventory Management and Leadership Management.

The information from the interview has enabled a template to be developed such that the extent of "Lean" in each enterprise can be identified and also the hindrance or shortfall the enterprise experiences in striving to be lean. This information will be helpful for formulating recommendations and solutions that can possibly address the weak or missing "Lean" aspect of each enterprise.

3.1 *Research questions and 8M framework*

(a) Survey Questionnaire

In order to better appreciate the analysis and findings of the study, it is pertinent to note the major characteristics of the questionnaire:

- In the questionnaire, one of every managerial aspect entails a few questions and business owner was expected to answer them on a scale of 1–10.
- Each question will hence be graded on a scale of 1–10 and the enterprise will be examined in terms of their level of "Lean" in the different aspects of management.
- Every question or aspect of the questionnaire entails a possible lean tool with it as a stepping-stone to embrace lean philosophy into his or her enterprise.

Outlets from both sectors are assessed and given the following lean grades*:

A — a score of 85% or higher
B — a score of 70–84%
C — a score of 50–69%
D — a score of 40–49%

*Supply Chain Management — 3 Questions, Service Management — 4 Questions, Inventory Management — 4 Questions, Leadership Management — 2 Questions.

From the percentage score of each managerial aspect, we would be able to identify the area of weakness holistically. Lean tools would then be recommended to each aspect that is 'not lean enough' for productivity upgrade.

3.1.1 *8M framework*

The research questions are underpinned by the basic technicalities of Lean Principle, creating value and cutting down of waste (Womack and Jones, 2005). Each question was crafted to cover every aspect of the 8M framework of Productivity Advantages. The 8M framework comprises of Management, Method, Make, Manpower, Market, Material, Message and Money. A closer scrutiny will allow us to discover the inextricable relationship between each element of the 8M framework and the productivity performance associated with it (Toh and Shandre, 2014).

Every question attached to each element of the 8M framework of productivity will be further broken down to four other categories that are indispensable for a competitive, strategic and productive business enterprise (Russell and Taylor, 2006). They are Supply Chain Management, Inventory Management, Leadership Management and Service Management. Table 1 summarizes how lean concept can be incorporated to the 8M framework. Following that, there is a detailed discussion of how each of the elements in the 8M framework are linked to the questions asked in the survey.

(a) Management

1. *What is the extent to which your company standardizes each of the service procedures? For example, are there any standard operating procedures when faced with certain situations?*

Positive management and exemplary leadership are paramount in standardizing work processes and in making processes which

Table 1: Integration of 8M Framework and Lean Principle

8 Ms	Meaning of M	Lean Approach	Lean Tools	Managerial Sector
1. Management	Organizational Culture, Philosophy, Behavior	Top management to set the ground for robust standard operating procedures (embracing lean philosophy from the top management). Standardizing can ensure better consistency. Continuous improvement (*Kaizen*).	VSM to create value flow TQM	Leadership Management
2. Material	Supplier Management	To be able to exercise JIT management in order to reduce inventory cost. To prevent excess items. Sorting out of materials to detect obsolescence, thereby allowing accurate ordering of items.	*Kanban* demand-pull system 5S	Inventory Management
3. Method	Technology & Innovation	To be able to engage efficient use of technology to cut down on waste. To be able to improve production and smoothen the service time to cut down on time lost due to poor customer service.	—	Service Management

4. Manpower	Human Resource: Mobilization, Development & Training	To ensure that employees are trained holistically; multifunctional. To inculcate the right mentality of removing slack during intervals and doing things right the first time to reduce waste on motion. Continuous improvement.	TQM	Service Management
5. Money	Finance, Working Capital, Investment	To have good financial management, cost control and credit cost and to prevent credit leakage.	*Kanban* demand pull	—
6. Make	Diversity of Products	To cut down on the non-value-added diversity of products to cut down on the waste. To be able to focus on fewer products in order to ensure quality assurance.	TQM	Service Management
7. Message	Advertisement & Promotion, Trust	Getting messages across to consumers at the lowest possible cost.	*Kanban* demand pull	—
8. Market	Segmentation and Revenue Sources; Customer Management	Segregating the consumer target group to produce what customers really want. Allows to cut down on waste.	*Kanban* demand pull	Inventory Management

are non-value-added in the VSM more visible. It also aids to develop team members' critical thinking ability for problem solving and to embrace *Kaizen* from the bottom level (Brennan and Gortz, 2008). The question on the implementation of a standardized value stream will allow us to check on the extent of Lean philosophy that the management level of the business organization has embraced.

(b) Material

2. *How often was your company faced with a problem of excess/shortage of supply?*

Material will involve the supplier management. It is imperative to manage the inventory space, which translates to higher inventory cost. JIT[1] would lower inventory holding cost that fundamentally boils down to the main concept of being lean, cutting of waste (Hernández, 2010).

(c) Method

3. *To what extent does your company utilize the current technology, such as self-checkout machines or an updated POS system, to cut down on service time?*

To incorporate Lean Principle into 'Method' of the 8M framework, an important aspect is that there should be efficient machineries and technologies to replace routine work of manual labor. Increased production capacity will increase productivity, decrease customers' turnover time and hence cut down the excess expenses on labor with technologies (MTI, 2015). By checking on the extent of use of the current technology, we will be able to ascertain the degree of understanding that enterprises have about efficient machineries and technologies in order to eliminate waste.

(d) Manpower

4. *Does your company advocate the idea of multifunctional teams i.e. training staffs to be functional in all aspect instead of specializing? (For example, taking orders, cashing out, serving food)*

5. *How often were you faced with problems such as: misinformation about when employees do hand/takeover of shifts, delay in service time due to inadequate understanding of job or extra effort due to work not done right the first time?*

Employees should be able to execute multiple job assignments and be multifunctional in terms of job skills. Human resources and mobilization of manpower would be highly relevant in order to remedy the problem of manpower crunch in terms of seasonal busy production period or during peak hours (Staff of Entrepreneur Media, 2015). Multifunctional teams would remove slack and create value out of their free time, which epitomizes the rudimentary concepts of Lean Principle which are to cut waste and create value (Womack and Jones, 2005).

(e) Money

To be lean in terms of financial management, cost control and credit cost management will be indispensable in a business enterprise in order to minimize payment leakages (McLaney and Atrill, 2010).

(f) Make

6. *To what extent have you checked on the popularity/demand of each variety of products to see if cutting down on the quantity of the less popular product lines can reduce additional cost or wastage?*

A diversity of products and services can allow business enterprises to stand out in terms of the varieties of product they can offer. However, market demand should be well researched and probed into before committing to a myriad of services and products. In order to effectively sell a diverse range of products in a business enterprise, one has to keep check on the suitability as well as the effectiveness of the variety of products and each of the products served (Charantimath, 2006).

To be lean, in terms of cutting waste, the enterprise should eliminate excess diversity of products and services to exercise waste control and quality assurance.

(g) Message

This primarily involves cutting down on promotion costs and getting the message across to customers at lower cost. The effective use of social media as a marketing strategy to communicate with the target audience can be one of the strategies to reduce cost and increase the proliferation of messages across the area. (Toh and Shandre, 2016, Chapter 7)

(h) Market

7. *Do you segregate your consumer target group to change production for certain groups to prevent overproduction of items which are not applicable to certain type of market group?*

Segmentation of the market to identify market groups can help to cut down on certain varieties of product which are less relevant in the area of business (McDonald, 2012). This would contribute to the efforts of cutting down waste.

4. Survey Results and Discussion

A total of 30 F&B and retail SMEs were interviewed in this evidence-based study. (i.e. 20 F&B outlets and 10 retail outlets). The individual percentage scores were collated for each managerial aspect and the two sectors will be analyzed wholly. Charts have been utilized to indicate the grade distribution for each of the managerial domains across companies. In the charts, the vertical axis indicates the number of enterprises with the particular grading, while the horizontal axis indicates the obtained grade under consideration.

Each question is worth 10 points, and hence a total of 30 points is allocated for the first section, supply chain management. Each enterprise has been graded according to the point system as mentioned above in this study (i.e. grade "A" is a score of 85% or higher).

4.1 *Supply chain management*

There are a total of three questions in this section of Supply Chain Management. Table 2 provides a breakdown on the allocation of points to questions regarding Supply Chain Management.

The total score out of 30 points (3 questions × 10 points each) will be tabulated. A percentage score will be given to each enterprise

Table 2: Score Sheet for Survey Questions on Supply Chain Management

0–2 (Very Weak) Points	3–4 (Weak) Points	5–6 (Average) Points	7–8 (Good) Points	9–10 (Excellent) Points
No standardization of procedures within the enterprise. Frequent excess/shortage of food/items.	Few standardized processes such as item delivery day or food order. Poor communication with supplier. Unable to execute JIT ordering. Occasional excess/shortage of food.	Several standardized processes, ranging from delivery day to coordination of JIT ordering. Mediocre communication with supplier. Occasional execution of JIT. Seldom excess/shortage of food.	Several standardized processes. Contingency plans for excess/shortage of products are well standardized. Several suppliers to cover up for possible mismanagement from the supplier side. Occasional execution of JIT. Seldom excess/shortage of food.	Mostly standardized processes. Detailed service processes such as scripted service processes are done. Well-managed supply chain, holding good relationship with supplier to entertain any JIT ordering. Frequent execution of JIT.

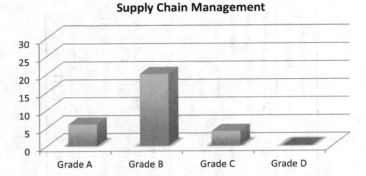

Figure 7: "Lean" Grade System of Enterprise for Supply Chain Management

Source: Survey results.

and will be further categorized into their respective grades. As seen from Figure 7, there were a total of six enterprises that scored "A", 20 scored "B", 4 scored "C" and 0 scored "D".

Case Study (1a): Hand-in-Hand Beijing Restaurant

It was evident through the interviews that the enterprises grouped under the grade "A" category maintained good relationships with suppliers who are willing to help the business owner to exercise JIT. Hand-in-Hand Beijing Restaurant is an enterprise which achieved grade "A" under the category for Supply Chain Management.

Based on the interview, the business owner claimed that having good relationships with the suppliers has allowed them to exercise JIT, and they are therefore able to keep their ingredients fresh and not lose customers due to insufficient supply of food. (i.e. *Muda*) Hand-in-Hand Beijing Restaurant also has a robust standard operating procedures (SOP) and contingency plan for their supply chain management. There is a fixed schedule of the week where supplier would supply them with the demanded amount of food. Furthermore, suppliers are informed of the potential *ad hoc* ordering of ingredients. As a result, Hand-in-Hand Restaurant is able to exercise JIT without the worry of facing overproduction or shortage of ingredients.

In congruence to the evidence of strong supply chain management in the company, they were aligned to the category of "excellent" as shown in Table 2.

Case Study (1b): One Man Coffee Café

As reflected in the score sheet, most of the enterprises that scored grade "B" have a mediocre relationship with their suppliers. They were faced with rigid schedule of items or food delivery, as a result of which most enterprises ended up with excess food or items. This case is especially prevalent for enterprises that face seasonal demand from the market. When the market is less predictable, enterprises will find it more difficult to order the right amount of inputs using demand information.

From the interview with the store manager of One Man Coffee Café at Upper Thomson road, it was revealed that the customer demand is unpredictable for them. Even with thorough market demand monitoring, they were unable to predict the correct amount of inputs per week. However, as most food items can be kept for more than a week, the excess or shortage of food ingredients faced were still kept reasonably low. Nevertheless, the owner mentioned that they do have certain contingency plans to deal with excess or shortage of food materials, and still execute good communication with its suppliers.

As such, the enterprise still has some evidence of good supply chain management, with individual scores for the interview questions under the category of "Good" as seen from Table 2.

Case Study (1c): YeShangHai Cuisine Pte Ltd

For enterprises that fell under the grade "C" category, there were no standard operating procedures in terms of supply chain management. Ordering of supply was mostly done *ad hoc*, and when the supplier fails to meet their last minute demands, they will be faced with a shortage of supply. Otherwise, these enterprises would usually order most items in excess, incurring unnecessary inventory cost. Failure to standardize business operations, in the case of supply chain management, will make supply of goods uncertain, hence leading to a frequent excess or shortage of supply.

From the interview with the business owner of YeShangHai Cuisine Pte Ltd, it was recognized that their F&B outlet TianXiang (that worked on *ad hoc* ordering) is occasionally faced with an excess of food items. This is due to the lack of proper VSM procedures and standardizing systems in the ordering of food items. As a result, there was a poor execution of JIT. They are also faced with problems such as higher incurrence of inventory cost due to the high amount of *Muda*. In addition, the manager mentioned that as they are not always able to determine consumer demand, and they also do not have close communication with the suppliers regarding consumer demand forecast.

Evidently, TianXiang did not fare well for the interview and found their enterprise falling between the categories of "Weak" and "Average" as shown in Table 2.

We can attribute the low revenue turnover to higher inventory cost, high customers' turnover rate due to shortage of supply and large amount of *Muda* due to excess of supply.

4.2 *Service management*

There are a total of four questions in this section of Service Management. Table 3 provides a breakdown on the allocation of points to questions regarding service management. The total score out of 40 points (4 questions × 10 points each) will be tabulated. As seen from Figure 8, there was 1 enterprise that scored "A", 12 scored "B", 9 scored "C" and 8 scored "D".

As mentioned in the Introduction, Service Management encompasses a standardized set of processes that would enable the company to meet the needs of the customer. It would also involve the utilization of technology to reduce the waiting time of customers and enhance customer satisfaction. Similarly, it would also require the company to review its product offerings to ensure that it is up to date with the market demand. By understanding the market demand, the company would be able to tailor the right product mix and level of service to meet the needs of its customers. Therefore, in Table 3, the score sheet for Service Management has included these aspects.

The evidence-based study on service management lies in line with the key issues highlighted by MTI in their annual report. Low adoption of IT technology has been one of the few problems that hindered the F&B and retail sectors from improving their productiv-

Table 3: Score Sheet for Interview Questions on Service Management

0–2 (Very Weak) Points	3–4 (Weak) Points	5–6 (Average) Points	7–8 (Good) Points	9–10 (Excellent) Points
No utilization of technology within the enterprise.	Very weak utilization of technology within the enterprise (e.g. only with an outdated POS system).	Average utilization of technology within the enterprise (e.g. POS system, social networking platform and cellphone apps for publicity).	Good utilization of technology within the enterprise (e.g. newer version POS system, website development and cellphone apps for publicity).	Excellent utilization of technology within the enterprise (i.e. Website development, mobile application, newest POS system and software application).
No intention of doing any market demand research to review their shop items.	No/very rare intention of doing any market demand research to review their shop items.	Rare intention of doing any market demand research to review their shop items.	Annual review of shop items with occasional market demand research.	Quarterly or recent review of shop items with frequent market demand research.
No training provided for newcomers.	Little training/advice for newcomers (i.e. learn on the job).	Some briefing/training for newcomers prior to service period.	Good discussion and Q&A session for newcomers prior to service period.	Standardize workshops and lesson plan for newcomers to be well trained enough before service period.

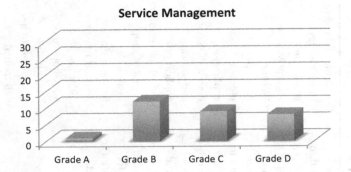

Figure 8: "Lean" Grade System of Enterprise for Service Management
Source: Survey's results.

ity (MTI, 2015). From our interview, it was deduced that most of the enterprises did not manage an "A" due to the inadequate use of current technology, such as an updated POS system which allows clearer stocktaking procedures, self-queue kiosk or self-ordering. This was mainly attributed to the high costs involved to set up such a system.

Most of the enterprises fall under grade "B". Most of them are cognizant of the importance of having multifunctional teams and market demand research work. Even unaware of Lean Principle, they review the popularity of each product regularly, and necessary adjustments are made to cut down on *Muda*. Enterprises from the grade "C" category would be those that fare poorly in terms of IT adoption, and hence failed to improve their productivity through the use of efficient equipment.

Case Study (2a): Premaas Cuisine Pte Ltd

From the interview with the business owner of Premaas Cuisine Pte Ltd, it is known that he has fine-tuned his organizational culture into a multifunctional one. He has ensured that newcomers are well coached and will always be present for work delegation purposes so that they are able to be multifunctional while on the job. With the multifunctional nature of his team, the delegator will be able to redirect manpower to wherever help is needed. Evidently, idle time (i.e. *Muda*) will be minimized with the multifunctionalism of his team.

Premaas Cuisine also reviews their menu regularly on a quarterly basis. They review the market demand of each dish on the menu in order to remove them from the menu and cut down on the cost of ingredients incurred. They have also segregated their market and have set their menu to cater to both vegetarian and non-vegetarians.

However, Premaas Cuisine fared poorly in terms of the level of technology embraced in their enterprise. They have a non-updated POS system that is incapable of stocktaking, inventory management and sales monitoring. Similar to other enterprises that fell under the grade "B" category, they do not have queue kiosk, iPad for food ordering or the use of technology for inventory stock counting.

From Table 3 as shown above, Premaas had their business strategy graded and categorized as "Average" based on the level of technology used in the enterprise. They fared better on aspects based on reviewing the company's competency to meet the market demand, categorizing them a grade "Good" in terms of Service Management. Overall, the company is in the "B" grade category.

Another problem identified by MTI was the high turnover rate of employees in the F&B industry. Through our interview, we found out that this problem is common in the industry and has caused perpetual low productivity level in the sector. Any enterprise that fails to standardize their operational procedures, such as "scripted" service procedures or having a workshop for newcomers, tends to face high level of *Muda*. *Muda* that is incurred due to the aforementioned inadequacies will lead to higher rate of defects, delay and lost opportunity due to customers' dissatisfaction. The distribution of grades "C" and "D" can be attributed to the high turnover rate of employees in the sector, which subsequently causes high rate of *Muda* throughout the industry.

Case Study (2b): Fat Boy's Burger Bar

As a company in the grade "A" category, we managed to interview the manager of Fat Boy's Burger Bar, a multichain F&B Restaurant in Singapore. They have a total of four outlets in Singapore and are reputed for their westernized cuisine and build-your-own-burger marketing strategy. Fat Boy outlets are equipped with one of the latest versions of POS system that is capable of viewing the current inventory status. They have a strong market research team that regularly reviews the market demand of each item on the menu and introduces new burger tastes to meet customer demand.

Furthermore, they have a robust training workshop catered for newcomers to enhance their competency level in terms of their menu and service processes knowledge. At every outlet, an expeditor will be present to ensure that employees there have a common agenda and direction to work toward. After every dinner service, After Action Review (AAR) is done, which involves all employees in the enterprise. Continuous improvement, which Fat Boy engages in, is essential for their business enterprise to continue growing (Brennan and Gortz, 2008).

The success of Fat Boy, evident by the yearly revenue turnover of more than SGD 300,000, can undoubtedly be attributed to the Lean management of their enterprise with their strong embracement of productive technological management systems (Bell, 2005).

As such, with the presence of detailed standardized procedures that allow the company to customize to customers' need, the company fared well enough to be categorized into the "A" grade category.

4.3 *Inventory management*

There are a total of four questions in this section of Inventory Management. Table 4 provides a breakdown on the allocation of points to questions regarding inventory management. The total score out of 40 points (4 questions × 10 points each) will be tabulated. As seen from Figure 9, there were 4 enterprises that scored "A", 7 that scored "B", 13 that scored "C" and 6 that scored "D".

As mentioned, Inventory Management involves the ability to monitor the flow of inventory and the use of items in its production line (Investopedia, 2015). It also involves having the ability to

Table 4: Score Sheet for Survey Questions on Inventory Management

0–2 (Very Weak) Points	3–4 (Weak) Points	5–6 (Average) Points	7–8 (Good) Points	9–10 (Excellent) Points
No scheduled date for cleaning up of warehouse/kitchen. Always faced with incorrect inventory. High excess/shortage of inventory.	Yearly spring-cleaning of warehouse/kitchen. Frequently faced with incorrect inventory. High excess/shortage of inventory.	Weekly cleaning of warehouse/kitchen. Random sorting out of hardware and equipment. Occasionally incorrect inventory. Mediocre excess/shortage of inventory.	Weekly cleaning of warehouse/kitchen. Scheduled date for recategorization stray materials. Seldom faced with incorrect inventory. Minimal excess/shortage of inventory.	Daily cleaning of warehouse/kitchen. Scheduled date for sorting, reorganizing and shining, and steps taken to sustain the shine. Rarely faced with incorrect inventory. Rare excess/shortage of inventory.

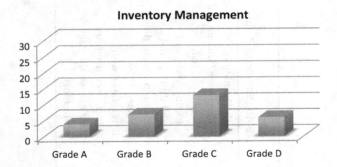

Figure 9: "Lean" Grade System of Enterprise for Inventory Management
Source: Survey's results.

have an optimal amount of inventory at any point, thus eliminating waste.

In general, Lean management appeared to be applied the least in the inventory management of the 30 SMEs interviewed. From the interview, we learnt that the crux of poor Lean management was the low or no implementation of Six Sigma[2] lean strategy. Shining, sorting or standardizing is not done regularly, resulting in high inventory cost. Furthermore, most enterprises use manual stocktaking techniques that result in frequent excess or shortage of items or goods in their warehouse.

Even though most enterprises are unaware of Lean Principle, some still have engaged Lean Principle to a certain extent. Enterprises with grades "A" and "B" are taking some efforts in alignment with Six Sigma tool to a certain extent, as weekly affair.

Case Study (3a): Countryside Café Singapore

Countryside Café Singapore, which uses the conventional manual stocktaking method, claimed that they were faced with occasional shortage and excess of stocks. The enterprise conducts its cleaning session once a week to sort out materials in its kitchen. Consequently, we can attribute the occasional excess food products to human error and poor management of the enterprise. Nevertheless, there are weekly inventory checks and some degree of organization in the store in order to keep up with the normal standards.

Countryside Café focuses on the sale of alcoholic beverages. As claimed by the business owner, beer is usually supplied in barrels. Since the beer barrels can only be monitored in terms of the amount of barrels, the amount of beer within the barrels would be uncountable and there would only be some instances of minimal miscalculation or over ordering.

However, items on their menu were mostly non-perishable, which explains the sustainability of the business. From the "Lean perspective", their business productivity can still be improved with better inventory management techniques. As such, Countryside Café would fall under the score category of "Good" as shown in Table 4, giving the enterprise an overall grade of "B".

Case study (3b): Pearl's Personality

Enterprises with grades "C" and "D" are those which sort their inventory only after long time intervals as a result of which they are faced with very frequent excess or shortage of inventory due to human error. Their situation worsens due to the fact that inventory is being managed manually by pen and paper.

Pearl's Personality is a retail company that is in the grade "C" category. From the interview with the company's manager, it was revealed that the company seldom does warehouse cleaning and reorganization. Pearl's does *ad hoc* checks on the inventory as a monthly affair and was hence is faced with occasional excess inventory. This has certainly increased unnecessary inventory costs that could have been minimized with proper inventory management.

As such, it can be seen that Pearl's has poor Lean management techniques in the managerial area of Inventory Management, with scores belonging in the category of "Average" as shown in Table 4.

4.4 *Leadership management*

There are a total of two questions in this section of Leadership Management. Table 5 provides a breakdown on the allocation of points to the questions regarding Leadership Management. The total score out of 20 points (2 questions × 10 points each) will be

Table 5:   Score Sheet for Survey Questions on Leadership Management

0–2 (Very Weak) Points	3–4 (Weak) Points	5–6 (Average) Points	7–8 (Good) Points	9–10 (Excellent) Points
No meeting held. Leader does not delegate instructions, does not motivate, and does not advocate the right mentality in employees. High idle time due to poor delegation of work.	Annual meeting. Leader delegates responsibility with sparse and unclear instructions. Leader does not motivate, and does not advocate the right mentality in employees. High idle time due to poor delegation of work.	Quarterly meeting. Leader delegates responsibility with clear instructions. Leader motivates employees to a certain extent but does not advocate the right mentality in employees. Average idle time due to mediocre delegation of work.	Weekly meeting. Leader delegates responsibility with clear instructions. Leader motivates employees, is clear of daily objectives, and occasionally advocates the right mentality in employees. Little idle time due to good delegation of work.	Daily meeting. BAR and AAR done religiously before and after service. Leader delegates responsibilities with clear, concise instructions. Advocates clearly the idea of continuous improvement within the workers and "do the right thing, right the first time" mentality within the workers. No idle time due to excellent leadership quality of leader.

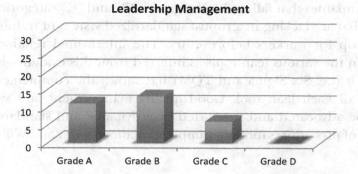

Figure 10: "Lean" Grade System of Enterprise for Leadership Management
Source: Survey's results.

tabulated. As seen from Figure 10, there were 11 enterprises that scored "A", 13 that scored "B", 6 that scored "C" and none that scored "D".

As mentioned earlier, Leadership Management involves management of the company and the workers, to collectively set the right organizational culture that would emphasis the importance of continuous improvement (*Kaizen*). This is pivotal as Lean management is an organizational strategy that should be supported with appropriate management style. For instance, workers should be trained with the mentality of continuous improvement as well.

Most enterprises fared generally well in terms of lean leadership management. Companies that scored grade "A" advocated the idea of 'do the right thing, right the first time, every time' strongly. These companies aspire to achieve the objective of positive cultural organization in the enterprise and have ensured tight quality management of their products. Concurrently, these firms are also engaging in daily meetings, and AAR before-action review (BAR) after and before daily service, respectively. Evidently, due to the positive culture of the organization (Burke *et al.*, 2012) and the motive of continuous improvement (*Kaizen*), these companies are those that are doing relatively well with an average revenue turnover of SGD 200,000.

Companies that fall under the grades "B" and "C" categories are those that are lacking in a robust standardized system of training or workshop for workers before entry. The intertwined relationship between the various lean tools as inferred from this evidence-based research (i.e. Six Sigma and TQM) has shown the complementary nature of each lean tool. Good quality management and system must be advocated and supported by a dynamic and standardized system of procedures for better implementation (Sayer and Williams, 2010).

Case Study (4a): Spring Summer Fall Winter

Spring Summer Fall Winter (SSFW) is one of the retail companies in Haji Lane that falls into the Category grade B. The owner believes strongly in setting the right mindset toward their employees and organizes weekly meetings to go through the firm's strategy and products with its employees. Despite these positive attempts, the owner still finds difficulties in inculcating a strategic mindset into their business culture. She attributed this failure to the high turnover rate of employees in her retail enterprise.

Therefore, it can be seen that she was not aware of the fact that the lack of a balanced approach via systematic procedures crippled her intentions of setting a positive cultural organization. From this case study, the importance of rapport, trust and coherence in aspiration among employer and employees within an enterprise is validated, as suggested by Oakland (Oakland, 2014).

Thus, with reference to certain positive attempts in Leadership Management, the company scored within the category "Good" in Table 5.

Case Study (4b): One Place Western Bistro

In contrast to the previous company, One Place Western Bistro is a company that exhibits strong Leadership Management and is within the "A" category. The manager mentioned that daily meetings are held and that the bistro also follows BAR. The presence of BAR ensures that each staff member is competent and prepared for the dinner service, and is clearly aware of tasks in different areas (e.g.

food preparation, serving of customers, billing of customers). Furthermore, the team is trained to be multifunctional and can perform different tasks if a certain area is short-handed. The ability of staff to switch tasks to meet the needs of the company enables the company to cut down on the idle time period of workers, hence increasing their productivity.

The presence of AAR/BAR provides a platform for the staff to provide feedback regarding the problems they face during the dinner service and to share their opinions on how they can improve the service and performance. This clearly shows the mentality of continuous improvement (*Kaizen*), which is aligned to Lean Management.

As such, the firm is able to meet almost all the criteria in the score sheet in Table 5, and hence this enterprise is in the category of "excellent" in terms of execution of the leadership aspect of Lean Management.

5. Conclusion and Recommendations

This study was conducted using an evidence-based study approach. From the research, it was evident that very few business owners are aware of Lean Principle. However, they are already applying Lean philosophies and concepts into their business to a certain extent.

From the survey results and case studies, we infer that Service Management and Inventory Management are the worst performing managerial domains out of the four. Service Management only has a score 1 "A" and 12 "B", while Inventory Management also fared poorly with a score of 4 "A" and 7 "B" . Supply Chain and Leadership management fared relatively well, mostly due to the positive mindset of business owners and the desire to progress toward building a good rapport with suppliers.

For Service Management, among the 30 retail and F&B enterprises interviewed, it was found that there IT technology was not utilized to the maximum level in business. First, sales of items are not being monitored closely as stores are often equipped with an outdated POS system. Without the competency to review their daily sales accounts, business owners were unable to conduct market demand research for their products religiously. This creates a ripple effect in the organization overall, as it results in weak waste control and poor quality assurance. This inability to cut down on product lines that are less popular handicaps the business with higher material and inventory cost.

Another reason for the poor ratings in Service Management is the high employee turnover rate. Keeping in mind the current manpower crunch, coupled with the foreigners–local employment ratio, enterprises find it extremely difficult to focus their attention on service excellence. Out of all case studies, only the Fat Boy case study is an exception as no significant manpower issues were highlighted during the interview. This could be attributed to its reputable success within the industry that allows the "inherent" attraction of employees to work in their enterprise without much marketing of jobs. As a result of the low job turnover rate, they were able to provide workshops for employees to understand the menu items and service procedures, hence allowing them to stand out in terms of Lean management, where service quality and competency of employees are the most important.

For Inventory Management, enterprises fared poorly mainly due to the unawareness of the importance of 5S. Amongst the 30 enterprises that were interviewed, only 4 cleaned their warehouse/kitchen daily. The extent of 5S in each enterprise has a close relationship with the occurrence of incorrect inventory in their enterprise. There has been a lack of understanding in the notion of 5S and, more importantly, the existence of 5S. Disappointingly, we found that none of the enterprises interviewed in the survey were aware of the existence of 5S.

In conclusion, recommendations include tackling the problem of poor utilization of IT technology, resolution or reduction of the problem of high job turnover rate and increasing awareness of Lean Principle to SMEs in both the retail and F&B sectors in Singapore.

Taking the challenges and inadequacies into consideration, this chapter provides a few possible recommendations and solutions for SMEs in Singapore to better embrace Lean Principle.

5.1 *Recommendations*

Based on the findings that we gathered from the interviews, this section proposes several recommendations that aim to improve the understanding of Lean Management, especially in the managerial domains of Service Management and Inventory Management. They include: An open letter to all SMEs, tax deductibility aspect of Lean Management-related workshops and trainings, advocating IT business solutions as well as advocating Lean qualifications.

(a) Suggested Approaches to Lean Management for Industries

Small retail enterprises should start small by using 5S to sort out their inventory or warehouse to allow the companies to visualize waste (e.g. obsolete items or loose items) easily. Given the poor knowledge of Lean Principle within the retail and F&B industry, we aim to improve on the "Message" component of the 8M framework to/get the message across the messages and ideas that Singapore Productivity Centre (SPC) has been spreading across to the relevant business owners.

Small F&B enterprises should kick off Lean implementation by understanding how to improve their business through Lean

Table 6: Approaches to Adopt Lean Management for Industries

Size/Industry	Retail	F&B
Small (= <10 workers)	To encourage the use 5S as a stepping stone	8M + Lean Management Template for them to cross-check and implement Lean
Medium (>10 workers)	To encourage Lean philosophy by encouraging them to consider the Uniqlo model (i.e. analyzing of value streams, flat hierarchy system to allow opinions from different perspectives for *Kaizen*)	To encourage Lean philosophy within the workers encouraging them to consider the Starbucks model (i.e. the importance of analyzing detailed processes and cutting of waste)

concept in a holistic manner. The 8M framework allows the enterprise to look at their business in a holistic manner while the Lean approach via the 8M framework allows the enterprise to see how Lean can actually tackle each aspect of their business. It is from this point that the government can invigorate the enterprise's inquisitiveness and encourage them to understand more about the Lean Principle and why the government is advocating such an approach nationwide. This approach is based on the belief that "Message" has been missing in all initiatives taken by SPC thus far. Hence, increasing awareness of all initiatives that have been taken by SPC/SPRING will not only make the current recommendation successful but also help to rekindle interest in the past initiatives taken by SPC.

Medium enterprises would want to work their way up the business ladder to emulate model enterprises in the industries, such as Uniqlo and Starbucks. The message that we would like to bring across to the medium enterprises would be that they should build on their current success and learn from enterprises that are bigger than them. Case studies and brochures can be provided to them to notify them of the available workshops conducted by SPC. The brochure should include step-by-step initiatives that the government is taking to ensure that by year 2018 (example) medium enterprises would be the first to adopt the Lean Principle. It is important that the brochures be self-explanatory, such that business owners understand the idea, even if they do not attend the workshops. Existing assessors like BCG and PricewaterhouseCoopers will be benchmarking and grading the medium enterprises to see if Lean implementations have been done correctly. In case business owners are clueless regarding the Lean revamp, consultation is always available at SPC and help is just a call away.

Compared to small enterprises, medium enterprises would have to take more effort to implement Lean, given their larger capacity. They should be on the first line of engagement of Lean principles in order for the small enterprises to follow suit. The assessment of Lean implementation would leverage on the existing initiatives that SPC has been doing and also shed light on some services that SPC has been providing to the SMEs but was not known of. This approach also acts as an impetus and opportunity for medium enterprises to climb up the ladder, hopeful of transcending their enterprise to a level equivalent to that of an MNC.

(b) Lean Area Networking Session

In our survey, it was found that only 2 out of 30 of the enterprises interviewed were aware of the workshops provided by SPC. Many initiatives have been taken by SPC in an attempt to encourage Lean implementation in the various sectors. However, the crux of the problem lies in the poor marketing of these initiatives to the SMEs, who are in fact the main target audience. A possible approach the Singapore Productivity Centre (SPC) or SPRING Singapore can take is to organize industry-specific networking sessions for business owners to build network and also invite guest speakers (Lean consultants) to discuss the commencement of an industry-wide Lean campaign.

The idea of a networking session hinges on the fact that business owners would want to maintain good relationships with other business enterprises in their industry and learn more about how peers are doing business. This would help to boost the turn-up rate for the workshop as well, which would be hosted along with the networking session. Lean workshops would be used as a medium to educate business owners and to raise awareness of business owners' understanding of Lean Principle.

(c) Tax Deductibility

The manager or business owner would be entrusted with the task of achieving Lean objectives, and hence he should receive sufficient support from the government through a sufficient budget (Bonaccorsi *et al.*, 2011).

While the government has provided productivity investment credit (PIC) to subsidize enterprises in procuring essential machine and equipment for productivity upgrading, it will also be relevant for companies that invest in adopting Lean initiatives and programs that transform processes and resource flow into higher level of efficiency and productivity. Apart from involving the business owners in the Lean workshops provided by the government, a budget can be made to factor in the tax-deductible aspect of Lena initiatives. This would encourage the SMEs to engage Lean consultancy firms in Singapore, such as Kaizen Consultancy Group (KCG), Kaizen Institute Singapore or Eagle Wings.

A more intimate engagement in terms of consultancy will improve the follow-up process to ensure successful implementation through the years (Paul *et al.*, 2012).

(d) Advocating IT Business Solutions

Based on the findings that we gathered under the managerial aspect on Service Management, there are many IT platforms that are not being exploited by business enterprises in Singapore. Business solutions such as website development, mobile application and POS system can be promoted to these enterprises. A checklist can be crafted and mailed to SMEs for cross-reference purposes. From our interview with the 30 enterprises, it was found that many enterprises were not aware of the various technologies available that can be used for the betterment of their business. The purpose of the checklist is to create awareness of the possible room for improvement in terms of business IT solutions for SMEs in Singapore.

The checklist can include the following items:

- Website development: space for information, product listing, conduct of e-commerce.
- Mobile Application: mobile apps and social media platforms for market expansion, testing products, B2B transaction.
- POS System: up-to-date point of sale (POS) systems to keep track of inventory and sales, cutting down waste and unwanted stocks.
- Software Application: generic and customized software than can help companies to streamline management operation and administration as in customers' orders, vendor information, sales order and delivery, human resource management, payroll system and customer relationship management.

(e) Advocating Lean Qualifications

SPC can provide incentives for enterprise owners to engage employees of higher management such as service managers or store managers with Lean qualifications (e.g. Green Belt or Black Belt). Incentives such as higher pay, which are subsidized by the government, can be provided to attract and retain the qualified employees. The importance of engaging Lean thinking requires the flow of Lean behavior from the top management in order for the implementation to be successful (Sayer and Williams, 2010).

There are several ways through which awareness of the Lean Principle can be increased and sustained. However, as it does take time and resources to establish a Lean model, it is important for the enterprises to remain committed to using relevant Lean tools to achieve excellence in Supply Chain Management, Service Management; Inventory Management and Leadership Management. The government can also play an active role in supporting the campaign towards the adoption of Lean management by offering grants, and tax rebates for accredited activities and programs as well as organization of targeted workshops and seminars that promote Lean thinking for productivity improvement.

Appendix: Scoring Scheme for Interview Questions

Score	Supply Chain Management
0–2 (Very Weak)	No standardization of procedures within the enterprise. Frequent excess/shortage of food/items.
3–4 (Weak)	Few standardized processes such as item delivery day or food order. Poor communication with supplier. Unable to execute JIT ordering. Occasional excess/shortage of food
5–6 (Average)	Several standardized processes, ranging from delivery day to coordination of JIT ordering. Mediocre communication with supplier. Occasional execution JIT. Seldom excess/shortage of food

(*Continued*)

Score	Supply Chain Management
7–8 (Good)	Several standardized processes. Contingency plans for excess/shortage of products are well standardized. Several suppliers to cover up for possible mismanagement from the supplier side. Occasional execution JIT. Seldom excess/shortage of food.
9–10 (Excellent)	Mostly standardized processes. Detail service processes such as scripted service processes are done. Well-managed supply chain, holding good relationship with supplier to entertain any JITordering.

Service Management

Score	
0–2 (Very Weak)	No utilization of technology within the enterprise. No intention of doing any market demand research to review their shop items. No training provided for newcomers.
3–4 (Weak)	Very weak utilization of technology within the enterprise (e.g. only with a outdated POS system). No/very rare intention of doing any market demand research to review their shop items. Little training/advice for newcomers (i.e. learn on the job).
5–6 (Average)	Average utilization of technology within the enterprise (e.g. POS system, social networking platform and cell-phone apps for publicity). Rare intention of doing any market demand research to review their shop items. Some briefing/training for newcomers prior to service period.
7–8 (Good)	Good utilization of technology within the enterprise (e.g. newer version POS system, website development and cell phone apps for publicity). Annual review of shop items with occasional market demand research. Good discussion and Q&A session for newcomers prior to service period.
9–10 (Excellent)	Excellent utilization of technology within the enterprise (i.e. website development, mobile application, newest POS system and software application). Quarterly or recent review of shop items with religious market demand research. Standardize workshops and lesson plan for newcomers to be well trained enough before service period.

(*Continued*)

(Continued)

Score	Supply Chain Management
	Inventory Management
0–2 (Very Weak)	Always faced with incorrect inventory. High excess/shortage of inventory.
3–4 (Weak)	Frequently faced with incorrect inventory. High excess/shortage of inventory.
5–6 (Average)	Occasional incorrect inventory. Mediocre excess/shortage of inventory.
7–8 (Good)	Seldom with incorrect inventory. Minimal excess/shortage of inventory.
9–10 (Excellent)	Rarely faced with incorrect inventory. Rare excess/shortage of inventory.
	Leadership Management
0–2 (Very Weak)	Very high idle time due to poor delegation of work.
3–4 (Weak)	High idle time due to poor delegation of work.
5–6 (Average)	Average idle time due to mediocre delegation of work.
7–8 (Good)	Little idle time due to good delegation of work.
9–10 (Excellent)	No idle time due to excellent leadership quality of leader.

Endnote

1. JIT means being able to produce just what is needed, just when it is needed and in just the amount that is needed.
2. Six Sigma is a disciplined, data-driven approach and continuous improvement methodology for eliminating defects (driving toward six standard deviations between the mean and the nearest specification limit) in product, process or service.

Chapter 2

Use of Self-service Technology in Supermarkets: Case Study of a Supermarket and Consumer Responses

1. Introduction

As technology improves, many manual tasks have been replaced by machines. This trend is also evident in the supermarket industry where the use of Self-service Technology (SST) is increasingly prevalent. The ease of technology adoption is somewhat facilitated by the increased literacy amongst Singaporeans.

However, the implementation of SST in supermarkets is not without its own set of challenges. Unlike other industries, supermarkets impact the lives of literally every man on the street; it is a place where many would have visited frequently to purchase daily necessities like food, beverages and household items.

This chapter includes a case study of the experience of NTUC *Fairprice*, which is one of the pioneers in the use of SST in Singapore. The study gathers information from both management and customers on the benefits and costs of SST, and the challenges faced during the change process. We also try to find out whether SST can be used more pervasively and, generally, to learn from the management's and customer's experiences.

1.1 *Goals of SST in the supermarket industry*

There are two main reasons for adopting SST in supermarkets. First, SST allows the customer to carry out self-directed tasks such as payment and scanning of goods. It can enhance the customer in-store experience and, at the same time, free up human capital to focus on other business functions. Second, SST increases productivity and reduces labor costs. Having to control operational costs is one of the main challenges of supermarkets, as the business typically runs on extremely low profit margins. To this end, some supermarkets have installed self-help equipment such as item locators and technologically advanced weighing scale on the shop floors (Hsieh, 2005).

1.2 *Types of SST*

In this study, we have identified three primary types of SST in the supermarket industry.

(a) **Self-service Checkouts:** These are computerized machines that allow shoppers to purchase tangible products using debit and credit card machines in a retail setting. Self-service checkouts allow supermarkets to reduce the number of staff needed, which leads to a reduction in human resource costs (Dabholkar *et al.*, 2003). For example, one staff member can assist customers at 4 to 6 self-service checkout lanes. This helps the supermarket to reap cost efficiencies and improve use of human resources. And, customers can benefit in the form of faster checkout time, efficient service and perceived privacy during the entire checkout process (Hsieh, 2005).

(b) **Interactive Self-service Installations:** These machines provide basic services such as helping customers determine the availability, location and price of a product. Examples include price checking kiosk, self-service weighing scale and self-testing station. These machines add a touch of interactivity to enhance the customers' overall shopping experience.

(c) **Interactive Voice Response System:** This technology is often used in hotlines to respond to customer queries by directing them to relevant departments such as billing, and conducting surveys at end of a call.

Of the above three types of SST, self-service checkouts and interactive self-service installations provide front-end service to customers, while Interactive Voice Response System provides support to the back-end function of the supermarket.

1.3 *Government support for SST*

In Singapore, one prominent organization encouraging the adoption of SST is the Singapore Productivity Centre (SPC). SPC is endorsed by the National Productivity and Continuing Education Council and SPRING Singapore. It aims to (1) promote better understanding of productivity measures, (2) improve productivity in companies and (3) train and build up in-house productivity competencies, so as to attain sustainable growth. SPC expects to help over 2000 companies to enhance their productivity through a series of workshops on topics such as *Self-service Technologies for F&B: A Solution for Manpower Crunch.*

Companies can also look to financial schemes offered by SPRING (a Singapore Government Statutory Board). SPRING aims to help local companies to grow by building their capabilities in all aspects of their businesses. One particular grant offered by SPRING is the Capability Development Grant (CDG). CDG is a financial assistance program which helps Small and Medium Enterprises defray up to 70% of their costs relating to consultancy, manpower, training, certification and upgrading of productivity such as implementation of SST.

At the global level, there are several established associations promoting SST. Some examples are Kiosk Marketplace and Self-service World. These associations link up suppliers of SST and retail companies through an established international network, publish white papers on the advancement of SST and organize conferences on a regular basis.

1.4 *Rising trends of SST usage in the supermarket industry*

SST is gaining pace in the supermarket industry, and more outlets are implementing SST in order to improve their operations. According to a survey conducted by Food Marketing Institute, while only 6% of the supermarkets in the USA had self-service checkouts lanes in 1999, that number has jumped to 35% in 2003 and has reached nearly 95% in 2007 (Grimes, 2004). Increasingly, self-service checkouts are handling approximately 15–40% of all daily transaction value and 12–30% of the daily dollar value of supermarkets (Kara *et al.*, 2013). In Singapore, large players in the supermarket industry such as NTUC FairPrice, Cold Storage, Sheng Shiong and GIANT have also adopted SST in their operations.

2. SST in the Supermarket Industry

This section examines the (1) main benefits for adopting SST in supermarkets, (2) challenges faced during implementation and (3) key performance indicators that supermarkets use to evaluate SST.

2.1 *SST and customer satisfaction*

With the rising degree of homogeneity among product offerings, supermarkets are increasingly capitalizing on customer service to gain a competitive edge in this highly oligopolistic industry. SST presents a possible means of enhancing the customer experience.

Many research papers have demonstrated the viability of using SST to improve customer satisfaction. Cronin and Taylor (1992) showed that customer satisfaction has a significant positive effect on purchase intentions, resulting in greater sales. Lee *et al.* (2009) demonstrated that the beneficial effects on service quality delivered by self-service kiosks lead to retail patronage intentions. This demonstration is substantiated by a study of 823 individuals on customer satisfaction with SST, which showed that 56% of the individuals described their encounters with SST as above satisfactory.

A study conducted by Marzocchi and Zammit (2006) collected data from users of self-scanning devices at a major Italian supermarket chain located in Northern Italy. The researchers analyzed 353 samples and found that sense of control and enjoyment significantly influenced satisfaction with self-scanning device. They also found that satisfied customers were willing to say positive things about the store and to visit the store more frequently (Cho and Fiorita, 2010).

Underpinning this outcome is the important and crucial use of SST, which increases the convenience and speed of information from the supermarket to the end customer. Now, kiosks can provide information (i.e. price and availability) to the shoppers. Supermarkets can provide unique information such as health content and recipes using standalone kiosks (Murphy, 2007). Technology can make the task of shopping easier and interactive. It shifts the dimensions of the usual shopping methods and revolutionizes the entire retail environment. As a whole, these features can distinguish one retailer from another.

2.2 *Balanced customer service strategy*

In order to reduce throughput time, supermarkets have looked to develop a balanced customer service strategy around their cashier lanes. With the use of self-service checkout stations, supermarkets are able to promote the perception of "fast checkout". Supermarkets redirect customers with fewer grocery items to pay using the self-service checkout, hence reducing their wait time. Supermarkets which are able to optimize shoppers' throughput while reducing long queues will outperform those that simply install self-service checkouts and save on human resources (Thom, 2006). Thus, the optimal balance ratio of cashier queues to self-service checkout stations will contribute to customer satisfaction.

2.3 *Challenges of SST*

Despite the rising trend of SST, it is not without its challenges. In 2013, three leading US retailers Costco, Jewel-Osco, and Albertsons removed SST machines from their stores, stating that they are not confident that SST had benefitted their customers, but instead might have created unintended consequences (Kiosk Marketplace, 2012).

According to a study conducted on 400 individuals in October 2013 by Tensator, a retail technology firm, one in three UK shoppers had left a store without purchasing the goods they intended to because of a negative experience they had with a self-service machine. The study further showed that 84% of those questioned needed staff assistance when using self-service checkouts and 60% preferred traditional staffed counters. Customers who prefer traditional staffed counters like the interaction with the cashier and feel that payment made is more secured (Tensator, 2013).

According to International Data Corporation (IDC), some shoppers find SST technologically intimidating, while a lack of knowledge of how to use SST prevents some from using them. Furthermore, when using SST, IDC reported that some shoppers experienced random security checks to ensure that payment and scanning procedures are correct. These inspections reinforced resistance against the usage of SST in the future.

Moreover, supermarkets tend to assume that with SST, shoppers are able to finish their checkout process faster. However, this is not always the case. IDC found that self-service checkouts are more popular among adults with children and the elderly regardless of the amount of goods bought. The former reasoned that children could learn and help with the scanning of goods. The elderly, on the other hand, prefer to slow down their checkout process so that they could pack their purchase and checkout at their own pace. These groups of slow shoppers end up delaying the checkout process, thus discouraging other shoppers from using it (Retail Systems, 2005).

One common concern of supermarkets is the problem of "shrink" or lost inventory caused by factors ranging from accidental failure to scan a product to intentional theft. Most supermarkets believe that "shopper-caused shrink" happens more easily in self-service checkouts. According to a study conducted by the Food Marketing Institute (FMI), overall shrink in 2006 made up 1.7% of sales. However, from the FMI report, 40% of the total shrink was employee-caused and 25% was due to cashier dishonesty. Hence, there is an ongoing dilemma for supermarkets whether self-service checkout is the main culprit (IBM, 2008).

In addition, Michelle Marian of Motorola Solutions' North American Retail and Hospitality arm shared that consumers usually have a very high level of expectation of positive user experience when they use technological aids provided by a business. Therefore, the supermarkets have to ensure that SST machines are user-friendly for all customers (Arnfield, 2014).

2.4 *Key performance indicators of SST*

Given that there are several types of SST installations within the supermarket industry, there could be different key performance indicators when it comes to evaluating the usefulness and success of SST. Customer adoption could be used as an indicator in the early stages of the implementation, while customer satisfaction and commitment to the usage of SST determine the success of SST in the long-term. In addition, a positive net present value and short payback period could render the SST investment financially sound (Cho and Fiorita, 2010).

3. Research Methodology

3.1 *Research objectives*

In this study, we seek to accomplish three objectives. First, we seek to better understand how supermarkets can improve their revenue performance and profitability with the use of SST. Second, we aim to investigate the challenges faced by both merchants and consumers when using SST. Third, we want to understand if SST could be used more pervasively in Singapore.

From this case study, we hope to suggest possible measures for supermarkets to increase their effectiveness in the implementation of SST and for the trade associations and government agencies to encourage the adoption of SST within the supermarket industry.

3.2 *Research Method*

As part of the scope of this study, we examine the sentiments of Singaporeans using SST, their overall perception of SST and its effectiveness. We adopt a convenience sampling method to collect the data through both face-to-face interview and an online survey. A website was set up to allow respondents to complete the questionnaire at their leisure. A total of 42 online responses were received, and 15 face-to-face interviews were conducted. The sample consists of individuals who are regular shoppers at mainstream supermarket chains, aged from 18 to 75. They are mainly female, quite young (mean age group of 36–45) and have college education. For the older generation, we conducted face-to-face interviews, translating the questions into the language/dialect that they are comfortable with. We also conducted an observational field study by visiting three types of NTUC FairPrice supermarkets, namely NTUC FairPrice, NTUC Finest and NTUC Xtra, to understand their operations better.

In addition, we also carried out an email interview with the management team of NTUC FairPrice to learn more about their experiences in adopting SST at their outlets.

4. Survey Findings

Through our survey, we sought to understand the various challenges faced by consumers in the use of SST, their responses to the use of SST and their overall satisfaction level. The results will help supermarkets to serve their customers better.

4.1 *Integration of SST in supermarkets and its challenges*

(a) Ease of Adoption

Of the 57 respondents, 86% are aware of the various SST available (Figure 1) while 57% do not find it difficult to use them (Figure 2). When asked about the difficulties of using SST, 45% state that they

Figure 1: Are You Aware of the Variety of the SST Available? E.g.: Self-service Checkout, Ability to Checkout Prices/Stock Available Via the Machine

Source: Survey and interviews.

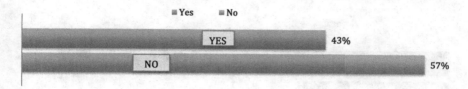

Figure 2: Do You Think it is Difficult to Use SST?

Source: Survey and interviews.

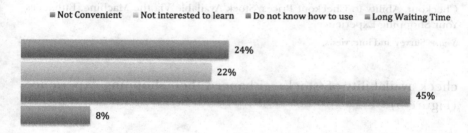

Figure 3: Why Do You Think it is Difficult to Use SST?

Source: Survey and interviews.

do not know how to use SST, 24% state that it is not convenient and 22% state that they are not interested to learn how to use SST (Figure 3). When asked to rank the ease of use of SST from 1 to 100 where 100 is most friendly, respondents gave an average score of 57.6 with a standard deviation of 23.65 (Figure 4). This shows wide disagreement between those who think that SST is user-friendly and those who think otherwise.

On the overall sentiment, 72% of the survey respondents acknowledged that the variety of SST available, for example self-service checkout, machines to check prices, machines to

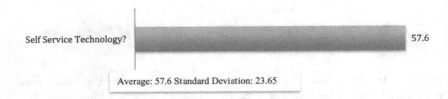

Figure 4:   How Would You Rank SST in Term of User Friendliness?

Source: Survey and interviews.

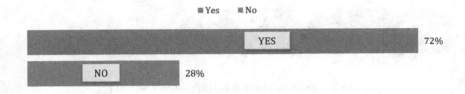

Figure 5:   Do You Think That the Variety of SST Available, e.g.: Self-service Checkout, Ability to Checkout Prices/Stock Available Via the Machine, Enhances Your Shopping Experience?

Source: Survey and interviews.

check availability of/stocks, enhanced their shopping experience (Figure 5).

4.2 *Self-service checkout vs. regular checkout*

Then, we narrowed the scope of SST to the use of self-service checkout because we felt that the payment stage is a vital component of the retail experience as it is the last point of sales contact between the supermarket and customers.

(a) Waiting Time

72% of the respondents felt that their waiting time to checkout was too long (Figure 6). The amount of time to checkout fell between 6 and 10 min (Figure 7).

(b) Shoppers' Preferences

Slightly more than half of the respondents (54% to be exact) prefer to use self-service checkout to regular checkout (Figure 8). This

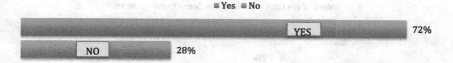

Figure 6: Do You Feel That Your Waiting Time to Checkout is too Long?
Source: Survey and interviews.

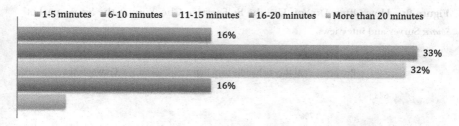

Figure 7: How Long Do You Wait to Checkout?
Source: Survey and interviews.

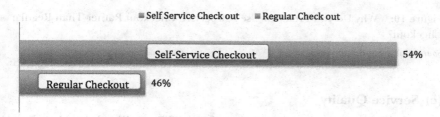

Figure 8: Do You Prefer to Use Self-service Checkout or Regular Checkout?
Source: Survey and interviews.

shows that there is mixed reception toward SST. Not all customers will choose to use the self-service checkouts when given the option.

Only 14% of the respondents stated that they used self-service checkout "most of the time", 19% indicated "often", 46% indicated "sometimes" and 21% indicated "never" (Figure 9).

We investigate the motivation behind the use of self-service checkout rather than the regular checkout. 59% of the respondents highlighted that "speed" was the main factor, 19% attributed it to "convenience", 17% indicated "ability to handle own items" and 6% indicated "privacy" (Figure 10).

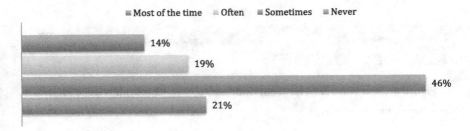

Figure 9:   How Often Do You Use the Self-service Checkout at the Supermarket?
Source: Survey and interviews.

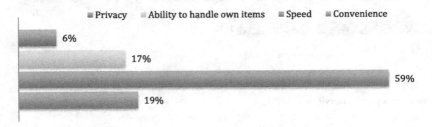

Figure 10:   Why Do You Prefer to Use Self-service Checkout Rather Than Regular Checkout?
Source: Survey and interviews.

(c) Service Quality

In order for customers to accept and use SST readily, the technology should meet certain service qualities. Service quality has been conceptualized as the difference between customer expectations of a service to be received and perceptions of the actual service received (Grönroos, 2001).

About 63% of the respondents stated that they encountered a bad experience at the self-service checkout (Figure 11). When asked what contributed to the bad experience, 31% state that they faced a breakdown in technology (Figure 12). This may mean that the respondents had problems using the machine and had to approach retail staff for help. The breakdown of technology reduces the efficiency of the self-checkout machine and increases the waiting time of customers. 27% state that the self-service checkouts are not user-friendly.

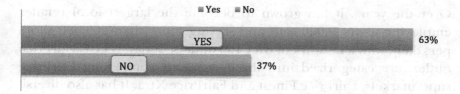

Figure 11: Have You Ever Had a Bad Experience at the Self-service Checkout?
Source: Survey and interviews.

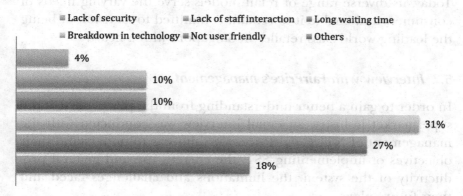

Figure 12: If Yes, What Aspects of the Encountered Had Made it a Bad Experience?
Source: Survey and interviews.

This may be because the machine uses English as the primary language and customers are more comfortable with other languages. 18% stated that there were other factors (e.g. error in pricing; cannot pay by vouchers; inconsiderate users) that contributed to the bad experience (Figure 12). Through our face-to-face interviews, some customers explained that they find machines less responsive and prefer the interaction in the regular checkout.

5. NTUC FairPrice

5.1 *Background of NTUC FairPrice*

The labor movement in 1973 founded NTUC FairPrice Co-operative Ltd, with a social mission to moderate the cost of living in Singapore.

Over the years, it has grown to become the largest local retailer employing about 9,000 staff and serving more than 400,000 shoppers daily, with a network of over 100 outlets. Today, NTUC FairPrice outlets are categorized into three segments comprising FairPrice supermarkets, FairPrice Finest and FairPrice Xtra. It has also diversified into the "convenience store" business, FairPrice Xpress and Cheers, with an established network spanning over 160 locations island-wide, 282 stores and serving over 100,000 shoppers daily. Today, its diverse range of retail models serve the varying needs of consumers and enable it to remain committed to its vision of being the leading world-class retailer in Singapore with a heart.

5.2 *Interview with FairPrice's management*

In order to gain a better understanding from the perspective of the supermarket industry, an email interview was conducted with the management of NTUC FairPrice. The aim was to understand their objectives of implementing SST, the current use and general productivity of the system, the limitations and challenges faced and their future plans.

5.3 *Objectives of implementing SST in NTUC FairPrice*

Implementing SST allows NTUC FairPrice to improve service levels by providing more options for checkout and payment. This is especially relevant in view of the industry-wide manpower shortage. The plan is to serve more customers with the same number of staff. Some of the cashiers can be redeployed to assist customers, and hence enhance customer service experience. Through the improvement in allocation of manpower resource and improvement in service quality, NTUC FairPrice hopes to improve its revenue performance and profitability in the long run.

5.4 *Current use of SST in NTUC FairPrice*

By the end of 2016, NTUC FairPrice has implemented 180 SST machines. There are two main types of SST installations in the stores (observed during our field research). They are (1) self-service checkouts and (2) interactive kiosks such as self-service weighing scales, price checkers and self-service testing station.

(a) Self-service Checkouts

Self-service checkouts are computerized machines that allow shoppers to purchase tangible products using debit and credit card payment machines. These checkout stations are aimed to serve customers with fewer shopping goods in order to reduce customer throughput. According to the management, supermarkets that experience higher customer traffic will place more self-service checkout counters in order to ease the long waiting time. Self-service checkout machines are stationed apart, but in the proximity of regular staffed counters. Customers who have less than 10 items are encouraged to use the self-service checkout machines to ease the long queues.

Currently, 20% of NTUC FairPrice's customers use the self-checkouts in stores where they are available. Young and technologically savvy consumers will proceed to the self-service checkout counters and pay accordingly. Employees are situated near the self-service checkout counters to assist customers who have trouble using the machine. Staff support is essential in the use of self-service checkout counters in supermarkets (Anitsal and Paige, 2006). In NTUC, friendly and well-trained staff provide quick and effective assistance. Anitsal and Paige (2006) conducted a study on consumer adoption and quality perception of self-service checkouts in US grocery stores. The study emphasized a pleasant environment, audible instructions and employee support services for positive consumer responses. Hence, by providing assistance to the shoppers, NTUC seeks to enhance the shopping experience and reduce possible service failure in the use of kiosks to the minimum.

(b) Interactive Self-service Installations

Similarly, the presence of self-service weighing scales, price checkers and self-service testing station allow customers the autonomy to conduct simple activities like weighing items, checking prices and testing products. 30% of NTUC retail outlets are equipped with the self-service weighing machine (see Figure 13). From the management perspective, SST reduces unnecessary manpower costs. In the past, staff are employed to do the job of weighing items. With the use of these free-standing installations, customers are now able to help themselves. To facilitate the use of these machines, detailed instructions are provided. Most of these instructions are only in English and may pose difficulty for some.

Second, interactive kiosks increase customers' autonomy and improve their shopping experience. In NTUC FairPrice Xtra, where electrical appliances are sold, a self-service testing station allows customers to test the electrical appliances. This contributes to a positive customer experience.

5.5 *Productivity of SST in NTUC FairPrice*

NTUC FairPrice perceives that SST can positively impact their business. Benefits include giving customers the choice of checkout methods, some control over the speed of transaction and the option of packing their own purchase. SST also enables the staffs to focus on service-oriented tasks instead of mundane job routines.

Figure 13:   Self-service Kiosks at NTUC Fairprice

Source: Courtesy of NTUC FairPrice Co-operative Ltd.

However, it is hard to attribute all sales improvement and all reduction in waiting time to SST alone. There may be other contributing factors. And, it is recognized that savings in manpower costs has to take into consideration the investment costs of SST. The average payback period in NTUC FairPrice is 3–5 years.

5.6 *Challenges of SST faced by NTUC FairPrice*

On the flip side, NTUC also faces challenges in the implementation of SST. First, there is the challenge of educating customers regarding its usage. To address this, simple instructions are programmed into the SST or printed and placed in full view. Second, there are instances of downtime due to technical issues, but no major incidents that have severely hindered the business.

From the perspective of NTUC FairPrice, there is still room for improving some aspects of SST to better integrate it into the retail process. One area worth noting is that cashless payments currently reside on two terminals, one for credit card and one for NETs payments. It will greatly facilitate customer adoption if the two terminals can be combined into one to make the whole process simpler.

The main consideration for installing SST in some supermarkets but not others is the receptivity of the regular customers. This in turn depends on the customers' technology savviness and openness to the use of new technology.

From our field study, we notice that older customers tend to shun SST. They will approach the retail staff for assistance when using SST. Studies have shown that younger customers are more receptive to using SST when shopping in supermarkets (Kara *et al.*, 2013).

Older customers are unable to see the incorporation of technology as an improvement (Meuter *et al.*, 2003). Although store assistants are stationed there to provide assistance, the older customers will avoid using the self-service checkouts. In Meuter's paper, this behavior is termed "Technology Anxiety". Their findings indicate that customers with higher levels of technology anxiety use fewer

SST. In addition, technology anxiety is also found to influence over-all feelings of satisfaction, intentions to repurchase and the likelihood of participating in positive word of mouth (Curran *et al.*, 2003). Hence, the presence of self-service checkout counters does not necessarily result in a positive outcome (Curran *et al.*, 2003). Uncomfortable feelings toward technology may result in a low rate of adoption of self-service checkouts counters. In addition, older customers may prefer to interact with familiar faces at the check-outs counters. Employee service is also important to incorporate the human touch and provide a point of differentiation between the supermarkets.

5.7 *Future plans for SST*

Having had positive customer reviews and good overall experi-ences with SST thus far, NTUC FairPrice ultimately finds that the benefits of SST outweigh the costs. In the long run, NTUC FairPrice believes that customers will learn to adapt to SST and it will greatly benefit the entire retail industry by alleviating the man-power crunch problem. In fact, NTUC FairPrice views SST as a means to enhance the customers' shopping experience rather than as a means to cope with manpower crunch. As mentioned, only 20% of customers use the Self Machine machines available. Therefore, NTUC FairPrice felt that there is still much potential to be realized and has made plans to further increase their invest-ment in SST.

6. Recommendations

The effort to implement SST effectively is a challenging task. In order to encourage the use of SST machines, it is important to devise and implement strategies that align SST to the goal of customer satisfac-tion and customer commitment. With these in mind, we will recommend strategies to first improve revenue performance and profitability with the use of SST. Second, we wish to resolve the chal-lenges faced by both supermarkets and consumers when using SST.

Third, we wish to increase adoption of SST. In crafting our recommendations, we will draw on the 8Ms productivity framework (Toh and Thangavelu, 2017, Chapters 2 and 3) and focus on five of the factors — Manpower, Message, Make, Method and Management.

6.1 *Improving the SST adoption rate through communication*

When faced with new technology, customers may be overwhelmed initially. According to NTUC FairPrice's management, only 20% of their customers use the self-service machines available. Only 14% of the survey respondents use self-service checkout "most of the time" (Figure 9). Given the low adoption rate, it is pertinent that supermarkets take an active role in encouraging customers to start using the SST machines.

Communication has been found to influence the adoption of technology (Lee *et al.*, 2002). Written and spoken communication from leading supermarkets like NTUC and Cold Storage can help to reduce the inertia of using SST and increase the pervasiveness of SST in supermarkets.

(a) Campaigns (Message)

Supermarkets can take on an active role and run campaigns to promote and increase the adoption rate of SST. In executing the campaigns, supermarkets can launch a "Do-It-Yourself" campaign to incentivize shoppers to utilize and provide feedbacks on the self-service installations. In the survey conducted, 46% of the survey respondents prefer to use regular checkout (Figure 9). This group of customers are comfortable with the conventional way of shopping for groceries. Through the campaigns, customer will have a better understanding of the variety of SST available and the ways to use it. This will encourage adoption and reduce the initial barrier of using SST. These supermarkets can seek financial assistance and advice from SPRING or SPC in order to run its promotional campaigns. As part of the promotional campaign, for a limited period, a discount on the purchase can be given to those customers who use the self-service checkout machines.

(b) Retail Staffs (Manpower)

Strategic manpower management can help in the adoption of SST. Supermarkets should train all retail staffs in SST, and station these staffs at SST locations to facilitate, educate and communicate the value of SST to the customer. Their presence can help to reduce "Technology Anxiety" and lower the inertia of customers. From our survey, 43% of survey respondents find it difficult to use SST. It is crucial that this group of well-trained retail staff are present to encourage the use of SST during the initial stages of implementation in the supermarkets in order to reduce the steep learning curve of users.

6.2 *Minimize the failure rate of SST (Method)*

Customer service failure can reduce overall customer satisfaction and subsequent repurchase behavior (Jones *et al.*, 2007). 31% of our survey respondents state that they have encountered a breakdown in technology while using SST (Figure 12). Often times, there is no recovery system when SST fails unexpectedly (Bitner *et al.*, 2002).

If the matter is not addressed promptly, service failures have been found to arouse anger and discontentment, leading to disastrous consequences for the supermarket (Chang *et al.*, 2008). Meuter *et al.* (2000) reveal that 43% of customer dissatisfaction was due to SST technical failure. Subsequently, 36% was attributed to process failure, 17% to technical design, and 4% to customer fault. Surprisingly, most customers attempt to rectify the error themselves instead of giving up, regardless of assistance from the staff (Nakata, 2003). In addition, Michel (2001), Halstead (1992) and Singh (1981) found that dissatisfied customers were more likely to repurchase when their complaints were dealt with satisfactorily.

Therefore, it is vital that supermarkets have a robust in-built recovery program to rectify process failure. In addition, staff should be on standby around operation hours to provide immediate assistance in case of a technical glitch. The measures mentioned above will reduce the resentment caused by the breakdown in technology.

6.3 *Increase relevance and user friendliness of SST*

(a) Simple SST Design and Useful Features (Method)

A well-designed SST interface should be simplistic and uncluttered, yet able to provide specific instructions for customers to complete a certain task on their own. According to NTUC FairPrice, their SST installations have a variety of features such as price check-up, searching products of different brands and allowing for different modes of payments. These features have to be regularly reviewed and updated for SST to remain relevant.

(b) In-built and Signage Instructions for SST (Method)

27% of the survey respondents state that the self-service checkouts are not user-friendly (Figure 12). Currently, the instruction for SST is primarily in English. If possible, the four main languages (i.e. English, Malay, Tamil and Chinese) should be provided. Alternatively, pictures can be used so that language will not be a barrier.

6.4 *Government online portal for SST*

Apart from monetary incentive to encourage the use of SST, government agencies such as SPRING and SPC, and trade associations can offer infrastructural support to relevant stakeholders of SST. An online portal can be created to allow exchange of ideas under headings such as (1) Seminars and Talks on SST, (2) Vendors of SST, (3) Grants and Incentives by Government and (4) Forum.

(a) Seminars and Talks on SST

This portal can serve as a go-to platform for seminars and talks on SST by big SST vendors such as IBM, international SST associations such as Self Service World and Kiosk Marketplace, and SST experts like Ryan W. Buell from Harvard Business School. Topics can range from breakthrough SST technologies to educational and training courses on SSTs. The target audience for these events can include foreign companies to encourage sharing of knowledge, partnership and exchange of technology and expertise.

(b) Vendors of SST

A consolidation of vendors that supply SST can potentially attract stakeholders to join the portal. Vendors can be charged a minimal fee to be listed on the portal. This fee revenue will help the portal to generate an income to sustain its operations.

(c) Grants and Incentives by Government

By having a significant number of local companies interested in SST on the online portal, it is easy for SPRING and SPC to inform and help these companies with financial and non-financial assistance. This can potentially help local companies to boost their productivity while fulfilling the mission of SPRING and SPC.

(d) Forum

A forum on the online portal serves as an avenue for stakeholders to discuss issues relevant to SST such as reviews of latest SST products and problems of SST. It is also a good platform for SPRING and SPC to observe the "real" needs of local companies to aid them in crafting effective policies and provide grants for supporting productivity initiatives.

7. Conclusion

In this chapter, we sought to better understand how supermarkets can improve their revenue performance and profitability with the use of SST. Based on the information collected from a survey of 57 supermarket shoppers, we reckon that shoppers are still quite ambivalent about using SSTs as part of their shopping experience. Only 57% of the respondents find it not difficult to use SSTs and only 14% use SSTs to checkout their purchase "most of the time". A high percentage (63%) of respondents reported that they had encountered bad experience in their use of SST checkout machines. This reflects either the lack of techno familiarity and sophistication on the part of the consumers or the SST machines are still not user-friendly enough.

The case study of the nation's premier supermarket had helped to ascertain the value and purpose of SSTs in enhancing service quality and providing relief to the pressure of manpower shortage. The use of SST can result in an improvement in productivity of manpower and increase the profitability of the firm. Nonetheless, successful introduction and implementation of SSTs requires concerted effort in educating and guiding the consumers and a reliable maintenance regime that minimizes technical breakdown of machines. More initiatives need to be taken for SST to be used more pervasively in Singapore. It is important that all stakeholders are able to work together and implement strategies that align SST to the goal of customer satisfaction and customer commitment.

Chapter 3

Seeking Productivity Improvement with Self Service Technology (SST) in the F&B Sector: Case Study of Six Restaurants and a Consumer Survey

1. Introduction

1.1 *Singapore food and beverage sector and present challenges*

The Food and Beverage (F&B) sector in Singapore is a key part of Singapore's economy. Together with accommodation, the F&B sector contributed to 2.2% of the nominal Gross Domestic Product (GDP) in 2016. Other than the economic perspective, the F&B sector also plays an important role in the vibrancy of the employment market. According to the Manpower Resources Guide for F&B Industry published by Ministry of Manpower in 2010, the industry employs about 213,300 workers or 8.0% of the overall service workforce.

The island's diverse food culture and Singaporean's increasing appetite for eating out has created a solid demand base for a thriving industry. According to statistics provided by the Standards, Productivity and Innovation Board (SPRING), Singapore, the number of establishments in the F&B sector increased from 6,462 in 2011 to 7,260 in 2015, which is an increase of 12.3% over the period. There is a wide variety of F&B outlets, ranging from fine dining eateries and restaurants to food trucks. On Singapore Stock Exchange (SGX), the F&B industry accounts for a diverse group of more than 60 businesses involved in different aspects of food production and distribution. Many of the local eateries have also ventured overseas through joint venture, franchising or corporate alliance. All of these suggest that F&B industry is an ever-growing sector with exciting prospects ahead.

Despite a positive outlook, the F&B sector faces a declining sales growth rate, which partially contributes to the slowing down of GDP growth rate in Singapore. The economy is expected to grow at only 2% to 4% this year despite a strong upward trajectory in external-facing activities. The slowing productivity growth in the domestic economy, particularly the F&B sector, is alarming and requires attention. Published figures from the Ministry of Trade of industry shows that the labour productivity of the F&B sector together with the Accommodation sector was declining at a rate of 1.7% per annum between 2013 and 2016, the second worse performing sector after business services sector.

The tightening of foreign labor employment regulations by the Singapore government may be one contributing factor to the productivity drop. Relevant regulations pose significant challenges to any labor-intensive sector like F&B. The curb on the inflow of foreign workers and higher levies, which were progressively introduced from July 2013, have forced a greater reliance on Singaporean workers. However, jobs in the F&B sector are hardly perceived to be the dream job for many Singaporeans. Since the end of 2009, about 20,000 to 37,000 new jobs have been published every three months. However, there have not been enough locals to fill the vacancies. Many of the restaurants surveyed by the Business Times in 2013 agreed they needed about 10–40% more staff to function optimally. The manpower shortage is commonly dealt with by tapping into the part-time labor pool, which is largely made up of students and those looking for a casual position to earn some extra cash. However, over reliance on this pool of workers puts businesses in a risky proposition as their availability is seasonal and their commitment period is erratic.

The impact of a severe manpower crunch is worsened by the high employee turnover rate. According to the figures published by the Ministry of Manpower, the average monthly turn-over rate (defined as the sum of recruitment rate and resignation rate) for the Food & Beverage Services in 2016 is 8% which is twice that of the economy wide figure. When employees including part time staffs leave frequently, the companies find fewer incentives to provide adequate training. Therefore, it is difficult to offer uniform and consistent service with good quality. This tends to affect both the productivity and sustainability of the companies in the F&B industry.

Keen competition in the sector has moderated the increase in the prices for food charged by operators. On the other hand, rising costs of ingredients, gas and electricity bills, and soaring retail rents exert substantial squeeze on the profit margin of the enterprises in the F&B sector. The Straits Times published in 2012 that the rental price has increased by almost three folds to $25–$35 per square foot a month from $9 to $12 per square foot in 1988. It currently still hovers around $30 per square foot per month. The Straits Times published in 2012 that the rental price has increased from $9 to $12 per square foot a month in 1988 to $25–$35 per square foot in 2012. The rising expenditures have forced many restaurants to either raise prices, reduce food portions or quality in order to stay competitive. This is likely to severely hamper the quality of their customer service, and therefore this affects the long term sustainability and productivity of the restaurants.

The foreign labor regulation, manpower crunch, high employee turnover rate, rising inflation, costs and rentals all collectively place significant pressures on the F&B sector and adversely affect the sector's productivity. Therefore, maximizing efficiency with limited manpower supply and maintaining competitiveness is the most important issue that needs to be addressed immediately.

1.2 *Objectives and organization*

One of the methods widely adopted to reduce dependency on manpower is the use of Self-service Technologies (SSTs). SSTs are technological interfaces that enable customers to produce a service independent of direct service employee involvement. The most commonly used SSTs can be categorized into three types including (1) self-service kiosk, (2) smart phone application or tablet PC and (3) conveyor belt or buzzer, etc. The study mainly presents analysis on SSTs through the three categories.

According to an annual survey conducted in 2015 by the Singapore Department of Statistics on the service industries, restaurants represent the largest segment in F&B services industry, accounting for 36.6% of the total number of establishments in 2012. Despite their significant presence in F&B sector, restaurants have recorded the lowest profitability ratio, suggesting high operational inefficiency. Therefore, this study focuses our studies on the restaurants in F&B industry and their adoption of SSTs. We mainly aim to evaluate the feasibility, benefits, hindrances and effectiveness in adopting the technologies to help boost productivity of firms in the F&B sector. Under the 8M Framework of Productivity Improvement, this study focuses on providing recommendations in the aspects of Management, Manpower and Method. The study also presents recommendations for companies and trade associations in F&B sector to improve productivity through the deployment of SSTs.

The chapter starts by presenting background information of the Singapore F&B sector and challenges ahead. The adoption of SSTs can be an important solution to current difficulties. Section 2 then displays secondary information on the general usage of SSTs across industries, especially in the F&B sector. It also presents findings from past studies on benefits and challenges of adopting SST. Section 3 analyzes findings from our company studies. Following that, the learning points from a survey of 46 consumers have been elaborated in Section 4. The case studies and consumer surveys provide pertinent inputs for the suggestions and recommendations relating to usage of SST in improving productivity in the F&B sector, and these recommendations are provided in Section 5. Section 6 concludes the chapter.

2. Usage of Self-service Technology

2.1 *Current usage of self-service technology*

There is a rising trend in adoption of SSTs in the F&B sector. Technology is increasingly playing an important role in the services sector and is dramatically changing the business transaction model. Technology is also changing the way services are delivered and the way companies are managed. We experience Self Service Technologies every day in our personal life as consumers — when we withdraw money from Automated Teller Machine (ATM); when we call an organization and are asked to navigate through a series of telephone menu options before talking to a person in the desired department; or when we book a taxi through mobile applications. The most common industries adopting SST are hotels, F&B, banks and entertainment enterprises.

The SSTs have also begun to infiltrate the food and beverage world in a way that is irreversible and all-encompassing, thereby saving labor, time and money for the owners. Due to the limited secondary information and research available in this field, we have conducted a sampling of 50 restaurants in Singapore to derive a illustrative overview of the usage of SSTs in Singapore. Our study found that 30% of the overall sample is currently using SSTs. Despite being a relatively smaller portion compared to those not adopting SSTs, it demonstrates the significant presence of SSTs' in the Singapore F&B sector. Indeed, there is a consistently growing number of hospitality operators deploying SSTs in their businesses as found in studies conducted by Hospitality Technology Magazine in 2009.

2.2 *Commonly used self-service technologies*

While some SSTs are very much welcomed by consumers, others take longer to be accepted and widely practiced. Some commonly used SSTs can include ATM, pay-at-the-pump gas terminals, movie ticket kiosks and automatic hotel checkout machines. SSTs practically exist in all industries today. The common SSTs observed in F&B sector include the iPad or other tablet PC for food ordering, self-service kiosk outside the shop for queue management, conveyor belt for food delivery and buzzer which rings when it is the customers' turn to collect the food.

According to Hotel Business Review, the latest trend in the F&B industry is to use smart phone applications as an order taking device since it offers a practical and cost-effective alternative to tablet PCs and the traditional handheld Point of Sale (POS) devices. Moreover, there are even more advanced technologies on the horizon. The next step in the SST industry is likely to be the migration of commonly used SSTs such as Self-Service Kiosks to more advanced and convenient technologies. For example, in near future, customers may be able to place orders through their car GPS system and make payments via self-swipe credit, debit card scanners and smart phones.

2.3 Benefits

Reduction in waiting time: Successful adoptions of SSTs have led to reduction in customer waiting time. For example, Yoshinoya, a Japanese restaurant, adopted self-service kiosks and observed that waiting time from order to delivery reduced by 17%. Jumbo Seafood reported a 50% reduction in customer waiting time after adopting wireless ordering. SSTs allow food orders to be delivered to the kitchen immediately. It also enables customers to complete all procedures such as queuing, ordering and making payment via one terminal, which highly improves the operational efficiency. This can also lead to a faster table turnover rate and therefore reduce customer waiting time.

Reduction in operational costs: Operational costs can be reduced through the adoption of SSTs as well. Deployment of SSTs can enable service at higher accuracy compared to human services. According to studies conducted by Hospitality Technology Magazine in 2009, over 64% of consumers in the study agree that one reason why they like to use self-service kiosks is its high accuracy. One successful example is the adoption of self-service kiosk in Yoshinoya, which has helped to eliminate wrong food orders. It has managed to reduce food waste by 24% and also reduce operational costs.

Improvement in customer service: The Hospitality Technology survey in 2009 found that improvement in customer service remains a key reason behind the implementation of SSTs. Furthermore many have agreed that, in terms of motivation to use SSTs, improving customer services is a more important factor than reducing operational cost. Meuter *et al.* (2000) found that SSTs can improve customer satisfaction whenever the customer perceives that the technology is a better alternative than the traditional face-to-face method of service delivery. Moreover, the reduced waiting time also contributes to improvement of customer service.

Reduction in reliance on manpower: Another major motivation behind adoption of SSTs is to provide customer service without tying up the company's human resources (Hsieh, 2005). According to the SPRING Singapore, it is a feasible solution for restaurants to implement an integrated "self-service" concept to overcome the difficulties posed by the tightening of foreign labor supply. For example, since the adoption of wireless ordering, Jumbo Seafood has observed 40% reduction in manpower from 5 to 3 staff needed at every station. Loof has observed a 28% reduction in manpower from 14 to 10 staff and 11% reduction in manpower costs after deploying similar SSTs. Therefore, SSTs can also be successfully utilized to reduce restaurants' reliance on manpower.

2.4 *Challenges and hindrances*

Difficult to change customer mindsets: A study conducted by *Today Newspaper* suggests, Singaporean customers' attitude toward self-service takes time to change. As explained by one restaurant owner, "there may be perception that if a customer is paying $15 for food at a restaurant, they won't have to do self-service as they are paying the service charge". Changing social norms and the general public's attitudes toward SSTs can be difficult, thus creating significant challenges for restaurant owners who intend to make use of such technologies. However, Bitner *et al.*'s (2002) study found that the combination of written and oral communication to customers can significantly improve their readiness to adapt to new technologies.

Different acceptance rates to new technology: Researchers have found that not all customers have the same level of acceptance to and expertise with various technologies. Predicting customers' appeal is not easy. "Neat ideas" may or may not add value to customers (Fickel, 2000). A study on SST adoption in Sweden also found that participants aged 20 to 30 years have greater inclination to use SSTs compared to other age groups (31–40 and 41–50 years old) (Bashir and Albarbarawi, 2011). Therefore, the adoption of SSTs may or may not be appealing to certain group of customers. Companies should carefully analyze targeted customer segments, their technological readiness and the type of SSTs they are likely to accept before proceeding with the project. More importantly, companies should not force all customers to accept SSTs. There should be alternative routes to prevent dissatisfied customers (Bitner *et al.*, 2002).

Limited technological options: Though there are various kinds of SSTs available in the market, companies still find technological limitation a significant challenge. For instance, there are some service options that are not suitable for SST due to security and privacy concerns. Moreover, there are also other issues such as the incompatibility of restaurant menus and the technological interfaces (Hendricks, 2002). The survey conducted by Hospitality Technology in 2009 indicated the top barrier to kiosk deployment in United States was that "Self-service does not fit in with my establishment's particular environment" with 49% of respondents citing this factor. This demonstrates how technological constraints prohibit companies from adopting SSTs.

Technology breakdowns: Studies done by Bitner *et al.* (2002) have found that the largest percentage of negative responses regarding SSTs was attributed to SST failure. Another study by Meuter *et al.* (2000) revealed that 43% of customer dissatisfaction was because of SST technical failure. These were followed by 36% due to process failure, 17% due to technical design and 4% due to customer fault. Therefore, technological breakdown is a significant challenge for companies intending to adopt SSTs. Firms need to deploy robust technologies, conduct regular maintenance as well as provide on the spot assistance with experienced staff.

2.5 *Measures adopted*

Many papers have provided suggestions and recommendations on procedures to adopt SSTs. First of all, Bitner *et al.* (2002) provided one useful diagnostic exercise for companies to evaluate the effectiveness of their current SSTs or to develop new SSTs. The diagnostic exercise includes the important questions that companies need to constantly ask themselves before the continuation of their SST projects. These questions include:

- What was the rationale for introducing SST?
- How would you rate the SST's success so far?
- What challenges are you facing in the future with this SST?
- Is your company providing excellent service to your customer via this SST?
- Are the basic requirements for customer satisfaction being met?
- Are customers likely to adopt this SST?

Iris Ong (2010) also proposed a conceptual framework in her study of Self Service Technologies in Singapore. A company intending to use SST is recommended to follow 6 basic steps:

(1) Define the current service flow
(2) Establish the risk and opportunity with using SSTs
(3) Determine factors that limit the adoption of SSTs
(4) Identify and assess (do cost-benefit analysis) the types of SSTs available
(5) Testing and Implementation
(6) Evaluate and monitor the outcome from using SST

Many Singapore companies have also readily made use of funding from Singapore government agencies to facilitate the adoption process. For example, according to *Today Newspaper*, in July 2014, more than 17,000 Singapore firms have benefited from productivity initiatives under the National Productivity and Continuing Education Council, such as the Productivity and Innovation Credit Scheme. It had paid out $1.5 billion in cash and tax savings as of 28 February 2014. In addition, more than 2,700 Innovation and Capability Vouchers (ICV) were also awarded during the second quarter of 2014. According to SPRING Singapore, the ICV is a voucher valued at $5,000, to encourage SMEs to take their first step toward capability development. SMEs can use the voucher to upgrade and strengthen their core business operations through consultancy in the areas of innovation, productivity, human resources and financial management. Apart from consultancy, ICV also supports SMEs in the adoption and implementation of simple solutions to improve business efficiency and productivity. Each SME is entitled to a maximum of eight vouchers. Each ICV project must be completed before the submission of a new application. All these funding schemes can be useful financial support to ensure proper and smooth adoption of SSTs to some extent.

3. Case Studies on SST Adoption by Restaurants in Singapore

3.1 *Research scope and methodology*

In order to provide a more detailed analysis of the adoption of SSTs in Singapore restaurants, we analyse the responses of 46 consumers in a sample survey, and also conducted case studies involving establishments from 6 restaurant holding groups. Face-to-face interviews were conducted with restaurant managers or owners in order to find out their perceptions and experiences of adopting SST. The companies include restaurants from diverse backgrounds ranging from fast food joints and cafés to casual dining with operational experience from less than 1 year to more than 10 years. Companies which have not adopted SSTs are also included in the case studies in order to help identify the factors that prevent them from using SSTs.

The consumer survey also targets people from diverse educational and age backgrounds. Both internet surveys and face-to-face interviews were carried out in order to reach different target groups. According to secondary information as discussed above, we presume that young people aged from 14 to 35 are the main users of SSTs and they are the critical group behind successful adoption. Therefore, 30 out of 46 consumers are allocated to represent this sample population.

A list of questions asked during the interview of restaurants' owners or managers as well as a list of questions included in the consumers' survey are presented in the Appendix to this chapter.

3.2 *Characteristics of sampled restaurants*

Characteristics of restaurant holding companies: We have interviewed six restaurant holding companies. They will be noted as Restaurant A, B, C, D, E and F, respectively, for confidentiality reasons. Among them, three operate casual dining restaurants and the other three are fast food restaurants. The years of operation of the restaurants range from 1 year to more than 60 years. A majority have only 1–3 outlets except for Company B, which is a large food holding company with 87 outlets in Singapore and more overseas. Table 1 below shows the background information of these restaurants holding companies studied.

Table 1:   Background Information of Restaurant Holding Companies

Company	Type of Restaurants	Years in Operation	No. of Employees	No. of Outlets	Usage of SST
A	Fast food	4–6 years	50	3	Using
B	Fast food	Around 60 years	No clear figure	87	Using
C	Casual dining	Above 10 years	12	1	Considered
D	Casual dining	1.5 years	50	3	Considered
E	Fast food	69 years	60	2	Not at all
F	Casual dining	1 years	12	1	Not at all

Source: Company interviews.

Among the six companies in F&B sector, two are currently using SST, two have considered adoption but have not yet done so, and another two have not considered using SST at all. Therefore, the analysis below categorizes them into two groups and evaluates them accordingly. This sample gives a diverse picture of restaurants at different stages of SST adoption. Therefore, it presents a more holistic view of possible measures to suggest to trade associations and agencies in order to encourage smooth adoption of SSTs in the F&B sector.

3.3 *Results and findings*

(a) Group 1: Have not adopted SST

Companies under group 1 include Restaurants C, D, E and F. Both Restaurants E and F have never considered adopting SSTs at all. Restaurants C and D have done some business analysis regarding this decision but eventually abandoned or postponed the project. As a casual dining eatery, Restaurant C offers authentic Italian food since 1995. Company D manages three outlets of Vietnamese Restaurants offering a variety of classic local dishes. Restaurant E has been distributing rice dumplings in Singapore for over 60 years. It also has been credited as one of the best restaurants in Changi Airport by Bloomberg and Reuters. Restaurant F was established last year in 2013. It is currently operating one outlet, which is positioned as a family-friendly bistro.

(i) Types of SSTs interested in:

Smart phone or tablet PC: Company C intended to adopt tablet PCs and POS system for food ordering and payment. The owner also hopes to do marketing through such technological platforms whenever there are new products coming up. The management is also interested in getting firsthand reports and feedbacks generated directly by the system.

Company D had a similar plan to install tablet PC for order taking. Company E, despite never considering adopting SSTs, also believes online application or tablet PC can be useful for their restaurants. The technologies can be used to take orders while people are queuing for seats outside the restaurant. In this way, table turnover rate is also likely to be improved.

Conveyor belt: Company F however finds conveyor belt, which can transfer food directly from the kitchen, is going to be very useful due to the ease of usage. It helps to reduce manpower reliance as waiters and waitresses no longer need to bring food from the kitchen. Operational efficiency is also likely to be improved. Minimum manpower can be effectively engaged to maintain the desirable service level.

(ii) Major benefits looking for:

To reduce customer waiting time: Company C believes that tablet PC supplemented with human service can assist in reducing customers' waiting time. With vivid pictures from tablet PCs and possible audio explanations of the menu, customers can make decisions faster. Therefore the table turnover rate can be improved significantly. This is consistent with findings presented in Section 2. There are many successful cases of reduced customer waiting time after adoption of SSTs. The manager from Company D also agrees with this point. She believes food orders can be sent faster to the kitchen through SSTs, and thus this helps to reduce customer waiting time.

To gather firsthand business data: The owner of Company C brings up another major reason for his intention to adopt SSTs. He hopes to get firsthand and quick updates on customer preferences and product consumption patterns. Web-based tablet PCs and kiosk ordering systems are usually able to record customers' consumption patterns, for example the most popular products in particular outlets. They can also help to consistently upsell higher margin products. Therefore, products with highest sales or profit margins can be easily identified; the inventory management process can be optimized with the better knowledge of product demand; and furthermore customer feedback can be gathered at a faster rate.

To reduce reliance on manpower: All of the four companies agree that reducing reliance on manpower is the major benefit they are looking for if they adopt SST in future. Due to the tightening foreign labor laws as explained in Section 1, Companies C, D, E and F have all experienced labor constraints. The manager from Company E recognizes that the reduction of reliance on manpower can boost the restaurant's productivity as well. The 8M Framework for productivity improvement provides the fundamental support for this view, since manpower is one major component behind productivity boost. Employees serving the customers can be involved in other functions of the company such as learning the skill in making a new cocktail drink, and operating equipment that assist in food ingredients preparation. Therefore, value-added per worker to the company can be increased due to improvement in choice of products offered and lower cost of food production.

(iii) Major reasons for not adopting:

Reliability: The manager from Company E reports that one main reason for not adopting SSTs is the lack of reliability of such technological devices. The potential cases of customers cheating and false payments can generate many disputes. This is likely to hamper the company's productivity instead of improving it.

Costs: High implementation cost is another reason brought up by Company E. Company F shares the same concern regarding high costs, especially since SSTs such as the installation of conveyor belts may require renovation of the entire restaurant.

Inadequate communication: Company C has seriously contemplated the adoption of tablet PCs and POS systems in its restaurant more than 7 months before the interview. Together with its technology vendor, it has approached SPRING Singapore to apply for assistance under the Innovation & Capability Voucher (ICV) scheme. The aim of ICV is to encourage Small and Medium Enterprises to take the first step toward capability development by using the S$5,000 voucher to engage consultants to help in upgrading and strengthening their core business operations in the areas of innovation, productivity, human resources and financial management.

After many months of waiting, Company C is still unable to get approval for assistance under the ICV scheme. The company has to abandon the project. The owner of Company F also mentioned the tedious paper filing process to apply for government grants has offset the incentives to adopt SSTs. These examples may well reflect bureaucracy in application and inefficient approval process, but could also be inadequacy of information provided by the applicant that stop the process from going forward. Care and prudence have to be exercised in expending taxpayers' money. Therefore, there is a need for better communication between applicants and grants giver to enable the objectives of the scheme be attained.

Difficult technological interfaces: The manager at Company D says they have examined many technology interfaces from various suppliers and found them incompatible with the menus. They find that these platforms are not user friendly enough to be adopted smoothly.

Technology breakdown: The manager at Company D also acknowledges high maintenance cost as another major hindrance. Their analysis presents that maintenance costs may not be justified by the costs saved from manpower reduction. On top of this, customers tend to remember their failed experiences with technologies rather than the happy ones. Adopting SSTs may lead to more dissatisfying customer services due to the technology breakdowns.

(b) Group 2: Currently using SSTs

Companies under group 2 include Companies A and B. Company A is a fast food restaurant with 4–6 years of experience. It was first established in Japan in 1990 and later expanded to Singapore. It has adopted SSTs at both outlets. The third one will be opening soon. Company B is another fast food restaurant with over 60 years of operation. It has more than 80 outlets in Singapore, which include both retail stores and dine-in restaurants. In recent years, it started to adopt SSTs in some restaurants.

(i) Types of SSTs adopted:

Smart phone application/tablet PC: Company A has adopted iPad for food ordering. It is the only method of placing orders in the restaurant, which also serves as an advertising tool whenever the company is rolling out promotion packages.

Self-service kiosk: Company B adopted a self-service kiosk outside some of its dining-in restaurants for customers to send orders, make payments, get the receipt and queue numbers.

Conveyor belt: Company A is proud of its conveyor belt delivery system, which the manager refers to as the Direct Train Delivery System. Once orders are sent from iPad, the kitchen will prepare the food, which will then be sent out later via plastic bullet train toy. The train stops in front of customers' table. Once they collect the food, they press a yellow button on top of the train and it will return to the kitchen for next round of food delivery.

(ii) Adoption process and frequency of usage:

Both companies find the adoption process moderately or very convenient. Both managers started the process by sourcing for appropriate technological devices which can fit in with their needs. They both provided employees with some training in using the SSTs to ensure they will be able to assist customers.

The manager from Company A finds it is relatively easy to teach customers on how to use these SSTs. Most adapt fast to the iPad ordering and Direct Train Delivery System with some to little guidance from the restaurant. The manager from Company B believes incentives are necessary to encourage customers to use the SSTs rather than the traditional human-assisted alternative. Therefore, for those choosing to order food through self-service kiosk, they get a $1 discount. The company finds this a very effective strategy to encourage smoother adoption and greater usage of SSTs.

In Restaurant A, all food orderings and deliveries are done through SSTs. Therefore, the usage is very high. On the other hand, in Restaurant B, the self-service kiosk is presented as an alternative to human service. The SSTs are still used very frequently even though there can be a slightly longer queue at the human counter sometimes.

(iii) Major benefits realized:

Reduced reliance on manpower: Both Companies A and B adopted SSTs in order to reduce reliance on manpower. This is the major benefit they are looking for. SSTs are considered not as a replacement of human service, but rather as an additional support to counter the effects of tightening foreign labor supply. This intention coincides with those of all four companies, C, D, E and F studied above.

Company A has adopted SSTs since the very beginning of its establishment. Therefore, the exact figure of manpower reduction is unknown. However, the manager agrees the adoption of SSTs has successfully helped them to reduce manpower reliance to some extent, such that they would have to hire more employees per store without the SSTs. Company B also agrees that the adoption helped to reduce manpower reliance significantly. Initially they required 15–30 staff per store. With the adoption of SSTs to take orders, collect payments and manage queues etc., they now only require 6–7 staff per store.

Improved customer satisfaction: The manager at Company A believes that the adoption improved dining satisfaction for some groups of customers, but not necessarily all the customers. He has observed that customers who are younger and more receptive of new technology tend to like the idea of Direct Train Delivery System. Parents are also more likely to take their children to revisit the restaurant because many like to see the toy train coming out of the kitchen. In this way, the SST has become a unique selling point of Company A and also helps to improve customer satisfaction.

The manager from Company B also agrees there is an improvement in customer satisfaction to some extent. Due to the adoption of SSTs, the customer waiting time is significantly reduced. Moreover, Company B gives $1 discount to customers using the self-service kiosk. Customers are also exempted from service charge if they do their own packaging. In this way, people who are more budget-conscious find the adoption of SSTs reasonable, and their satisfaction levels increase accordingly.

Both companies agree there may not be improvement in customer satisfaction for all type of customers. Instead, adoption of

SSTs may have an adverse impact on customer satisfactions for those who are less receptive to new technology or who are slow in learning to use the SSTs.

Improved operational efficiency: Company A finds a positive correlation between technology and operational efficiency. An increased investment in SSTs helps to raise the efficiency ratio for both outlets such that greater revenues can be generated with lesser inputs in operation. The manager at Company B explains that SSTs help to reduce the number of employees needed per store. Therefore, the unit cost invested in people is reduced but their revenue does not decrease accordingly, which leads to an improvement in operational efficiency as well as profitability.

(iv) Major challenges encountered:

High maintenance cost: Company A finds that the biggest challenge lies in the regular maintenances of the SSTs. Adopting iPads in restaurants for commercial purposes is very different from its domestic usage. The frequency of touching the screen can be 50 times more. Therefore, the company needs to service these technologies once per week. The manager reports that 50% of the cost saved from the reduction of manpower has been incurred on the technology maintenance.

Difficult to change customer mindset: On the other hand, Company B states that the greatest challenge lies in changing customers' mindset toward SSTs. As indicated above, customers' perception toward SSTs is a significant factor that affects the successful adoption of SSTs in restaurants. The manager at Company B observes that customers always hesitate to try the new technology regardless of age. Young people however have faster rates of adoption, while the older generations still tend to queue up at the human counter. Many customers still prefer human interactions. Some important elements of the human services, such as warm smiles, polite greetings etc. cannot be easily replaced by technology. Therefore, due to the difficulty in changing customers' mindsets, the perceived service quality of the restaurant may possibly decrease rather than increase.

Technological constraints: Company B finds another big constraint posed by SSTs is the technological interfaces. The self-service kiosk adopted only accepts card payments right now. Due to this technological limitation, the cash option is not available. This has posed quite a number of problems for customers who prefer to use cash or are buying small quantities. Therefore, technological limitations place constraints on restaurants who want to encourage better adoption of the SSTs.

4. Consumer Opinions on the Use of SST in Restaurants

4.1 *Characteristics of consumers sampled*

A total of 30 customers completed the online questionnaires, and 16 of them participated in the face-to-face interviews. The proportion of male respondents (57%) was slightly higher than the proportion of female respondents (43%). The largest group of respondents was between the age group of 20–35 (57%). However, the sample includes customers ranging from under 20 years old to above 60 years old, as shown in Figure 1. In terms of education, 48% of the respondents had college education background, as shown in Figure 2.

Overall, the respondents were relatively younger with higher education level compared to the general public. We note that though our samples may not be representative of the whole popula-

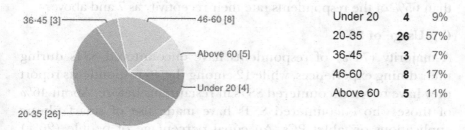

Under 20	4	9%
20-35	26	57%
36-45	3	7%
46-60	8	17%
Above 60	5	11%

Figure 1: Question 2 "Please Indicate Your Age Group", Survey Questions to Consumers, 2014

Source: Consumer survey.

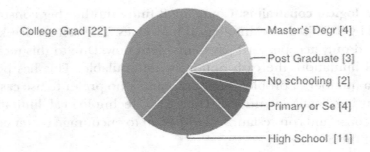

Figure 2: Question 3 "What is the Highest Degree or Level of School You Have Completed? If Currently Enrolled, Highest Degree Received", Survey Questions to Consumers, 2014

Source: Consumer survey.

tion, a large portion of the sample consists of young and educated respondents who are likely to be potential users of SSTs.

4.2 *Findings from consumer interviews*

(a) High receptivity to new technology and SSTs

The majority of the sampled customers (92%) rate their comfort level with new technology higher or equal to five upon ten. More than half of them (55%) provide a rating higher than 7, which indicates that they are quite comfortable with new technology.

Sampled customers also have high receptivity to SSTs at restaurants. Over 90% of them rate their openness to SSTs above average. More than 65% of the respondents rate their receptivity as 7 and above.

(b) Usage of SSTs

A majority (74%) of respondents have encountered SSTs during their dining experiences, while 12 among the 46 respondents report they have never encountered SSTs in restaurants before. About 46% of those who encountered SSTs have made use of smart phone applications or tablet PCs. An equal percentage of people (26%) used either self-service kiosk or conveyor belt at restaurants. Among them, about half use the SST every time there is one available. However, 35% of those who encountered SSTs in restaurants only use the technologies as an alternative to avoid long queues or other dissatisfying factors in human services.

36% of respondents use SSTs at restaurants for food ordering, while 25% use the technologies for take-away orders. Another 17% stated that the SSTs they have encountered are used as a queue management system.

(c) Perception of SSTs

- ### Perceived benefits

User-friendly technologies: A significant portion of customers (86%) who have made use of the SSTs in restaurants consider the technologies moderately or highly user friendly. Only a small percentage of them (6%) find SSTs not user friendly at all.

Reduced waiting time: 92% of the respondents believe SSTs have reduced their waiting time by providing better queue management, faster table turnover rate, faster food ordering and payment process, and higher operational efficiency within the restaurants. Moreover, 22% of them believe that their waiting time has been reduced to a large extent.

Improved dining experience: Over 63% of the respondents believe that their dining experiences have been improved to some extent or more through SSTs. 78% in total find that SSTs contribute positively to deliver good services. However, it is notable that 3% of the respondents who have made use of the SSTs believe that their dining experiences will be more satisfying without SSTs.

- ### Perceived challenges

Technology breakdown: About a quarter of the respondents (25%) stated that one major challenge they have encountered is technology breakdown. As supported by findings from Section 2, customers always tend to remember their dissatisfying encounters with technologies rather than the "happy memories". Once a customer has an unhappy experience due to a technology breakdown, it significantly downgrades his perceptions of SSTs and the restaurant.

Not at ease with new technology: Despite a generally high rate of receptivity to new technology, 22% of the respondents who have encountered SSTs still find themselves not at ease with the new technology. In the new information era with rapid development of technology, people may have significantly improved their openness to new technologies, but still feel uneasy over learning and adapting to new things.

Do not know how to use: 16% of the respondents perceive little knowledge of how to use the SSTs as another major challenge. Many people are uneasy over new technology because they do not know how to use them. It is human nature that many are unwilling to learn and explore things outside of their comfort zone. Some believe the struggle to explore or to learn how to use the SSTs may demonstrate stupidity in public and thus increase their stress levels. Such perceptions result in many unhappy dining experiences because of SSTs. A few recommend that guidance from the restaurant or convenient technology interfaces can be very useful to overcome this uneasiness.

Prefer human interaction: Despite respondents' openness to new technologies and SSTs, majority of them (64%) still prefer human interactions instead of SSTs once they are asked to choose between the two. Human interactions always form the basis of service industry. Technologies fail to provide the kind of connections and bonding that can be achieved through a friendly smile, a polite greeting or other forms of human interactions. Furthermore, SSTs in restaurants can sometimes alienate customers instead of forging the kind of attachments human interactions can give.

Overall, the adoption of SSTs in restaurants can generate several positive benefits such as the reduction of reliance on manpower, improved customer satisfaction and operational efficiency, etc. The sampled customers show strong receptivity to SSTs. They have also recognized SSTs' user friendliness and their contribution to less waiting time and more efficient services. However, restaurants still need to take actions to overcome the challenges posed by SSTs, such as frequent technological breakdowns, customers' uneasiness over new technologies and their preferences for human services. The next section will provide recommendations for restaurant owners and trade associations to ensure proper adoption of SSTs in the F&B sector.

5. Recommendations

As analyzed in Section 3 and 4, the three major steps in adopting SSTs lie in the adoption process, changing customers' mindsets, and the management of SSTs. This section provides recommendations for both the restaurant owners and trade associations on how to encourage wider and smoother deployment of SSTs in the F&B sector.

5.1 *Issue 1: Adopting SST and recommendations*

(a) Recommendation for restaurant owners

Choose simple and compatible technological platforms: Restaurant owners are recommended to choose simple technological platforms which best fit in with their business needs. The SSTs commonly found in F&B sector include self-service kiosks, smart phone applications, tablet PCs, conveyor belts and buzzers, etc. However, the kinds of SSTs available are not restricted to this list. The type of SSTs chosen must fit in with the company's objectives, restaurant nature and targeted customer segments. Based on findings from secondary research, our surveys and case studies, the following table (Table 2) provides a list of various SSTs and the corresponding situations they are most suited for.

As indicated in Table 2, there are many different options of technological platforms and interfaces to choose from for each type of SST. As discussed by the manager from Company D, one major reason for not adopting the tablet PCs is the absence of a simple technological interface which can be compatible with their menus. Therefore, restaurant owners should be extremely careful when choosing the type of SSTs and the technology platforms to be adopted. This is usually the most important consideration while adopting SSTs.

Table 2: Choice of SSTs for Different Functions

Types of SSTs	Functions of SSTs	Business goals of SSTs	Restaurant Nature	Suitable Customer Segments
Self-service kiosk	• Queue management • Automatic payment • Food ordering	• Reduce queuing time • Reduce customer waiting time for food • Reduce manpower reliance • Improve operational efficiency	All types of restaurants, commonly in fast food restaurants	Prefer younger generation workers with some educational background
Smart phone application/tablet PC	• Food ordering • Marketing & advertising	• Improve operational efficiency • Reduce customer waiting time • Reduce manpower reliance	Casual dining, café or bistro	Prefer younger generation workers with some educational background
Conveyor belt	• Food delivery • Food display	• Improve operational efficiency • Reduce manpower reliance • Unique selling point of the restaurant	Fast food or casual dining	Suitable for all types of customers
Buzzer	• Queue management	• Improve operation efficiency • Reduce customer waiting time • Improve customer satisfaction level	Fast food, casual dining, café or bistro	Suitable for all types of customers

Source: Compiled from secondary sources, surveys and case studies.

(b) Recommendation for trade associations and agencies

Cooperate with technology companies: Trade associations and agencies are recommended to cooperate with technological companies to develop more SSTs with greater functionality and variability in order to meet different business needs.

As indicated by the manager at Company B in Section 3, the kind of self-service kiosk they have adopted faces several technological constraints such as not being able to accept cash and certain types of credit cards. The manager at Company D also recommended government agencies to work with technological companies to develop simpler interfaces or solutions which can adapt to their restaurants' menus. These technological limitations inevitably pose challenges to customers, and therefore slow down their acceptance rates. In order to encourage greater usage of SSTs at restaurants, there should be more types of technologies with more functions in order to address the varying restaurant requirements.

Government agencies can start by cooperating with several top SST providers in Singapore such as CrimsonLogic Pte Ltd; SR Data Dynamic; or Astra Singapore. It is recommended to bring on board technology experts in the industry together with these companies to form a SST Solution Committee. This committee can attend to various SSTs projects in F&B industry and serve as a technology consulting team for SSTs adoption in restaurants. It will mainly provide technological developments and amendments on top of the already existing SSTs to fit in with different companies' needs. For example, the committee, with sufficient funding from technology companies, government associations and agencies, can help Company B in our case study to develop a self-service kiosk which can accept cash as a mode of payment. Upon successful development, this can be a major breakthrough in the SST industry, which can possibly lead to considerable profit opportunities. Other than major projects like this, the committee can also work on SST adoption projects together with the respective restaurants to develop customized technological solutions that specifically meet the restaurant's requirements. One example can be to simplify the technological interface of the tablet PCs and customize them for Company D's menu.

An annual Food Technology Fair exhibiting both technologies used in the restaurant kitchen as well as front-end technologies that are customer facing will be useful in promoting SST in the F&B sector. It will be an event that restaurant operators, SST manufacturers and consumers can attend in order to interact with and understand the needs and preference of stakeholders.

Organize Seminars, Talks and Exhibitions on SSTs in the F&B Industry

Trade associations and agencies are recommended to organize seminars, talks and exhibitions for both technology vendors and restaurants to facilitate better understanding of the SSTs and their applications in the F&B industry. It is recommended to establish a committee in charge of organizing such events so as to promote the sharing of ideas, good practices and innovations that can be adopted.

Trade associations and Government agencies can also organize talks by inviting experienced professionals in the SST industry or F&B sector to share their knowledge and experiences with SSTs.

Another way to forge a connection between restaurant owners and technology vendors is through trade fairs or exhibitions, where potential buyers and sellers gather for a 2–3 day event. The fair can be international, regional or national, and there is a display of various SST products and demonstration regarding their usage. The selling parties at the trade fairs can include manufacturers, traders, suppliers of SSTs, suppliers of services, technical cooperation agencies, institutions, press and other media. The buying parties can include any restaurant owner who is considering adopting SSTs or is interested in exploring the technologies. The motivation driving technological companies are the opportunities to: showcase their products and reach the targeted audience; create or reinforce their visibility and raise awareness about new products; attend to inquire and disseminate information; strengthen relationships with existing customers and identify new ones; as well as meet potential business partners. Restaurant owners or other buy-side participants may join the exhibition because they are interested in exploring the markets and observing the trends; exchanging experiences; gathering useful information on latest technological developments; comparing qualities, prices, and functions of different products; and establishing business connections with reliable suppliers.

5.2 *Issue 2: Changing customer mindsets and recommendations*

(a) Recommendation for restaurant owners

Utilize written and spoken communication to facilitate greater acceptance: As alluded to in Section 2, some SSTs receive wider acceptance among customers, while others do not. Consumers' readiness to accept and use SSTs depend on ability (their perceived ability to perform the behavior), role clarity (them knowing what to do) and motivation (perceived benefits to using the SSTs) (Bitner *et al.*, 2002). Therefore, in order to encourage greater acceptance of SSTs, it is important to address all three aspects of the customers' mindsets. As found in our secondary research and case studies, written and spoken communications from formal institutions have a positive impact on the customers' decision to adopt a new technological innovation. Therefore, the restaurants which just adopted SSTs are strongly recommended to provide clear written and spoken communications in guiding and motivating customers to use the SSTs.

First, communication is vital to let customers know that SSTs are there. As mentioned by the manager at Company B, when they first started adopting the self-service kiosk, they engaged employees to stand beside the kiosk and guide people from the human counter to the kiosk. Written guidelines are placed on the kiosk, which has helped some group of customers as they find this a better way to learn compared to oral communications. Both written and oral communications help to boost their confidence to use the SSTs. Moreover, these enable them to know clearly what to do with the technology, which addresses the role clarity part.

Written communications can include signs and symbols to attract customers' attention to the SSTs. Words and pictures can also be utilized to explain the proper ways of using SSTs. Written communication can be found within the restaurant, outside the restaurant and on social media, press or other communication channels. Oral communication may involve waiters or waitresses explaining directly to customers, promoting the SSTs and providing guidance. It can also be adopted as a marketing strategy to spread the news of newly adopted SSTs through word of mouth. Financial incentives can be provided to encourage customers to share their dining experiences with friends or family members through social media. As discussed in Section 2, the combination of information from firms, family and friends have the strongest impact in improving customers' readiness to use SSTs. Therefore, restaurants can use both written and oral communications to encourage better acceptance of SSTs among customers.

Provide various motivation plans targeting different types of customers: As discussed in Bitner's paper, customers' acceptance of SSTs also depends on their motivations, and their perceived benefit from the adoption. As indicated in the interview with Company B, financial incentives do have notable positive impacts to encourage greater usage of SSTs. Even though it only provides a $1 discount for every use of SSTs, it has successfully attracted many customers who are budget conscious to make use of the machine. This helps to create more satisfying services since these customers find their waiting time reduced and money also saved. Therefore, restaurants intending to adopt SSTs can develop a detailed motivation plan targeting different types of customers. Table 3 provides an example of various motivation plans to encourage usage among different groups of customers.

Table 3:   Type of suitable SST classified by customer segment

Types of Customers	Types of Motivations Suitable
Children	Token or trophy for participation; toys or other gifts
Young people and working adults	Gift cards; financial incentives including cash and discount; merchandise rewards ranging from small branded keychains to high-end electronic products
Consumers aged 50 and above	Financial incentives including cash and discount; gift cards; small gifts

Source: Author's compilation.

Therefore, in order to improve customers' readiness to try the new technologies, restaurants adopting SSTs can develop various customer motivation plans to target various groups of customers with different acceptance rates.

5.3 *Issue 3: Management of SST*

(a) Recommendation for trade associations and agencies

Provide more financial support: As explained in Section 3, the manager from Company A brought up the issue of high maintenance costs after successful adoption of SSTs. SST management, regular checks, continuous improvements and constant updates all impose significant financial burdens on the restaurants. Furthermore, as discussed in Section 2, SST maintenance is indeed a critical part of the sustaining the use of SSTs. People are very unforgiving of confusing or unreliable SSTs. One bad encounter with the SSTs tends to create a long-lasting impact on customers' perception of the technologies and therefore reduces their usage and acceptance significantly. Therefore, it is critical for restaurants to invest heavily into the management and maintenance of SSTs.

According to the case studies of the six companies, most of them found they can only apply for one type of grant for one project, for example, the Productivity and Innovation Grant. In most cases, they find the grant insufficient to cover both the adoption and maintenance of technologies. Moreover, it is has been noted that the current financial support is given out on a per-license basis. This poses problems to companies managing restaurants under different names. Since they only have one license, the funding that they are allowed to apply for is insufficient to cover the adoption and maintenance of SSTs in all branches.

Therefore, the trade association and agencies are recommended to cooperate with the government sector to roll out more financial assistance plans to companies in F&B sector. This can help to increase the adoption of SSTs and thereby improve the productivity of the sector. There can also be other kinds of financial assistance options with less stringent application requirements to address the needs of different companies.

6. Conclusion

The usage of SSTs has begun to infiltrate the food and beverage sector, saving labor, time and money for the owners. Based on a survey of 50 restaurants, only 15 of them use SSTs in their business operations. This indicates that there is still room to increase adoption of SSTs to improve the productivity and revenue performance of enterprises in the F&B sector. A survey of 46 consumers together with case studies of six restaurants, including those that have adopted and those that have not done so, have yielded insights on the problems and challenges in the adoption and usage of SSTs in the F&B sector. Other than the problem of cost of SSTs, which could exceed the amount enterprises may be willing to invest, there are problems in using SSTs. These include the reliability of the equipment, training of staff to be familiar with equipment, acceptability by consumers and accessibility to government funding schemes. This study indicates that restaurant owners should be extremely careful while choosing the type of SSTs and the technology platforms to be adopted. The suitability of a particular type of SST varies depending on the size and mode of operation.

SST has the potential to be a major factor shaping growth in productivity and improvement in restaurants services. As SST continues to become more acceptable, convenient and efficient, companies can embrace it to operate more efficiently and to serve their customers better. This is particularly the case in countries like Singapore with limited labor supply, increasing industry competition and rising consumer demand. However, the adoption of SSTs still faces several constraints and needs the cooperation of restaurants, technology companies, trade associations and public agencies in order to facilitate an encouraging environment.

Appendix

Interview of Restaurants' Owners/Managers

Interviews are conducted at the site of the restaurants. The owners or managers are asked to indicate their current usage of SSTs, types adopted as well as those which are being considered for adoption in the future. The managers were then asked the purpose of adopting a particular type of SST, steps taken to ensure proper adoption and consumer usage. Restaurants not adopting any SSTs, they were asked to share reasons for non-adoption.

The list of questions asked during the interview of restaurants' owners or managers:

- Has the SST contributed to improve customer satisfaction?
- Has the SST contributed to increase operational efficiency?
- Has the SST helped in manpower staffing?
- Has the SST contributed to increase profitability of the restaurant?
- What is the biggest benefit of adopting SST?
- Have you encountered any of the following difficulties while adopting the SST such as technology breaking down; costing too much; customers not knowing how to use it; customers being uncomfortable with new technology; customers preferring human interaction, etc.?
- How did you solve the problems?
- How well do you feel that the SST serves its purpose?

Consumers' Survey

In the consumer's survey, the following questions were designed to discover a detailed picture of the perceived effectiveness:

- How user-friendly is the SST?
- How well do you feel it has served your needs?
- Has the SST reduced your waiting time?
- Has the SST improved your dining experience?
- Have you encountered any of the following difficulties while using the SST such as technology breaking down; costing too much; customers not knowing how to use; customers being uncomfortable with new technology; customers preferring human interaction etc.?
- Please rank your receptiveness of SST at restaurants.

Chapter 4

Integrating the Supply Chain with RFID: A Study on Boosting Productivity in the Retail and F&B Sectors

1. Introduction

Increasing productivity is one of the challenges that every business firm will face. In a fast paced business environment, it is both crucial and essential to stay ahead of the game and maintain the competitive edge in terms of superior productivity.

According to recent studies, productivity of the food and beverage (F&B) sector has been lagging behind that of other sectors, falling a cumulative of 3.3% over the past 2 years (Singh, 2015). A similar trend has also been observed in the retail sector. According to studies done by the Ministry of Trade and Industry, the productivity of these two sectors has also been experiencing negative growth and has been falling behind those of other industries (Ministry of Trade and Industry, 2014). Furthermore, with the recent foreign worker curbs, the outlook for firms in these sectors has dampened in anticipation of a further decline of productivity (Singh, 2013).

1.1 *What is RFID?*

Radio frequency identification (RFID) is a technology that is able to provide real-time information about supply chain operations. RFID technology is not new; it was first used in 1945 for military purposes, but has since evolved to encompass wide areas of usage and implementation. In the recent years, RFID technology has been used by warehouses and logistics enterprises to achieve reduced shrinkage, improved material handling and tracking as well as higher accuracy in data collection.

A simple RFID involves an RFID chip implanted into a tag, which is then tagged onto the item of interest. The RFID tag can be detected by an RFID reader, and data is then sent to a control and management system. The scanning of tagged items can be done automatically, whereby line of sight is not required and multiple items can be scanned together at the same time.

It should also be noted that RFID technology can be differentiated into passive and active RFID technology. Passive RFID systems have tags that have no internal power source and have only a microchip and an antenna. They wait for an interrogating signal from the RFID reader in order to send data contained in the tag. On the other hand, active RFID tags possess their own power source and transmitter, enabling the tag to broadcast its signal actively. They are hence commonly used as "beacons" to track the real-time location of assets (Thrasher, 2013). We believe that the implementation and integration of this active technology into the supply chain will help firms improve the accuracy of tracking their goods and also increase productivity through the use of more accurate and timely information (Figure 1).

RFID has the potential to increase visibility of merchandise in the supply chain through its tracking capabilities. This would not only grant more precise control to supply chain management, it would also help reduce costs to the firm via multiple avenues, one of which is the reduction in shrinkages. Logistics and inventory management could also be carried out more efficiently and accurately as data about tagged items are reflected in real time to the

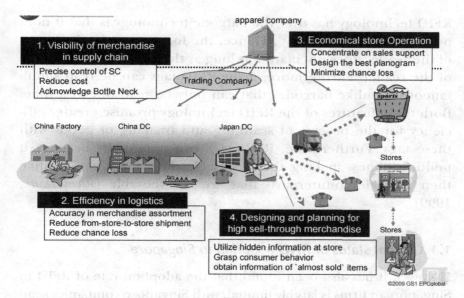

Figure 1: Potential Areas Where RFID Could be Used in the Supply Chain

Source: RFID Implementation in Japan, EPCglobal Japan.

overarching inventory management system. At the store front, RFID technology can also help reduce incidents of theft and lost items via its tracking capabilities. RFID technology can also help reduce the time and manpower allocated to inventory management and stock-taking, and this would help to free up more staff to providing customers with a better shopping experience. Last but not least, one benefit of using RFID technology is access to its data storing capacity. This would help firms keep track of consumer behavior such as allowing them to see which goods are the more popular or less popular ones among consumers. This would help them forecast future trends and better streamline their sales and production plans to meet these demands.

1.2 *Key differences between RFID and barcoding technology*

It should be noted that RFID technology is vastly different from the commonly seen barcoding system. One major advantage that

RFID technology has over the barcode technology is that it does not require 'line of sight'. Hence, the location and orientation of the reader does not matter as long as the tags are within range of the reader. Furthermore, many RFID tags can be read simultaneously, unlike barcodes that can only be read one at a time. Both these features of the RFID technology promise greater efficiency for the process of scanning and tracking of goods with these tags. Furthermore, RFID tags can potentially be written multiple times, making them reusable data containers, unlike their barcode counterparts that are not reusable (Raza *et al.*, 1999).

1.3 *Current status of RFID adoption in Singapore*

However, it has also been found that the adoption rate of RFID in Singaporean firms is largely limited, with Singapore companies scoring 55.5 out of a total of 100 for the Information Maturity (IM) Index and 55.1 for the Digital Engagement (DE) Maturity Index.[1] The Awareness Technologies Index score, which includes use of machine-to-machine technologies such as RFID sensors and GPS chips, rated slightly lower at 47.4. Figure 2 compares Singapore's performance with that of other countries such as the United States, Australia and Japan.

1.4 *Significance of study*

The integration of RFID in the supply chain of firms, especially in the case of small and medium enterprises (SMEs), will greatly boost productivity of these firms. However, there seems to be a fair amount of inertia in the adoption of RFID despite the list of potential benefits that this technology offers. This study seeks to explore the obstacles deterring a greater rate of RFID adoption by Singaporean SMEs, especially in areas of inventory management and tracking. Through this study, we also hope to formulate possible suggestions of how Singapore SMEs can use RFID technology to achieve a leaner

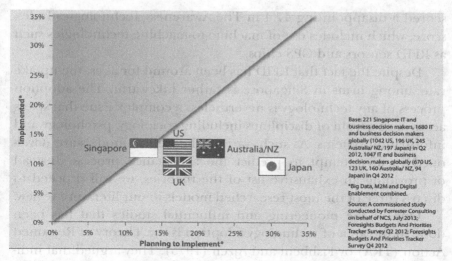

Figure 2: Singapore Lags in Terms of Emerging Technology Adoption Plans
Source: Solutions for the Urbanised Future, Volume 2, NCS.

supply chain and achieve sustainable increases in productivity in the face of productivity slowdown in the F&B sector as well as the curb on foreign manpower.

2. Literature Review

Since the inception of RFID in 1926, the presence of computers and information technology has dramatically enlarged their sphere of influence in our daily lives. At the same time, technology alone does not ensure productivity growth. Acceptance of the new technology must take precedence and is a continual process that takes place at both the individual employee and the organizational levels. As mentioned previously, RFID is not a new technology; however, the adoption of RFID by various industries is an emerging phenomenon that is slowly gaining momentum. Similarly for Singapore, there is some level of reluctance by firms, or best described as a "wait and see" approach, toward the adoption of RFID. This is supported by recent evidence where Singapore firms scored a disappointing 47.4 in The Awareness Technologies Index score, which includes use of machine-to-machine technologies such as RFID sensors and GPS chips.

Despite the fact that RFID has been around for ages, the uptake rate among firms in Singapore is rather lukewarm. The adoption process of any technology is nevertheless a complex issue that spans across a spectrum of disciplines including sociology, psychology and information systems. As such, various theoretical models are developed in an attempt to predict the acceptance process. Instead of providing an exhaustive list of the theories, we will proceed to discuss three of the most researched models in our literature review.

One of the pioneering and influential studies that has been done in the area of technology adoption is the Theory of Reasoned Action (TRA) by Fishbein and Ajzen (1975). They argued that individual human behavior is constantly influenced and shaped by various factors which include subjective norms and their attitude toward one's behavior. Subjective norm is defined as "the person's perception that most people who are important to him think he should or should not perform the behavior in question" (Fishbein and Ajzen, 1975). In a review conducted by Ajzen (1991), subjective norms are reaffirmed to be one of the crucial determinants that heavily influence one's behavior (Ajzen, 1991). Consider the application of this theory into the area of technology adoption. Regardless of the source of the normative pressure, be it from one's peers or superiors, we can expect the continual usage of technology (RFID in this case) by one if one's act of adoption is favorably accepted by one's peers. However, other authors have presented empirical evidences that point little toward the importance of social norms in Technology Acceptance Model (TAM). For instance, Mathieson (1991) found social norms to be statistically insignificant. Fulk *et al.* (1987) and Venkatesh and Morris (2000) also found that social norms tend to play a small role in influencing technological adoption.

Shortly after the conception of TRA model, Davis (1989) developed the Technology Acceptance Model (TAM) which is based on the general concepts developed in TRA, to explain computer usage behavior (Davis, 1989). According to TAM, an individual's inclination toward new technology is guided by two fundamental factors: perceived usefulness and perceived ease of use. Perceived usefulness is defined as "the degree to which a person believes that using a particular system would enhance his or her job performance" (Davis, 1989). Perceived ease of use is then defined as "the degree to which a person believes that using a particular system would be free of effort" (Davis, 1989). Empirical studies by Chau (1996) and many others have found strong and statistically significant evidence that points toward the importance of these two factors in technology adoption (Chau, 1996).

Last but not least, there is the Innovation Diffusion Theory (IDT) by Rogers (1962). Rogers took a particularly different slant of analyzing the phenomenon of technology adoption (Rogers, 1962). Rogers argued that the process of adoption is one that is characterized by information gathering by the individual to mitigate any uncertainty that may arise due to initial adoption. This information is often relayed within one's network of personal contacts via different communication media platforms. IDT also further predicts that the process of information gathering will be the stage where the individual forms his/her perception of the innovation. This ultimately affects the adoption behavior. IDT also predicts that the rate of diffusion may be expedited if initial adopters perceived the innovation to have the following:

1. **Relative advantage:** The degree to which an innovation is perceived as being better than its precursor.
2. **Ease of use:** The degree to which an innovation is perceived as being difficult to use.
3. **Image:** The degree to which use of an innovation is perceived to enhance one's image or status in one's social system.
4. **Visibility:** The degree to which one can see others using the system in the organization.
5. **Compatibility:** The degree to which an innovation is perceived as being consistent with the existing values, needs and past experiences of potential adopters.

6. **Results demonstrability:** The tangibility of the results using the innovation, including their observability and communicability.
7. **Voluntariness of use:** The degree to which use of the innovation is perceived as being voluntary, or of free will.

All the models mentioned above represent the wealth of knowledge that may assist in predicting the variance in the technological adoption process. These theories also provide the evidence that the adoption process of any new technology/innovation is not solely determined by one but by a spectrum of factors. The next portion of the literature review will delve into some of the common barriers to RFID adoption that are found by various academic authors.

2.1 *Authors and selected readings to identify the potential barriers to RFID adoption*

In the tables below, we attempt to summarize the major studies performed to address the different barriers to the adoption of RFID. Table 1 provides a listing of the authors of the articles referred. Table 2 identifies the barriers highlighted in the articles. These include the lack of an international standard, the cost of RFID hardware and software, incompatibility of RFID with current technology and the perceived complexity of RFID technology.

Table 1:   List of Authors and Articles Referred to in Table 2

(A) Aberdeen Group (2005)	(J) Attaran (2012)
(B) Huber *et al.* (2007)	(K) Bhattacharya *et al.* (2007)
(C) Michael and McCathie (2005)	(L) Thiesse *et al.* (2011)
(D) Juban and Wyld (2004)	(M) Chen *et al.* (2005)
(E) Wang *et al.* (2010)	(N) Tajima (2007)
(F) Ngai and Gunasekaran (2009)	(O) Shih *et al.* (2009)
(G) Narsing (2011)	(P) Strueker and Gille (2008)
(H) Wu *et al.* (2006)	(Q) Matta and Moberg (2006)
(I) Davison and Smith (2005)	(R) Kim and Garrison (2010)

Table 2:   Barriers to Adoption of RFID Highlighted in Articles Referred to in Table 1

Barriers to RFID Adoption	A	B	C	D	E	F	G	H	I	J	K	L	M	N	O	P	Q	R
Inaccuracy of tag read rate	✓		✓			✓		✓	✓	✓	✓		✓	✓	✓	✓	✓	
Lack of global standards	✓		✓	✓	✓	✓		✓	✓	✓	✓		✓		✓	✓	✓	
Lack of awareness		✓		✓														✓
Perception of RFID benefits (lack of)				✓								✓						✓
Size of firm					✓													✓
Integration challenges			✓	✓	✓			✓			✓		✓		✓	✓		✓
Implementation challenges			✓			✓												
Privacy issues			✓	✓		✓			✓	✓	✓		✓	✓	✓	✓		
Security issues				✓		✓				✓			✓					
Cost of RFID tags	✓	✓	✓	✓	✓	✓	✓	✓	✓	✓	✓							
Cost of hardware (infrastructure)	✓	✓	✓	✓	✓	✓	✓	✓		✓	✓	✓					✓	
Cost of software, training			✓		✓						✓	✓						
Management of the vast volume of data is an issue									✓						✓	✓		

(*Continued*)

Table 2: (*Continued*)

Barriers to RFID Adoption	A	B	C	D	E	F	G	H	I	J	K	L	M	N	O	P	Q	R
Lack of RFID expertise						✓				✓						✓		
Lack of senior management support												✓	✓		✓			✓
Employee reluctance to adapt to changes											✓							
Uncertainty of ROI										✓			✓	✓				
Incompatibility of RFID with current technology																		
Satisfied with current level of technology (barcodes, etc.)									✓									
Overhaul of existing business design process									✓		✓							
Immaturity of RFID technology					✓		✓	✓										
Lack of business value/value proposition	✓	✓						✓										
Perceived complexity of RFID technology					✓													

3. Methodology

In an attempt to better understand the potential barriers that may hinder the uptake of RFID technology among the F&B firms in Singapore, we have prepared a questionnaire which concerns the common barriers to RFID adoption, mentioned by various authors in the academic realm. A questionnaire comprising 27 questions is crafted so as to get a better understanding of the various constraints that may impede the adoption rate of RFID for firms. With these findings, we hoped that we would be able to recommend policies that are to be targeted and streamlined to enable firms to overcome these constraints. We decided to conduct random door-to-door interviews in ION Orchard shopping mall which houses a wide range of retail and F&B companies. In total, we managed to intensively interview 15 companies over the span of two weeks. Despite the small sample size of our interviewees, most of their responses provide sufficient material for empirical verification and analysis. As such, the findings remain highly relevant and significant to policymakers.

4. Benefits and Potential Areas of Application of RFID

In order to convince the companies to adopt RFID technology, it is important for us to help the companies to see how RFID technology can help them achieve other objectives in tandem with the push toward higher productivity. The purpose of this section is to explicate the benefits of RFID technology, specifically RFID tags, and their relevance in addressing real-life productivity issues faced by retail and F&B sectors in Singapore today.

Individual case studies will be used to highlight a range of productivity issues faced by companies and firms that have yet to adopt RFID technology in their businesses. We will seek to address these issues via RFID-orientated solutions, thereby drawing attention to the relevance and feasibility of RFID technology. Productivity growth will also be analyzed according to the 8M framework (manpower, material, method, money, make, management, market and message) in order to give a holistic and complete approach in tackling productivity improvement.

We will also include case studies on companies that have adopted RFID solutions to address their productivity issues in order to showcase the competitive advantage that this revolutionary technology can bring.

4.1 *Reduction in operational costs*

Reduction in operational costs can come in several forms. First, the most direct and obvious example would be the reduction in manpower. One major difference between RFID tags and the traditional barcode is the breaking away from the line-of-sight scanning procedure necessary for the latter. This means that products embedded with RFID tags do not have to be physically orientated to be scanned. Due to this, many products can be scanned together at the same time regardless of tag orientation. As such, this signifies the ability to automate much of the common supply chain management labor-intensive activities such as checking and scanning incoming inventory. Moreover, in general, one of the major cost components for distribution centers is labor, which alone accounts a lion share of 50-80% of the total distribution costs (Twist, 2005). RFID offers a plethora of cost-saving advantages via unprecedented automation. Keith *et al.* (2002), found that with RFID technology, receiving check-in time of inventories can be effectively cut down to a margin of 60–93%. These improvements from the barcoding system translate into time and labor savings.

Another form of cost savings could come through accurately predicting sales and thereby allocating and transferring the correct amount of goods to individual branches of the company. If the cost of transportation of goods is high, transporting too many or too little of goods to a certain store branch might result in additional costs when companies try to rectify this problem. It is one of the important practices in Lean Management.[2] Firms might be forced to clear goods at a discounted price, thereby incurring some loss. RFID technology allows for assessment of consumption and purchase pattern of certain goods by monitoring sales trend over time.

This allows companies to accurately predict the amount of goods to allocate to its stores, creating a leaner supply chain, and this translates into money savings.

Case Study 1: Paul Frank (Fashion Accessories Store)

Paul Frank has benefited greatly from the implementation of RFID and the Intrasys' Inventory Management and Stock Take Solution.

The Paul Frank Warehouse is issued with two mobile RFID readers installed with Intrasys' Inventory Management System. All items are being tagged individually and mass consigned by RFID scanning. On picking up of any inventory, data from the reader is transferred to the central Inventory Management Database, and so these item details can be retrieved in real time from anywhere.

All Paul Frank retail stores carry a Mobile RFID Reader (Figure 3). Upon receipt of inventory, the staff stocks in by scanning all items in the shipment. This improves communication along the supply chain by making information received by the front-end retail stores from back-end warehouses more accurate and in real time.

Figure 3:   Mobile RFID Readers Picking Up Real-time Information on Products
Source: Leading retail apparel Paul Frank Singapore implements RFID for Inventory, Intrasys.

In retail stores, store operators benefit from the increased efficiency in stocktaking processes. What used to take eight employees and 4 hours now only requires two employees and is completed in half the time, achieving 800% increased efficiency. Reducing manual stocktaking and replacing it with an inventory management system also reduces worker fatigue, allowing for increased quality of work such as increased focus for longer of periods of time and reduction in human error arising from labor fatigue. Quirk and Borrello (2005) predicted a 90% reduction in location and human errors as a result of the usage of RFID, which greatly reduces labor intensity in processes of stocktaking. This result can be clearly observed in the case of Paul Frank Company.

Case Study 2: Cold Storage (Retail, Supermarket Business)

Cold Storage launched and completed its first RFID inventory and supply chain management trial in 2007 which involved two processes, one to study how to use technology in Singapore's business field and the other to research on the potential business benefits and returns on investment that could be reaped via greater efficiency of the tracking of pallets and goods which RFID tags offer.

Due to the lack of a backroom that can be used for storing goods, most of the products delivered to the store goes directly onto the shelf for sale rather than to the storage. With the implementation of RFID tags, cold storage has seen a marked improvement in inventory tracking, a reduction in inventory levels needed on-site, reduced stock-outs, faster throughput and reduced demand for labor-intensive stock checks. All these factors served to increase overall productivity of the company.

Case Study 3: Uniqlo and Optical 88

Uniqlo is a Japanese multinational company that specializes in the sale of clothing and apparel. However, it has been observed that the stocktaking process of Uniqlo is both time consuming and cost inefficient. Uniqlo employed the barcoding system coupled with their personal database system. The stocktaking process requires staff to scan each and every one of the barcodes, which will indicate the details of the product on the scanner. Each and every good has to be scanned during the stocktaking process, and a manager will be required to repeat the process after the staff has done it so as to assure that the results are accurate. We found that this process was both time consuming and inefficient.

Furthermore, the process of stocktaking requires smaller firms to close down its shop front for a few hours during weekends (staff indicated that it is usually on a Sunday afternoon) in order to facilitate the stocktaking process. Hence, there is a loss in potential sales that the store could have made should they have stayed open for business during those few hours. For larger stores, overnight stocktaking process is required. However, this process is outsourced to a specialized company and not done by Uniqlo staff. This process would incur additional costs to Uniqlo as it is now outsourcing its stocktaking processes to an outsider firm.

Should Uniqlo and Optical 88 replace their barcoding system with an RFID system, stocktaking would require less labor and, furthermore, less time could be allocated for the process of stocktaking. Stocktaking becomes an easy and painless process. Smaller stores might consider remaining open for the process of stocktaking. Alternatively, with the use of RFID tags, stocktaking processes can be done in a flexible manner, such as when human traffic is low. These improvements would translate into cost savings as sales could potentially be increased. The ease and convenience of stocktaking with RFID could also mean that larger stores might not need to outsource this task to another company but could undertake it themselves. This would allow cost savings, as they no longer have to employ another company for stocktaking. Our short interview with the staff of Uniqlo and Optical 88 revealed that they were keen on implementing RFID in their businesses should the opportunity arise.

As seen in Figure 4, products are tagged with RFID tags. These tags are simple and easy to implement and could be used in conjunction with existing barcode tags.

The optical shop, Optical 88, also faces a similar situation as Uniqlo in terms of stocktaking processes. Staff expressed that stocktaking was a tedious and time-consuming process that was

Figure 4: RFID-tagged Items in a Retail Store

Source: RFID Implementation in Japan, EPCGlobal Japan.

conducted once every 6 months. This large volume of goods to stock and lack of manpower make the exercise rather onerous.

Should Optical 88 adopt an RFID solution, stocktaking would be a much easier process and could be done more regularly. One benefit of this would be that the firm would be able to gain knowledge of which products are facing higher demand, and so make the necessary arrangements in order to avoid a stock-out scenario.

Case Study 4: Lacoste and Folli Follie

At the time of interview, the Lacoste at ION Orchard is currently planning to move out of the premises in the next few months. We observed that there was a 50% sale going on for most products, and staff told us that there was a need to clear existing stocks, hence the need for a 'clearance sale'. This could be attributed to the fact that as it is too expensive to move the goods to another location, the company would rather clear its stock by selling it off at a lower price.

We identify the problem here as an inaccurate forecast of the demand for goods. Too many products were stocked up at this particular branch and this resulted in the need to sell them off at much lower prices in the event that the store closes down, since transport costs are high.

Should Lacoste adopt an RFID solution, there would have been potential cost savings for the company. RFID tags have the ability to monitor sales trends. This would ensure that there is no oversupply of goods. This would eliminate the excess stock of goods that the Lacoste store at ION Orchard now faces. The store could have transported less goods to this particular branch if they observed low sales and hence avoided the need for a 'clearance sale' that could be interpreted as a loss on sales.

Folli Follie is a fashion and jewelry company based in Hong Kong, but has branches in the South East Asia region, specifically one at ION Orchard. Staff told us that sales have been slow in the recent times, not just for their store but for retailers in the area in general. They noted that the appreciation of the Singaporean currency has resulted in a loss of consumption, especially that of tourists. As a result, sales have taken a dip and staff do not seem optimistic about business in the near future.

Our suggestion for Folli Follie would be similar to that of Lacoste. Should the company adopt an RFID system, it would be able to track and monitor trends in sales across regions. They would be able to predict a dip in sales due to the appreciation of the Singaporean currency and act accordingly. They could supply less goods to Singaporean branches with the knowledge that sales in the region will be slow and divert these goods to branches where they predict a depreciation of local currency. This would avoid the situation whereby goods are held in the Singaporean branches where sales are low, when they could have been at another place where there is higher traffic. All these measures are likely to result in potential sales increases.

4.2 *Enhancement in information accuracy*

An advantage that RFID has over the traditional barcoding technology is the ability to monitor sales trends, and this allows for accurate forecasting of future trends. RFID is a technology that is able to store up to 40 times more information than the traditional barcoding technology, and this advantage could be used to prevent out-of-stock scenarios which would then translate into potential loss in sales (Singh, 2003). Singh (2003) predicts that due to the enhanced information storage capability, RFID is able to overcome the issue of information inaccuracy that has plagued the conventional barcode technology. The problem of information inaccuracy can be highly detrimental to any businesses as it can lead to loss in potential sales. According to a recent worldwide study of causes of retail out-of-stock situations by Gruen *et al.* (2005) retailers, on average, lose nearly 4% of sales to out-of-stocks. In addition to this, the out-of-stock impact is found to be 50–100% higher for high-velocity items.

Moreover, inaccuracy of information can lead to issues such as inventory inaccuracy. In the conventional supply chain, manufacturers often adopt the push method where products are manufactured and pushed to the sales front-end. In a study, RFID systems are shown to enhance product demand forecasts by 10–20% as compared to conventional systems. RFID systems also helped to lower inventory levels by 10–30% and increase sales by 1–2% through reduced occurrences of out-of-stock scenarios (Zebra Technologies, 2004).

This function of RFID technology is particularly applicable and important in companies that have many branches and hence need to communicate and transfer stocks across branches. Inaccuracy in information can lead to inventory inaccuracy. As in a conventional supply chain, many companies interviewed stated that companies often adopt the push method, whereby products are pushed to the sales front-end from the headquarters. As such, stores merely act as receivers of these goods from the headquarters. However, information lags and demand uncertainty often leads to the swelling of inventories in warehouses and distribution centers. This is supported by findings by Kang and Gershwin (2005) for a global retail store. They found that inventory accuracy is only 51% on average for 500 stores (Kang and Gershwin, 2005). Some of the companies that we interviewed revealed that there might sometimes be an error in the amount or kind of products that is being pushed down from the company headquarters. This results in inventory inaccuracy, and stores might take some time to rectify this matter.

RFID helps to address the issue of high inventory by facilitating a seamless flow of information which is always kept up to date so as to assist the supply chain managers to make better quality decisions. With accurate information input, RFID will also help to enhance the accuracy of demand forecast. As such, RFID helps to reduce incidences of stock-out scenarios while ensuring the leanness of the supply chain.

An important aspect of productivity growth is using the most efficient machinery or technology method. The data storing potential of RFID tags allows for a more efficient allocation of resources, ensuring that goods are delivered to areas where they matter the most. Data analytics can be applied to increase efficiency and profitability.

The following case studies further elaborate on the application of RFID to enhance information accuracy for business operations, as well as possible challenges that could arise.

Case Study 1: The North Face

The North Face is a multinational American company that specializes in outdoor gear and has many branches across the globe, including a few in Singapore. We interviewed the store manager of the ION Orchard branch, and he expressed that the company is in the midst of RFID trial that is yet to be implemented across all branches of the company. However, he seemed optimistic about the potential benefits that RFID technology could bring for the company.

One issue that he raised was the shortfalls of the top-down push method whereby goods are pushed from manufacturers to stores. He noted that in some occasions, products are wrongly sent to particular stores. In such a scenario, stores make sure that they have the right amount of products, regardless of the kind of products. For example, the store was supposed to receive 10 of the same product, 5 in red and 5 in blue, but it receives 10 red and 0 blue products instead. In such a scenario, the store manager said that it was acceptable as long as the total amount of goods was correct. They will then make sure that the misplaced products are indeed in another store and not missing and unaccounted for.

However, we feel that such inaccuracies in inventory management would result in stock-out scenarios that firms should seek to avoid. Although inventory records indicate a particular number of each different product, the actual numbers might differ. Should North Face adopt RFID technology and tags, these situations could potentially be avoided. The North Face company headquarters would be able to track the number of products pushed out to each of the branches. Even if there is a mistake in the product numbers, real-time RFID inventory management systems will allow store managers to update the number of goods in their stores to avoid an inaccurate inventory record. Then they could restock on products that are running low in their individual stores as they deem fit.

Case Study 2: EDIT/Mitju

Information inaccuracy issues are not only a problem for large companies, they might pose as an even more severe problem with smaller firms. EDIT is a small company with two branches in Singapore, one in Bugis Street and one in ION Orchard. When we interviewed the store manager in ION Orchard, it was revealed to us that inventory inaccuracies pose a huge problem for the company. As the size of the store is small, there is usually only one staff that is tending to the store. In the case of a stock-out, the staff would need to replenish the stock by making his way down to the other branch or meeting his colleague at the nearest MRT so as to collect any stock. In such a scenario, he would need to close down the store for the time being while he attends to the replenishing the stock. This is a huge issue for the company as potential sales are lost when the company closes its storefront during business hours.

Due to the shortfalls in stocktaking procedures, the store manager reveals that stocktaking does not take place on a regular basis. Stocktaking only takes place at the store when there is a request sent from their company headquarters. As such, there might be a lag time before any discrepancies in inventory are discovered.

Furthermore, because EDIT has such a small shop, the store manager tells us that most products are stocked by keeping an arbitrary number of products in the store. For example, he makes sure that there are 5 of every product at any time in the store and would seek to replenish them as soon as he sees them starting to deplete. One possible issue that might arise here would be that the store would be unable to cope to unexpected surge in demand. When this happens, the store manager would have to close the store for a short period of time in order to replenish the stocks.

For the case of EDIT, we would highly recommend RFID tags as a solution to solve its stocktaking and inventory management systems. The data storing capabilities of RFID would prevent a stock-out scenario in this company. It is highly unlikely that all goods would be equally popular with customer, as some will be more popular as others less. Therefore, we think that it is inefficient to keep the same amount of stock for each and every good in the store. The data storing capabilities of RFID would be able to help EDIT record past sales trends and forecast future sales trends, so that the company will be able to better meet the needs of its customers.

The active RFID technology would also be able to notify the store manager when the stocks are running low, instead of needing him to visually check and verify the amount of stocks. As the store manager has to perform all the duties of the store by himself, it is inevitable that occasionally human errors will be made in the areas of stocktaking and keeping track of the inventory. With the help of active RFID technology, he does not need to keep track of the inventory, rather the system will notify him whenever a particular product is low in stock. This would increase the overall labor productivity as he can now devote more time to other areas of the company such as serving his customers.

4.3 *Significant reduction in shrinkage*

Shrinkages arise in the event of stock loss, which may give rise to inventory inaccuracy. Some common forms of shrinkage includes loss of items, shop theft and spoilage. This could be seen as a form of material cost. Shrinkage can have a crippling effect on any businesses. Twist (2005) estimated shrinkage alone cost US retailers $30 billion a year. Empirical studies conducted by Fleisch and

Tellkamp (2005) estimated that shrinkage alone accounted for 2–4% of US retail industry in 2001.

One common form of shrinkage faced by retail companies is shop theft. This poses a problem because not only does it translate into a loss on profit, it could also cause inaccuracies in inventory records. This problem is further worsened when the period between each stocktaking process is long.

Another problem that is often faced by F&B sectors is product spoilage. This problem could be severe when companies are dealing with highly perishable goods. Any overstocking of goods without selling them would mean loss on company profits should these products expire.

RFID technology can address the issues of shrinkage as it has the ability to track movement of products and inventories accurately. This would mean that stores would be able to track their product movement and reduce the amount of shop theft incidents. Furthermore, RFID provides users with real-time information and a helicopter view of all the inventories in its warehouse. Lee and Ozer (2007) conducted a study on the effects of RFID on the shrinkage and found that the original shrinkage was effectively reduced by 10–66% with the implementation of RFID system. With the proper inventory management system, the company would be able to track the exact position of each and every one of its tagged goods.

The active RFID technology would also mean that RFID tags could be programmed to alert users when the perishable goods that they are tagged onto are about to expire. This would allow management to take the most appropriate course of action with this information instead of allowing the products to go bad. This would reduce shrinkage and subsequently reduce loss.

Case Study 1: Stereo

Stereo is a retail company that specializes in the sale of headphones and audio peripherals. The store manager at the ION Orchard branch reveals that shrinkages due to loss of items could be a potential issue for the company as some of the items and peripherals that the store handles could be very small. Small items such as replacement ear buds could easily be misplaced during stock check or during processes where the products are moved from one place to another.

Should the company adopt RFID tagging of their products, shrinkages due to losses could be reduced as tagged items can be easily located and tracked with RFID technology. This would result in less shrinkage and thus higher productivity for the company.

Case Study 2: Ng Ai Muslim Poultry

Ng Ai Muslim Poultry has greatly benefited due to the implementation of RFID and the Intrasys' Warehouse Inventory and Rack Management Solution.

Forklifts are equipped with four RFID antennas, and mounted with a RFID reader, positioned strategically to cater for pallets and rack layout. All pallets are tagged with Intrasys' Pallet Tags, integrated with RFID technology (Figure 5). On picking up of a pallet,

Figure 5: Forklifts Equipped with RFID Antennas and Reader; Pallets with RFID Tags

Source: RFID-enabled High Density Racks Improves Productivity in Cold Store Warehouse, Intrasys'.

data from the reader is transferred to the RFID System to provide real-time feedback on the pallet information.

An obvious benefit of employing an RFID system in this case would be the ease and simplicity of integrating RFID technology with existing warehousing procedures. Pallet tags are inexpensive and can be readily applied to existing pallets. Furthermore, RFID readers can be easily mounted onto forklifts and powered by the forklift's power source, forming a simple yet complete RFID closed system.

With the use of the RFID system, manual logging and updating of pallet location is no longer needed; this means that the operators can be freed up for other tasks.

Furthermore, management now has 100% visibility of the warehouse. Operators and employees are able to easily locate items, and management is able to have accurate, real-time information on warehouse inventory. This complete warehouse visibility greatly boosts productivity; it helps prevent costly mistakes, improves ability to find inventory and provides useful data for the optimization of the warehouse process.

Due to the success of the Intrasys' Inventory and Rack Management Solution, Ng Ai is considering to deploy the same setup for its future warehouses.

Case Study 3: Aeropostale and Pedro

Aeropostale and Pedro are 2 of the companies that we interviewed with regard to shrinkage due to shop theft. The former is a multinational American apparel company, whereas the latter is a company that specializes in leather goods in the Southeast Asian region.

Both stores that we interviewed faced similar situations: they face some form of shrinkage in the form of shop theft every financial year. A quick survey of the shop front indicated that there were no security barriers installed at the entrances. Store managers revealed that theft is discovered only if store attendants visually see the crime being committed. They also admitted that although there are security cameras installed in the stores, they are often too late as a measure to prevent shop theft from taking place.

Furthermore, missing products are only discovered during the stocktaking process that takes place once every 6 months. In the event that theft has taken place, it is often too late before it is discovered that the goods are missing.

We believe that RFID tags would be an appropriate solution in addressing the shrinkage issues of Aeropostale and Pedro. Should an RFID tagged product be taken out of the store without being paid for, the active RFID tag would be able to send a signal to the inventory management system, indicating the location of the product, similar to the pallet tracking system utilized by Ng Ai Muslim Poultry. The company would then have to react quickly to recover the product and prevent the theft. Such measures would prove effective in reducing the amount of shrinkages due to theft each year.

4.4 *Quality management*

The enhanced traceability that comes with RFID technology would allow companies to track and monitor goods in real time as goods move through different stages of the supply chain. This would improve the consistency of products and would reduce the incidences of spoilage. This would be particularly applicable in the F&B industry as spoilage of products and consistency are issues.

Due to the information capacity of RFID tags, they are able to track multiple indicators such as temperature and humidity. Combined with the active notification functions, this would notify the company whenever the quality of the products risk being compromised. This is of utmost importance when dealing with highly perishable food items. RFID technology is also better poised than traditional barcode technology as RFID tags have displayed higher durability than the latter when exposed to natural elements.

Case Study 1: United Biscuits

United Biscuits is a British food manufacturing company that exemplifies the use of RFID to monitor and track production process in order to ensure consistency and quality of products.

The application of RFID technology in its food manufacturing plant presents interesting lessons because it is an environment that involves moisture, metal, and variable temperatures. United Biscuits uses RFID technology to control movement of raw materials and in the weighing, mixing and baking processes involved in the preparation of biscuits, cakes and prepared foods in its Ashby, U.K., plant.

RFID tags are attached to stainless steel carts at the beginning of the food processing sequence, as these are used to carry materials through the processing facilities, including weighing, preparation, mixing and baking. This ensures that there are no human errors. Raw materials and finished products are tracked as they travel throughout the entire plant. Human operators are informed through the use of overhead displays that either things are going smoothly or that there are food processing problems to attend to. United Biscuits has reported improved efficiency in the manufacturing process, improved information accuracy, enabled better tracking of the food products, and observed a decline in incidence of errors. There has also been improved stock control, improved control over material usage and improved product traceability and reporting.

Case Study 2: ADM Cocoa and Swiss Bake Ltd

ADM Cocoa and Swiss Bake were 2 of the food distributing companies that we interviewed. They are both suppliers of food products and materials to large organizations. ADM Cocoa produces cocoa products that are distributed both locally and internationally. On the other hand, Swiss Bake is a company that manufactures pastry goods for large supermarkets such as Cold Storage.

One large similarity between both companies is the use of the barcoding technology, which requires manual scanning of a large amount of goods. Also, both companies handle food products that need to be transported and distributed elsewhere.

We believe that RFID technology and RFID tags would be able to help companies such as these in several ways. First, when goods are shipped to many parts of the world, they are often exposed to elements of the nature that can affect the quality of the goods. RFID tags would be able to track these changes and companies can make adjustments to ensure the integrity of their products. This is especially applicable in the case of ADM Cocoa that ships its products internationally.

Second, RFID tags are also better suited for goods that have long transportation time as RFID tags have higher durability than traditional barcodes when exposed to the elements. Issues can arise should barcodes be damaged or destroyed during the movement process. Harsh environment conditions can also damage these barcodes. This is because barcodes have to be applied onto the surface of the products to ensure that line-of-sight scanning can be carried out. However, with RFID tags, line-of-sight scanning is no longer required, and so the tags do not need to be on the surface of the goods and exposed to the elements. It would greatly decrease the chance of these tags being damaged.

4.5 *Increased supply chain visibility*

RFID promises greater visibility of supply chain for management across different parts of the supply chain. With RFID, companies no longer need to stick to the conventional push down approach whereby stores merely act as receivers of goods pushed down from the manufacturing end of the supply chain.

Poor visibility of the supply chain can have debilitating effects on any business. The annual loss faced by the U.S. retail industry as a result of poor supply chain visibility is estimated to be at US$70 billion (Teresko, 2003). 42% of this figure is an unintended consequence from the product not being on the retail shelf for consumers. RFID promises greater visibility of the supply chain via enhanced information accuracy and better information sharing among stakeholders.

To increase productivity, one of the key areas of improvement is in the area of business management. RFID technology and monitoring systems can aid management personnel to achieve a greater degree of precision and control in managing their products. Greater visibility of supply chain allows for greater coordination between different arms of the company, resulting in a leaner and more efficient supply chain. This can be done by adopting an inventory management system whereby data from RFID tagged goods can be updated in real time in a central system.

Case Study: Paul Frank

Paul Frank Company uses an inventory management system that allows for real-time updating of product information such as product location and quantity of each product. As mentioned before, different parts of the supply chain are integrated via a central RFID-orientated inventory management system. As such, Paul Frank no longer needs to perform manual logging and updating of inventory, as this is done in an automated manner via the Mobile RFID system. The management now also has complete visibility of warehouses and stores, and this can be managed via Paul Frank's RFID integrated inventory management system.

This allows all Paul Frank staff to access and track goods as long as they have access to the inventory management system. Information lags and inaccuracies are eliminated as a result of real-time tracking and updating of the database.

4.6 *Enhancement in customer service*

The benefits of RFID are not just confined to the areas of supply chain management as mentioned above. RFID brings along a plethora of positive externalities to the frontline such as superior customer service. RFID helps to free sales staff from the menial and labor-intensive tasks such as counting of inventories, and enables to redeploy them to the frontline in tending to the needs of customers, thus creating a better shopping experience (Roberti, 2003).

The integration of RFID technology can also create a more holistic in-store experience for customers. For instance, the leading Italian fashion retailer, Prada, has implemented the RFID system in its New York branch where it tracks the products the customer takes to the changing room and automatically displays additional information about the garment (Jones *et al.*, 2004). It will also recommend related products to the customer. RFID tags will also be able to detect and store customers' tastes and preferences and recommend similar items. No doubt, this will create a more holistic and personalized shopping experience and at the same time create for opportunities to increase company profits.

Case Study: TUMI

TUMI is a high-end American manufacturer of suitcases and bags for travel. We spoke to the store manager of its Takashimaya branch, and she revealed that TUMI is currently using a form of RFID technology, but not being used for tracking or inventory management purposes. Furthermore, there is not much need for RFID tracking of the store's goods as products come in a very limited amount (less than three pieces) and it could be said that in such cases the full benefits of RFID tracking could not be tapped.

However, we feel that RFID technology still has a lot to offer for high-end retailers such as TUMI. For example, TUMI could adopt RFID integration methods such as that of Prada, which would allow for a more tailored and holistic shopping experience for TUMI.

A retail store with fully integrated RFID systems will provide customers with a unique and personalized shopping experience from choosing of products on the shelves, to the fitting room and all the way to checking out at the point of sales (Figure 6). Smart shelves

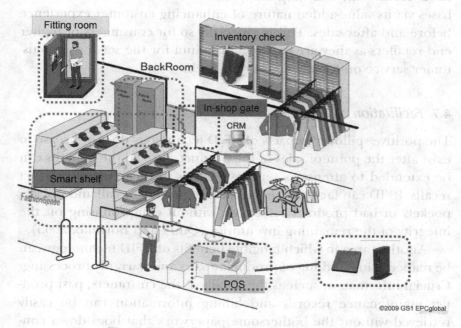

Figure 6: A Fully RFID-integrated Retail Store

Source: RFID Implementation in Japan, EPC Global Japan.

could detect items that are being chosen and removed from the shelves and suggest similar items or other items that are compatible with the chosen item. This would provide a tailored shopping experience for the consumer as well as open up new opportunity for the firm to increase sales. This process can also be replicated at the fitting rooms when scanners detect the items that are brought into these fitting rooms.

Another way of increasing productivity is through product innovation. RFID tags are also highly programmable, and this could serve as a plus for high-end retailers. TUMI could help customers reprogram their RFID tagged luggage and bags so that customers themselves would be able to track their bags after the point of sales. This after-sales service could serve as an additional selling point for high-end retailers.

To meet the challenges of increasing competition, firms in retail and F&B sectors often have to not only retain their existing consumer base but also penetrate into new markets. We believe that RFID technology can help companies reach out to new customer bases via its value-added nature of enhancing customer experience before and after sales. This is especially so for consumers of higher end retailers as they are paying a premium for the service and customer service on top of the product itself.

4.7 *Facilitation of after sales services*

The positive spillover impacts of RFID technology does not cease to exist after the point of sales of the product. Instead the benefits can be extended to after-sales services such as in the areas of product recalls. RFID can facilitate the process of product recall and isolates pockets of bad products effectively without compromising on the integrity of the remaining inventories (Quirk and Borrello, 2005).

Another area in which tangible benefits of RFID technology can be reaped is in handling of product repairs and warranty processing. Crucial information such as the details of the customers, past product maintenance records and billing information can be easily retrieved without the bothersome paperwork that bogs down conventional systems (Kärkkäinen and Holmström, 2002). Therefore, all these contribute to enhance and facilitate a seamless experience for all customers.

Companies interviewed opined that they have not encountered any major problem relating to after sales services to customers. Generally, they do feel that the advantages of RFID have not been fully exploited in the whole retail value chain.

5. Findings and Discussion

Having looked at the plethora of benefits that RFID can bring to retail and F&B companies, we will now focus on the potential barriers which companies may face in the Singapore context. Even though the sample size of our interviewees is small, they have been carefully chosen so as to give us an accurate representation of the retail and F&B industries in Singapore. Moreover, the questionnaire findings reaffirmed the common barriers as identified in the literature review. As such, these findings remain highly relevant and representative of the actual sentiments faced by companies.

The novelty of the adoption of RFID among F&B and retail firms in Singapore inevitably gives rise to a range of potential barriers toward initial adoption. These barriers may be systematic, while others are the consequence of limited awareness of RFID technology. In order to further refine our discussion and crystalize our findings, we have decided to segregate these barriers into six categories: technological constraints, cost and ROI, privacy and security concerns, implementation constraints, organizational concerns, and human resource constraints.

5.1 *General questions (regarding awareness and general attitudes toward RFID)*

1. Are they aware of RFID technology?
2. Are they aware that certain firms in Singapore have adopted this technology?

3. On a scale of 1–10 (1: most negative, 10: most positive), what is their general stand on implementation of RFID?
4. Which part of their firm do they think will benefit the greatest from RFID implementation?

About 40.0% of our respondents are aware of RFID technology and the fact that certain firms in Singapore have adopted this technology. 46.7% of our respondents are highly positive toward the implementation of RFID. 53.3% of our respondents are neutral toward the implementation of RFID. Common areas in which the respondents felt that RFID has positive benefits are the following: inventory and stock management, demand forecast, point of sales and reverse logistics.

5.2 *Technological constraints*

1. Do they believe that RFID technology will provide additional value if deployed within the F&B/retail sector?
2. Is the lack of global standards a hurdle for their firm in adopting RFID technology?
3. Do they believe that RFID is suitable for product assortment?
4. Is poor reader accuracy a barrier for their firm in adopting RFID technology?
5. Do they believe that RFID systems are too complex for users?

86.7% of the respondents believe that RFID technology will provide additional value if deployed within the F&B/retail sectors. 26.7% of the respondents feel that the lack of global standards may pose a hurdle for their firm in adopting RFID technology. 80.0% of the respondents strongly believe that RFID is suitable for product assortment. All of the respondents were satisfied with the accuracy of RFID readers. 20.0% of the respondents believe that RFID systems may be too complex for users, especially for the senior workers.

Discussion: It is highly encouraging to find that most companies which we surveyed strongly believe that RFID has potential to provide additional value. One of the more interesting finding from this questionnaire is the fact that few of the respondents felt that the lack of global standards will pose a hurdle for their firm to adopt RFID. This finding may be attributed to a variety of reasons. First, this finding may be located in the larger context of the streamlining of the RFID bandwidth as a result of the establishment of the agreed protocols spearheaded by EPCglobal in June 2004. Second, we feel that the finding may not accurately reflect the actual sentiments due to a small sample size. Moreover, some of the companies that were interviewed are SMEs which may not necessarily have a high overseas presence. Therefore, they may not run into the issues of the lack of global standards in the short run, thereby introducing downward bias into our findings. Further research may be warranted in this case.

Another area of interest is that some of our respondents believed that RFID systems may be too complex for users, specifically the senior workers. Our interview with the Uniqlo branch manager shed light that senior workers are not rostered to do stocktaking as they display steeper learning curves in using scanners to do stocktaking. Their concern may be held in the larger context of an aging population in Singapore. As Singapore's labor force continues to grey without definite replacement, this may pose a barrier toward adoption of RFID for companies. As such, this may warrant the intervention and continued investment by the government in areas such as retraining and education. This is further developed under the following section of policy recommendations.

5.3 *Cost and return to investment (ROI)*

1. Is the high cost of RFID hardware and infrastructure a barrier for their firm in adopting RFID technology?
2. Is the high cost of RFID software, integration, service and support a barrier for their firm in adopting RFID technology?
3. Is the high cost of RFID tags a barrier for their firm in adopting RFID technology?
4. Is uncertainty in return on investing in RFID technology a barrier for their firm in adopting RFID technology?

About 93.3% of the respondents believe that the high cost of RFID hardware, infrastructure, software, integration, service and support, and the price of RFID tags are potential barriers toward adoption of RFID technology. 86.7% of the respondents feel that the uncertainty in return on investing in RFID technology is a barrier for their company to adopt RFID technology in the foreseeable future.

Discussion: The cost and ROI are two highly relevant areas of investigation to determine the potential barriers toward RFID adoption. A significant number of our respondents believe that the cost of adopting and implementing RFID may be too costly. Despite the fact that price of tags has decreased significantly from their time of inception, they still represent a significant cost. Passive tags may cost as little as US$0.50 per piece (Table 3), but this is only applicable for bulk purchase in excess of a million tags.

Moreover other costs include that of infrastructure, software implementation, integration and training courses as well as the various hidden costs that arise from the integration of RFID technology in the SCM. AMR Research estimated that the cost of implementing a fully integrated RFID system is between $13–23 M (Zaheeruddin, 2005). The breakdown is as given in Table 4.

Table 3:   Costs of Various Types of RFID Tags (USD)

Tag	Unit Cost (minimum of 100 pieces)*
23mm Read Only Glass Transponder	$3.26
32mm SAMP Glass Transponder	$5.71
12mm Read Only Wedge Transponder	$3.16
Read/Write Card Transponder	$4.18
30mm Read Only Disk Transponder	$4.24
Read Only Key ring Transponder	$4.56
85mm Read/Write Disk Transponder	$7.19
120mm Read Only Cylindrical Transponder	$8.64
Read Only Mount-on-Metal Transponder	$8.90

*As of January 2005 for Texas Instruments

Table 4:   Cost of Shipping 50 Million Cases Per Year (USD)

Tags and readers	S5M to $10M
System integration	S3M to $5M
Changes to existing supply chain applications	S3M to $5M
Storage and analytics of the large volumes of data.	S2M to $3M

Source: AMR Research, McClenahen (2005).

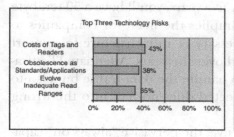
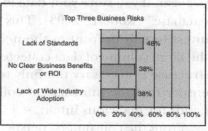

Figure 7:   Top Three Technology and Business Risks
Source: Forget Wal-Mart, Mark Hall (Computerworld, 2004).

Given the fact that the implementation of RFID technology is relatively new among industries, there is a certain degree of uncertainty. Figure 7 captures the expected risks that may arise from both business and technological perspectives. As such, both high costs of RFID tags and uncertainty surrounding the application of RFID may impede firms from adopting RFID technology readily.

5.4 *Privacy and security concerns*

1. Do they believe that consumer privacy is a concern with the implementation of RFID technology?
2. Do they believe that RFID security is a concern with the implementation of RFID technology?

About 60.0% of the respondents strongly believe that consumer privacy may be a concern with the implementation of RFID technology. 46.7% feel that RFID security may be a key concern with the implementation of RFID technology.

Discussion: Another area which we consider as a potential barrier toward adoption is both the privacy and security concerns attributed to the pervasiveness of the "always on" capability of RFID technology. Inevitably after implementation of RFID, enormous amount of data will be collected. To this end, the RFID Journal (2003) estimated for a consumer goods manufacturer "tracking all its items from production to point of sale would generate 10 terabytes of data per year. If you store your data for five years, you'll have a 50-terabyte database" (Roberti, 2003). This implies the need for companies to invest heavily upfront in the necessary IT infrastructure to support the large volume of data collected over the years. Adequate IT infrastructure is necessary not only to handle the data traffic but also to ensure that the information collected does not fall into the wrong hands for malicious intent.

From the consumers' perspective, the pervasive "always on" capability of RFID tags can be a thorny issue that needs to be addressed in the near future. Based on the questionnaire, most of the companies believed that consumer privacy is a concern with the implementation of RFID technology. Take for instance, the case of TUMI where the manager revealed that she is particularly concerned that the tracking capability of RFID tags may not sit well with some of her high net worth customers. Moreover, with the establishment of the Personal Data Protection Act in 2012, this has raised a definite level of awareness among both the businesses and the consumers. Nonetheless, cost of managing information can be lessen if company can make use of the vast amount of data collected to conduct business analytics that can improve sales performance.

5.5 *Implementation constraints*

1. Do they believe that the compatibility and integration of RFID technology with other technologies is a barrier for their firm in adopting RFID technology?
2. Do they believe that data synchronization between RFID systems and other systems is an issue?

3. What do they think will be some of the major issues that their firm will face specifically with regard to RFID implementation?

About 73.3% of the respondents believe that the compatibility and integration of RFID technology with other technologies is a barrier toward adoption of RFID. 66.7% of our respondents believe that data synchronization between RFID systems and other systems may be an issue.

Discussion: Implementation constraints such as integration issues can serve as an impediment toward widespread adoption of RFID in any industry. Integration issues are often highlighted as one of the common barriers, and this is highlighted by our questionnaire findings. The adoption and implementation of RFID technology should not be seen as an off-the-shelf solution. Significant challenges are posed to users who want to integrate RFID solutions to their business models. These challenges include that of antenna configuration and deciding on the most optimal location to place the RFID tag so as to maximize the data collection. All these require considerable level of engineering and programming skills.

Currently, there is also a limited pool of third-party vendors who can supply the necessary software to help companies to fully integrate RFID technology into their existing SCM. An interview conducted by RFID Journal in 2003 highlighted the challenge of implementing RFID in a major aerospace company which hired a large IT consulting and systems integration company to do the coding. Two of the company's own programmers wound up spending five months creating a custom application that could route RFID data to the right application in the right format. And that was just for phase one of its project. Moreover, the implementation constraints may be attributed to the lack of skilled RFID personnel who are trained in the areas of specialized troubleshooting and maintenance of the RFID ecosystem.

5.6 *Organizational constraints*

1. Do they believe that a high degree of business process change required as a result of the adoption of RFID technology is a barrier for their firm in adopting RFID technology?

2. Do they believe that a lack of awareness in RFID technology is a barrier for their firm in adopting RFID technology?
3. Do they believe that a lack of identifiable business need is a barrier for their firm in adopting RFID technology?

About 73.3% of our respondents feel that a high degree of business process change required as a result of the adoption of RFID technology is a barrier for the firm in adopting RFID technology. 60.0% of our respondents feel that a lack of awareness in RFID technology is a barrier for the firm in adopting RFID technology. 46.7% feel that a lack of identifiable business need as a barrier toward adoption of RFID by their company.

Discussion: Organizational constraints such as the inclination of the organization toward innovation may impede the smooth assimilation of RFID technology in their business model. In a survey conducted by Deloitte (Figure 8), it was found that the culture of the fear toward change was pervasive among the retailers, accounting up to approximately 30% of the respondents (Abbott, 2004).

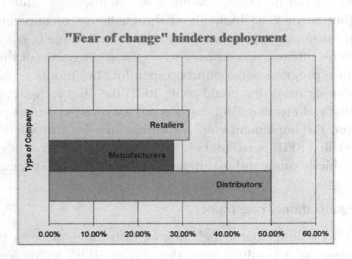

Figure 8:   Fear of Change Hinders Deployment of RFID

Source: RFID: How Far, How Fast: A View from the Rest of the World, Deloitte.

From our questionnaire, we identified that a high proportion of our respondents believed that a high degree of business process change, and a lack of awareness in RFID technology posed a barrier for their companies to adopt RFID technology. In order to overcome these organizational constraints, it is crucial for us to first raise awareness about the benefits of RFID for both retailers and F&B businesses.

5.7 *People constraints*

1. Do they believe that a lack of willingness among customers and suppliers to use RFID technology is a barrier for their firm in adopting RFID technology?
2. Do they believe that a lack of senior management support is a barrier for their firm in adopting RFID technology?
3. Do they believe that a lack of a skilled pool of RFID personnel is a barrier for their firm in adopting RFID technology?

About 26.7% of our respondents believe that a lack of willingness to use RFID technology is a barrier for their firm in adopting RFID technology. 13.3% of our respondents believe that a lack of senior management support is a barrier for their firm in adopting RFID technology. 33.3% of our respondents believe that a lack of a skilled pool of RFID personnel is a barrier for their firm in adopting RFID technology.

Discussion: From our questionnaire finding, a small proportion of the respondents believe that a lack of willingness among customers and suppliers to use RFID may serve as a potential barrier to adopting RFID. It is critical that both the customers and suppliers be on board with the adoption and implementation of RFID as the plethora of potential benefits that RFID technology offer can only be fully unleashed if it is integrated in the whole supply chain. These benefits in turn will have positive spillover into the areas of significant cost savings, faster decision making by management and assurance of a lean supply chain.

One of the positive findings from our questionnaire is that 87.7% of our respondents have the strong backing of senior management in adopting RFID technology. The minority who believe that there is a lack of senior management support may be attributed to the size of the company. There seems to be a correlation between the size of the company and the willingness of the company to adopt RFID. This can be partly explained by the fact that if the company is too small, it may not be able to fully reap the benefits of RFID, let alone justifying the ROI of the investment in RFID.

6. Policy Recommendations

Having analyzed the current situation of RFID adoption among Singaporean firms, we observed that there are indeed many productivity issues faced by firms, which RFID technology can help to address. Hence, we have come up with a list of plausible suggestions that might make it easier for firms to take up RFID technology in their supply chain. These policy suggestions range from more direct top-down approaches implemented by the government such as subsidies and mandates to less direct means such as setting up of information booths to spread awareness and educate people about RFID technology. Some policies will also touch on the international aspects of RFID technology such as the streamlining of global RFID spectrum, which we believe will also help to increase productivity among firms. These policies will be further discussed in detail below.

6.1 *Subsidies via the enhanced PIC scheme*

The key motivation for the case of government subsidy is that we can look at RFID technology as a merit good with positive externalities with enhanced productivity and ensuring a lean supply chain for all stakeholders involved. In the framework of goods with positive externalities, the issue at heart is underconsumption and as such market equilibrium is less than the socially optimal level of output. The final outcome is inefficient, and welfare loss ensues.

Moreover, government subsidies helped to shoulder the uncertainty of investment that shrouds RFID. To this end, global analysts Frost & Sullivan highlight the considerable support offered by government in the form of direct funding for vendor initiatives or subsidies to end users intending to adopt this technology. Their report on the Asia-Pacific RFID Market highlights that government subsidies are a powerful driving force for RFID adoption. As a result of government subsidies, market earned revenues in Asia Pacific are projected to be boosted from US$569.7 million in 2008 to US$2.17 billion in 2015.

Currently, the Singapore government is offering allowances up to 100% if the expenditure is incurred on or after 15 Dec 2010: Automated system for storage and retrieval of information, including RFID system and bar-coding system. It is highly positive that the Singapore government recognized the importance of subsidies to encourage companies to take up RFID technology. However, we believe there is room for improvement so as to ensure a higher take up rate among both the F&B and retail firms.

First, a handful of respondents were unaware of these policies. One of the respondents, Mr Ho from ADM Cocoa Pte Ltd lamented that he would like to see some form of subsidies for adoption of RFID in the areas of inventory management. In order to prevent the dislocation between the policies and their targeted audience, it is crucial for policymakers to ensure that policies are properly communicated to their targeted audience. This point is further elaborated in the later segments.

Second, in order for companies to reap the full range of the benefits offered by RFID, it is important for them to fully integrate RFID at every juncture of the supply chain. As such, we propose for a progressive allowance subsidy vehicle that offers differentiated levels of subsidies for varying degrees of integration of RFID. This serves as an additional incentive for companies to look at how they can actively apply RFID solutions in every aspects of their supply chain. This proposal helps to mitigate the issue of moral hazard on the company's part where they adopt a "slap and paste" mindset.

Third, we feel that the current PIC may not adequately address the daily concerns of smaller companies which may face a tighter cash flow due to a sluggish global economic growth. Currently, a business may convert up to $100,000 of its eligible PIC expenditure into cash on an annual basis at a rate of 60%. Hence, for $100,000 of expenditure, the business may apply to the IRAS to receive cash of $60,000 in lieu of tax benefits.

However, the cash benefit is small compared to the potential benefit of up to $272,000 in terms of tax savings. With the low conversion rate, the cash benefit option would make sense only in cases where the business has significant amount of tax losses.

6.2 *Raising awareness of RFID technology*

Currently, 60% of our respondents are not aware of RFID technology. We believe that ignorance of the technology and its benefits can be a potentially huge barrier toward RFID adoption. Firms tend to be more apprehensive with a technology that they are unfamiliar with or have not heard about before. But after a brief introduction about RFID and its uses and benefits, most of our respondents demonstrated a certain degree of willingness in wanting to adopt this new technology. Most of them even believe that RFID can boost productivity of their business and push the company toward a leaner supply chain.

There are several ways in which awareness can be raised about RFID technology. First, education can take place in a top-down manner initiated by the government. For example, government newsletters could publish articles to educate firms about RFID. In addition to newsletters, they could also direct firm owners to websites set up by the government especially to explain the uses of RFID technology and its potential benefits.

Second, education can also take place through sharing and interaction on a common platform that firms share. This is often in the form of unions or organizations that firms are members of. For example, the Singapore Food and Beverage Management Association is an organization formed with the purpose of serving as a hub for its members to network and exchange business ideas and practices in the F&B industry. Forums or talks held as part of the program during a regular organizational meeting could reach out to many potential firm owners who have yet to learn about RFID.

Third, education could also take place through mass media. Here, the target audience is not merely restricted to firm owners and business owners but to the general public as well. This would also help reach out to small business owners who might not be members of unions and organizations. Forms of mass media could include publishing articles about RFID in the TECH or IT columns of widely read newspapers such as the Straits Times. Journals or scholarly articles could also be published in local IT magazines to further reach out to business owners keep to find out more about RFID and in greater detail. Furthermore, our study has found that 60% of the respondents are concerned that consumer privacy might be a potential problem that they might face when choosing whether to adopt RFID technology. Such potential concerns of consumers might be addressed in articles found in the mass media, and this would help to dispel any ungrounded worries. Favorable public opinion might even be a push factor for firms to adopt RFID.

Fourth, knowledge about RFID could also be promoted during conventions and local IT shows. This would help to target small business owners who might happen to attend these conventions, who are not part of any union or organization. As IT conventions are often ideal places for unveiling of new technology, we believe that this is a good avenue to educate the public about RFID technology. Interactive display centers could be set up for people to learn more about RFID technology and its benefits.

We believe that through education about RFID and its potential benefits, firms would be in a better position to decide whether RFID is a technology that is suitable for their company. We have confidence that with the proper form of education, they will be more receptive and willing to adopt RFID into their supply chain. In the long run, a more educated industry would also foster an environment whereby RFID technology can be easily taken up by firms that are yet to do so.

6.3 *Education and retraining of workers*

When a company decides to adopt RFID technology to streamline its supply chain, having just the hardware and equipment is not sufficient. They would also need the technical know-how and workers who are trained to operate these systems efficiently. 33.3% of our respondents believe that a lack of a skilled pool of RFID personnel is a barrier for their firm in adopting RFID technology. Furthermore, through our interview, we found out there is a limited interest among senior workers toward using this technology. Due to an aging demographic profile and initiatives for older workers to continue to upgrade and stay relevant in the workforce, we believe that any policies recommended will have to take into account this crucial group of workers.

First, one policy recommendation that we would like to suggest is the setting up of specialized training centers where workers could be trained and equipped with the technical know-hows of operating RFID systems. Companies could either send their workers here to be trained or they could hire trained professionals straight from these centers. With the setting up of such facilities, we believe that it would address the concerns that some companies might have regarding the lack of a trained workforce to operate their RFID systems. With this boost in confidence, we believe that we will observe an increase in the willingness to adopt RFID technology.

Second, we need to address the issue of training older workers to be familiar with the system. We can do this by ranking RFID operating tasks into different levels of complexity that requires different levels of technical knowledge. For example, a highly complex job would be that of troubleshooting and repairing faulty RFID systems. Such jobs require a high degree of technical knowledge that might need long periods of training and might not be suitable for older workers. A less technical-intensive job would be monitoring of goods and tracking of locations of goods. These can often be monitored via a computer screen and all the information can be retrieved easily should there be an inventory management program being used. An even less technical-intensive job would be that of scanning of RFID-tagged goods. These jobs require minimal technical knowledge of RFID operating systems, as they are often self-contained to scanning of RFID tags with a handheld scanning device. We would suggest that less technical-intensive tasks be allocated to elderly workers in order to shorten the familiarization process and at the same time ensure minimal work stress in the adaption period. Special retraining programs could be set up in order to cater for these.

Third, we would suggest that subsidy schemes be set up for the retraining of workers. We could engage the help of organizations such as NTUC Employment and Employability Institute (e2i). e2i is an institute which seeks to create solutions for better employment and employability among workers. Recently, it has achieved much success, seeing more than 51,800 workers undergoing its training programs, attaining a 36% increase in workers from 2013 (Today, 2015).

A similar initiative can be set up for workers taking courses on RFID usage, and this can help push firms toward RFID adoption as the costs of retraining workers have now been reduced.

7. Conclusion

We believe that RFID technology is a solution that can help to address many productivity issues that firms in Singapore are facing today. The numerous benefits of RFID can help to impact firms through various channels such as reduction of manpower needed and more efficient and accurate tracking of inventory to reduce shrinkage. These benefits are not just limited to a certain stage of the supply chain, rather its impact can be felt at each and every stage of the supply chain.

Through our studies, we have found out several potential barriers that are holding back RFID adoption in Singapore. These factors range from concerns about organizational changes and a deficit of a trained workforce to manage RFID systems to a simple lack of knowledge about RFID technology which results in uncertainty and unwillingness to adopt RFID technology. For any progress to be made in the RFID adoption rate among F&B and retail sectors in Singapore, these problems will first have to be addressed.

As such, we have drafted several policies that are tailored to address these potential problems. If these are implemented, we believe that these would greatly help in fostering a business environment that is welcoming to RFID technology. The potential benefits of RFID has been proven to be real, and what is left for firms to do now is to embrace and make the fullest use of this technology.

Endnotes

1. The IM Index encompasses big data, business intelligence, analytics as well real-time data processing, while the DE Index includes mobile, social and online applications of services.
2. The application of Lean Principle and Management among Singapore SMEs in F&B and Retail Industries is considered in Chapter 1.

Chapter 5

The Role of Shared Services in Improving Productivity in the Food Services Sector

1. Introduction

1.1 *Overview of F&B services sector in Singapore*

Singapore's Food and Beverage (F&B) Services sector is a key part of Singapore's economy. Together with accommodation, it constituted 2.09% of Gross Domestic Product (GDP) in 2014. Under the Singapore Standard Industrial Classification (SSIC), the F&B Services sector consists of restaurants, fast food restaurants, food caterers, café & snack bars, food courts and others. F&B services play an important role in the job market, employing about 199,400 workers or 5.51% of the total employment count (Ministry of Manpower, 2015).

Between 2013 and 2016, the number of establishments in the F&B had increased by 974 reflecting a vibrant average growth of 3.6% per annum (Department of Statistics: *Annual Survey of Services*). However, the growth in terms of value-added and operating surplus (profits) over the same period were 3.8% and 2.0% per annum respectively. These indicate that business expansion had not brought about significant improvement in productivity measured per establishment basis.

On the whole the productivity performance of the F&B sector is still languishing behind other sectors in the economy.

1.2 Challenges of F&B services sector

There are a few key mitigating factors that are faced by the F&B services sector. These include labor shortage, increasing fixed costs, poor capital intensity, inadequate skilled labor, antiquated HR practices and sub-optimized capacity (Euromonitor International, 2014).

Labor shortage continues to plague F&B services, with a job vacancy rate of 5.3% in 2014, the fourth highest rate of all industrial classifications. The government has tightened the Dependency Ratio Ceiling (DRC), meaning that business would need to hire six locals in order to be eligible to hire a foreigner (Ministry of Manpower, n.d.). Locals are also reluctant to work in F&B services due to the negative perception of working in the sector (Staff Reporter, 2013). Many F&B establishments therefore now face the issue of understaffing. For example, it was reported this year that Old Hong Kong Kitchen had to turn away diners at least once a week when a staff does not show up for work. This resulted in an estimated loss of revenues of $2,000 each time. Kilo and Relish also experienced a similar situation. This issue will only be further exacerbated with the new DRC enforced on existing F&B services in July 2014 as well as increases in work permit levy rates in 2016.

Other than labor shortages, F&B services also experienced *increasing Operational Expenditures* (OPEX). Industry wide OPEX increased by 3.6% per annum between 2013 and 2016, while the corresponding operating receipt registered growth of 3.3% per annum. This reflects a rather marginal growth of profit over the same period. The increase in OPEX can be attributed partially to the labor shortage as well as rising rental. Rising OPEX has forced many F&B services to either raise prices and/or reduce food portions or service quality in order to stay competitive. As a consequence, smaller F&B players who are less able to internalize the costs will likely be the most affected, resulting in market exits and industry consolidation. According to the F&B Services Survey conducted by

Singstat (2013), small F&B establishments[1] recorded the lowest Depreciation–OPEX Ratio at 0.170. (Department of Statistics Singapore, 2013).

The low OPEX ratio implies *poor capital intensity.* Small F&B establishments on aggregate also recorded negative operating surplus. (Department of Statistics Singapore, 2013). At the outset, this suggests that larger F&B establishments (based on the magnitude of operating receipts) reap greater operating surplus by substituting capital equipment for manpower, thereby utilizing greater capital intensity to achieve economies of scale.

(a) *Analysis of F&B services sector*

Summarily, these changing regulatory measures and rising operation costs have had substantial impact on the bottom line of F&B establishments. However, F&B SMEs, particularly SMEs with one or two F&B establishments, have been hit the hardest. From a cost perspective, F&B SMEs are unable to compete against hawker centers on a low-cost proposition. On the other hand, these SMEs operate in an environment where only large F&B groups can achieve cost efficiency. Hence F&B SMEs are relegated to be price takers, leading to a decreasing operating surplus in light of rising costs and their inevitable predicament in these absorbing costs.

These small F&B establishments face a dilemma in that they are inherently unable to achieve economies of scale from greater capital intensity due to the indivisible nature of (high) sunk costs as well as the minimum efficient scale often required.

One solution to increase operational efficiency (and hence productivity) would be for smaller F&B establishments to externalize business processes through Shared Services. The adoption of Shared Services allows small F&B establishments to bypass these scale limitations and yet realize the cost efficiency benefits by pooling together similar business processes across the industry.

Given the challenging business environment, it is imperative to devise solutions that help smaller F&B establishments increase operational efficiency. Failing to do so would reduce the heterogeneity of the F&B services sector. This would be a highly undesirable consequence given the role of a diverse food culture in positioning Singapore as an international culinary hub.

1.3 *Definition of shared services*

Shared Services is defined as the sharing of facilities or business processes to reduce per-unit operating costs and also to lessen the need to incur high sunk costs for capital investment. In context of its usage, we mainly refer to the *externalization of business processes by Small & Medium Enterprises (SMEs) to external service providers or* alternatively through collaborative industry projects.

Large F&B groups are inherently able to internalize business processes among their multiple outlets with sufficient scale. The internalization model adopted by large F&B groups such as Suki Group is similar in many ways to the externalization model for SMEs, albeit without the central managing authority. Hence, it is important that our study encompasses both SMEs and large F&B groups for comprehensive analysis.

For this study, our scope of Shared Services will encompass Centralized Kitchen, Centralized Dishwashing, and Part-Time Pool Program.

1.4 *Report objective and organization*

The main objective of this study is to understand the role of Shared Services in improving productivity of F&B establishments. In the case of Singapore, the government has put in place different schemes and grants[2] that will help private enterprises to develop or adopt Shared Services for better business performance and productivity improvement. We seek to evaluate the feasibility, benefits, hindrances and effectiveness in adopting each Shared Service to help boost the productivity.

Under the 8M Framework of Productivity Improvement (Toh and Thangavelu, 2017, Chapters 2 and 3), this study focuses on providing recommendations in the aspects of Manpower, Management, Material and Money. The study also presents recommendations to the various stakeholders (F&B establishments, trades associations, and government) to improve productivity through the adoption of Shared Services.

For the subsequent two section(s), we will first review the literature on the concept of Shared Services, its development globally and its applicability to the value chain of Singapore's F&B sector. This is followed by a summary of our research approach, methodologies and highlights from survey results.

In the fourth section of the study, we will discuss four key Shared Services in the sector in detail, their effectiveness and usage, as well as issues faced, using results from surveys, interviews and secondary research. This is followed by an exploratory discussion on potential Shared Services that could be implemented. The study concludes by providing actionable recommendations to increase the effectiveness of Shared Services in helping the food service industry to improve productivity.

2. Overview of Shared Services

2.1 *Literature review*

Since the 1990s, the concept of Shared Services has gained traction as a solution to larger business entities. In the literature, Shared Services refers to the practice of business units, operating companies and organizations sharing a common set of services instead of having duplicated services (Quinn *et al.*, 2000).

Organizations have decentralized operations as they expanded, which inadvertently duplicates job tasks (Shah, 1998). A trend toward integration of shared services, outsourcing and offshoring has also been observed since 2000s (Kearney, 2004). By 2000s, organizations that have consolidated the full back-office began to use Shared Services for managing Enterprise Resource Planning (ERP) systems such as SAP (Leknes and Munkvold, 2006) and Oracle (Sedera and Dey, 2007).

Shared Services have been adopted by major corporations globally including Fortune 500 companies and other smaller organizations (Wallace, 2011). Some scholars argued that the adoption is often limited to larger and more complex organizations with over \$2 billion in revenue and with multiple business units (Schulman, 1999).

Shared Services are widely applied across various sectors. The cost reduction and service improvement aspects are among key factors which motivate the governments of various countries, especially in Europe and America, to adopt Shared Services in the public sector (Kearney, 2007). Besides being implemented to improve administrative efficiencies in government functions, Shared Services are also widely adopted in healthcare and education sectors. There has also been an ongoing discussion regarding the application of Shared Services into non-profit sector (Walsh, 2006).

In the F&B industry, for example, some businesses have adopted models to streamline the food production process, as observed in cases such as Operation Slam[3] by Burger King. Fast food restaurants served as a model for food operators who adopt its method of outsourcing food production to a specialized factory or setting up its own centralized food production facility.

Financial reasons, such as cost reduction, productivity improvement and better economies of scale are often the main reasons that drive sharing of services (Holzer and Issacs, 2002). Nevertheless, Shared Services have other benefits such as increasing service quality, process, improving span of control, knowledge transfer and the ability to leverage technology (Redman *et al.*, 2007; Bergeron *et al.*, 2003, Schulman *et al.*, 1999).

2.2 *Value chain analysis in F&B*

In order to ascertain areas where Shared Services can help increase productivity for F&B enterprises, a value chain analysis has been carried out. Typically, areas in the value chain where Shared Services can be used are: food processing, food procurement and food storage. Areas in the sales side may also include the expansion into food delivery services and online ordering systems. The value chain of a typical F&B enterprise is shown in Table 1. The feasibility of using shared services at each link is considered.

Table 1: Summary of Salient Features in Activities in the F&B Value Chain That Can be Classified as Shared Services

	Value Chain for F&B		
	F&B Activities	Shared Service?	Description
Primary Activities			
Inbound Logistics	Purchasing ingredients for menu items	Yes	Shared service is possible for inbound logistics as F&B operators can do bulk orders together for certain menu items.
Operations	Item Preparation Method		
	Dishwashing at outlets	Yes	Due to a shortage of dishwashers, companies can consider outsourcing dishwashing together.
Outbound Logistics	Food Serving Protocol	Yes	Labor constraints may lead to companies adopting a similar manner of serving food using technology (e.g. self-collection, robot food servers).
Sales & Marketing	Product Placement Strategy	Yes	F&B operators can consider partnering with those offering complimentary products to save on marketing fees (e.g. discounts and promotions for F&B operators in the same mall).
	Sales & Offers	Yes	
Service & Support	Customer Service Practices		
	Home Delivery	Yes	Delivery service and online ordering systems can be shared between F&B operators on a same, outsourced platform.
	Online Ordering System	Yes	

(Continued)

Table 1:   (*Continued*)

	Value Chain for F&B		
	F&B Activities	Shared Service?	Description
Secondary Activities			
Infrastructure	Funds Collection		
	Administrative Tasks		
Human Resource Management	Employee Scheduling		
	Appraisal/Reward System		
	Hiring/Firing of Staff	Yes	Regarding hiring, the F&B operator may outsource it to an agency if current methods of recruitment do not do well, given our labor crunch.
Technology Development	Customer Feedback System		
	Product Development		
	IT Software System	Yes	IT platform can be provided by software companies so F&B operators need not spend too much time creating one from scratch.
Procurement	Global Product Acquisition	Yes	To enjoy bulk order savings, F&B operators may look into shared procurement.
	Local Product Acquisition	Yes	

Source: Author's compilation.

3. Methodology

3.1 *Research approach and methods*

In order to provide an understanding of the role of Shared Services in productivity improvement for the F&B sector in Singapore, the research focuses on two main aspects in evaluating existing Shared Services: *Usage and Effectiveness.* Potential Shared Services would also be explored. Below are the set of questions that guided researchers in research and in report writing.

1. What is the current usage and scope of application for the existing Shared Services in the F&B sector in Singapore? [Usage]
2. How do those Shared Services help F&B businesses improve productivity through 8M and according to productivity measurement? [Effectiveness]
3. What are the issues and concerns regarding adopting existing Shared Services? [Challenges]
4. What could be the potential Shared Services for the F&B sector? [Suggestions]
5. How could the government and different stakeholders help the F&B sector to further improve productivity through Shared Services? [Suggestions]

Besides engaging secondary research through trade journals, databases, magazines and newspaper articles, we mainly focused on primary research to gather insights regarding the situation of Shared Services in Singapore. Methods for primary research included surveys, interviews and site visits. Both shared service providers, food operators and other industry practitioners were interviewed.

In this study, we used both *case studies* and *survey results* to support the evaluations on each shared service. The survey is conducted either through short interviews with outlet managers on-site, or through sending an online questionnaire for business owners to fill in. The purpose of the survey would be to collect information on outlet operations, in order to evaluate the feasibility of existing Shared Services, and also to understand the usage of Shared Services by F&B establishments in Singapore.

3.2 *Demographics of survey respondents*

A total of 44 F&B enterprises were included in the surveys. They were selected to provide a representative sample relevant to the F&B sector in Singapore. Responses were obtained through sending online questionnaires to 1,000 SMEs in the F&B sector and by conducting on-site interviews with outlet managers.

Figure 1 illustrates the demographics of the F&B establishments surveyed, while Figure 2 shows the number of outlets that the surveyed enterprises have.

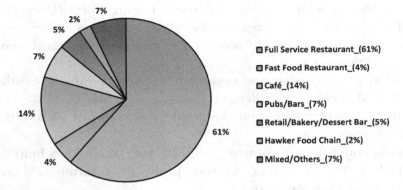

Figure 1:   Types of F&B Establishment

Source: Surveys and interviews.

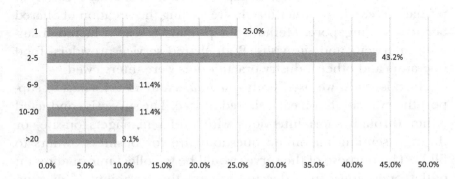

Figure 2:   Number of Outlets

Source: Surveys and interviews.

(a) *F&B enterprises for case studies*

Table 2 shows the profile of the eight F&B enterprises selected for case studies and their respective status of adoption for different Shared Services. We share insights gathered through interviews with business owners and managers/directors later in the chapter.

4. Evaluation of Shared Services in Singapore

4.1 *Central kitchen*

(a) *Situation and development of central kitchens in Singapore*

The concept of Central Kitchen (CK) is not new in Singapore. As early as 1986, a local brand Old Chang Kee had started its own CK (Weizhen, 2014). By 1987, Bengawan Solo became the first among the Singapore confectionary industry to utilize a CK, which was opened on a 9,500 square foot plot at Harvey Road (Chua, 2010). In 1991, Jack's Place set up its own CK at Defu Lane to centrally produce the main sources and soups, as well as to cut the steak (The Business Times, 2011). Moving into early 2000s, successful SMEs or large foodservice groups, such as Select Group (Select Group, 2010), Sakae Sushi (Sakae Holdings, 2013) and Komala's, have set up their own CKs during the time of expansion.

A big wave of establishing or upgrading CKs came around the 2010s among big restaurant groups, in a move toward automation to tackle the labor crunch and to reduce kitchen space at the outlets (Min, 2014). Large companies such as Breadtalk, RE&S, Japan Food, Sakae Sushi and Tung Lok had refurbished and upgraded their CKs with state-of-the-art facilities to improve efficiency.

In a call for greater productivity in the sector, government agencies such as SPRING also supported many other SMEs, such as Soup Spoon and Pu Tien to establish their own CK. Multiple grants or assistance in other forms have been provided for F&B companies to purchase equipment, re-design workflow, implement 5S practice (Lean Management) as well as obtain Hazard Action Critical Control Point (HACCP) and ISO certification for their CKs. CKs have also been adopted by some hawker food chains such as Tian Tian and Lor Ke (Kim, 1995) Chicken Rice, as well as few social enterprises for training ground.

Table 2: Profile of F&B Enterprises for Case Studies

Company	Type of F&B Service	Type of Cuisine	Number of Outlets	Years in Operation	Central Kitchen	Dish-washing	PPP	F&B Market
A	Mixed	Japanese	30+	>10	Yes	Yes	Yes	No
B	Fast Food	Indian	8	>20	Yes	No	No	No
C	Hawker Food	Local	4	>10	No	Yes	No	No
D	Casual Dinning	Western	5	>15	No	No	Yes	No
E	Pub/Bars	Western	1	<5	No	No	No	Open to consideration
F	Casual Dining	Local	2	<5	Yes	No	Yes	No
G	Full-Service	Korean	2	<5	No	No	No	Open to consideration
H	Dessert Bar	—	2	<5	No	No	No	No

Note: PPP: Part-time pool program for engagement of workers.

Source: Surveys and interviews.

Currently, most of the CKs are located in Tai Seng, which is designated as a food zone in Singapore. Large groups such as Breadtalk Group, RE&S, Sakae Sushi, and Suki Sushi have standalone buildings for their headquarters and CKs in Tai Seng. The Kampung Ampat Foodlink, a six-story building that is designated by the Agri-Food & Veterinary Authority of Singapore as a dedicated food facility, hosts the CKs of several companies including popular food chains such as Soup Spoon and Awfully Chocolate (Mapletree Industrials, 2012). Common locations for CK also include Woodlands and Bedok.

The use of CK to improve productivity has been proven effective, with newspaper articles or online reviews citing many examples for its importance in ensuring consistency, as well as helping to reduce number of service staff, kitchen space required, and the skill level required for the kitchen staff. As such, CK and automation have been a popular strategy among large restaurant groups. Nevertheless, small businesses are still unable to tap on productivity improvement through CK and automation because of the volume requirement (Jessica Lim, 2013). Also, about 42% of companies in the foodservice industry are micro-companies, with less than $1million in annual revenue.

The concept of CK has been rather popular in the F&B sector. But CK today still tends to serve restaurants within the same group. CK can expand to become a general supplier (blogtkz, 2013). There is much potential in further exploring the idea of CK, such that smaller establishments could also benefit from the productivity improvement through CK.

(b) *Different forms of food preparation for F&B establishments*

CK is a facility that centralizes procurement and common food production process across the outlets within an F&B group and is an internal service provider. It is one of the four forms of food processing that is normally adopted by F&B enterprises in Singapore. Smaller scale restaurants would usually purchase raw ingredients directly and do all food preparation at the outlet, which is the conventional way. Larger establishments with CK centralize some food production for their outlets, such as baked goods, sauces, soup, and sliced meat, before they are sent to the outlet kitchens where food is served to customers. The ready-prepared system is more commonly adopted by fast food restaurants for which food is produced either on-site or off-site, chilled, stored and either reheated or processed simply before serving to customers. Outsourcing food preparation, especially for the non-core menu items, is widely adopted compared to the rest. In response to the labor crunch, such a mode of food preparation would continue to be on the rise (see Figure 3).

(c) *Survey results for state of adoption of central kitchen in Singapore*
(i) By size
The likelihood of adopting of CK is hugely influenced by the size of the F&B establishments, especially in terms of number of outlets. A sample of 92 foodservice companies, including 50 large establishments and 40 from the surveys is analyzed for the state of adoption of central kitchen according to the number of outlets they have.

    Smaller establishments are much less likely to have standalone central kitchens compared to larger establishments, unless the

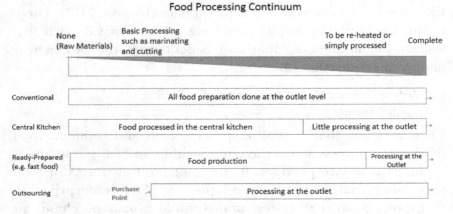

Figure 3:   Different Forms of Food Preparation Systems in Singapore
Source. Adapted from introduction to foodservice system.

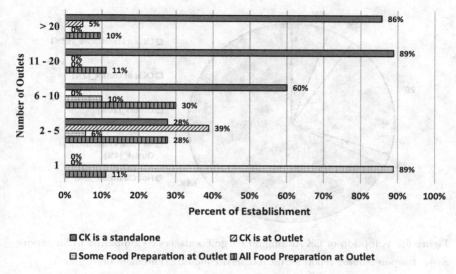

Figure 4: Adoption of CK Based on Number of Outlets

Source: Company Survey.

establishment also has catering as one of their core businesses. Examples are Laksania and Argentum Kitchen, which each have catering arms in addition to their two outlets. Establishments with 2–5 outlets are more likely to adopt a CK at one of their outlets as an alternative of *having a standalone CK*. Examples are Bricks n Cubes Café and Pita Pan, which prepare some of their food items at their main outlets before sending them to the other outlet(s) (see Figure 4).

In general, we observe that *very few F&B establishments outsource* their food preparation. As pointed out during the interview with the owner of F&B establishment E, he is more willing to establish a CK at his main outlet rather than outsourcing, due to the small scale and quality concerns such as freshness.

The use of CK has been *common* among *larger-scale establishments* in Singapore. Figure 5 shows the detail of the state of adoption of a list of 50 large food service companies in Singapore. The list is adapted from Passport Industry Report for the Foodservice Industry in Singapore (Euromonitor, 2014).

In total, 70% of them have established a CK. A majority (68%) of restaurants have standalone CKs, except for Han's, whose CK is at

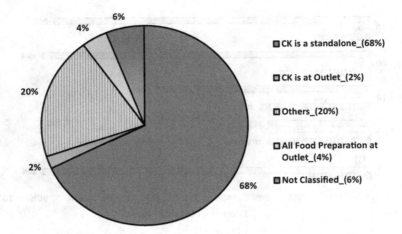

Figure 5: Adoption of CK Among 50 Large Foodservice Companies in Singapore
Source: Passport industry report for the foodservice industry (Euromonitor).

two of its outlets to utilize the existing space. It is noted that, despite having over 20 outlets in Singapore, Thai Express does not have its own CK. Ten of the large F&B groups (20%) are fast food franchises or international food chains, such as McDonald's, Subway and Starbucks, who adopt the readymade food preparation system. They may choose to use only common warehouses or cold rooms for their outlets for storing raw materials, but food processing might be largely outsourced to overseas manufacturers.

(ii) By categories

The decision of whether to adopt CK is also largely dependent on the business model and the type of F&B establishments. For catering business, it is imperative to have CK due to the lack of retail space. CK is also very commonly adopted by food retail chains or snack bars chains, such as Mr. Bean, Old Chang Kee, Lao Ban Bean Curd, Udders and Twelve Cupcakes, which require limited or even no kitchen space at the retail sites.

However, for full service or quick casual restaurants which are cook-to-order, having a CK is less of a necessity because of the existing kitchen spaces and the requirement to maintain food freshness for a shorter time. Having a CK is very beneficial for establishments with a franchise model since a CK is critical in ensure food consistency across all outlets. An example would be Char-Grill Bar, which managed to turn itself into a franchise model after adopting a CK (Keeping it Simple, 2014).

(d) *Impact of central kitchen*

(i) 8M framework and productivity benefits

According to the 8M framework, centralized activities like centralized dishwashing and centralized kitchen improve productivity through the following:

- Management: Management practices for CK such as 5S and HACCP ensure food quality and improve efficiency at the backend.
- Manpower: Reduces manpower needs and skill requirement to cope with labor crunch.
- Method: Investing in machineries and technologies such as ERP systems helps to streamline production and improves efficiency.
- Materials: Centralizing production allows CK to enjoy bulk purchase during procurement; material wastage is also reduced with machineries.
- Productivity Benefits: According to our observation and analysis, CK has tremendous impact on productivity benefits for an F&B establishment in Singapore in many aspects along the value chain.

First and foremost, it helps F&B enterprises to *improve the bottom line* by *reducing costs* through economies of scale, which allows firms to enjoy bulk discounts for purchasing. CK also helps the big groups to *increase revenue streams* by expanding to catering or supplying to other SMEs. It would potentially increase sales by improving customer experience by ensuring food quality consistency and reducing the food preparation time at the outlets. CK has also been critical in supporting the firm's expansion. By utilizing machines and other technologies, which is made possible by obtaining sufficient scale through centralizing food production, the requirement for back-end kitchen staff at the outlet level could be significantly reduced. This also brings along other benefits such as reducing kitchen space

Finance and Accounting	Huge upfront investment results in high CAPEX, less rental costs			
Technology Development	Centralisation allows for implementation of ERP system to streamline production, automation			
Human Resources	Less labour requirement, **more effective recruitment strategy** due to less skill requirement and training for kitchen staff			
Infrastructure	**Less kitchen space and equipment** required at the outlets			

Procurement (Inbound Logistics):	Operations (Centralised Food Preparation)	Delivery to Outlets (Outbound Logistics)	Operations (Food Preparation at Outlet)	Service and Sales
•Allowing for centralised procurement to enjoy **bulk discounts**	•Centralising Equipment and Labour •**Obtain Sufficient Scale for Automation** •Control Food Quality •Reduce Material Costs	•Additional labour and trucks required for delivery	•Simplify food preparation procedure •Less labour hours and skills requirement •Faster food preparation time	•Ensuring food **consistency** across the outlets •Less customer complaints •**Increase revenue stream** through expanding to new segments such as catering and sales to other SMEs •Consolidation of business processes to allow more efficient expansion

Figure 6:   Impact of CK on value chain

Source: Author's compilation.

and equipment. As a result of automation and productivity improvement, the worker's wages would be increased as well.

Figure 6 summarizes CK's impacts on different aspects along the value chain of a typical F&B enterprise that adopts CK in Singapore.

However, a downside of CK is that, as noted during interviews with Companies A and C, it results a perceived loss of quality due to automation. Customers might still prefer the "authentic taste" of dishes that are fully prepared by hand. Furthermore, with a centralized food system, the impact of equipment malfunction could be significant, and thus preventive maintenance is important.

(ii) *Case studies of Singapore firms*

Company A is a good example to illustrate the impact of CK on a company's whole value chain. By centralizing food production, A is able to purchase raw ingredients in bulk and to import them directly from overseas suppliers, resulting in 20–30% cost savings. Automation through implementing rice cooking machines and vacuum tumblers results in a 35% productivity improvement and 12.6% increase in wages. About 3–4 staff are saved at each outlet for kitchen operations,

Table 3:   Examples of F&B enterprises that benefited from implementing CK

Companies	Impact
Tunglok	• Implemented robotics to do the job of three men at its CK.[4] • Artificial Intelligence Cooking Machines (AICs) cook 100 kg of fried rice in an hour instead of 30 kg if cooking manually.[5] • Ability to tap into new business opportunities in catering with kitchen innovation launched BellyGood Catering in 2013.[6]
Pu Tien[7]	• Reduce staff strength by four per outlet. • Cut the size of each outlet kitchen by 10% while increasing seating capacity.
Char Grill Bar (Keeping it Simple, 2014)	• Kitchen space reduced from 60% of the outlet space to 30%. • Requires a kitchen helper with 15 days of training instead of an experienced chef with 5 months of training; cheaper labor and easier to find staff. • Allows franchise to consistently produce quality products.
Soup Spoon	• Cost savings of 66% in terms of kitchen equipment investment. • Kitchen size is reduced by 66% at the retail store.

Source: Company surveys and interviews.

and less space and equipment are needed at the outlet. Most importantly, as pointed out by the director, CK helps to ensure food consistency. CK also allows A to increase revenues streams by selling to customers or other SMEs half-processed food ingredients.

The experience of other companies in the usage of CK is summarized in Table 3.

In summary, for F&B enterprises that have sufficient scale to implement a CK, CK could have tremendous impact on cost savings and productivity improvement along the value chain.

(iii) Central kitchen and social enterprises

Some social enterprises use CK as a way to train special groups to integrate into the workforce. A case in point, Laksania established in 2008 with a social mission to help people with mental or physical disability to gain employment (Laksania, 2014). At CK, some jobs could be monotonous, but in a positive light they could be suitable for people with disabilities. Furthermore, as revealed during interviews, CK could provide a relatively sheltered training environment for this special group of people before they seek open employment.

Another example in Hong Kong would be the Hong Chi Gourmet Central Kitchen (Social Enterprise, n.d.). News reports in early 2015 indicate that Breakthrough Mission was also planning to set up a CK to train former drug offenders (Goy, 2015) and to provide gainful employment.

(e) *Issues associated with central kitchen*

(i) Reasons for not adopting central kitchen (see Figure 7)

• Lack of sufficient scale

According to the survey, lack of sufficient scale has been cited the most number of times as the reason for not adopting a CK, especially among the smaller-scale establishments. Operating a CK requires *high monthly overhead costs* for rental, utility and labor expenditure. Machines would also incur extra depreciation cost in accounting. The costs would outweigh the benefits brought by CK in productivity improvement if the F&B establishment has not obtained sufficient scale. Furthermore, from manpower saving perspectives, it may be offset by the need of workers to run the CK, and additional labor for logistics and transportation.

As shared by the owner of Company C, for the CK he was looking at, the utility and rental alone would cost him $15k per month. Having only four outlets at the moment, he would need 6 more outlets to support the high monthly overhead costs. Thus, despite knowing that the CK would help to save 85% in terms of labor

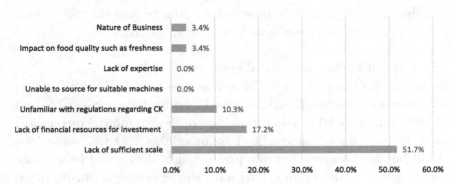

Figure 7: What Are the Reasons for not Adopting a CK?

Source: Company survey and interview.

hours, he did not invest in a CK. For Company D, which owns an international famous franchise brand, management also cited lack of sufficient scale as a reason for not having a CK for the five outlets that they manage directly. Nevertheless, they are looking into purchasing ready-made dough directly in the near future, instead of having all food preparation done at the outlet.

The lack of sufficient scale is the most critical reason stated by SMEs for not being able to leverage CK and automation to improve productivity like the bigger establishments.

- High capital requirement

Investing in a CK incurs *large amount of sunk costs* upfront in purchasing the machines, renovating, and designing workflow and layouts. The initial investment was S$10–12 million for Company A, which is a larger-scale establishment with 30 outlets. Despite having a relatively small scale for using CK to support four outlets and to cater to a few other organizations in the past, Company F incurred an initial investment of S$1–2 million. Besides equipment costs, Company C would also incur higher cost in re-innovating the CK to fulfil the requirements specified by AVA if it were to invest in a CK. According to the owner of Company C, it would cost him S$150,000–S$200,000 to just renovate the CK and another S$40,000 to purchase machines of second rate.

Given the large amount of capital requirement, smaller establishments are often unable to invest in a CK or machineries due to the *lack of sufficient financial resources.* Even for those with sufficient resources, some may not favor investing in CK due to *the additional CAPEX involved,* as pointed out by the managing director of Timbre Group, Edward Chua (blogtkz, 2013).

- Nature of business model

Given the diversity of F&B enterprises in terms of type of food served and the operating model, CK is not suitable for every enterprise, even for those who have obtained sufficient scale and financial resources. F&B outlets that cater to fine dining and boutique style enjoyment will not be suitable for CK.

(ii) Challenges when implementing central kitchen

Technical staff are required when setting up a CK since machine operations and procedures designed at CK require expertise knowledge. Accredited expertise knowledge may also require for HACCP certification to ensure food quality, as well as initiatives to streamline and improve kitchen operations. It is also noted that foodservice operators face constant challenges regarding where and how to source for suitable machines, since most have to be imported from overseas.

Challenges regarding food safety, storage and packaging, as well as order and logistics management would also arise during transportation to outlet kitchens from the CK. Considering CK's impact on the whole value chain, changing the way the company does things would be a huge challenge (Keeping it Simple, 2014).

(iii) Potential issues with government grants

The government has heavily subsidized certain F&B establishments to promote CK and automated food processing equipment. However, as CK is still more applicable to large establishments due to high monthly overhead costs and capital expenditure, multiple grants have ended up benefitting big F&B groups the most. For example, Tunglok received an undisclosed government grant capped at 70% for purchasing a robotic arm costing $150,000 in its CK (Straits Times, 2013). SPRING has also funded other larger F&B establishments such as Paradise (about $200,000 out of $300,000 project costs) (Route to productivity Paradise, 2012).

By helping larger establishments lower their CAPEX and operating costs, the government risks causing a pricing distortion in the market. Large F&B groups tend to have monopolistic pricing power. The price of the final consumer product could be artificially lowered by subsidized cost margins. SME F&B establishments who do not receive such subsidies face the threat of diminished operating margins.

Small F&B enterprises should be encouraged to collaborate and amalgamate their operations such that centralized kitchen could be implemented. In this regard, government agencies and trade associations may foster the use of CK to a greater segment of the F&B industry.

(f) *Discussion on other possibilities*

Since smaller-scale establishments are unable to obtain economies of scale to implement CK to improve productivity like the big restaurant groups, this section would discuss other possibilities to improve productivity through potential Shared Services or other ways for food preparation. Table 4 shows some of the possibilities:

(i) Sharing equipment and kitchen spaces

Sharing of kitchen equipment and spaces has been a common practice in the United States. By nature, it can be considered as an industry shared service to help F&B operators to lower equipment cost. There are commercial kitchens or food incubators available for smaller establishments, food trucks and entrepreneurs who could rent the space and equipment for use for a certain period of time. This allows individual food operators to use relatively costly equipment and machineries without investing in them on their own while also maximizing the capacity. Such practice is seldom observed in Singapore except for very few food incubators in bakery (Bake, n.d.). Perhaps the use of overly expensive equipment for food preparation and cooking is not pervasive in Singapore.

Co-sharing of CK between foodservice operators is another possible option. We observed interests in co-sharing of CK through online forums and interviews with foodservice operators. There are instances of foodservice operators partnering with each other or suppliers to share a CK to improve productivity in Singapore. However, such an option may be challenging due to government regulations and concerns regarding issues such as hygiene,

Table 4:   Alternatives to CK

Sharing Equipment and Kitchen Spaces	Outsourcing Food Preparation
• Commercial Kitchen/Food Incubator	• Outsourcing Processed Food Items from Food Manufacturers
• Sub-leasing or Co-leasing of Kitchen	• CKs as General Suppliers
• Leasing of Machine and Equipment	

cross-contamination and exposing the company's recipe. Kitchen facilities in universities and polytechnics may also be utilized during their closing hours.

Leasing of machine or equipment from existing owners or a service provider is another plausible option. It could be on a pay-per-use basis. But the equipment must be in proximity to be convenient.

(ii) Food preparation outsourcing

Outsourcing of food preparation to food manufacturers was once a Collaborative Industry Project (CIP) in 2013 spearheaded by SPRING and Restaurant Association of Singapore (RAS), and participating foodservice companies could get subsidized up to 70%. The project was not well received as restaurants have idiosyncratic preferences and preparation practices that are deemed as areas of product differentiation and competitive advantage.

In practice, it might be difficult for smaller-scale establishments to outsource part of the food processing, such as buying marinated meat. This is because manufacturers would not want to receive customized orders if Minimum Order Quantity (MOQ) is not reached (Jessica Lim, 2013).

Further, foodservice operators may not wish to purchase standardized stock items due to the need to differentiate themselves in a competitive industry.

Existing CKs could also sell some of their processed food items to other SMEs, which is practiced by Company A. Nevertheless, this depends on the capacity of the company and the profit margins.

4.2 Centralized dishwashing

(a) *Introduction to centralized dishwashing in Singapore*

Under the operations section of the value chain, dishwashing is a common activity that is shared by numerous F&B enterprises as majority would require the use of dishware and crockery when serving. Apart from retail outlets, bakeries and fast food restaurants that require no use of containers or use disposable items, there are possibilities of sharing this activity among the rest of F&B enterprises.

Table 5:   Mode of Dishwashing

		Utilization of Labor Resource in Dish Washing	
		In-Sourcing Company-Employed Labor	Out-sourcing Externally Employed Labor
Utilization and Ownership of Dishwashing Facilities	Company-Owned Dishwashing Facilities	1. Own Staff, Own Machine	2. External Staff, Own Machine
	Externally-Owned Dishwashing Facilities	3. Own staff, External Machine	4. External Staff, External Machine: (a) On-site (b) Off-site
	100% Manual Washing	5. Own Staff	6. External Staff

When it comes to dishwashing, there are two key input factors to consider: *labor* and *facility*. Facility refers to the use of dishwashing machines, which has been highly supported by the Singapore Government as a key initiative to improve productivity. In terms of extent of sharing for these two input factors, we figured out there are six ways in which dishwashing is currently practiced by F&B establishments in Singapore (Table 5).

Currently there are two ways of shared dishwashing being practiced in Singapore: on-site and off-site (Category 4 in Table 5). It is classified according to the distance of the dishwashing facility from the F&B outlets.

On-site centralized dishwashing: applies to *clusters of F&B establishments,* such as food courts, canteens and hawker centers, where there are shared premises for dishwashing facilities near F&B establishments.

On-site centralized dishwashing is currently provided by cleaning companies under contract, who would also be responsible for collecting and returning trays, and cleaning tables.

Off-site centralized dishwashing refers to the practice in which dirty dishes are transported to *another location* to be washed, which requires more time and transportation requirement. All the shared dishwashing services are currently managed by external companies.

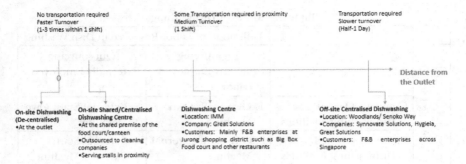

Figure 8:   Types of Shared/Centralised Dishwashing in Singapore

Currently for off-site dishwashing, there are three major players: Synnovate Solutions, Hygieia and Great Solutions (SPRING, 2015). Figure 8 below shows the different players for shared dishwashing according to their distance to the F&B outlet. For shared/centralized dishwashing, *proximity* to the outlet is an important factor because it would imply additional *transportation and logistics handling,* costs, as well as the turnaround time for dishwashing.

The following section focuses on evaluating off-site shared dishwashing services and also discusses on-site shared dishwashing and its impact on the other.

(b) *Situation and adoption of off-site centralized dishwashing in Singapore*

Our online and fieldwork survey showed that non-Sharing (using on-site dishwashing machines and insourced labor) is still the most dominant mode of dishwashing in Singapore, which is practiced by 60% of the sample of 41 F&B enterprises surveyed. Approximately 22.8% of them still use manual dishwashing. Around 23.8% have outsourced labor to external service providers. None of the F&B establishments in the sample engage in off-site dishwashing (see Figure 9).

The profile of F&B enterprises that engage in dishwashing services provided by specialized companies include large F&B establishments such as Paradise Group, Ding Tai Fung and Suki Sushi, smaller establishments with 1–4 outlets, as well as several food courts. Interviews with industry practitioners have also revealed that

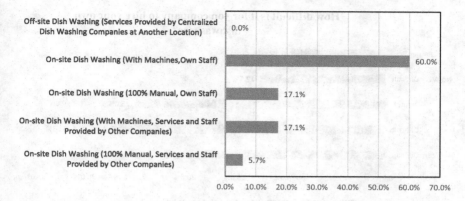

Figure 9: Distribution of Mode of Dishwashing of F&B Enterprises Surveyed
Source: Company survey.

off-site dishwashing has very limited adoption among F&B enterprises in Singapore, despite heavy subsidization by the government.

A director of a major service provider commented that there could be *excess supply* of off-site shared dishwashing services in the market. Several cleaning companies had been closed down as observed by the interviewee. Site visits to three dishwashing sites showed that none of them are running close to full capacity. One of the sites, which opened 9 months ago, only uses 3 out of the 7 dishwashing lines.

Next, we examine the issue of the relatively low adoption rate of off-site centralized dishwashing in Singapore.

(c) *Evaluation of centralized dishwashing in Singapore*

(i) Benefits of centralized dishwashing
According to the 8M framework, centralized dishwashing improves productivity through the following:

• **Manpower**
Centralized dishwashing can help in reducing manpower requirement.

Hiring and managing dishwashers often present a challenge for F&B enterprises due to the manpower crunch. According to our survey, 53.2% of the F&B enterprises find it either difficult or very

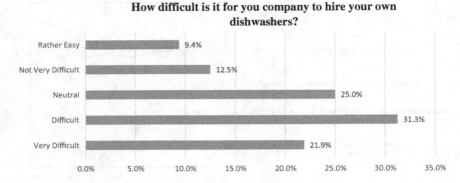

Figure 10:   Difficulty in Hiring Dishwashers

Source: Company survey and interviews.

difficult to hire their own dishwashers. Owner of Company E also commented that his bar almost had to be shut down because of the difficulty in hiring dishwashers.

Managing dishwashers could also be a huge challenge for F&B enterprises since dishwashing is a very critical activity that must be carried out at the outlet on a daily basis. However, as pointed out by an industry practitioner, given the tough nature of the job and the low-skill labor force, the issue of no-show or high turnover could be rather prevalent in the industry. As shared by director of Company A, dishwashers on leave could become a huge problem for F&B operators on that day, and even managers might have to wash the dishes themselves (see Figure 10).

The dishwashing service totally eliminates the need for F&B enterprises to manage their own dishwashers. Both companies A and C cited it as the most important benefit for such a service. Besides savings on tangible costs such as recruitment and the administrative duties, it saves the hassle of hiring and managing dishwashers and ensures that there is reliability for getting dishwashing done. And these are benefits that cannot be quantified based on a productivity measure.

• Method

Investment in machineries and technologies such as robotics augmented dishwashing systems to improve efficiency (SPRING, 2015). Similar to Central Kitchen, shared dishwashing saves the kitchen space and equipment costs for dishwashing facilities. Much cost-savings would be realized, especially for large restaurant chains which have not yet invested in dishwashers at the outlets. Having no dishwasher at the back-end also frees up more kitchen space for other kitchen staff. This is especially relevant to Company C which operates in a stall environment, where space is a constraint.

• Materials

Shared/centralized dishwashing allows for bulk purchase of dishwashing chemicals and utilities, and dishwashing chemical usage is also optimized.

• Money

Eligible companies can apply for CDG and IDG grants from the government to defray a substantive part of the cost of adopting centralized dishwashing.

From the industry standpoint, using off-site centralized dishwashing is more productive than each individual restaurant outlet having their own dishwashing equipment. This is because each restaurant outlet could save the equipment costs, while being able to enjoy lower costs from labor, chemicals and utility savings due to economies of scale. Nevertheless, from an individual foodservice operator's point of view, such a service may not necessarily be more productive due to other operational concerns. These include investing in extra sets of crockery and unique shapes and pattern of bowls and plates used by restaurants that may not be amenable to general dishwashing machines.

The dishwashing machine at the off-site centralized dishwashing site is able to wash 3,000 plates per hour, compared to 400–600 plates (20–30 racks) per hour of a typical under-counter dishwashing machine installed at the outlet (Protek). About 3–5 people are required in operating each machine at the off-site dishwashing site.

According to a service provider, F&B enterprises would save 15–50% in operating costs in dishwashing. However, in the case of Company A, according to the director, the actual cost saving with one of the service provider is around 5–8%. The director commented that the service is charged on a per tub basis, making it expensive to wash crockeries that do not fit properly into the tub.

(ii) Reasons for not adopting centralized off-site dishwashing

- **Insufficient scale**

Off-site shared dishwashing is not necessarily cheaper for smaller establishments because of the additional transportation and logistics involved. Such fixed costs are indivisible and must be spread over a large inventory volume. Using on-site automated machines would often suffice for establishments with sporadic or limited dishwashing volume. For them, a standalone under-counter dishwashing machine that can wash around 400 plates per hour would suffice, and it does not take much time and costs to do dishwashing with the machines with the small volume.

- **Not suitable due to nature of operation**

Some F&B enterprises use special types of crockeries with special handling requirements, making it unsuitable for using off-site dishwashing services. For example, as shared by a staff at a Thai Express outlet, the restaurant use hotpots, which are heavy and it is troublesome to transport them to be washed at another location. Certain restaurant concepts of Company A included not using the dishwashing service because their crockery were imported directly from Japan and because it would take a long time to replenish the crockery that could be broken or damaged in the dishwashing process.

To cope with manpower challenges, Companies B and E have opted to use disposable crockeries to minimize dishwashing. As a casual dining restaurant, Company E only spent about S$100 on disposable crockeries, which is in fact more cost-effective than using any dishwashing services.

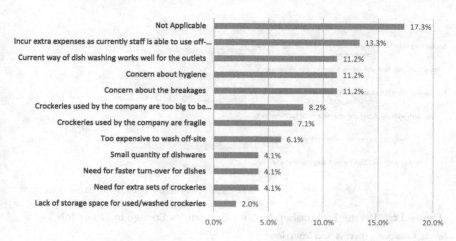

Figure 11:　Reasons for Not Adopting Centralized Off-site Dishwashing

Source: Company survey and interview.

• Manpower: Flexible task assignment

Through interviews and surveys with various F&B operators, we find that operators considered off-site centralized dishwashing services not suitable for them because their staff engaged in dish-washing also engaged in other tasks, and so their role cannot be simply eliminated. According to our survey, 48.6% of the enterprises in the sample have dishwashers who are also engaged in other job tasks. As such, outsourcing dishwashing would means redeployment of labor and readjustment of duties. Some F&B enterprises are unwilling to go through the hassle of redeployment even though outsourcing dishwashing would lessen the burden for the staff (see Figure 12).

Some enterprises rotate dishwashing duties among full-time staff who would use *off-peak hours* to do the dishwashing, such as Nando's and Company G.| As such, outsourcing dishwashing would in fact incur more costs for them. Case in point, Company G spent only $40 daily to incentivize full-time staff to do the dishwashing, and this is a much cheaper option compared to a normal contract of $3,000 (Jianwen, 2013).

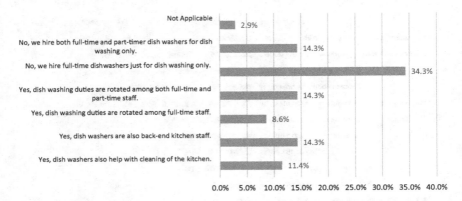

Figure 12: Do the Dishwashers in Your Companies Engage in Other Job Tasks?
Source: Company surveys and interviews.

- **Additional operation costs with off-site dishwashing**

Need for Extra Sets of Crockeries:

Using off-site shared dishwashing requires F&B operators to purchase extra set of crockeries for the *whole* shift. Some may even need three sets to account for the one set in transit. However, if dishwashing is done on-site, dishes can be reused for 3–4 rounds during peak time, according to an owner who operates a western restaurant and bar with a capacity of 100 persons. In the case of Company D, the additional amount of dishware required is unimaginable to the operations director, as the three restaurant outlets serve around 10,000 customers per day. This would incur much more costs and management issues. Even through the government subsidies for purchasing the extra set of crockeries, the director of Company F said that such a practice is not favorable as it would add on to the inventory holding costs.

Lack of Storage Space:

The operating model of off-site shared dishwashing is such that dirty dishes are usually collected by the service operator at the end of each shift (lunch/dinner) while clean dishes in tubs are returned to the outlets. This means restaurants would need to have space to store more than one set of crockeries required for the whole shift. For company H, high sunk costs had already been incurred in designing kitchen layout and it is almost impossible to change the layout for the storage space. According to the director of company A, lack of storage space is still a concern, and a few other large establishments that used off-site shared dishwashing also mentioned the same concern.

- **Slow turnover of clean crockeries**

A limitation of off-site shared dishwashing is that it is often difficult for it to provide the flexibility for faster turnover during festive periods to F&B establishments, when there is surge in demand for dining out. The demand for crockeries tends to vary a lot between weekdays and weekends, as well as different periods, and there is a concern whether shared dishwashing could cope when there is a surge in unexpected demand. Companies D and G also rejected the use of the service on the basis of turnover.

Quality Concerns:

Some foodservice operators felt that they were unable to control the dishwashing process if they were to outsource dishwashing and thought that quality concerns would rise. Company F no longer used shared dishwashing due to breakage and hygiene reasons. The breakage rate was 5–8% for A which utilized off-site centralized dishwashing provided by a company. It is also difficult to conduct QC activities such as counting plates and assessing cleanliness. Hygiene control and crockeries breakages come up to be big issues for owners of G and H for using such a service.

- **Perceived risk toward off-site shared dishwashing**

In general, we have observed skepticism and aversion toward off-site shared dishwashing among foodservice operators due to perceived *marginal long-term risks and operational risks.*

Contractual liability for lease space, depreciation cycle of kitchen equipment and trending demand of food fads are some of the long-term risks that enterprises face. F&B enterprises, particularly SMEs, are unwilling to absorb *marginal long-term risks* in terms of contractual liability for dishwashing and additional inventory of crockeries.

This is inherently important given that closure rates of F&B entrants have cumulated to about 50% within the past 5 years (Ang, 2015).

Operationally, off-site shared dishwashing involves a multitude of uncertainties for F&B establishments. Uncertainties include the *hygiene standards* of dishwashing, increased *breakage rate, compatibility* of existing crockeries and, particularly, the *reliability* and *turnover frequency* of the service. If the current process of on-site dishwashing suffices, the perceived operational risks incurred by management to overhaul the work process is too high, particularly when there is no contingency if service quality of shared dishwashing is unsatisfactory for the duration of contract.

(d) *Issues regarding government grants*

(i) Early termination of dishwashing contracts
Currently, SMEs in the F&B sector that outsourced dishwashing are eligible for funding for 12 months under SPRING's Capability Development Grants (CDG). The grant is capped at 70% of the operating costs. However, it turns out that some restaurants simply terminated the 2-year dishwashing contract at the end of the grant period. According to the CEO of a service provider, surprisingly 9 out of 10 of clients who applied for grants dropped out after first year. Nevertheless, most of the long-term clients who can benefit from dishwashing services, such as Ding Tai Fung, need not claim the grants. Thus, subsidies are wasted to some extent in encouraging operators to adopt the service.

(ii) Overcapacity for off-site centralized dishwashing
Excess operational capacity has been observed at such centralized facilities. While F&B enterprises have been lagging behind in adopting centralized dishwashing, centralized dishwashing facilities have continuously sprung up. Case in point, a centralized dishwashing facility recently opened[8] at IMM, Jurong East spearheaded by CapitalMall Trust and Great Solutions. As a result, supply for centralized dishwashing has outstripped demand from F&B enterprises. Productivity gains, from shared dishwashing can only be realized when there is *widespread adoption* to realize economies of scale.

There is also an *incongruence in promoting centralized dishwashing.* Under SPRING, the adoption of centralized *outsourced* dishwashing is incentivized via CDG on costs charged by service providers. On the other hand, subsidies can also be claimed for *insourced dishwashing* via E2I's Inclusive Growth Programme (IGP) (SPRING 2015). Furthermore, F&B enterprises are subsidized under the PIC grant to purchase their own automated dishwasher.

The decision to adopt centralized, outsourced or insourced dishwashing are mutually exclusive. When large F&B groups opt for centralized insourced dishwashing, demand for its *substitute,* outsourced dishwashing, would decline. Lower demand for centralized outsourced dishwashing results in higher unit costs which are absorbed on the demand side by F&B enterprises in terms of operating costs and on the supply side by dishwashing workers of service providers in terms of lower wages. In fact, the management of a Centralized Outsourced Dishwashing Facility noted that they would have to decrease a worker's wages in future due to lack of demand.

There is also a disconnect between government agencies and the industry in the push for productivity. Many F&B enterprises remain skeptical and have avoided centralized dishwashing thus far. Without prior agreement by majority of F&B enterprises, service providers supplying infrastructure capacity have borne sizeable market risk to *achieve minimum efficient scale.* This has arguably resulted in numerous closures of cleaning companies; a poor optimization of taxpayer money given the wasted subsidies granted to these cleaning companies.

4.3 *Part-time pool program*

(a) *Manpower challenge in F&B sector related to part-time staff*

(i) Manpower crunch
As discussed in Section 1, manpower crunch presents a constant challenge for F&B sector. One of the solutions would be to tap into part-time staff (PTs) to cope with the challenge.

(ii) Commitment of part-time staff

The commitment of PTs often presents a big challenge for foodservice operators. In the case of company D, despite having a total of 90 PTs, only 4–5 of them are active. Outlet mangers of Papparich and Eighteen Chefs commented that they still prefer hiring full-time staff for their commitment level. Most PTs are students, and they are unable to commit during exam period though the business needs to be run as usual.

(iii) Tedious and costly hiring process for part-time staff

The process of managing PTs could be tedious and frustrating. It costs $300 to $500 per insert to advertise in newspapers for hiring PTs, yet there still could be insufficient responses. Operators need to advertise, screen, interview, train and manage other administrative tasks for the PTs. The process itself is tedious, and the high drop-out rate and short commitment of PTs further add on to more costs and workload for the Human Resource (HR) team.

(b) *Introduction to part-time pool program*

Human resources is a potential area to be shared among F&B enterprises. Theoretically, developing a sustainable trained pool of labor could benefit all the F&B enterprises for helping them to lower recruitment cost, deployment cost and training costs.

Part-time Pool Program (PPP) was developed out of the idea that by having a common pool of trained part-timers managed by external recruitment agencies, F&B enterprises could tackle the manpower challenges mentioned above. It was initiated in 2011 by SPRING, but it has been put on hold for review since September 2014.

The operational model of PPP is as follows:

- Foodservice operators submit details for manpower requirement schedule to recruitment agencies.
- Recruitment agencies recruit, screen and select for PTs:
  — Training of PTs conducted at Restaurant Association of Singapore (RAS).
  — PTs pay $27 per person upfront for the training.

- Certification is awarded at the end of the training.
- PTs are deployed to different F&B enterprises by the recruitment agencies.
- Foodservice operators could obtain 70% of the funding for the first year, but capped at S$10,000 if they commit to certain number of slots for PTs.

(c) *Adoption of part-time pool program*

According to the media report, by May 2013, over 120 companies and 3,000 workers in both the retail and foodservice sector participated in the Part-time Pool Program. From the interview with General Manager Mr. Frey Ng of TCC Solutions, it was revealed that TCC had a total of 200 clients in the F&B and retail sector in PPP, while 60 clients remained at the end of the program. Approximately 60% of the clients were from the F&B sector. TCC was one of three main appointed service providers for PPP and was the only one that stayed throughout the program. Others include Achieve Group, BCG and GMP. F&B clients such as Jumbo Seafood would hire part-timers for only peak hours during lunch and dinner time. Some took PTs from PPP regularly, while some only took PTs during special periods such as exam periods or during the opening of new stores.

(d) *Benefits and productivity improvement of part-time pool program*

According to the 8M model, PPP achieves productivity through *management, market and manpower*. PPP allows enterprises to minimize *management* costs by outsourcing recruitment process to agencies. It also creates a part-time labor *market* that F&B and Retail enterprises can tap into, to plug *ad hoc* labor gaps in the work schedule. Augmenting full-time (FT) staff with PT labor from PPP also alleviates the workload for full-timers. This allows FT staff to enjoy greater work–life balance and other fringe benefits. In the long run, this would be beneficial for retaining and attracting *manpower* to the F&B industry.

A reliable service provider would ensure that PTs would be supplied according to operators' need and the administrative tasks would be taken care of. This saves the company the hassle of managing PTs and avoids no-shows of PTs that could affect sales. Soup Spoon used PPP for better flexibility in work arrangements, and the proportion of part-timers doubled from 30% in 2010 to 60% in 2013.

(e) *Evaluation of the program design and structure*

In essence, the program is about government agencies working with trade associations to provide *training and certification* for part-time workers. Furthermore, *subsidies* are provided for foodservice operators who take in these part-timers from the recruitment agencies. Training and certification was meant to assure the confidence of the F&B operators and to lower their training costs, while the subsidies are meant to be used to increase the demand for part-time workers from foodservice operators by lowering the costs, and to encourage recruitment agencies to expand the pool of part-time workers to include mature workers and housewives.

(i) Training and certification

Though it may seem like training and certification could increase the confidence of foodservice operators and hence the demand for part-time workers, survey results show that such standard training and certification are not necessary for foodservice operators. Only a small proportion of 12.5% deem it necessary.

The reasons for this are that the F&B industry itself is *very diverse* in nature with different restaurant concepts, cuisines and operating models. A one-size-fits-all training course would not be able to meet the requirements of individual F&B operators. Interviews with A and D indicate that the companies still have to retrain the part-timers from PPP *according to their specific restaurant concepts and requirements.*

According to an interview with Mr. Frey Ng, General Manager of TCC Solutions, most if not all of the part-timers deployed from PPP would work in the service line, and this does not require much technical skills. Most outlet managers surveyed, such as managers of Table@Pips, Astons and Manhattan Fish Market believed that on-the-job training for part-timers would suffice. It was also found that larger F&B chains such as Seoul Gardens, Ichiban Boshi and Sakae Sushi tend to have their structural training at the corporate

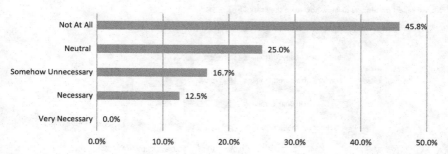

How necessary do you think is the standard training course and certification of part-timers to you (if that would mean slightly higher cost for hiring part-timers)?

Figure 13: Survey Result Regarding the Necessity of Training and Certification for F&B Operators

Source: Company surveys and interviews.

office to orient new part-timers. In the sample, 43 out of 44 restaurants said they would provide their own training for part-timers but none of them engaged in any standard industry training courses. The training and certification process *might be redundant,* especially if it would incur extra costs for F&B operators and has *little value-addition.*

Companies A and D commented that training should be focused on the soft skills of PTs and managing PT's job expectations instead. The owner of company E commented that industry-wide standardized training for back-end staff would be helpful, though it was not so helpful for training service staff.

(ii) Subsidizing for outsourcing to recruitment agencies

The subsidy would help F&B enterprises to lower the costs of using the recruitment and deployment services provided by recruitment agencies, and hence increases their consumption for the service. From an economic perspective, the subsidy increases the welfare of both the F&B enterprises (the consumer) and the recruitment agencies (the supplier) but is *at the expense of large amount of spending by the government.* The large amount of subsidy ($10,000 per year) is only

Does your company provide trainings for new part-timers?
What kind of training is provided?

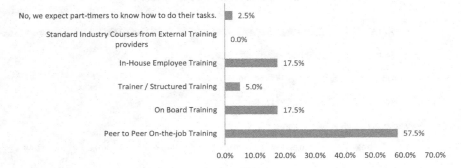

Figure 14:   Training Provided for Part-Timers

Source: Company surveys and interviews.

justified if consumption of such service could add much more benefits to the society. Otherwise, the society as a whole might incur a
deadweight loss due to unnecessary consumption at the subsidized
rate. Furthermore, such a practice is *not sustainable*. The dropout
rate from PPP of one of the agencies is 60%.

Another issue is that the one-year deployment grant of $10,000
is inflexible. The amount of grants is fixed; however, the relative
benefits will inherently vary depending on the size of the SME and
the usage rate of PPP. Larger establishments may find $10,000 insuf-
ficient to defray the costs.

(iii) Use of recruitment and deployment services by agencies
Authorities must understand that using recruitment agencies is
merely one of the many alternatives F&B establishments use to manage part-timers. Normally, referrals is the most common way by
which F&B companies obtain part-time staff, accounting for 58.5%
of the survey respondents. It is also the most effective and cheapest
way according to many, such as D, E and Astons. Hiring through
walk-in interviews comes next. Only 14.5% of the respondents
reported using job agencies.

The use of recruitment agencies for hiring and managing part-
timers is *not suited for every company* in the F&B sector because

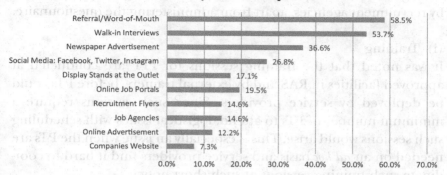

Figure 15: Part-Timer Recruitment Channels
Source: Company surveys and interviews.

different companies have different operating models and different needs. Smaller establishments such as F and *Table@Pips* tend to satisfy their demand for PTs easily through referrals or walk-in interviews at lower costs, since only a small number of employees is required. Large establishments, such as Seoul Gardens and Sakae Sushi, may prefer to have their own HR team to manage the PTs. Since *cost* is always a concern in the competitive F&B industry, some would shun away from outsourcing PTs due to high mark-up charged by agencies. Nevertheless, some companies may still out-source if managing their own PTs indeed incurs higher cost to them for the tedious process, or the current HR team lacks the capacity for it. Some, such as company A, may only use recruitment agencies when they find it difficult to get sufficient PTs, such as during exam period or opening of new outlets.

Furthermore, F&B establishments may see service staff as a way to differentiate themselves in the competition and would want to hire and train their own service staff instead of sharing PTs with others.

(f) *Evaluation of program execution*
In this section, we discuss some of the issues or potential issues that could arise during program execution. In our case studies, only A and D have participated in PPP. We have also interviewed several outlet

managers on their experience or opinion on using services provided by recruitment agencies, apart from administering the questionnaire.

(i) Training

It was noted that the training sessions for PPP are conducted at approved facilities in RAS and by external trainers, before PTs could be deployed by service providers. Since such sessions require a minimum number of PTs to attend, logistical issues with scheduling such sessions would arise. This is especially an issue when the PTs are needed on an *ad hoc* basis and service providers find it hard to coordinate such training sessions at such short notice.

According to A and D, the *classroom training* provided in PPP has not been very helpful because the training was too generic and did not meet their needs. Company A commented that the PTs are unable to do basic tasks such as greeting the customers in Japanese. The HR Manager of D felt that even after training, some PTs were still unclear of the expectations, such as the fact that they might need have to do table cleaning. Such classroom training did not guarantee the quality of PTs.

(ii) Deployment of part-time staff

In PPP, service providers would decide the deployment of PTs for F&B establishments. Both A and D commented that the service provider rotated PTs too often and they have to keep re-training the PTs. The *lack of consistency* resulted in higher training costs for the companies and is counter-productive. The Director of A noted that PTs were sometimes deployed to locations far from home, which affected the moral of PTs to remain in the job.

Another issue with the deployment by recruitment agencies is the *lack of flexibility*. F&B establishments could not rotate the PTs from PPP among the outlets according to their needs, as the arrangement had been fixed. This was noted in the case of D.

(iii) Costs to F&B establishments

According to A and D, the main reason for dropping out of the program is the *cost* of using PPP. F&B establishments are willing to pay only upward of \$12/h on normal days for an agency-sourced PT. According to the MOM Occupational Wage Table 2013, the median hourly rates for FT amount to \$8.52 compared to the \$12 ceiling by F&B establishments and \$15 rate from PPP. Hence, this shows that the costs of PPP is too high and only large F&B establishments with sufficient volume may be able to absorb such high costs.

High cost of hiring PTs from PPP would also upset wage structure. The director of F commented that an assistant manager is only paid at \$11 per hour and so it is not possible for them to hire an inexperienced PTs at a higher rate than that.

(g) *Conclusion and further discussions*

Through the research conducted, we conclude that PPP has not been very effective in helping F&B establishments to tackle manpower challenges and productivity improvement given its limited applicability and adoption. The important reasons for this are that authorities have failed to take into consideration costs of the middle-man and that they lack the understanding of the operating nature of F&B enterprises. Nevertheless, it may still be crucial to have a constant pool of PTs for F&B enterprises to tap into and to lower their costs of recruiting and deploying PTs through some infrastructure. The idea of PPP might be good, but the actual program design could be modified. Government agencies should implement initiatives that are more catered to the needs of F&B enterprises and must explore cheaper options.

It is also important to note that the root cause of the manpower crunch is not solely the fact that government had reduced DRC. Local F&B enterprises need to change their mind-set from relying on the use of cheap labor for *volume growth* to a more sustainable *quality growth* model that focuses on providing quality service and improving staff's welfare. There has been always a large pool of potential part-time staff in the society that local F&B enterprises could tap into, such as *students, housewives, mature workers and people with disabilities*. But in order to engage a pool of constant part-timers, the industry as a whole needs to improve workers' benefits to attract more people.

According to the feedback we gathered from the industry practitioners, *improvement of HR practices* by F&B operators could help to alleviate the manpower crunch by attracting more people to work in the industry. Firstly, service staff have not been paid enough compared to other developed countries, given the harsh nature of the jobs in the industry. Local wages for service staff have been stagnant over the years because of reliance on foreign labor and low operating margin resulting from high rental. Secondly, the staff are overworked while management is still unwilling to outsource some activities to save costs. For example, a staff member in Brick n Cube was involved in managing much paper work for invoices besides servicing customers, but an E-procurement system, which could have been used instead, is not implemented because of the additional costs. Thirdly, certain practices are inconsiderate to the staff. For example, the split shift arrangement for PTs, adopted solely to reduce costs, makes PTs end up wasting hours. Some F&B operators have provided no transport disbursement despite workers working late into the mid-night. On the other hand, we noted during on-site surveys that Astons did not face much problem of hiring sufficient PTs in general, because of their good HR practices. Besides having a buddy system, outlet managers have also strived to make the environment pleasant for young PTs to work in, and thus most of the PTs stayed on for a long time with the company.

In conclusion, tackling the manpower challenge in F&B sector requires collaboration from different players in the industry: government agencies need to understand more about operations of F&B enterprises and their needs; and service providers should strive to provide more value-added services; and F&B operators should strive to improve HR practices to attract and retain more PTs.

5. Recommendations

5.1 *Recommendation to government agencies*

The Government has a wide range of schemes to help businesses manage challenges and tap opportunities for growth. The Productivity and Innovation Credit (PIC) provides support for businesses as they restructure and innovate. All businesses are eligible for PIC tax deductions. The Capability Development Grant (CDG) helps SMEs defray up to 70% of qualifying project costs in 10 areas including business strategy development, human capital development and productivity improvement. CDG grants are awarded based on project proposals submitted by businesses. SMEs can receive funding for adopting ICT in specific areas such as tailor-made solutions for integrated point-of-sales, mobile sale and customer relationship management. The Collaborative Industry Projects (CIP) was launched in 2013 and expanded in 2015, where SPRING collaborates with Trade Associations and Chambers, Centres of Innovation, productivity centers and solution providers to develop solutions that will help SMEs reap overall innovation and productivity improvements. All these have sparked some interest among industry players. However, the plethora of schemes and grants have also generated some confusion and abuse. To help enterprises, agencies should have open communication channels and should *proactively* understand the situation on the ground.

For the traders and bosses of companies, stereotype assumptions and beliefs relating to government help (such as cumbersome paper work, multiplicity of condition) has stifled their enthusiasm in the application for government help and grants. On the other hand, the government agencies can possibly increase their outreach programs to increase the awareness of the schemes, grants and help available for SMEs. In the implementation of schemes, the government agencies in-charge are criticized for being "half-hearted" and over-reliant on market forces to yield the targeted result. As a specific example in this study, a consortium set up to jumpstart the dishwashing industries has promulgated the development of a monopoly which has over-invested in hardware (machineries) — resulting from the generous subsidy available in the purchase of the capital equipment. The monopolistic power exercise in charging relatively high fees for the dishwashing services have contributed to the low take-up rate among the restaurants, while the dishwashing consortium has to bear with excess underutilized capacity. It is certainly not an ideal situation with obvious wastage, and furthermore, economies of scale cannot be realized.

What would be a more appropriate arrangement is the co-ownership of the dishwashing enterprises by the government, guiding the operation not purely based on short-term profitability but on long-term vision of developing a new system of dishwashing that can help in sustaining and uplifting the productivity of the F&B sector at large. It is not an advocacy for more government participation in commercial activities, but a recommendation for the public sector to take on a strategic role in guiding and developing the sector to the right size and potential so that the seeds for productivity are sowed and planted. The government can then relinquish its role for private enterprises to sustain and enhance productivity in the new platform.

5.2 *Recommendations specific to the shared services*

(a) *Central kitchen*

(i) Startup incubator

The concept and working of a central kitchen may still be abstract and unclear for some restaurant operators. SPRING or RAS may organize visits to such establishments in Singapore and overseas to enhance the familiarity and knowledge of central kitchen. In some other countries such as the U.S., shared Central Kitchen is being used as a start-up incubator. Like the effort made at Block 71, a shared CK could be created solely for SMEs.[4] It could be a testing ground for interested entrants to test-run the viability of their F&B concept in a controlled environment.

(ii) Shared equipment for F&B clusters

Shared equipment may also be plausible for clusters of F&B establishments. For basic food processing, sharing processing equipment does not impinge on intellectual property.

For example, in a locality (such as Dempsey Road or Clarke Quay) designated for conglomeration of F&B establishments and food services companies, operators could reach an agreement to lease an ice making machine for the use of establishments within the neighborhood. If greater cooperation is feasible, the concept of centralized dishwashing can also take root in such locality.

(iii) Lowering minimum efficient scale for central kitchen

Central Kitchen remains prohibitive due to sunk costs and scale concerns. To widen the scope productivity benefits, the minimum efficient scale for CK has to be lowered. One such way would be the standardization of the work processes in the CK. Industrial sites specific for CK should be equipped with approved pre-fab CK solutions to eliminate the need for renovation and interior design.

(b) *Shared dishwashing*

(i) Storage space
On-site shared dishwashing has the greatest marginal benefits in terms of labor/cost savings. There has to be greater cooperation and communication between restaurants, service providers and shopping malls in negotiating needed storage space for extra crockeries.

(ii) Greenfield market segment
Shared dishwashing provides productivity benefits across the industry. Hence, service providers could expand their service offering to school canteens and office cafeterias. Admittedly, some of these market segments require the approval of government ministries such as MOE.

(iii) Off-site centralized dishwashing
For the off-site centralized dishwashing to be adopted more pervasively, the business model may have to be modified. It is perhaps best to think about the Xerox business model used in leasing out Photostatting machines to enterprises. In contrast to the current practice of restaurants sending their owned crockery to the dishwashing establishment, restaurants have to be convinced to use standardized set of crockery provided by the dishwashing companies. There are choices among the standardized sets. Restaurants buy the services of usage of clean utensils, and payment can be negotiated based on piece rate basis or standard packages like those used in peddling mobile phone services by the telcos.

In the new business model, restaurants will enjoy cost saving for not needing to maintain stock of crockery. The payment for the services of crockery usage could be much less than the wages needed to engage workers to do dishwashing. Besides establishing a new business activity, the dishwashing companies will enjoy higher capacity utilization of the relatively expansive equipment. While the companies have to bear the cost of holding the crockery, they also have the greater flexibility in higher turnover in the usage of the crockery.

(c) *Part-time pool program*

(i) Improve the training to focus on soft skills and job expectations
    of part-timers

Since the F&B industry is quite diverse in nature, having standardized industry-wide training courses for part-time service staff may not serve the needs of individual foodservice operators. Instead of providing classroom training, it is more important to manage the expectations of the part-timers regarding the job scope and commitment, and train them for soft skill such as greeting the customers.

(ii) Online system to allocate part-timers

A more efficient online system could be developed for signing-up and allocation to coordinate rotation of PTs among different F&Bs effectively. This would reduce the administrative costs at agencies, which can then be passed on to F&B establishments.

Part-time recruitment channels tend to be informal due to the *ad-hoc* nature of such jobs. Similar to National Jobs Bank managed by WDA, a singular channel for part-time jobs can be set up. This would reduce the recruitment costs incurred by F&B establishments. In this regard, a portal can be set up by the Restaurant Association of Singapore (RAS) and WDA.

(iii) Vocational education and professionalism

Working in the F&B industry remains a stigma. The younger generation should be culturally receptive toward F&B workers. Schools could provide students with internship attachments to better understand the industry.

6. Conclusion

In this study, we have considered Shared Services: Centralized Kitchen, Centralized Dishwashing, and Part-Time Pool Program in F&B sector. By means of the survey and case studies, we have delineated some salient issues encountered in the adoption and usage of Shared Services in the F&B sector. Some suggestions and recommendations have been proposed to improve the benefits that can be obtainable for the usage of Shared Services considered in this study.

Shared Services help to achieve productivity improvement through economies of scale and reduction of manpower. Effectiveness of different Shared Services varies. Due to the diversity of F&B enterprises, it is unlikely to have an industry shared service that would fit all needs. There is always a limit to the scope of application. As such, *the scope of subsidies must be sensitive to the different needs* as Shared Services is not a one-size-fits-all.

Government subsidies for Shared Services is a short-term solution. In the long run, government agencies could help by providing more research and analytics to help both restaurants and shared service providers to help both parties improve so as to facilitate adoption. Examples of value-added research to business owners could be cost of overhead space, pricing/revenue optimization and annual industry updates.

Cost is always the key consideration for adopting any new initiative for F&B. Productivity improvement through Shared Services must be translated to significant cost-savings for F&B.

Endnotes

1. Defined as those with less than 1 million annual operating receipts.
2. Various assistance schemes and grants are managed by SPRING Singapore. On 1 April 2018, SPRING and International Enterprise Singapore merged to form a one-stop business development agency, Enterprise Singapore (ESG). Details on grants and schemes are available at: https://www.enterprisesg.gov.sg/financial-assistance/grants
3. Burger King undertook a massive overhaul called "Operation Grand Slam", and franchising arrangements were changed, marketing strategy was altered, and food production and labor operations were overhauled to increase profitability.

4. Block 71 is a factory building located in Singapore's Ayer Rajah Industrial Estate located at 71 Ayer Rajah Crescent or one-north. Blk71 has built up a strong innovation and entrepreneurship community, where entrepreneurs, investors, developers and mentors within the interactive digital media space are within close proximity to each other. Blk71 is home to more than 100 startups, venture capital firms and tech incubators.

Chapter 6

3D Printing as a Means of Improving Productivity

1. Introduction

Contrary to what most people think, Additive Manufacturing (AM) technology, commonly known as printing, is not new. The earliest form, which was called Rapid Prototyping (RP) technology, first became visible in the late 1980s when the first patent application was filed in Japan. Since then, the 3D printing sector has grown as various AM technologies and processes emerged over the years even though the heavy focus on industrial applications still remained. The technologies mainly refer to Selective Laser Sintering (SLS) and Fused Deposition Modeling (FDM), which is more commonly termed as rapid tooling or rapid casting today due to its primary prototyping applications (3D printing industry, 2015).

Since then, 3D printing has increasingly been used in various fields and industries, one of which is the retail sector. While the usage of 3D printing in retail is still nascent, it has generated excitement and interest among retailers as 3D printing is set to revolutionize the industry by disrupting the entire supply chain, opening new markets and satisfying consumers through mass customization.

Across the world, many companies are setting up 3D printing stores to make the technology known to the general public. In Denmark, 3D Printhuset just opened the largest 3D printing store in Copenhagen to cater to customers looking for unique and customized products. They are also offering classes and open areas for consumers to try out the new technology. Elsewhere in Milan, 3D printing shops are also being set up with the focus of increasing consumer knowledge in 3D printing, which is lacking at the moment. Most companies who have chosen to set up a store have felt that a physical retail shop was important in building trust and confidence, especially for new and emerging technologies.

3D printing has also revolutionized the retail industry by placing a stronger emphasis on innovation and mass customization while creating new business models, products and services. For example Argos, UK's online retailer is testing out a new business model to produce 3D printed jewelry for consumers. This would enable consumers to play a role in designing and customizing their own products instead of buying off-the-shelf end products. Another example would be Amazon, which has filed for patent application to patent the method for purchasing printed items in a bid to expand its business model and be a complete provider of 3D printing services (3D Printing Industry, 2015).

This new technology has also opened up new possibilities for many retailers. Much excitement was created at the New York Fashion Week Spring 2015, when a 3D printed dress was showcased using materials previously not possible with other methods of production. As the technology continues to develop, it brings much anticipation as an alternative to mass production while requiring more skilled employees with relevant expertise. According to an employment analysis, job postings that require 3D printing skills have increased more than 200% over the last 4 years. Hence, more has to be done to enhance the productivity of the retail sector and to ensure that future needs are met.

Major 3D printing companies are also collaborating with retailers as more companies discover the potential that this new technology brings. In fact, 3D printing technology is creating downstream linkages to small companies that could work with larger retailers to customize the products according to the preferences of customers. This allows larger retailers to use online shopping to reach out to larger local and global customers. For instance, Target worked with Shapeways to allow consumers to design and personalize their own jewelry charms and pendants, allowing them to choose the material, size and even color (KDM, 2015).

Therefore, we can see that there is still much growth potential for 3D printing in the retail sector as the technology continues to develop.

This study sought to analyze the current market trend for additive manufacturing, while exploring the usage and future potential of 3D printing in the retail sector in Singapore. As the current usage of 3D technology in the retail sector is still in the early development stage, particularly in Singapore, this study attempts to bring in current sentiments and perceptions from local 3D printing companies, while presenting the various opportunities and challenges that may arise from this growing and emerging technology as it is increasingly used in various fields.

We will then draw up some policy suggestions which focus on the various roles that business associations, companies and the government can play to stimulate and grow the sector further after analyzing the problems and challenges companies are facing through the 8M framework.

2. Literature Review: Understanding the Market

2.1 *Overview*

Traditionally, additive manufacturing has been used to create prototypes as companies or manufacturers use them to test and try out new designs before proceeding on to mass produce parts. Today, this technology has grown in its usage in various industries with widespread applications.

Figure 1 shows the key sectors in which this technology is currently used globally. The automotive, medical, industrial, aerospace

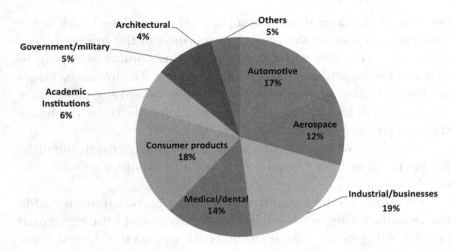

Figure 1:   Industries Using AM

Source: MIT Technology Review 2014, adopted from Wohlers Associate.

and consumer products industries account for more than 60% of the entire market.

A review from Massachusetts Institute of Technology (MIT) showed that additive manufacturing has been increasingly used to create functional products and parts instead of the initial prototyping testing stage as the technology continues to develop and patents for key processes expire. However, key hurdles such as cost, speed and material compositions still remain, which prevents widespread adoption of this technology beyond the prototyping stage.

The list below provides some examples to illustrate the application of additive manufacturing in various industries mentioned in Figure 1.

(a) Automotive — interiors, exteriors, seating components
    Examples: dash boards, mirror holders, bumpers, car seats.
(b) Aerospace — jet engine components, turbine parts, interior
    Examples: gas turbine, cockpit equipment, belt buckles, cable
        ducts.

(c) Industrial — manufacturing, robotics
    Examples: mounts for sensors, air ducts, fluid lines, heat
        exchanger.
(d) Medical, dental
    Examples: hearing aids, knee/spine/hip components, organs.
(e) Consumer products
    Examples: electronic goods, jewelry, fitness equipment, fashion.

In industries such as automotive, aerospace and manufacturing, advancements in 3D printing have made a significant impact on the industries as most manufacturers adopt these new processes to make prototypes. As a result, newer, lighter and safer products can be produced. The ability to print parts rapidly has also been an effective tool in delivering customer specific components while decreasing time to market. For instance, Ford Motor Company produced a rubber connector used to protect wiring in car doors in just 7 hours as opposed to 22 hours with traditional methods (Fortune, 2015).

Interestingly, other uses of this technology have also gone unnoticed over the last decade. In the medical and dental industry, the vast majority of hearing aids in the world today are actually 3D printed, with more than 10,000,000 3D printed hearing aids circulating worldwide (Forbes, 2013).

2.2 *Market analysis: Growing demand*

The global additive manufacturing market is expected to grow exponentially in the next few years. According to a market researcher, Gartner, the market is projected to grow from $1.6 billion in 2015 to $13.4 billion in 2018, with a CAGR of 103.1% (Forbes, 2015). By 2025, the direct economic impact is estimated to be around $230–$550 billion as the usage and applications of additive manufacturing increases (James *et al.*, 2013) and many experiments and figures out how they could use this technology in their production process.

One prominent area is the growth of consumer 3D printing market as additive manufacturing moves toward mainstream adoption after patents that once held back its development (for instance, selective laser sintering) expired in 2014. Technological developments have since enabled the production of increasingly complexed and innovative products, accompanied by decreasing production cost. Now termed as the 3D consumer revolution, the rise of cheaper and higher quality 3D printers have made the technology accessible to the masses, with printers that cost as low as a few thousand dollars, as compared to a few hundred thousand dollars in the past.

This has generated much hype and interest worldwide as consumers become intrigued by the endless possibilities with 3D printing. As said by President Barack Obama, "3D printing has the potential to revolutionize the way we make almost everything" (CNN, 2013). The novelty of this technology has gradually made its way into the retail market, as the demand for consumer 3D printers increases exponentially fueled by increasing awareness of this technology.

Figure 2 shows the projected sales of consumer 3D printers in 2018, which would exceed over 1 million units (Gartner, 2014).

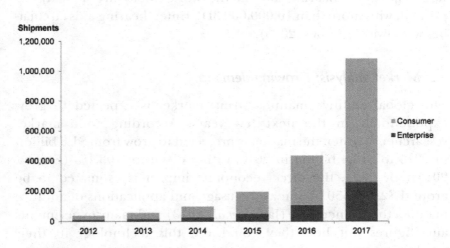

Figure 2:   Sales and Projected Sales of Consumer 3D Printers from 2012 to 2017

Source: Gartner Research by Pete Basiliere, 14 February 2014.

3. 3D Printing and Retail

3.1 *Overview*

Having looked at the general market outlook for additive manufacturing, the following segments delve deeper into the retail industry.

The rise of additive manufacturing in the retail industry is a recent phenomenon, over the last 2–3 years, and much can still be expected as expectations continue to rise, as illustrated by Figure 3.

According to Figure 3, market expectations of technological development follows a particular hype pattern before they reach maturity. Beginning with the innovation trigger, it reaches the peak of inflated expectations before falling into the trough of disillusionment where consumers come to a realization that they might be expecting too much from the technological innovation. This is followed by enlightenment, where consumers become more aware and conscious about the applications of the technology, before it finally reaches a plateau.

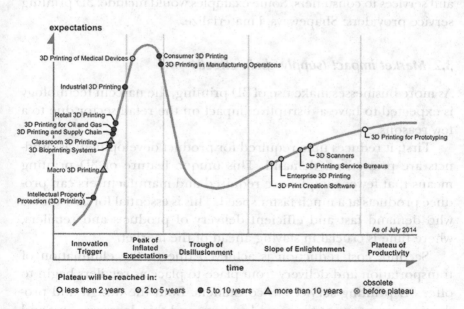

Figure 3: Hype Curve for 3D Printing, 2014

Source: Gartner (2015).

At one end, we can see that expectations for other applications such as prototyping, scanners and service bureaus will be reaching a plateau in 2–5 years, while expectations for macro 3D printing and classroom 3D printing still have a long way to go (over 10 years).

However, retail 3D printing, like most uses of 3D printing are still in the initial stage: innovation trigger, where expectations on the various applications are still increasing exponentially before reaching a plateau in 5–10 years. As technology develops, fueled by reduction in cost and increase in quality, we can expect to see 3D printing used more widely in various industries and applications, for example, 3D bio-printing systems, 3D printing for oil and gas industry and even intellectual property protection.

Many countries have since seized the opportunities to develop the retail industry to realize the market potential that additive manufacturing presents (beyond prototyping) to produce products such as fashion apparel, footwear, electronic devices, tools and toys. Many companies have also entered the market to offer new products and services to consumers. Some examples would include: 3D printing service providers: Shapeways, i.materialize.

3.2 *Market impact (supply chain effects)*

As more businesses make use of 3D printing, the nascent technology is expected to have a disruptive impact on the retail sector due to a few reasons.

First, it reduces time required for product development as products are printed on demand. This unique feature of 3D printing means that fewer samples are required and manufacturers can produce products at a much faster speed. This is essential for consumers who demand fast and efficient delivery of products and retailers, where time is crucial in staying ahead of the market.

Second, cost reduction is achieved due to the elimination of transportation and delivery from place to place as retailers begin to offer 3D printing services to consumers. Both the design and production can occur at the same location, and this decreases cost and shortens the existing supply chain significantly, even allowing retailers to take on the roles of being a designer and manufacturer.

An example of the impact of 3D printing on the supply chain:

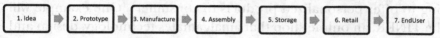

The flow chart above illustrates an example of the disruption that 3D printing can do to the supply chain. From the time the idea was generated to the end user, 3D printing can eliminate the intermediate steps 4 and 5 entirely, shortening the entire production process.

Another possible future scenario with the rise of consumer 3D printing is the direct flow from Steps 1 to 7, eliminating all other steps including the retail sector. Therefore, this poses new challenges to retailers in future who have to find new ways and business models to innovate.

This disruption provides ample opportunity for retailers to break into the retail supply chain and reduce their cost of production. By eliminating the assembly and storage cost, retailers could save significant cost of production. In addition, 3D technology also allows retailers to directly link up with manufacturers with specific consumer preferences that will create a larger consumer market for their products.

4. Singapore's 3D Printing Market in Retail

4.1 *Market competition*

To cater to the growing demands of 3D printing in Asia, major international 3D printing companies such as Stratasys and 3D Systems have also set up subsidiaries or engaged resellers locally. More local companies have also entered the market to provide 3D design and printing services at the retail level. Other than the pioneering few companies (Portabee, 3D Matters), more companies have opened up online stores and/or brick and mortar stores offering a range of products and services from selling 3D printers to providing 3D printing services. Some examples would include: 3D printing studio, Meka 3D Printing, Simplifi3D, Zelta 3D, 3D Hut, 3D printing Singapore, Pirate 3D, etc.

Some innovative startups have emerged to make use of 3D printing to offer personalized products to consumers. One example will be TINKR, an online shop that amalgamates technology, design and fashion to create innovative prints like calligraphy pendants to personalized figurines. Another example will be Polychemy, which offers customized 3D printed jewelry. Its designs are unique and are based on the trending designs and consumer preferences as elucidated from a Google search.

This emergence of new startups entering the market has been strongly supported by government agencies, such as SPRING Singapore which has been playing an active role in providing financial support and grants to capitalize on this growing market. SPRING has recently set up a $75 million co-investment fund in June 2015 to look for accelerators to invest in startups in several emerging sectors including clean technology and advanced manufacturing (robotics, additive manufacturing). This is with the hope of encouraging more and more startups to take advantage of the opportunities presented by the growing global market.

4.2 *Challenges*

Having understood the current global and local market for 3D printing, we will now analyses some of the problems and challenges faced in this emerging sector which affects productivity.

First, the retail sector lacks the necessary skills and infrastructure for adopting the new technology. Skilled designers trained in 3D printing are currently lacking in this industry, as mentioned in the earlier sections. Time would be needed to build the relevant skill sets required to fully leverage on this new technology, while companies will also need to continue experimenting and look into possible applications of 3D printing in various markets.

Second, the literature review pointed out the lack of consumer awareness on 3D printing. This has compelled many 3D printing companies to set up physical brick and mortar retail stores in order to educate and raise awareness on this new technology. It is often easier to explain to consumers face to face as human interaction is crucial in building trust among consumers. The presence of a shop front will enable one to experiment and be able to view how 3D printers work first hand.

Third, 3D printing technology requires high capital expenditure. 3D printers have become increasingly cheaper over the years, but printers which are of higher quality, resolution and capacities are still expensive. This high financial outlay is often difficult for new startups to afford due to the lack of financial resources. For instance, a decent 3D printer called Ekocycle Cube from 3D Systems costs around $1,200, while other higher-end printers can cost up to tens of thousands.

The materials used are also much more expensive than raw materials used in traditional manufacturing. For instance, the cheapest standard materials used ranged from $25 to $45 per kg, depending on the quality and manufacturer (CNN, 2013) which is much higher compared to traditional manufacturing. Hence, the overall cost is still high.

Apart from costs, there is also another challenge of managing consumer expectations. Consumers usually expect high-quality, efficient and affordable prints which are difficult to create and obtain at this moment owing to the current limitations in technology. The most common materials used today are plastic and metal (more for industrial purposes due to high cost), which is not durable and can be flimsy. Time is also a factor. Consumers often have to wait at least a few hours for the printing to be completed, and in the case of difficult and complex prints, it might even take a day or two. Hence, companies have found it a challenge to meet expectations with regard to the price, quality and time required.

Worldwide, there have been high expectations for 3D printing to transform the entire manufacturing process. However, owing to the limitations of the technology (as mentioned above), this overly optimistic view of being able to print almost anything and everything may not be possible in the near future. Even if this were to occur, companies have to decide whether it is commercially viable and feasible to 3D print every object given that mass production is still a much faster and cheaper process. The challenge would then be to decide how to best use 3D printing in their new business model.

Last but not least, the rise of mass customization brought about by 3D printing presents retailers with new challenges that they have to face. First, retailers have to constantly innovate in order to differentiate their products and services from their competitors as the market becomes increasingly competitive. Second, the need to create and adopt new business models becomes a necessity as 3D printing is set to disrupt the entire supply chain, thereby shortening and eliminating the need for storage and transportation. Third, it also questions the viability and sustainability of setting up brick and mortar retail stores as consumers can now take part in the design process instead of buying off-the-shelf products in shops. This issue becomes more prominent as the growth of E-commerce allows many to make use of online platforms to source for products and services with the click of a button instead of spending time in shops. Examples include 3D printing marketplaces such as myminifactory, 3dagogo and 3D printing networks: 3D Hubs and Ormakexyz, whereby consumers can upload their design and print their products worldwide, regardless of where they are. This presents a threat and a challenge to retailers as consumers may stop going to the store to purchase items and, instead, 3D print their own replacement parts.

5. Case Studies: Interviews with 3D Printing Retailers/ Companies

In the next segment, we will be analyzing some of the problems faced by retailers/companies in the 3D printing industry. We interviewed six local 3D printing companies to find out their business sentiments and understand some of the difficulties and challenges that they faced.

It was difficult to find any retailers that focused mainly on the consumer market unlike our western counterparts, as Singapore's 3D printing consumer market is still new and emerging with only a small number of market players. Each company interviewed was uniquely different from the other, and most catered to different customer groups ranging from commercial, industrial to consumers. The nature of 3D printing being just one of the many production process methods also meant that companies may not be solely focused on 3D printing, and often offered a wide range of products and services.

The following provides a list of the companies who agreed to the interview. A short description of each company and the products or services offered are as follows:

(1) Protoking is an integrated design firm that focuses on manufacturing techniques such as additive manufacturing or computer numerical control (CNC) processes to produce innovative products for consumers. The firm is capable of providing a comprehensive service to customers starting from designing, prototyping to the eventual production and manufacturing of goods in larger quantities.

(2) Meka is an online retailer that not only supplies 3D printing materials or 3D printers but also provide 3D printing design services, courses and training for educational institutions or anyone who is interested in learning more about 3D printing.

(3) 3D printing studio is a relatively new start-up in Singapore that provides a wide range of services and products for consumers. The company has a retail shop front in Burlington Square which sells 3D printers. It also provides 3D design, printing services and courses to those interested.

(4) Simplifi3D is one of the pioneers in the field which supplies 3D printers and materials while providing 3D printing services to consumers and industrial players. The company also conducts workshops for educational institutions, corporations and agencies. Now, they focus more on providing back end maintenance and support for 3D printers to their customers.

(5) Polychemy is a start-up that customizes 3D printed jewelry based on big data. The company is currently working with Walmart to cater to customers in the United States before entering the local market.

(6) PrintStone Private Limited is a start-up that provides both 3D printing services and commercial printing services. The company has a shop front in Peace Centre catering to students or

Table 1:   Products and Services of Companies in the Survey

Company	Services		Products		
	3D printing	Courses	3D printers	3D materials	Jewelry
Protoking	✓				
Meka	✓	✓	✓	✓	
3D Printing Studio	✓	✓	✓		
Simplified3D	✓	✓	✓	✓	
Polychemy					✓
PrintStone Private Limited	✓				

Source: Company Interviews.

companies who are looking to design or print unique products for any events or functions.

Table 1 provides a summary of the type of products and services that each company offers.

5.1 *Survey framework and methodology*

Face-to-face interviews were carried out as it enabled interviewees to express their thoughts, and it was found to be the most suitable way as questions were adjusted and tweaked accordingly depending on the nature and type of products and services that the company offered. This enabled us to get a first-hand account of their experiences and difficulties that they faced, while gaining new insights that may not be reflected from the literature reviews due to the lack of information available in the market.

The main interview can be broken down into three different segments.

(1) Understanding their operations:
  (a) How companies were using 3D printing technology (product, services offered)?
  (b) Motivation behind their business (management);

(c) Reasons behind setting up a brick and mortar store or going fully online;

(d) Extent of marketing and branding undertaken by the companies.

(2) Difficulties/challenges faced:
(a) Manpower;
(b) Main cost drivers (material, money).

(3) Sentiments and future plans of the company:
(a) How aware are consumers toward 3D printing;
(b) Future area of application that the companies were considering;
(c) Suggestions from companies.

The results will be presented through the 8M Framework. (Toh and Thangavelu, 2017, Chapters 2 and 3)

(1) Understanding their operations

(a) *Management*

All companies (except 1) were startups formed within the last 2–3 years. A strong entrepreneurial spirit was evident as many shared their passion behind starting a business either motivated by a gap in the industry which they hope to fill or purely based on interest. Most had no prior experience in 3D printing and had to pick it up from scratch.

Faced with this new risky venture which does not have an established market, many of them are still struggling to form the foundation of their business and rely largely on self-learning or expertise from other industries. Many are also engaging in their own form of research given the lack of information available. For instance, Polychemy is a 3D printed jewelry online retailer started by a 25 year old entrepreneur who shared how he first started off with hand phone covers but soon discovered that it was only economically viable to use 3D printing for highly complex and customized items (such as jewelry) and not the rest.

Most of the startups are also looking into new areas that they can expand or venture into. As such, it would be appropriate to provide relevant assistance and tie ups, as many cited the lack of time and financial capabilities in doing so, in order to increase productivity of the companies. Workshops or seminars can be organized to help those who are eager to gain industrial knowledge while allowing them to make better management decisions by decreasing asymmetrical information.

(b) *Market*

From the literature review, we also noticed an influx of competitors entering the retail scene and the need for companies to engage in different marketing strategies. This is not the case locally.

In Singapore, 3D printing is still mainly used to produce prototypes in various industries, and most interviewed companies shared that they usually have a spread of customers ranging from SMEs looking for low-volume prototyping to consumers such as students who are working on architectural design projects (students from LASALLE) or educational institutions. Many also have clients overseas in neighboring countries such as Malaysia, Australia, etc. due to the small domestic market.

At this point in time, marketing and branding to increase market reach is also not a key focus for local companies. All companies interviewed rely heavily on word of mouth, referrals and returning customers for business, and most do not intend to invest much due to a few reasons. Firstly, 3D printing is an area whereby those who need it for various purposes would know who and where to find them. Hence, it was unnecessary to reach out to the main population. Second, the cost of marketing is too high and many lack the financial resources to do so. Many rely solely on Facebook, social media or educational institutions who work with them. Third, one company owner mentioned her failure in reaching out to suitable companies. She said that they have tried sending emails but received a low response rate. Last but not least, it is too time consuming for most companies to engage in it at present.

Another question that we focused on was the reasons behind setting up a physical store or an E-commerce online shop given that the trend worldwide for 3D printing seems to be toward E-commerce. The reaction was mixed. Many felt that a physical shop was still important in establishing a trust relationship with the customer, especially in providing services, consultancy and expertise despite incurring high rental cost. This was evident for companies that dealt more toward providing 3D printing services to domestic end consumers, while others who provided a variety of products and services felt that it was neither profitable nor necessary to set up a physical store as their pool of customers were regulars and preferred to rely mainly on online orders. However moving forward, most expressed their intentions to have a heavier emphasis on E-commerce as the technology develops.

(2) Difficulties/challenges faced

(a) *Manpower*

Most companies have few employees given that they are still in the start-up phase. Despite this, many expressed difficulties in finding suitable candidates for the job.

Spatial awareness and design capabilities are important for 3D printing, which many companies expressed is missing among most locals, who either do not have the necessary skill sets as they were mostly not taught in school or that they were unable to think out of the box. This means that companies often have to train workers from scratch. The suitable candidate pool is also made even smaller as startups are often unable to pay for locals who expect a higher pay.

As a result, most of them rely on part-timers or on full-time employees who are willing to accept a lower pay. This lowers productivity as companies have to channel more resources to teach repeatedly and are unable to progress further with limited resources and manpower.

(b) *Money*

One main aim of the interview was also to understand the underlying cost drivers of businesses. For majority of companies, other than rental and manpower which is a common factor, the biggest cost factors were equipment and freight costs.

An average 3D printer costs at least $20,000–$30,000, which is expensive for most companies who lack financial resources. Many commented that despite having the support of the Productivity and Innovation Credit (PIC) in defraying cost, many were still finding it difficult to cope as they were in the start-up phase. One interviewee also mentioned that they did not qualify for PIC as they fell short of the basic requirement to have at least three full-time local employees.

Also, the benefits of having greater communication among designers and manufacturers, as mentioned in the literature review, cannot be reaped in Singapore. Instead, many companies have their own production facilities or engage contract manufacturers abroad due to high operating cost and a small domestic market. This results in many companies having to outsource manufacturing while providing only the design services locally. The long lead time and high freight cost in shipping materials back and forth lowers the profit margin for companies. This is an issue as products are usually printed on demand for 3D printing; thus, this time is an unavoidable problem.

(c) *Material*

This comes hand in hand with the high cost of equipment. Most new materials are expensive, such as carbon fiber infused, wood and ninjax flex. Another concern regarding materials is that they are not durable or long lasting. This is especially a problem in Singapore as can be affected by the weather, prone to crack and change colur a lot faster under the humid weather.

The limitations of current materials are not known to consumers who lack in-depth knowledge on 3D printing. In general, consumers are not particular about the type of material used as long as the product serves its purpose, and an interviewee even mentioned how she would often recommend the cheapest material that is more cost-efficient and common.

In general, materials are still a main concern for many, although it is limited by the state of the current technology.

(3) **Sentiments and future plans of the company**

(a) *Consumers*

One concern that surfaced from the literature review was the current need to increase 3D printing awareness among consumers. However, having sought opinions from different local companies, the consensus is that consumers do not lack awareness on 3D printing, but rather they do not understand the uses and applications of 3D printing. Companies often find that they have to play an additional role of educating the public by organizing courses or workshops for those interested in order to increase market demand and awareness. In fact, many felt that consumers do know about 3D printing and that it is reaching saturation point due to the hype created over the last few years.

The lack of correct awareness also leads to an issue of managing expectations. Consumers do not understand the limitations of the current state of 3D printing technology in terms of speed, cost and quality and are, therefore, unwilling to pay high prices at this stage. This poses another challenge to companies in increasing productivity.

(b) *Make — product innovation*

As mentioned under manpower, the lack of skillful employees is a problem for companies who would want to differentiate themselves from overseas competitors. Most felt that the nature of innovation, which is important in 3D printing, is lacking among locals when compared to our western counterparts such as Europe or America.

More can be done in this area, as a few of the interviewees commented that the way forward would be to provide design expertise and consultancy for consumers who lack the basic modelling skills or design capabilities. Companies with a retail store have seen a small percentage of consumers bringing the physical item that they wish to 3D print into the store, without knowing much about 3D printing. Hence, employees have to be trained in order to meet the demands from consumers.

Another factor that influences innovation is culture. Locals tend to be more conservative and risk averse when faced with a new technology. From the interviews, many were afraid to innovate and did not want to take the risk given the current dominance of established companies from abroad such as Shapeways. However, many expressed that they were working on or intending to explore new areas of development that have not been unexplored locally. For instance, one is looking to expand into the medical industry, another is experimenting with new materials, while still others are considering different business strategies for expansion.

(c) *Message*

The focus of 3D printing over the last thirty years has been on industrial and manufacturing industries in Singapore. Significant effort and resources have been put into research institutions like NUS, NTU and AStar. In July 2014, the NTU additive manufacturing center was set up to focus on 4 industries that were important to Singapore, mainly aerospace and defense, building and construction, marine and offshore, and manufacturing (EDB, 2015).

It is only in the last few years that 3D printing for retail and fashion industry has become increasingly important. Hence, most companies felt that more could be done to ensure that information is disseminated through associations or government agencies. In particular, industry-specific training on standards were lacking given that 3D printing requires specific knowledge of particular industries or sectors. Relevant workshops or training can be provided to equip companies with the relevant knowledge, and, in particular, the training of companies on various industry standards is required.

(4) Looking ahead to the future

As discussed in the literature review, 3D printing has significantly disrupted the retail chain and is expected to further do so as the technology develops. We were interested to hear the sentiments of local companies regarding this, a question we also asked as part of the interview, to understand their expectations and thoughts about the future development of 3D printing with regard to retail.

As technology develops, most do not foresee 3D printing replacing mass production in the future due to various reasons such as cost, time, economic viability and, more importantly, the fact that 3D printing is more of a want than a need. The move toward mass customization will remain, and companies feel a greater need to provide professional services for customization and design in future.

Many also felt that the hype for 3D printing is dying down after the initial few years and it is reaching a saturation point whereby 3D printing has to deliver what it promises to the market. Many are also uncertain given the recent pessimistic events. In June 2015, Pirate3D, a local retailer selling 3D printers faced problems of delivering their printers on time to market after being successful on Kickstarter (Kurohi, 2015). In April 2015, Makerbot, a global leader in the retail of 3D printers, has also closed down all of its brick and mortar stores while laying off 20% of all workers (Zaleski, 2015).

However, as mentioned earlier, many companies are still optimistic about the possible growth and development of the industry as consumer 3D printing is still in the infancy stage. Hence, many are still experimenting and discovering new areas in which they could possibly expand into in future.

6. Policy Suggestions and Recommendations

The chapter provides an overview of the 3D printing industry and its development in the retail sector. A qualitative survey was also undertaken to understand the key challenges facing the retail sector. Although 3D printing technology and its impact on the retail sector is at the initial stage, there is great potential for the 3D technology to change the customer to retail and retail to manufacturer relationship.

6.1 *Future of retail*

Inevitably, 3D printing will disrupt the retail supply chain by eliminating the need for intermediate processes such as warehouse storage and inventory as the technology continues to progress. More companies will adopt 3D printing as a business strategy to differentiate themselves from their competitors while providing unique products to consumers. One example mentioned earlier, was Amazon, which has since patented its 3D printing business model. Another is Walmart, the world's largest retailer, which is intending to acquire a 3D printing company to produce replacement parts (Bloomberg, 2014). This will allow them to shorten the delivery and process time before the product reaches the customers while decreasing their own production cost.

Apart from existing established retailers, it is likely that 3D printing will spur more startups to establish themselves in areas where there is currently a market gap while making use of E-commerce or online platforms in a bid to lower start-up cost. This trend toward E-commerce is notable even among existing companies who have a retail front. Many companies who currently have a shop front have expressed interest or possible plans in the future to move toward online platforms due to rising cost.

Therefore, with 3D printing technology, many companies, especially in retail, have to adapt and evolve rapidly in the future in order to capture a significant market share. As the 3D printing market continues to be dominated by a few larger companies such as Shapeways and Stratasys, companies in Singapore will have to be strategic in differentiating themselves, especially in a small domestic market.

6.2 *Efforts for growth*

Locally, the 3D printing industry is still growing as the government continues to support the development and upgrading of skills in advanced manufacturing, which includes the 3D printing industry. In the Budget 2013, $500 million was set aside over five years to support research and development and encourage companies to utilize such disruptive technologies such as robotics and 3D printing in their manufacturing process under its "Future of Manufacturing" program (EDB, 2013).

Since then, many initiatives have been in place. In May 2015, the Global Additive Manufacturing Centre of Excellence (CoE) was opened by a US global safety consulting and certification company, Underwrites Laboratories (UL), which aims to provide services for the industry while enhancing further collaboration with local research institutes to transform Singapore's manufacturing industry (EDB, 2015). The first of its kind, this initiative supported by EDB will focus on training, materials, process validation programs and advisory services to promote a vibrant industry both locally and regionally. So far, UL has promised $8 million to the global center here.

In universities such as NTU, an additive manufacturing center has also been set up in 2014 to develop new additive manufacturing application for industries such as aerospace, automotive and even future applications such as food printing. This complements Nanyang Polytechnic's Additive Manufacturing Innovation Centre which has been around for the last 10–15 years, catering to a growing market need and demand.

Efforts have also been put in place to equip the workforce with 3D printing-related skills under the Workforce Skills Qualification (WSQ) framework rolled out by the Workforce Development Agency (WDA). More than 50 employees from different precision engineering companies underwent training in 2013 to upgrade their existing skills enabling them to stay ahead in this growing market.

The largest 3D printing event worldwide, Inside 3D printing Conference and Expo, has also been held in Singapore over the last 2 years. This enabled many to receive updates on 3D printing, meet professional industrial players and listen to sessions conducted by industry experts in the various fields.

Future plans to build an advanced manufacturing hub near NTU are also in place to enable closer collaboration between research institutions, innovation centers and companies to develop these new technologies further across a wide range of industries (EDB, 2014).

6.3 Recommendations

The following section will highlight some recommendations that businesses, associations and the government can undertake to mitigate some of the problems and minimize the challenges faced by the industry in trying to promote productivity.

(a) *Necessary skills and infrastructure*

(i) Lack of information on industry standards

In order to promote the adoption of 3D printing in existing companies, more can be done in the retail sector to enhance the necessary skills and existing support structure for the smaller companies. Despite much effort in research and development in the 3D printing market over the last few years, many smaller companies at the end of the supply chain do not feel the benefits of such research which is often concentrated among the larger companies and research institutions.

In particular, the lack of information with regard to industry standards was highlighted during the interviews we had. More workshops and talks conducted by industry experts can be organized specially for the smaller companies who have a different focus and target market than the bigger 3D printing companies. This will be important in increasing their industrial knowledge while enhancing their capabilities to design and print products that are of a certain standard and quality.

This task of increasing industrial knowledge can be undertaken by the newly opened Global Additive Manufacturing Centre of Excellence alongside various government agencies such as SPRING Singapore and EDB. As the Centre aims to be a global provider for advisory, research, training and process qualifications in 3D printing, they will be best suited to provide the relevant expertise for the various companies. SPRING Singapore and EDB can also continue to foster greater collaboration between industries in order to minimize the asymmetrical information present at the moment.

(ii) Upgrading of skills

In terms of upgrading and equipping employees with the relevant skills, the Ministry of Manpower (MOM) can work with current institutes for higher learning or polytechnics such as Nanyang Polytechnic, which has an Additive Manufacturing Innovation

Centre, to conduct courses for employees to obtain relevant basic additive manufacturing skills under the Singapore Workforce Skills Qualifications (WSQ) scheme. However, as companies do not only need to know the technical skills but also the relevant design skills, which is important in catering to consumers at the retail level, this collaboration should also include design schools in Singapore such as LASALLE and Singapore Fashion & Design School. This collaboration will benefit multiple parties, including students who will have a chance to work with companies from an early stage. This will also alleviate the manpower shortage that many companies are facing currently by encouraging more students to enter the 3D printing market once they gain relevant experience and expertise from a young age.

(b) *Collaboration and partnerships*

Currently, there is also only one maker consortium, Onemaker Group, which comprises of 6 prototyping companies (including Simplifi3D, a company interviewed in this study). The aim of the consortium was to bring designers and makers together, to form partnerships and also to provide an area for hobbyists to learn and try out 3D printing (One Maker Group, 2015). More partnerships can be formed at the retail level to create a larger consortium, to allow even more companies to work together and consolidate their resources. This joint platform will help companies decrease the time and resources used in organizing their own educational workshops for consumers, thus allowing them to spend more time in innovating and coming up with more products for consumers.

This effort has to be taken on by companies who have to take a more proactive role in sourcing for possible partnerships and collaborations in order to promote greater efficiency and productivity through sharing of common resources and space.

In addition to business partnerships, a possible suggestion mentioned earlier was collaborations between businesses and design schools. This will promote greater innovation and creativity within the industry as companies struggle to find the resources and time to develop new products given manpower and financial constraints.

Competitions or larger-scale projects can be organized to incentivize companies to collaborate with schools, research institutions or even entrepreneurs to explore new developments, something that the companies interviewed are already doing individually. This will help to minimize risk and provide possible business strategies for further expansion.

(c) *Safety guidelines and regulations*

As sophisticated products are increasingly being 3D printed, for instance, acoustic guitars, camera lens, shoes, sculptures and even firearms, the government will also have to come up with safety guidelines and regulations with regard to 3D printing, in order to safeguard the interest of multiple parties. This is especially the case for products that might cause harm to the individual, like firearms or any other illegal items. The issue of intellectual property rights was highlighted by the companies interviewed, who felt this will be a cause for concern and a possible obstacle that they will face in the near future as the market continues to expand. In the International Traffic in Arms (ITAR) regulations, proposed changes are being made to ban the printing of 3D printed gun parts after printable blueprints of guns were published online sparking outrage in the United States (Fox News, 2015). Such issues are likely to become more prominent and common as the production process becomes more mainstream.

Also, 3D printing has drawn heavy scrutiny from regulators in different sectors as issues about safety and quality of the product surfaced due to the different nature of this process as compared to traditional manufacturing. Regulators are finding it a challenge to evaluate the process due to their unfamiliarity, and the process of deciding and coming up with regulations for products can be long and challenging due to the inherent uncertainties in the technology (Financial Times, 2014). In the aviation sector, companies such as GE Aviation and Custom Control Concepts are finding it difficult to win approval from the US Federal Aviation Administration, while the same constraints are faced in the healthcare industry due to the strict regulations from the US Food and Drug Administration.

Locally, companies interviewed mentioned that they do not know of any safety regulations or quality certifications required at the moment. As research institutions (NTU) and the Global Additive Manufacturing Centre of Excellence spearheaded by UL continue to research and come up with the best practices for the industry, efforts can be put in place to ensure that information is passed down the supply chain to the retailers.

One concern that companies raised in the interview was that strict regulations will only stifle innovation and creativity at the moment as the technology is still in the developmental stage. Such concerns will have to be addressed as the technology matures and government agencies can work together to come up with a framework for the various industries.

Table 2 provides a summary of the actions that can be taken by the various parties as described in this section.

Table 2:   Summary of Key Opportunities and Challenges Facing 3D Retail

Challenges	Recommendations	Actions Taken By
Lack of information on industry standards	Greater collaborations between industries and companies	Global Additive Manufacturing Centre Government Agencies: SPRING, EDB
Lack of relevant skills	More courses conducted under the Singapore Workforce Skills Qualification (WSQ) scheme to provide technical skills while working with design schools to provide design expertise	Government agencies: Ministry of Manpower Educational Institutions: LASALLE, Singapore Fashion & Design School
Manpower Shortage	Greater collaboration will also curb manpower shortages and promote 3D printing as a possible career path	

(*Continued*)

Table 2:   (*Continued*)

Challenges	Recommendations	Actions Taken By
Insufficient resources and more time spent on educating the public	Formation of a larger consortium to consolidate and pool resources together	Businesses
Lack of innovation and creativity in coming up with new products	Organize competitions or larger-scale projects among entrepreneurs, schools, etc. to provide new ideas and possible strategies	Educational Institutions and Government agencies
Lack of safety guidelines and regulation	Come up with best practices and framework for the various industries while ensuring proper dissemination of information	Global Additive Manufacturing Centre of Excellence and Government Agencies

Source: Author's compilation.

7. Conclusion

The development of 3D printing technology is still in the early stages, and much can still be anticipated from this growing industry that will possibly revolutionize the entire retail sector. In this chapter, we have identified some key problems and challenges that companies are facing based on the 8 Ms framework that affects productivity at the current stage while concluding by providing some possible actions that can be taken by different parties, including educational institution, companies and also government agencies.

As 3D printing has widespread applications in many different industries, we recommend that the government and the Global Additive Manufacturing Centre of Excellence play a key role in stimulating and promoting productivity in the industry due to the lack of current trade associations and business associations in the related field. As much work is still done on the research level, we foresee that more and more retailers will be adopting this technology within the next 5–10 years as the technology process matures, leading to greater efficiency and productivity.

7.1 *Limitations and further studies*

This study focused more on the perspectives and sentiments of the companies interviewed due to the lack of available information in the market. The small and newly emerging 3D technology in the retail sector has only been around for the last 2–3 years and much is yet to be observed or seen as companies slowly adapt to the new process. Hence, a case study approach was used to find out some of the problems that companies are facing at this current stage. A more in-depth study can be done at a later stage as the industry matures and as more research is done locally and internationally.

Chapter 7

M-commerce as a Strategy to Increase Productivity in Singapore

1. Introduction

As technology advances, Omni-channels will be able to enhance not only consumer experience in retailing but also bring about increased opportunities for profitability, revolutionizing ways for merchants to engage customers. Omni-channel retailing refers to "merchants participating in every aspect to reach out to consumers (Diamond *et al.*, 2015)" or more specifically, "an integrated sales experience that melds the advantages of physical stores with the information-rich experience of online shopping (Rigby, 2011)." It focuses on a seamless approach for retailers to interact with consumers via various shopping channels, which includes the traditional brick and mortar stores, mobile commerce and E-commerce. This implies, "exposing consumers to a blend of offline and online information and letting them purchase products from either traditional or online channels (Brynjolfsson *et al.*, 2013)."

Traditional retailers can expect many benefits from Omni-retailing. One such benefit is that retailers with a strong online and physical presence will strengthen the retail brand, hence increasing sales from both platforms. One example would be Macy's, a fashion brand which started from a physical store, saw a 3.7% year over year growth in comparable store sales by optimizing Omni-channel strategies. In addition, the increased sales were not only driven by the additional online channel but also from the physical stores (Diamond *et al.*, 2015). One such online channel under Omni-channel is mobile commerce.

M-commerce is not only defined as any form of mobile communication with customers but is also tied to transactions conducted through mobile devices. Hence, it consists of both content delivery, such as notification and reporting, as well as transactions including purchasing and data entry (Leung and Antypas, 2001). M-commerce includes all transactions conducted by all mobile devices, such as laptops or handheld terminals but excludes those where the terminals are non-mobile yet wirelessly connected (Veijalainen *et al.*, 2006). It is worth noting that most commonly used mobile devices are mobile phones and smartphones (Kiba-Janiak, 2014). Some of these M-commerce applications include M-marketing, M-shopping and M-payment, which will be elaborated in the later part of the chapter.

Here in Singapore, mobile commerce is seeing phenomenal growth. According to the Infocomm Media Development Authority (IMDA) there are more than 8 million mobile subscriptions in Singapore with a mobile penetration rate of 149.8% as of December 2016. It is thus not surprising to find increasing number of consumers relying on mobile commerce for shopping. A PayPal survey revealed that in just one year, total spending on M-commerce increased from S$43 million to S$328 million in 2012 and is estimated to increase to S$3.1 billion in 2015 (Lee, 2012). Among the categories, consumer spending on fashion and accessories were the highest for smartphone users at S$39 million. The growth potential for M-commerce is significant and will be able to raise productivity among retailers as well.

Currently, Singapore has been leading the way in Asia in mobile commerce with many startups engaging in providing goods and services on the online platform, especially in mobile commerce. However, not all enterprises have been investing in mobile commerce, especially those enterprises in traditional retailing. In addition, M-commerce strategies may benefit a variety of retailers via business-to-business channels or business-to-consumer channels. However, as the scope is too wide, we will only be focusing on retailers with a physical store and who are in the process of improving business-to-consumer channels. Therefore, this study aims to examine *how M-commerce as a strategy in Omni-channel can be a strategy for retailers with physical stores to improve their revenue performance and profitability and how to increase adoption of mobile commerce.* We will also be focusing on retailers only in these 3 categories: fashion and beauty, entertainment and lifestyle, and electronics.

This study gathers information from merchants on the advantages and disadvantages of using M-commerce as well as possible challenges on the adoption of using M-commerce or the obstacles that prevent firms from actually adopting them and generally learning from their experience in M-commerce.

The study makes several contributions. It contributes to the additional literature on understanding the costs and benefits of mobile retailing from the merchants' perspectives by interviewing them and understanding the various challenges of using mobile commerce by surveying consumers who engage in mobile shopping.

The chapter is organized in six sections. Section 2 starts off with a literature review with regard to two different business models: traditional retailing model and E-commerce business model. Section 3 touches on trends of M-commerce as compared with the rest of the world. Section 4 covers the methodology, while Sections 5 and 6 evaluate our research findings. Lastly, Section 7 includes policy recommendation to aid in increase adoption of M-commerce.

2. Literature Review

Existing literature provides some insights on the (1) rise of Omni-channel and revenue models of M-commerce, (2) types of M-commerce applications and M-shopping, (3) unique features of M-commerce (4) a comparison between M-commerce and E-commerce and lastly (5) processes of M-commerce.

2.1 *Rise of Omni-channel and revenue models of M-commerce*

Omni-channel retailing is an evolution of multichannel retailing, where the latter treats individual channels as separate business segments to target different group of consumers. These two differ mainly by taking into account the fact that consumers do not "exhibit a constant preference regarding the channel through they purchase goods." In other words, in the case of Omni-channel, consumers will interact with a company using several different channels before making their final purchase, creating a seamless interaction between retailers and consumers. For instance, "a customer may visit a physical store to inspect merchandise before ordering that same product online (Dorman, 2013)."

M-commerce has altered consumer's behavior in shopping, as well as changed expectations of interaction with retailers. However, adding a new channel, i.e. M-commerce, will only increase revenue if this platform "allows the firm to access a customer segment that was not previously served." Einav *et al.* (2014) also proved empirically that mobile shopping application increases both short- and long-run total platform purchasing. Moreover, they concluded that there is no evidence that "mobile application purchases are simply purchases that would have been made otherwise on the regular Internet platform." Hence, M-commerce reaches out to new customer segment and is profitable for merchants.

2.2 *Types of M-commerce applications and mobile shopping*

There are various types of M-commerce applications including M-shopping, where purchases are made on mobile devices; M-marketing which disseminates information through the use of mobile devices; M-information services where customers are able to compare prices or read about product reviews on their mobile devices (Kiba-Janiak, 2014).

Mobile shopping would require multiple applications for it to function. M-shopping requires not only mobile financial application but also mobile advertising. The former includes mobile money transfer when consumers buy a product through their mobile devices, changing the way businesses are conducting their transaction, while the latter has features to track "the current location of mobile users" (Varshney and Vetter, 2002) to target specific group of customers and may possibly increase the effectiveness of advertisement. In addition, mobile inventory management may be affected as tracking of goods will be possible through the mobile application. For instance, an application called "rolling inventory" allows for stores to locate trucks, which are carrying large amount of inventory, when a store needs certain items/goods. Table 1 summarizes the different applications, definition and interaction of usage for the application (e.g. business-to-consumers or business-to-business).

2.3 *Unique features of M-commerce*

In general, literature concurs to *five* unique features of M-commerce that make them different from the traditional retail models, despite them having different names and slight difference in classification. Lim *et al.* (2001) first noted four unique features of M-commerce that merchants can provide to consumers: (1) ubiquity, (2) personalization, (3) flexibility and (4) dissemination, while Ding *et al.* (2004) further added (5) convenience as the last feature of M-commerce.

M-commerce can also be thought of as wireless E-commerce, which engages consumers 'on the go' while doing transactions online (Lee and Benbasat, 2003). It is a relatively new phenomenon as compared to traditional retailing models, where retailers sell products and services directly to buyers at a mark-up from the actual cost. This mostly consists of traditional brick and mortar stores. Table 2 summarizes the main differences between traditional retailing and M-commerce.

Both M-commerce and E-commerce are considered non-traditional retail models, where they include features of traditional retailing models but go beyond individual transactions to maximize

Table 1: Application of M-commerce/Details and Networking Requirements of M-Commerce

Class of Applications	Details	Examples
Mobile financial application (B2C, B2B)	Applications where mobile device becomes a powerful financial medium.	Banking, brokerage, and payments for mobile users.
Mobile advertising (B2C)	Applications turning the wireless infrastructure and devices into a powerful marketing medium.	Users specific and location sensitive advertisements.
Mobile inventory management (B2C, B2B)	Applications attempting to reduce the amount of inventory needed by managing in-house and inventory-on-move.	Location tracking of goods, boxes, troops, and people.
Product locating and shopping (B2C, B2B)	Applications helping to find the location of product and services that are needed.	Finding the location of a new/used car of certain model, color and features.
Proactive service management (B2C, B2B)	Applications attempting to provide users information on services they will need in very-near-future.	Transmission of information related to aging (automobile) components to vendors.
Wireless re-engineering (B2C, B2B)	Applications that focus on improving the quality of business services using mobile devices and wireless infrastructure.	Instant claim-payments by insurance companies.

(*Continued*)

Table 1: (*Continued*)

Class of Applications	Details	Examples
Mobile action or reverse action (B2C, B2B)	Applications allowing users to buy or sell certain items using multicast support of wireless infrastructure.	Airlines compacting to buy a landing time shot during runway congestion (a proposed solution to air-traffic congestion problem).
Mobile entertainment services and games (B2C)	Applications providing the entertainment services to users on per event or subscription basis.	Video-on-demand, audio-on-demand, and interactive games.
Mobile office (B2C)	Applications providing the complete office environment to mobile users any where any time.	Working from traffic jams airport, and conferences.
Mobile distance education (B2C)	Applications extending distance/virtual education support for mobile users everywhere.	Taking a class using streaming audio and video.
Wireless data center (B2C, B2B)	Applications supporting large amount of stored data to be made available to mobile users for making "in-telligent" decisions.	Detailed information on one more products can be downloaded by vendors.

Note: B2C: business-to-consumers, B2B: business-to-business.

Source: Varshney and Vetter (2002).

Table 2: Comparison of features of traditional retail model and M- commerce

Traditional Stores	M-commerce
Physical stores only	Ubiquity — use of M-commerce anywhere, on-the-go
No personalization of information	Personalization
Transactions at points of sales only	Flexibility of transactions
Customer services through salespersons	Dissemination of information based on location
One-sided information	Convenient access of information

Source: Mobile Commerce: Promises, challenges and research agenda, Lim *et al.* (2001).

customer lifetime value (Noren, 2013). Hence, retailers are embracing Omni-retailing where customers are provided with various platforms to conduct transactions for a more wholesome shopping experience.

2.4 *Process of M-commerce*

M-commerce changes the way businesses are conducted through (1) the key players involved in a business and their interaction, (2) profitability and productivity improvement through using M-commerce, (3) issues that merchants or key players may face through using M-commerce. Our study focuses mainly on the relationship between businesses-to-consumers (B2C).

(a) M-commerce value chain

M-commerce value chain offers an alternative route where manufacturers are able to directly deliver products to consumers.

Since M-commerce alters industry value chain, the individual firm value chain also changes (Figure 1). Some of these primary activities that are transformed include both in- and outbound logistics, operations, sales and marketing and after-sales. Hence, M-commerce helps to restructure the organization to make it more productive and effective. One example is that M-commerce "provides users with more differentiated and high-value products." In addition, more inventories (i.e outbound logistics) can be stored

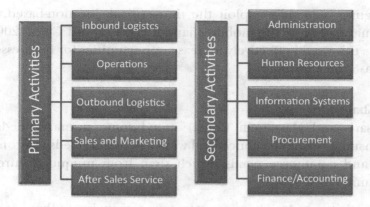

Figure 1: Individual Firm Value Chain

Source: Laudon and Traver (2014)

in warehouses as compared to traditional retail stores where space constraints are an issue. Furthermore, by taking note of user's preference online (i.e after-sales service), recommendations can be made to buyers, which help to increase sales of the business.

(b) Productivity improvements and challenges faced

Developing a successful M-commerce application would mean that businesses are able to understand the needs of customers, thereby improving customer service and obtaining a competitive edge over other businesses.

(i) Productivity improvements

M-commerce allows for access to wireless networks communications anytime and anywhere through mobile services. This alternate means of connectivity is *another profit stream* for businesses without being physically connected. In addition, it also allows instant communications if customers were to request for it, and this would provide a competitive edge for businesses (Frolick and Chen, 2004).

Secondly, M-commerce is a valuable channel to *enhance customer relationships and for advertising*, such as direct marketing and promotional activities. It has been noted that "the key to effective mobile marketing is to fully exploit the time-critical, location-based, and personal nature of the mobile channel (Frolick and Chen, 2004)." Hence this would effectively increase opportunities for businesses to increase their revenue.

(ii) Challenges

Coursaris and Hassanein (2002) noted some primary needs an M-consumer would be concerned with. Two main needs are connectivity and commerce needs, which stem from unique features in M-commerce.

Connectivity needs: There are two connectivity issues that consumers are concerned with, and they are also the challenges that merchants face. Firstly, consumers are concerned with privacy issues, and this fear increases with the increased degree and sensitivity of personal information exchanged. Secondly, download time is another concern. Web transfer rates may not be as fast when connected wirelessly; hence, the need for speed without sacrificing content is important.

Commerce Needs: M-commerce is the conducting of businesses on mobile apps; hence, payment is usually done by mobile payment. However, it has also been researched that consumers are highly unlikely to buy tactile goods or very expensive items online or on mobile devices (Coursaris and Hassanein, 2002). Secondly, security concerns also exist and are complementary with the privacy concerns as mentioned above.

2.5 *Advantages of using M-commerce*

There are plenty of advantages in using M-commerce that help increase productivity of retailers. We have classified these advantages by using the 8M productivity framework.

(a) Greater outreach of customers [Message]

Businesses are able to reach out to a greater number of customers with M-commerce. This improves communication between businesses and customers. Since users are also able to search directly for what they need regardless of where they are, M-commerce effectively provides customers with information that they need. Hence, consumers not only get personalized tailored promotional messages but also have the flexibility to read these messages when they have the time to do so.

(b) Getting useful information or real-time data [Money]

M-commerce is productive when businesses are able to get more information about their customers. This is especially so when "employees [are able] to access real-time data to make timely decisions that either decrease costs or increase revenues (Balasubramanian *et al.*, 2002)." One example cited is that when a field salesperson recommends suitable alternatives of a product that is not in stock when a user's information such as purchase history is revealed to the salesperson.

(c) Convenience [Make]

M-commerce is able to change the way customers experience retail by eliminating "some of the labor of life's activities (Mahatanankoon *et al.*, 2005)." Customers who are waiting are able to use the M-commerce application to pass time may "recognize a special comfort that could translate into an improved quality of life." By making transactions easier, consumers may possibly be loyal to the retail store by being repetitive customers.

(d) Innovation [Market]

Reinartz *et al.* (2011) mentioned that innovation in retailers is vital to break through to mature markets, such as Singapore. The need for IT-integrated lifestyles, heterogeneity in taste and individualization are some of the consumer-based challenges based on environmental trends (Reinartz *et al.*, 2011) that M-commerce is able to overcome. With the development of M-commerce, consumers are flexible in terms of where to purchase the products and how to purchase them. Therefore, M-Commerce could be a way through which retailers could break through mature markets.

(e) Complementary to E-commerce

M-commerce features are actually complementary to the E-commerce. Einav *et al.* (2014) compared a user's activity on both

M- and E-commerce before and after the introduction of M-commerce. Their findings suggest that adoption of the mobile shopping application is positively correlated with "immediate and sustained increase in total platform purchasing." Hence, introducing M-commerce to the already established E-commerce platform does not lead to a decrease in sales.

2.6 *Disadvantages of M-commerce*

Despite the numerous advantages of M-commerce in productivity improvements, there are still some challenges that M-commerce brings about.

(a) Usability (User adoption of shoppers)

One of the main challenges of M-commerce is that interaction is limited to the small screen and keypad on mobile devices, making it demanding for customers to find information or browse through data. A recent PayPal survey discovered that an estimated 66% of mobile shoppers in Singapore stopped a mobile transaction due to the hassle of entering financial details on their small screen (Loh, 2012).

There has been mixed evidence that consumers are likely to use M-commerce to buy products. A study conducted by Anckar and D'Incau (2002) on 485 Finnish respondents found that there was a low willingness among users to use some of the suggested M-commerce applications. Among the categories, buying products online scored a mean score of mobile willingness of only 2.65 out of 5. However, after splitting respondents into E-commerce adopters and non-E-commerce adopters, the mean score increased to 3.11 on the willingness to buy products using M-commerce. In another study, Mort and Drennan (2005) found that adopters of M-commerce were strongly correlated with certain consumer characteristics. For instance, people who love to shop and users who have a strong need to belong are more likely to use value-added shopping mobile services.

(b) Technical

As mobile phones are small, there is limited "memory and computing power, insufficient bandwidth and limited data transfer capacity

(Ding *et al.*, 2004)." In addition, according to a survey by MasterCard, there have been concerns of security in handling sensitive information during mobile payment, and the fragmentation of cash transactions online makes mobile commerce less appealing (Velasquez, 2014). Unless there is a team of software and mobile application developers within the company, such technical issues usually involve third-party companies such as Paypal to provide necessary expertise and software. It also involves partnerships with banks to establish credit payment accounts online for online transactions, which is a multilayered transactional process.

2.7 *Future of retailing*

Manley (2012) states that "Today, E-commerce is not just killing some stores — it is killing almost all stores." In addition, Dorman (2013) also emphasized that "members of the retail industry have openly predicted the demise of brick and mortar retail, which the Burning Platform (2012) describes as 'a slow motion train wreck'." Manley (2012) also concurred to this view by stating that the small profit margins made by retailers would diminish when there are smaller in-house purchases, as well as higher leverages as compared to other channels with lower fixed costs, such as M-commerce. With several trends converging to make M-commerce a profitable businesses, it seems that retailers would have to "adapt or die" (TechinAsia, 2013).

This phenomenon is not unfounded as many papers have cited the dangers of physical retailers not keeping up with technology. Firstly, Van Baal and Dach's (2005) paper concluded empirically that brick and mortar stores are likely to be used as show-rooms for customers to view the products before deciding to purchase it online. This free-riding behavior produces a suboptimal economic outcome. Furthermore, retailers are most susceptible to free riding because they are unable to differentiate online customers from in-store customers. Therefore they cannot prevent the former from entering their stores.

Secondly, Brynjolfsson *et al.* (2003) investigated the impact of online retailing on book retailers. They found that through location-technology services, customers prefer buying books from the website to shopping from physical stores as it was easier to identify their books. Hence, this decreased retailer's power in determining prices (Dorman, 2013), making the industry more competitive and closer to a perfect competition model.

3. Trends in Mobile Commerce

3.1 *Smart phone penetration rates*

As mentioned, one of the reasons why M-commerce is taking over the retail scene is due to the high rates of mobile penetration. Smartphones provide consumers access of being connected wirelessly, hence making mobile shopping possible. Figure 2 shows that Singapore ranks fourth in terms of smartphone penetration with a

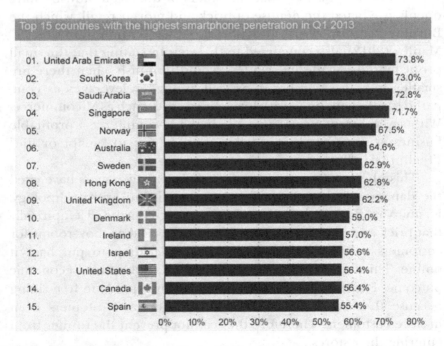

Figure 2:   Top 15 Countries with the Highest Smartphone Penetration in 2013

Source. The 15 countries with the highest smartphone pentration, Zoe Fox (Mashable).

Smartphone Shopping across Asia Pacific
Percentage of respondents who have made a purchase with a mobile phone in the past 3 months

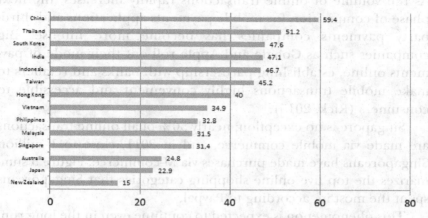

Figure 3: Number of People Who Made a Purchase Cia M-Commerce

Source: 60% of Chinese online shoppers have made purchases via smartphones, The Next Web.

penetration rate of 71.7% in 2013, while Hong Kong and United States are ranked eighth and 13th, respectively.

In addition, as can be seen from Figure 3, around one-third of Singaporeans have made a purchase with their mobile phones within three months, and these numbers are expected to grow.

3.2 M-commerce in the retail sector

Many businesses have jumped on the M-commerce bandwagon as consumer spending increases on mobile online shopping. This is evident in Japan and US, where consumer spending increased by three times reaching $10 billion and $1.2 million from M-commerce, respectively, in 2009 (Islam *et al.*, 2011). This is especially so in the retail sector where mobile traffic accounted for a high 52.1% of online traffic on Thanksgiving day in 2014 in the United States.

In addition, mobile sales on Black Friday accounted for 27.9% of total online sales, which is an increase of 28.2% from 2013 (IT Online, 2014). Figure 4 shows the increase in mobile commerce traffic and sales from the recent Black Friday sales. Consumer spending is expected to continue to rise even further in the future. As the volume of online transactions rapidly increases, the next phase of competition for mobile payments applications and third-party payments companies has become more intense. Big companies such as Google and Apple roll out their mode of payments online, establishing partnership with banks and retailers to make mobile transactions highly convenient and accessible to consumers (Rick, 2015).

Singapore is no exception; nearly 50% of all online transactions are made via mobile commerce, and in 2011, close to 1 million Singaporeans have made purchases via M-commerce. Figure 5 summarizes the top five online shopping categories that Singaporeans spent the most in, according to Paypal.

This phenomenon is expected to continue even in the long run, where the growth potential is significant. Figure 6 reports the rising

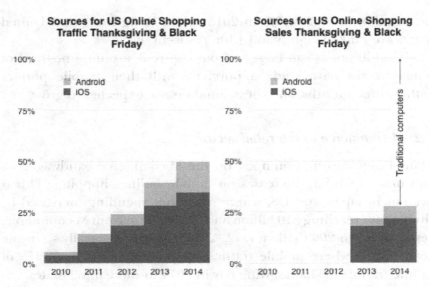

Figure 4:   M-Commerce Taking a Bigger Part of Online Shopping Traffic and Sales During Thanksgiving and Black Friday

Source: Online Retailers and Festive Season Hiccups, IT Online (2014).

Figure 5: Top Five Spending Categories in Singapore

Source: Paypal (2011).

U.S. Retail M-commerce Sales Via Smartphones & Tablets 2014-2018

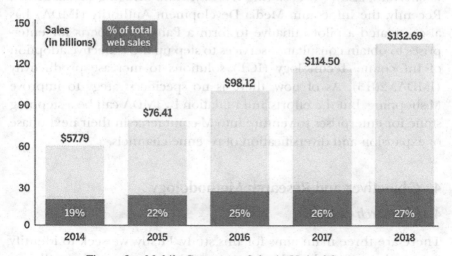

Figure 6: Mobile Commerce Sales in United States

Source: U.S. retail M-commerce sales via smartphones and tablets 2014–2018, Internet Retailer.

trend of M-commerce retail sales in the United States. In addition, Singapore's mobile commerce "is expected to grow 10-fold to reach S\$3.1B (US\$2.45B) in 2015, indicating that shopping on mobile devices has become mainstream due to the ubiquity of such devices (Lee, 2012)."

3.3 *Government role in M-commerce*

M-commerce, being an extended version of E-commerce, can help in reducing manpower and rental rates, which are the two main common challenges for retailers in Singapore. An example would be the use of QR code by Golden Village, which allows purchases of ticketing for cinemas but also the access of entry through QR-code-technology-enabled gates (Reed, 2012). Thus, since the early 2000s, the Singapore government has encouraged and aided retailers to engage in E-commerce by implementing 6 strategies to foster online E-lifestyle.

These six strategies include (1) Laying foundations for E-Businesses, (2) Catalyzing the digital transformation, (3) Spurring consumer demand, (4) Branding Singapore as a trusted global 'Dot.com' Hub and an E-Businesses Thought Leadership Centre, (5) Attracting top talents and, lastly, (6) Fostering E-lifestyle and bridging digital divide. Recently, the Infocomm Media Development Authority (IMDA) has also initiated a pilot initiative to form a Panel of Experts for enterprises to obtain consultancy services to step up the collective adoption of Infocomm Technology (ICT) solutions to increase productivity (IMDA, 2013). As of now, there is no specific strategy to improve M-shopping, but the efforts and initiation by IMDA can be a stepping stone for enterprises to venture into M-commerce in their next phase of expansion and diversification of revenue channels.

4. Objectives and Research Methodology

4.1 *Research objective*

There are three main aims for this study. Firstly, we seek to identify factors that affect the adoption rate of M-commerce. Secondly, we aim to understand both current and future challenges of adopting mobile commerce for both merchants and consumers. Lastly, we intend to find out how mobile commerce can be used more pervasively in Singapore.

4.2 *Research methodology*

According to the 8M Framework (Toh and Thangavelu, 2017, Chapters 2 and 3) developed, management, material, manpower, money, make, method, market and message are important factors to raise productivity level in a business. This framework was adopted to provide a general understanding in how retailers view M-commerce.

We conducted a survey for stores in a shopping mall (Tampines Mall) and shops along the main streets in a residential neighborhood. A total of 30 face-to-face interviews with questionnaires were collected among the fashion and beauty industries as well as electronics industry, as they were the two main industries most likely to venture into M-commerce first. This is because their items are light-weight, making delivery more feasible. This is also consistent with a recent Paypal study in 2011 where these two industries ranked among the top five categories among online shoppers in Singapore. Our interview focuses mainly on SMEs in Singapore.

5. Survey Findings

5.1 *Opinions on using M-commerce*

Merchants are generally receptive to the idea of using M-commerce, with a mean of 3.90 out 5, when asked about the likelihood of the company implementing M-commerce. This result is 1% statistically significant from choosing the 'neutral (3)' option. Figure 7 also

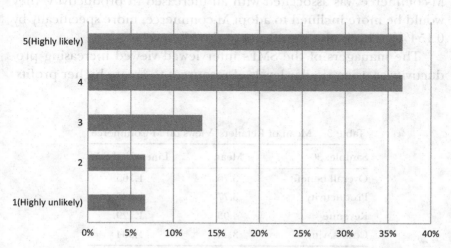

Figure 7:   How Likely is Your Company to Use M-Commerce?

Source: Field survey.

shows that more than 70% of managers indicated that their company is willing to use M-commerce in the future; some of them are already at their initial planning stages.

5.2 *Perceived benefits of M-commerce*

Retailers were also asked how likely they are to benefit if they were to adopt M-commerce in terms of productivity, revenue, cost savings and overall benefit, indicating a Likert scale number between 1 (little benefits) and 5 (strong benefit).

(a) **Mean of perceived benefits**

Retailers perceived that M-commerce can generally have a positive impact on their business in all 4 aspects, where the mean was 3.43 –4.03, at 5% statistical significance. The table of perceived benefits also explained that they would be likely to use M-commerce in the future if they have not implemented it (see Table 3).

(b) **Productivity in M-commerce**

In addition, we also found out how likely each benefit would affect the probability of retailers choosing to adopt M-commerce. Productivity ranked first. This means that if retailers felt that M-commerce was associated with an increased in productivity, they would be more inclined to adopt M-commerce, more specifically by 0.154%). This is also significant at the 5% level.

The managers of the SMEs interviewed viewed increasing productivity as using similar levels of resources to create higher profits.

Table 3:   Mean of Retailers' Views on M-Commerce

Sample: 30	Mean	Linearized S.D
Overall benefit	3.76	1.165
Productivity	3.77	1.135
Revenue	4.03	1.129
Costs savings	3.43	1.304

Source: Field survey.

Similar resources to them include mainly manpower and capital used for daily business operations.

However, this increase in productivity is also associated with challenges in implementation and that will be further explored in Section 5.3.

5.3 *Challenges in M-commerce*

Retailers were also asked to rank the possible obstacles or hindrances when using M-commerce. The three main obstacles as shown in Figure 8 are (1) Money — e.g lack of volume and money matters, (2) manpower — capable IT team and (3) methods — logistics related. Hence, these three categories will be discussed in this section.

(a) Money

Having a lack of volume in transactions is the most challenging factor in implementing M-commerce. About 23% of retailers mentioned this as the main obstacle. Lack of volume in transaction is classified under money category, since retailers explained how having a lack of transactions would lead to a decrease in revenue

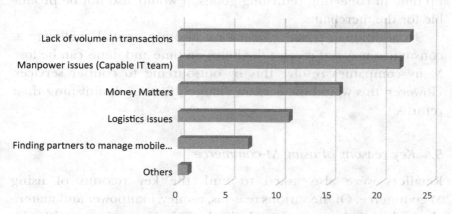

Figure 8:   Main Challenges Faced When Implementing M-Commerce
Source. Field survey.

earned. Hence, they are afraid that M-commerce may not be a suitable platform for transactions as it is not profitable enough to include in their business.

(b) Manpower

Secondly, the lack of manpower in forming a "capable IT team" might discourage the merchant from adopting M-commerce. Since M-commerce is a relatively new phenomenon, existing traditional retailers have to extend their resources to form a new team in planning for M-commerce. This also includes additional manpower for delivery, strategic planning of M-commerce. Such planning will take time and huge investments before it becomes profitable. Hence, this is also linked to the first challenge where merchants are concerned with the lack of transactions resulting in long time-span to break-even.

(c) Methods

Lastly, the factor methods includes having substantial logistics area to store their warehouse items and having a centralized point to put the goods together.

In addition, retailers were also very concerned with 'return policy' for consumers. Retailers prefer not to have to deal with return goods via courier services. This is because this would not only take up time in collecting returning goods, it would also not be profitable for the merchants.

In additional, postal services are also a potential challenge as consumers may not receive the items on time and items can be lost. Many companies resolve this by outsourcing to courier services. However, this would incur extra charges, further diminishing their returns.

5.4 *Key reasons of using M-commerce*

Retailers were also asked to rank the key reasons of using M-commerce. Of the various reasons, money, manpower and materials ranked first, second and third. This is consistent with the challenges mentioned in the earlier section. This should be the case since merchants would want to adopt M-commerce for these key reasons which are currently lacking in their businesses. Therefore, using the 8M framework, we are able to understand what kind of challenges the SMEs are facing in this environment and the reasons for SME's interest in adoption of M-commerce, which are both consistent in our interviews.

(a) Money

Retailers would be likely to use M-commerce if they could earn money from it. As with our previous results, the managers of SMEs interviewed acknowledge the profitability and the potential of using M-commerce. Therefore, money is the primarily reason why M-commerce is used as part of diversifying their business strategies. At the same time, money is also one of the challenges faced by the SMEs, due to the concern of the lack of volume transacted on M-commerce which they hope to overcome. In this case, both challenges and the key reason for M-commerce adoption are consistent.

(b) Manpower

Retailers will be more likely to use M-commerce if they could find a way of allocating manpower to increase productivity. Manpower in this case is more specific in terms of the IT capabilities of the current manpower or the establishment of an IT team within the company. Most of the SMEs interviewed indicated their intention of starting or planning to open up their business online first before venturing into M-commerce. This is in line with our literature review that M-commerce is viewed as an extended version of E-commerce. However, they lack the capabilities to expand further due to limited expertise within the company. IT expertise is therefore highly sought after by SMEs as 43.3% of the interviewees recommended solutions for IT expertise in M-commerce. They expressed that they long for IT capabilities for daily maintenance and use of M-commerce.

(c) Material/Supplier

Retailers will more likely to use M-commerce if they have the physical and technical capabilities in IT to expand their businesses. Similar to the factor of manpower, most of those interviewed mentioned the lack of resources for a capable IT team. Besides bringing in the manpower and the know-how, the SMEs also do need to have the physical resources and capabilities to ensure management of the IT solutions for the SMEs. Such resources may include but are not limited to acquisition of software, online websites and IT solutions for online marketing and secured payments. These business services could be outsourced to third parties such as PayPal, VISA or MasterCard. However, the SMEs faced a high cost of transaction with these third parties.

5.5 *Assistance requested by the merchants*

From Figure 9, we can see that the most popular recommendation as suggested by merchants was that retailers wanted websites that are publicly endorsed by government. This is indicated by 20 out of 30 retailers. Other recommendations raised were having online expertise and a platform for online secured transactions. This section gives us insights in helping to craft feasible recommendations for merchants to use M-commerce more pervasively in Singapore. It will be further elaborated in Section 6.

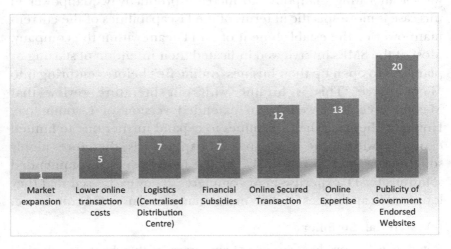

Figure 9:   Recommendations by Retailers

Source: Field survey.

6. Consumer Survey

6.1 *Objectives and methodology*

After interviewing merchants, we understand that one of the main challenges that retailers are concerned with is the lack of volume in transactions. To address that issue, we would have to find out and involve the perception of consumers' in the adoption of M-commerce. In this section, we would like to know (1) the responsiveness of consumers in using M-commerce and (2) the factors that could determine one's use of M-commerce.

To assess the preference of consumer for M-commerce, we solicited information from consumers using questionnaire survey, interviews and on-line query and response. The study was conducted by asking respondents aged 16 and above to answer survey questions either via an online website or face-to-face interview at NEX shopping mall. A total of 124 questionnaires were collected, with 102 online respondents and 22 face-to-face interviews.

6.2 *Survey findings*

(a) Adoption rate of M-commerce

According to age category, we find respondents in the age groups 20–30 and 30–40 are more receptive to M-commerce with a mean of 3.19 and 3.18, respectively (see Table 4).

Table 4:   Adoption of M-Commerce (overall) by Age Group

Age Category	Mean	Standard Deviation
16–20	2.96	1.07
21–30	3.19	1.29
31–40	3.18	1.22
41–50	2.3	1.70
Above 51	1.8	1.26

Source: Field survey.

(b) Using M-commerce with the help of others

Respondents above age 51 were mostly receptive to the idea of having someone they know purchase items for them despite them having a low willingness to use M-commerce. 52% of the respondents indicated that they were willing to engage in M-commerce with the help of others. This shows that they could be indirect users of M-commerce. Therefore, when websites or mobile apps are introduced to these elderly, they are unlikely to use it themselves but would get help from a third party to purchase items. Hence, we cannot ignore their opinions on the use of M-commerce.

(c) Factors affecting the adoption of M-commerce

We also tested how individual factors could affect adoption of M-commerce. We found out that the three most important factors that consumers seek are (i) secured online payments, (ii) buying with online sales promotions and (iii) the ease of using credit cards.

(d) Relevance to merchants

In our survey, we find that there are indeed consumers using M-commerce, with the younger generation being most proactive. This result is consistent with Lim (2014) where "the age of the consumer [has] an impact on the adoption of M-commerce application with those growing up in the age of technology more inclined to use M-commerce." However, our survey also shows that we cannot ignore the elderly as at least half of them may request their friends to purchase items for them.

Secondly, we also found that consumers were most concerned with the security of online payments, followed by the use of sales promotion online. Lim (2014) classified the above two factors as key "perceived ease of use" factors that will motivate consumers in using M-commerce. Hence, merchants can use sales promotion as a tactic to overcome the other factors that might influence the adoption of M-commerce, such as perceived ease of use of M-commerce.

Thirdly, our results were also in line with existing research where "usefulness, satisfaction (i.e. the purchase must fulfil all expectations), and trust in the M-vendor are critical determinants for consumers when considering repeat purchases in M-shopping

(Groß, 2015)." Hence, it is important for merchants to identify these factors to increase customer satisfaction.

7. Recommendations

The efforts to increase the use of M-commerce would be intensive. Based on the above findings, we have drawn a few recommendations and categorized them according to our aims of research. There are two parts to the recommendations: (1) to resolve challenges faced by merchants found in Section 4, (2) to instill trust in consumers and retailers in using M-commerce found in Sections 4 and 5.

7.1 *Resolving challenges faced by merchants*

(a) Associations
(i) Furnishing information
As mentioned, one major challenge perceived by merchants in M-commerce is the lack of transactional volume in M-commerce. However, supplementing results from the consumer survey, we can conclude that Singaporeans are moving toward the use of M-commerce. In the technology sector, there is a huge advantage to "first-movers", hence it is important for retailers to start planning at an early stage. Hence, associations could help to convey such findings to retailers.

Most SMEs are unable to conduct business analysis independently and, therefore, are unable to move forward and ride on to new business trends. Associations can help in providing general business information for retailers to be more informed in deciding their strategy for their businesses. Thus, information sharing between associations is important in determining retailers' adoption of M-commerce.

(ii) Capable IT management
As IT management is one of the retailers' major obstacles in adopting M-commerce, there is limited IT capability that SMEs can rely on for maintaining their businesses online, especially in M-commerce. Therefore, it will be beneficial if business associations engaged in

electronics, fashion and beauty can provide training courses and awareness to the retail merchants for them to improve and upgrade their IT capabilities.

Furthermore, business associations should be more proactive in engaging the retailers to share their expertise and know-how with new entrepreneurs, especially in IT management. The lack of such capabilities has severely limited the expansion of retailers' business in M-commerce. Unless more can be done to provide the IT expertise for the retailers through either training of staffs or promoting the IT sector to young Singaporeans, this factor will most likely remain a huge hurdle for retailers to overcome in adopting M-commerce.

(b) Government

(i) Money

In the 8M Framework, Manpower and Materials were the top two concerns for retailers. As the amount of money spent on hiring extra people and implementing new technology is a large sum of money, SMEs hope that the government could help them in certain form of subsidies to ease the burden if they were to implement M-commerce. These subsidies will aid the transition from the traditional retailing model to an E-commerce/M-commerce platform. An example will be the use of subsidies for the training courses held by associations in IT management. The financial aid will thus provide a temporary relief for the retailers when they are going through the transitional period in their organization of businesses.

(ii) Finding capable IT groups

One of the concerns expressed by retailers is the lack of capable IT members. Therefore, there could be a need to train and promote more Singaporeans in this sector. Furthermore, as the talent and the human resource is limited locally, the costs of establishing and starting an online business strategy become significantly larger as the returns of online business become uncertain due to the high risks involved. Therefore, it is also important for the government to educate the retailers on the risks and nature of online businesses while assisting in improving the IT capabilities of the SMEs.

7.2 *Forging trust in M-commerce platforms*

One of the main concerns for both consumers and retailers is the trustworthiness of using online platforms to purchase goods.

(a) Associations

(i) Campaigns/advertisements

Associations can help in setting up online campaigns or advertisements to instill trust in consumers. Since traditional stores already have some credibility, consumers using M-commerce would have a certain degree of trust with these brands.

(ii) Creating common portal/website

Associations can use a portal to link all retailers' website and have consumers rate the products they receive based on a few criteria such as authenticity, delivery and item quality. These customers' reviews will not only instill trust in consumers but will also help retailers to track their M-commerce progress.

(b) Government

(i) Legislation

Consistent with retailers' recommendations and consumer's survey, both sides were equally concerned about secured payments. Retailers felt that more rules and regulations can be put in place to ensure consistent and stable platforms for secured payments. As consumers and retailers place great faith in Singapore's government, they hope to seek assurance from the government to implement new legislation to regulate the payments online and work with third parties such as PayPal, Visa, and MasterCard and banks to ensure secured transactions online.

(ii) Government-backed cards

Retailers would also hope to promote the use of eNETs payment and gradually turn into M-commerce in a government-endorsed protocol. This will greatly alleviate the authenticity issues, as those with bad records and reviews will be dealt with more information availability. As the endorsement from the government serves as a signal effect for both customers and retailers to confidently do transactions, this will significantly increase their confidence and eliminate a major fear within M-commerce.

8. Conclusion, Limitations and Future Research

In conclusion, M-commerce as a strategy can increase productivity and profitability of retailers. Most retailers acknowledge the potential benefits of M-commerce. However, challenges like lack of trust and low transactional volume continue to prevent retailers from implementing the strategy. Hence, it is vital that merchants, associations and the government come to work together to overcome these challenges. Since this study focuses mainly on research from the B2C point of view, future research can be looked into, with the view of helping retailers from a business-to-business (B2B) relationship perspective.

Chapter 8

Effectiveness of Cash Management Technologies and Cashless Payments in Retail and Food Services Sectors

1. Introduction

In a recent KPMG study, it was reported that Singapore's consumers have a unique payment preference among all developed nations. Cash (referring to only notes and coins in this study) in circulation still forms about 8.8% of GDP *vis-a-vis* Australia and Sweden, which stand at 4.4% and 2.1%, respectively. The amount of currency (notes and coins) in active circulation has been rising, reaching the all-time high of S$ 35.48 billion in July of 2016 as shown in Figure 1. An article in the Economist magazine in 2016 reported that contrary to the common belief that countries tend to move away from cash as they become more developed and affluent, the amount of cash used in transaction has been increasing.[1]

The findings of a survey presented in the "Singapore Payments Roadmap Report", published by Monetary Authority of Singapore (MAS) in August 2016, showed a similar observation. It reported

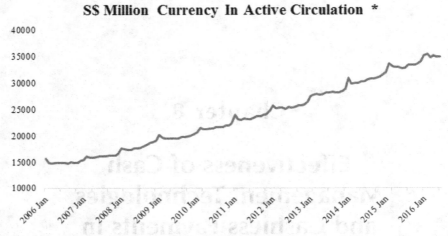

Figure 1: Amount of Currency in Active Circulation in Singapore from 2006 to 2016

Source: Monetary Authority of Singapore.

that cash was the second mostly widely used instrument after store-valued facilities (SVF), and consumers used cash in 60% of non-SVF transactions with 1.4 billion payments in 2015. The majority of cash payments were made for small-value transactions in places such as food stores, hawker centers, convenient stores or small shops.

However, cash handling can be costly to both businesses and the economy. Coins need to be minted and notes need to be printed, which require resources.[2] According to MAS, cash handling costs Singapore about S$2 billion per year, and this account for 0.79% of Singapore's GDP.[3] This amount is higher than that of countries such as Denmark (0.48%), Belgium (0.58%) and Australia (0.77%) which have similar share of transactions conducted in cash (between 50 and 60% of total value of all transactions).[4] Finland and Norway are the most efficient countries in handling cash as their handling costs account for only 0.12%[5] and 0.15%[6] of the countries' GDP. The "Singapore Payments Roadmap Report" also found that by eliminating cash at hawker centers and in taxis, Singapore economy could save S$150 million each year. This implies a huge opportunity for productivity improvement and cost savings in cash handling in Singapore.

Businesses in retail and foodservice sector generally have high volume of cash usage; hence, improving efficiency and reducing costs in their cash handling process can bring positive externalities by reducing the overall cost of cash incurred to the society. Furthermore, this can also help to alleviate the common issues of labor shortage and lack of productivity faced by businesses in these two sectors.

1.1 *Importance of productivity improvement in cash management to businesses*

At the micro level, cash management is highly important to businesses as it involves channeling the money received from customers to support investments and expenses in daily operations and business expansion. A bank is usually involved in this process to facilitate various transactions. The process is illustrated in the cash flows diagram of a typical company in Figure 2. The efficiency of managing cash will affect the liquidity of a company, which will in turn influence its business operations and investments.

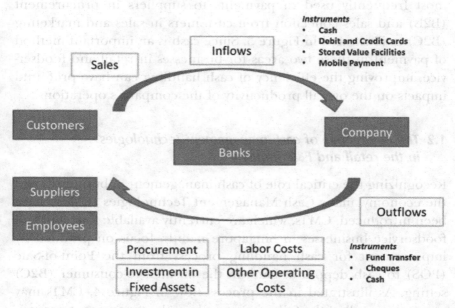

Figure 2: Cash Flow Process of a Typical Company

Source: Literature Review, Industry Publications.

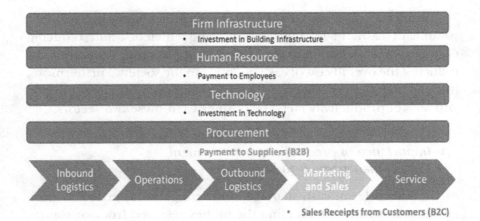

Figure 3:   Cash Handling in the Value Chain of Retail and F&B Businesses
Source: Value Chain Analysis, Industry Publications.

A value-chain analysis for retail and F&B businesses using data from "Singapore Payments Roadmap Report" reveals that cash is most frequently used in payments to suppliers in procurement (B2B) and sales collection from customers in sales and marketing (B2C) as illustrated in Figure 3. Since cash is an important method of payment in these two areas for businesses in retail and foodservice, improving the efficiency of cash handling can have profound impacts on the overall productivity of the company's operations.

1.2 *The emergence of cash management technologies in the retail and F&B industry*

Recognizing the critical role of cash management in businesses and the economy, many Cash Management Technologies (CMTs) have been introduced. CMTs, which are currently available for retail and foodservice businesses in Singapore mainly, focus on productivity improvement for cash handling process from the Point-of-Sale (POS) to cash deposit at bank in the business-to-consumer (B2C) setting. As illustrated in the process flow in Figure 4, CMTs may cover part or all of the following steps in cash management process:

Figure 4: Components of CMTs

front-end cash management, back-end cash management and cash-in-transit (CIT). CIT may also involve services provided by external parties to ensure the safety of cash transported between banks and businesses.

CMTs were considered as game-changing technologies that could automate and control cash processing procedures by SPRING Singapore in March 2015. The organization also launched the Call-For-Collaboration (CFC) to seek perspectives on CMTs in the retail and F&B sector. While CMTs have been adopted by retailers in other parts of the world including Europe and Japan for over the past 20 years, they were only introduced to Singapore with Cold Storage pioneering the implementation of an automated cash management system at its store at Sime Darby at the end of 2014.

Currently, major local supermarkets and retail chains such as Cold Storage, Sheng Siong, Cheers, and Yue Hua Chinese Products have implemented CMTs in their stores. Nevertheless, the adoption of CMTs has been rather limited in Singapore, especially among small and medium enterprises (SMEs).

(a) *Objectives of the study*

Improving productivity among SMEs has been a key agenda for government agencies such as SPRING Singapore. In light of the importance of productivity improvement in cash management, this study aims to understand how businesses can improve productivity through using CMTs and assess the effectiveness of these technologies so as to provide recommendations to companies in the retail and F&B sector as well as to trade associations and government agencies.

This chapter is organized as follows: Section 2 provides an overview of the cash management process as well as CMTs through secondary research. Section 3 presents the methodologies used in primary research and the research results gathered from interviews and surveys of companies, technology providers and customers. Finally, Section 4 concludes the study with recommendations and action plans for different stakeholders involved.

2. Overview of the Cash Management Process and Cash Management Technologies

2.1 *Cash management practices among businesses in retail and foodservices sector*

As discussed in Section 1, it is important for businesses to improve productivity in cash management. The traditional cash management process is often considered tedious and labor intensive, and thus there is room for productivity improvement in the current process. In this section, we will consider how cash is usually managed among retailers in Singapore.

According to literature review and interviews with industry practitioners, the cash management process (for notes and coins) starting from receiving money from customers to depositing at banks involves three major components: front-end cash management, back-end cash management and cash-in-transit. Cash needs to be counted, replenished, securely kept and deposited in the bank. The main activities of cash management are summarized in Figure 5.

In the front-end retail space, the process in which each cashier is responsible for the money in the cash registers is called "balancing cashiers' tills". Cashiers are given a certain amount of cash of various

Figure 5:   Cash Management Activities from Point-of-Sales to Deposit at Banks

Sources: Interviews with Industry Practitioners and Literature review.

denominations at the beginning of each shift and managers would count the cash and compare the amount against the sales for each cash register at the end of the each shift. Extra cash would be collected and kept in the back-end cash office. As such, the amount of cash in each cash register is the same as at the beginning of each shift. During each shift, cashiers need to ensure that they give customers the right change, or else they may be required to pay for the losses. When notes and coins of a certain denomination run out, the cashier needs to inform the managers, who would then withdraw the cash from the float in the back-end cash office.

At the back-end cash office, accountants count the cash and record the cash collected each day to ensure the amount tallies with the sales figures from POS system. Notes and coins would be separated according to denominations, and those with smaller denominations can be recycled to provide customers with change at the POS.

Cash is securely kept at the back-end cash office until it is deposited at the banks. Cash is usually deposited at the banks by staff or through cash-in-transit (CIT) services provided by a third party.

In general, the manual cash handling process has the following concerns:

(1) **Repetitive and time-consuming tasks:** Manual cash handling involves many repetitive and time-consuming tasks, such as cash counting and reconciliation. To ensure that the right amount cash is received from customers, cash is counted several times a day by different parties including cashiers, managers and accountants, as a mechanism to ensure no cash is lost in the process. Staff's working hours can also be spent on queuing at the bank to request for changes.
(2) **Prone to errors:** Manual cash handling is prone to errors since cashiers may give the wrong change to customers.
(3) **Risk of cash shrinkage[7] and theft:** Cash may be lost during the process due to various reasons such as misplacement, counting errors, and internal and external theft.

2.2 *Cash management technologies*

(a) *Introduction to cash management technologies*[8]

To improve efficiency in cash handling and to reduce labor hours required and errors, businesses can consider adopting CMTs.

CMTs are currently available in a wide degree of automation and sophistication. Businesses of large format and with high volume of cash transactions, such as supermarkets and departmental stores, may choose to implement a fully integrated cash handling system to close the loop and totally eliminate manual processing, as illustrated in Figure 6. On the other hand, businesses of smaller format, such as bakeries, pharmacies and convenience stores, may choose to implement part of the system, such as cash recyclers and/or cash management software to improve efficiency, as illustrated in Figure 7.

Typical cash handling automation systems include *cash recyclers, smart safes and cash management software.*[9]

Cash recyclers staying at the *front-end* of the cash handling process are able to accept, authenticate and sort by denomination currency notes received from customers. They are able to provide customers with change automatically from the stock of notes and coins that have been fed into the machine. Cash recyclers have wide application

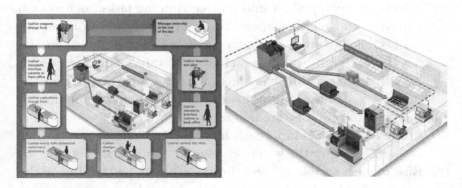

Figure 6: Example of Closed Cash Management System (Full System) Implemented in Retailers of Large Format

Source: Glory.

Front-end Cash Management Solutions at a German Shell Petrol Station	Front-end Cash Management Solutions at a Bakery in Montpellier, France

Figure 7: Examples of Front-End Cash Management Solutions Implemented in Retailers of Small Format

Source: Wincorf Nixdorf and Glory.

at check-out counters of different retailer formats. For example, Cold Storage and Fair Price are using the Glory CI 10 cash & coin recycler cash recycler to handle the cash exchanged during customer transactions, while Far East Orchid is using the CashGuard machine named Premium Note & Coin Recycler for the same purpose (refer to Figure 8 for detailed illustration).

Cash recyclers and Smart Safes staying at the *back-end* of cash handling process are usually used at the cash office. The back-end hardware helps to collate cash from different points of sales and reflects a collective summary of cash movement for the whole store. The available examples of back-end systems are Glory CI 100 cash & coin recycler and CashGuard Presidio (refer to Figure 9 for illustrations). Some models may also include a *Note Mover* which collects cash from the front-end system and then deposits it into the safe securely.

With the combination of different technologies at both front-end and back-end, the cash cycle at the retail store can be made closed loop, and all manual cash handling is eliminated.

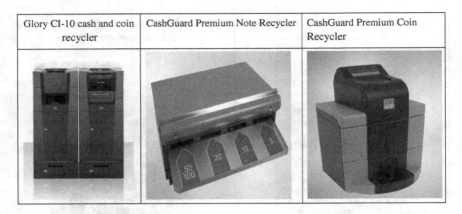

Glory CI-10 cash and coin recycler	CashGuard Premium Note Recycler	CashGuard Premium Coin Recycler

Figure 8: Example of Models of Front-End Solutions Available in the Market
Source: Glory and Strong Point.

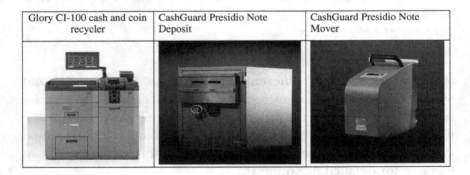

Glory CI-100 cash and coin recycler	CashGuard Presidio Note Deposit	CashGuard Presidio Note Mover

Figure 9: Examples of Models of Back-End Solutions Available in the Market
Source: Glory and Strong Point.

In addition, *Cash Management Software* allows real-time tracking of cash inventory and sales at each cash recycler and cassette. It also allows the manager to perform reconciliation through the cash flow statistical reports from the software.[10] Figure 10 provides illustrations of the interface of the software provided by different players.

By implementing CMTs, cash counting is eliminated throughout the cash management process. In the front-end operation, all cash counting is eliminated and managers can monitor the cash

Glory CI-SERVER	CashGuard Store Manager Software	CashGuard Store Manager Mobile Application
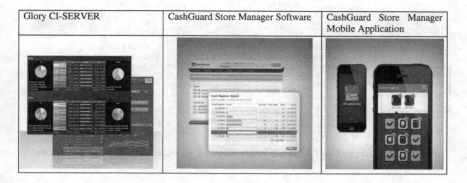		

Figure 10: Examples of the Interfaces of Cash Management Software
Source: Glory, Strong Point.

level at different cash registers easily through cash management software to decide when to replenish cash. Cash recyclers at the front-end retail space dispense cash automatically, leading to a faster check-out process and less errors. In the back-end cash management, it takes lesser time for cash reconciliation, since the report of total amount of cash available in the store can be easily generated from the system. During the cash-in-transit stage, companies can reduce the frequency of depositing cash at the bank, and eliminate cash counting before passing the money to third-party service provider.

The impact of CMTs on the cash management process is summarized in Figure 11.

(b) *Application of cash management technologies globally*

Despite CMTs being relatively new to businesses in Singapore, it has been over 20 years since the first CMTs were implemented in the world. In the mid-90s, motivated by security reasons, Swedish cash automation pioneer StrongPoint started to implement the first cash handling system at local supermarket check-out counters. Over the past 30 years, market leader Glory has implemented more than 200,000 systems in Japan where retailers are driven to provide customers excellent service.[11] According to StrongPoint, there are about 25,000 StrongPoint retail cash management systems installed

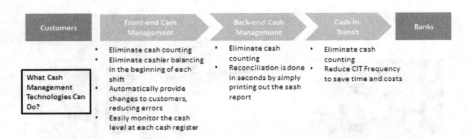

Figure 11:   Impact of CMTs on Each Stage of the Cash Management Process

in supermarkets all over the world.[12] Gunnebo installed 7,500 of its Safepay Systems in Europe in 2014.[13] In Europe and the United States, CMTs have been widely adopted by major retail stores, petrol stations and self-service restaurants, such as IKEA, Carrefour, Shell, Statoil, Tesco, SPAR International, 7-Eleven, KFC, McDonald's, and Burger King.[14] Nevertheless, such systems have relatively weak presence in the Asia Pacific.

Retailers need CMTs that are customized to their needs. Most applications of CMTs so far are seen in supermarkets, petrol stations, or large international retail or self-service restaurant groups. According to a report published by Planet Retail, big opportunities await retailers of smaller formats who are yet to adopt such CMTs.

Major CMT providers in the world are: Wincor Nixdorf, StrongPoint, Scan Coin, Glory and Gunnebo.[15] Examples of technology providers who have entered the Singapore market include Wincor Nixdorf, Glory and StrongPoint.

(c) *Benefits of cash management technologies — Overseas case studies*

Internationally, there are several companies that are known to have successfully implemented CMTs to improve productivity. Most tend to be big corporations who adopt the closed system including cash recyclers, smart safes and cash management software. The following section discusses a few such companies.

IKEA selected Wincor Nixdorf's Cineo line of cash recycling systems to automate cash handling across its operations overseas.

As of 2014 data, the retailer has been rolling out the system in about 300 stores in 25 countries. The technologies result in a time-saving of about 40–50%, as well as a complete elimination of the back-office errors in cash operations, as the process is completely closed.

Carrefour first enhanced its cash handling procedure in its hypermarket at Cesson-Sevigne (France). All of its 35 check out points are equipped with automated machines from SCAN COIN to receive cash from shoppers and provide change automatically. Carrefour's staff members are now able to safely deliver cash to their back office, and are assured that they will have sufficient cash to operate, with the help of security firm Brinks. After Cesson-Sevigne, six more stores of the company were also equipped with similar technologies.

Another retailer implementing these technologies overseas is Norges Gruppen, a Norwegian retailer. They use the services of StrongPoint and have recorded a shrinkage of 0 after the implementation of the system. Furthermore, Kurt Thomassen, the head of retail security, notes that the instances of staff made redundant due to theft or fraud has reduced by 30%.

Tesco uses the cash handling solutions by Cummins Alison in its UK operation. The system is able to count about 4,100 mixed coins in a minute, with 99.995% accuracy. Furthermore, the system has a total footprint of less than 1.22 square meters, requiring minimal retail space.

Through the overseas case studies, it is evident that CMT has improved efficiency, accuracy as well as security in the companies' operations. Given the proven benefits of CMTs and their wide application in other developed countries, the next section will examine the application of CMTs among businesses in Singapore.

2.3 *Adoption of cash management technologies in Singapore*

While there have been multiple successful examples of CMT applications among businesses in retail and F&B industry overseas, the number of companies in Singapore that have adopted CMT remains relatively low for both large corporations and SMEs.

Within the retail sector, the adoption is mainly concentrated among supermarkets, convenience stores and departmental stores, which have a large volume of cash transactions. For example, Fairprice, Cold Storage and Sheng Siong are currently automating all or part of their cash management process. Fairprice is also collaborating with Glory and CISCO to pioneer a fully integrated cash management system from front-end to back-end and cash-in-transit. In the foodservice sector, only a few operators of food courts, fast food chains and casual dining restaurants piloted the technologies. Some examples are The Soup Spoon and Japan Food Town, both of which have implemented Glory's solutions to automate part of their cash handling process.

Regarding the choice of technologies, businesses with multiple POS are more likely to implement back-end CMTs which consolidate sales from different POS and store the cash securely. Having back-end CMTs also encourages companies to engage third-party cash-in-transit services since the frequency of cash-in-transit decreases while volume of cash to be deposited at the bank per trip increases. Businesses with small retail space, such as convenience stores, casual dining restaurants, and food courts tend to choose only the front-end solutions which automate coins and notes dispensing.

As shown in Figure 12, there is a wide variety of businesses that have implemented CMT, yet the number of adopters within each category (except for supermarkets) is rather small. This implies a huge market potential for CMTs, especially among food courts, casual dining operators and SME retailers if cash remains popular in Singapore for the next 3 to 5 years.

Companies presented in Figure 12 are using CMTs provided by either Wincor Nixdorf, Glory or StrongPoint except for Ci Yuan Hawker Center, which implemented self-payment kiosk for each store. Figures 13 and 14 show examples of how the front-end cash management solutions are implemented.

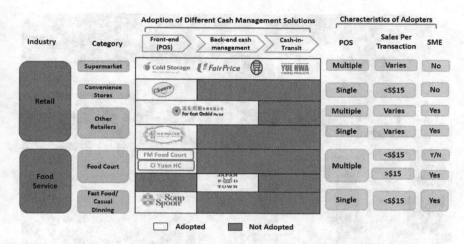

Industry	Category	Adoption of Different Cash Management Solutions			Characteristics of Adopters		
		Front-end (POS)	Back-end cash management	Cash-in-Transit	POS	Sales Per Transaction	SME
Retail	Supermarket	Cold Storage / FairPrice		YUE HWA CHINESE PRODUCTS	Multiple	Varies	No
	Convenience Stores	Cheers			Single	<S$15	No
	Other Retailers	远东朗廷名雅有限公司 Far East Orchid Pte Ltd			Multiple	Varies	Yes
		THE PARLOUR			Single	Varies	Yes
Food Service	Food Court	FM Food Court / Ci Yuan HC		JAPAN FOOD TOWN	Multiple	<S$15	Y/N
						>$15	Yes
	Fast Food/ Casual Dinning	Soup Spoon			Single	<S$15	Yes

☐ Adopted ▨ Not Adopted

Figure 12: Profile of Companies that have Adopted CMTs in Singapore (As of August 2016)

Figure 13: Self Payment Kiosk at Ci Yuan Hawker Center

Source: Internet.

Figure 14: Front-End Cash Management Solutions at FM @ Mapletree Business City

Source: Glory.

3. Research Results

3.1 *Research methodologies and survey profile*

To achieve the objectives mentioned in Section 1.3, the study sought to answer the following questions: (1) How did CMTs help the companies who have adopted it? (2) What are the current issues that non-adopters face in their traditional cash management process and what is the potential of CMT for improving their productivity?

To answer these questions, this study utilizes a combination of primary and secondary sources to gather data. Under primary research, site visits, on-site interviews, in-depth interviews and surveys were conducted. For secondary research, the information was gathered mainly through industry journals, databases, press releases and information sheets issued by technology providers.

Specifically, the study incorporates the perspectives of four stakeholders in the retail and F&B landscape: Adopters of CMT, non-adopters, technology providers as well as customers. In order to gather insights from the adopters of CMT as well as the technology providers, in-depth interviews were conducted with the managers at those companies. On the other hand, surveys were conducted in order to collect information from the non-adopters and customers. A summary of our methodology as well as details about the exact sample size of each group are provided in Table 1.

The following sections provide a brief overview of the profiles of the companies as well as customers that were interviewed/surveyed for the purpose of this study.

(a) *Profile of adopters of CMT interviewed*

In total, there were five interviews conducted with the management of adopter companies in order to gather insights about their

Table 1:   Summary of Research Methodology

Research Focus	Methodology	Target Achieved for Primary Research
How have CMTs helped companies	1. Case studies — interviews with adopters 2. Interviews with technology providers and CIT service providers	1. Case studies of 5 adopters of CMT (3 large retail companies and 2 SMEs) 2. Interviews with 2 major technology providers and 1 CIT service provider in Singapore
Potential of CMT in Singapore	1. Survey with non-adopters 2. Survey with customers on their payment habits	1. On-site surveys with 26 non-adopters of CMT 2. Online surveys with 60 retail and F&B customers
How are CMTs compared to its alternatives?	1. Case studies of companies using cashless transactions for productivity improvement 2. Secondary research on costs and efficiency of these alternatives	In-depth interviews with 4 retailers and 1 bank in China on the usage of mobile payment

adoption process, productivity improvements and challenges faced. These five companies were: Cold Storage, Fairprice, IKEA, Far East Orchid and Pink Parlour. Three of them (Cold Storage, Fairprice and IKEA) are large stores, while Far East Orchid and Pink Parlour can be classified as SMEs. Cold Storage and Fairprice are both large supermarket chains in Singapore, while IKEA is a large furniture retailer. Far East Orchid is involved in fresh flowers retail, and Pink Parlour provides beauty services. This study will therefore provide adopters' insights across different segments as well as company sizes.

(b) *Profile of non-adopters of CMT surveyed*

We conducted on-site surveys with store managers of companies who have not yet adopted CMT. The following figure sheds light on their profile.

- There are representatives from both retail and F&B industry, with the majority of the non-adopters representing retail industry and about 25% representing F&B industry (Figure 15(a)).

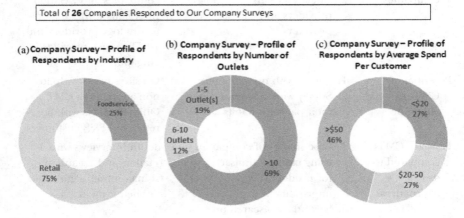

Figure 15: Profile of Non-Adopters of CMT Surveyed

Source: Survey of companies who have not adopted CMTs.

- About 70% of the non-adopters surveyed are part of a large chain of stores. This means that the parent company of the company surveyed has about 10 other branches in Singapore. This indicates the size of the company (Figure 15(b)).
- About 50% of the companies sell products that have high value (above $50 on average), and the rest of the companies sell products that are relatively lower in value (Figure 15(c)).

(c) *Profile of technology providers*

Two cash-management technology providers, Glory and StrongPoint, and a cash-in-transit service provider, CISCO, were interviewed to obtain information on their products and services. They also provided insights on the status of adoption of CMT in retail and foodservice sectors in Singapore. The aforementioned information was gathered through in-depth interviews conducted with the management of the three companies.[16]

(d) *Profile of customers*

We surveyed several customers to understand their perspectives of payment systems. More details about their profile are given in Figure 16.

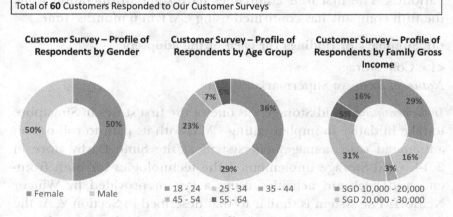

Total of **60** Customers Responded to Our Customer Surveys

Figure 16:   Profile of Customers Surveyed

Source: Survey of customers.

The following key observations can be made regarding the profile of customers surveyed:

- The survey respondents consist of an equal mix of both genders (Figure 16(a)).
- In terms of age, there are representatives of all age groups, with the younger generation (18–34) accounting for about 65% of the respondents (Figure 16(b)).
- There is an even distribution of respondents across various income brackets (Figure 16(c)).

3.2 Results of primary research

This section presents the information gathered from adopters and non-adopters of cash management technology. The data and information were obtained through site visits and interviews with executives and representatives of companies.

3.2.1 Adopters of CMTs

There are 5 adopters of CMTs in our sample of 31 companies. They are: Cold Storage, Fairprice, IKEA, Far East Orchid and Pink Parlour.[17] The first four companies have CMT in operation while the fifth company has confirmed using CMT in 6 months' time.

(a) Summary of findings for each of the adopters

<1> Cold storage
Nature of Business: Supermarket Chain.

Implementation: Cold Storage was one of the first stores in Singapore to take initiative in implementing CMTs with its plan to roll out an automated cash management system at the Sime Darby store in 2014. Cold Storage implemented the technologies for both front-end and back-end activities using a system provided by Wincor Nixdorf. The system is similar to that described in Section 2. At the front-end, the system automatically calculates and dispenses change when the cashier inserts money into the machines installed at the

Table 2: Key highlights of Productivity Improvement and Benefits Achieved by Five Selected Adopters

	Cold Storage	Fairprice	IKEA	Far East Orchid	Pink Parlour
Company Profile	A local premier supermarket chain	One of the largest local supermarket chains	An international furniture chain (to adopt technologies by year-end)**	An SME in Fresh Cut Flowers Wholesale Center	An SME in beauty service sector
Motivation of Adopting Technologies	— Lack of manpower	— Lack of manpower — Inaccuracy in processing payments	— Customer service — Rising labor costs	— Efficiency — Inaccuracy in processing payments — Customer service	— High labor costs and lack of manpower — Inefficiency
Key Productivity Improvement Highlights	— Total savings constitute 1.3% of total sales for a selected outlet — Expected to pay back the investments in 4 years — Headcount reduced from 25 to 11 for the outlet	— Cashiers' time spent on counting cash is cut by about 35% — Chief cashiers save 5 hours on average in cash reconciliation and 50 mins on average in cash replenishment each day	— Save about 4000–5000 hours per store a year	— Save 26 hours per week — Expect to pay back in 2–3 years	— Save at least the salary of a manager — Already get back the return based on monthly payment

(Continued)

Table 2:   *(Continued)*

	Cold Storage	Fairprice	IKEA	Far East Orchid	Pink Parlour
Additional Benefits	— Greater accuracy in giving change — Corporate branding — Greater employee satisfaction	— Greater accuracy in giving change — Offer more flexibility at work for cashiers — Allow cashiers to expand their skillsets through multi-tasking	— Greater accuracy in giving change — Staff can spend more time improving customer experience	— Greater accuracy in giving change — Cashiers can have more interactions with customers — Customers are impressed by CMT	— Greater accuracy in giving change — Manage money with ease — Being more mobile at work — Reduce repetitive work for employees who can now take on other roles

**Since the technologies have not yet been adopted, the productivity figures are estimates for IKEA.

POS. At the back-end, it helps to simplify and keep track of cash replenishment, cash collection as well as cash reconciliation. In the future, Cold Storage is planning to implement the system at more stores across the country.

Productivity Improvements: The key productivity benefits can be summarized as follows:

- Cashiers now focus on scanning, packing and up-selling grocery items, enabling the checkout process to take only 10 s per transaction, 60% shorter than the manual process.
- The greatest impact across different components of cash management is on the cash replenishment task. Before the implementation of the system, cash replenishment was performed at the beginning of the day and during the day. The withdrawal of float bags took 20 min and required at least one supervisor to be present. However, after the implementation, only one person is required to help with cash replenishment once per week. This has led to money savings amounting to approximately $44,700 per annum.
- Overall, one of the biggest benefits is cost saving on manpower, with a reduction in headcount from 25 to 11 staff at the Siam Darby outlet. With the new system, the cashiers can multi-task; for example, they can be a self-checkout assistant during their idle time.

Concerns: In terms of concerns, Cold Storage expressed their concerns in the area of availability of capital, especially since they are in the phase of expanding their adoption of CMT. They did not specifically record any implementation-related concerns.

<2> Fairprice
Nature of Business: Supermarket Chain.

Implementation: Fairprice's iCash program is another initiative toward automation of cash handling process. At the time this study was conducted (July 2016), Fairprice had deployed the system at 19 Cheers outlets and nine Fairprice outlets. The company plans to expand the system to 30 Cheers outlets (front-end) and 29 Fairprice outlets (both front and back end) by the end of 2016. Glory Global Solutions provided the technologies used in this system. The front-end is slightly different from Cold Storage's system. While cashiers are still the ones scanning and packing the items, customers are the ones inserting cash into a machine instead of handing the money to cashiers. The correct change in both notes and coins will then be released.

Productivity Improvements: The key productivity benefits can be summarized as follows:

- The system eliminates 40–60 min spent by chief cashiers on manually replenishing and verifying cash.
- CMT has reduced the cashiers' time spent on counting cash by about 35% — about half an hour of time savings for each cashier daily.
- Although the headcount remains unchanged, iCash allows Fairprice to optimize its workforce. The cashiers can multi-task and be cross-trained as both as cashiers and as retail assistants. This benefits them as they will have the opportunities to expand their skill sets and improve their employability.

Concerns: In terms of concerns, similar to Cold Storage, Fairprice also cited the cost of the CMT as a cause of concern. For implementing the system at a particular Fairprice store, the one-off cost is around $100,000, and significant maintenance cost is also incurred every year. The estimated cost to replicate these technologies at multiple stores amounts to millions of dollars. Other than the cost-related issues, Fairprice also expressed concerns over the lack of standardization in CIT process. Cassettes are different across different retailers, making it hard to integrate retailers' system with CIT provider's system. The closed-loop system is not entirely closed since cash still needs to be counted again at their CIT provider's place, leading to a delay in cash handling.

<3> IKEA
Nature of Business: Furniture Store Chain.

Implementation: IKEA in Singapore currently does not have any CMT in place; however, they have plans to adopt CMT by the end of this year. Specifically, they aim to install 2 back-end cash handling systems at their cash offices at the Singapore outlets. Since the system is only at the back-end, the cash management process would not be completely closed loop. However, they are currently conducting a feasibility study of a complete closed-loop solution in their Thailand operations and look forward to implementing it in Singapore if it proves successful.

Productivity Improvements: As the system is still in the process of installation, productivity improvement statistics are not available. However, IKEA expects that the purchase of the cash recycler will save about 4,000–5,000 h per store a year, of which the organization could redeploy staff to other roles. These savings are mainly recognized for the cash office.

Concerns: In terms of concerns, IKEA expressed similar concerns as other retailers. IKEA recognizes that the CMTs are not cheap to adopt and that complete adoption across all stores would cost a huge sum of money.

<4> Far East Orchid (FEO)
Nature of Business: Wholesale Floral Center.

Implementation: FEO implemented front-end CMTs for three front-end check-out counters and one cash collection point for sales from delivery at the end of 2015. In mid-2016, they purchased the back-end cash management solution to ensure that cash is securely kept. FEO was introduced to CMT by SPRING Singapore, and they applied for a grant from the government, leading to a subsidy of 70% of the investment. Currently, FEO is considering adopting cash-in-transit (CIT) services after which they would be able to have a fully integrated cash management system.

Productivity Improvements:

- FEO saves 26 h per week in cash handling, and the manager expects that the company would have sufficient cost saving to cover the cost of the machines in 2–3 years.
- Through recycling small changes, the frequency of cash replenishment is reduced from a couple times per day to only three times a week.
- Cash is now deposited at the bank twice a week as compared to once a day before implementation of CMT. The role of the cashiers has evolved into facilitators of transactions, and this has allowed cashiers to have more interactions with customers.

Concerns: Currently the POS system is not integrated with CMT. They also note that while the grant from the government is extremely helpful, the grant application process can be more efficient with less paper work required.

<5> Pink Parlour
Nature of Business: Salon Chain.

Implementation: Pink Parlour implemented StrongPoint's CashGuard front-end cash management technology (Premium Note recycler) for all six branches in Singapore one year ago. CashGuard Premium Note Recycler supports Pink Parlour's staff in calculating and dispensing the correct change. It can store a large number of notes within the machine, which strengthens security and reduces the number of bank visits to deposit cash. With a very technology-driven CEO — Mr. Derrick Seeto — Pink Parlour is heading on the path to adopt the technology in all branches in ASEAN. (Currently, the company has branches in Singapore, Malaysia, Indonesia and Philippines.)

Productivity Improvements:

- With the implementation, cash is only deposited at the bank once a month compared to once a week before, which reduces deposit fees paid to the bank.

- Pink Parlour is able to redeploy one accountant to other managerial tasks since reconciliation and verification of cash only takes couples of minutes.
- Employees at Pink Parlour branches are very satisfied with the advanced system, as they can return home earlier instead of staying one or two hours to deal with cash after closing.
- Mr. Seeto mentioned that he can manage cash at ease with CashGuard's mobile app, and risk of theft or being robbed is also reduced.

Concerns: Pink Parlour does not accept coins from customers. However, they have to buy the entire CashGuard system including the unused Premium Coin Recycler. They also express hope for the grant application to be more efficient.

Since the study has furnished the case studies and experiences of every individual adopter, the next section consolidates the key productivity benefits and concerns regarding the technologies across all five cases.

(b) *Benefits of CMTs — A consolidated overview*

Findings from the case studies show that CMTs have indeed brought significant benefits to the adopters. All of the companies included in the case studies reported that they were satisfied with CMTs and would expect their return on investment to be in the range of 2 to 7 years.

In terms of time savings, the results are similar to that of overseas companies. CMTs eliminate cash counting and reduce frequencies of cash replenishment and cash-in-transit. Cashiers do not have to repeat the same routine of withdrawing float bags and balancing cash registers at the beginning of every shift. Reconciliation becomes much easier, and the workload is also significantly reduced. For supermarkets, CMTs can help save 50% of the time in cash reconciliation.

Companies are motivated to adopt the system due to manpower issues and their drive to improve efficiency in cash handling and customer service. The impact on customers and employees is also important to the adopters. CMTs reduce the amount of repetitive work performed by cashiers and widen their roles to enable them to interact more with customers.

(c) *Challenges of CMTs — A consolidated overview*

Below is a summary of the feedback received from the adopters of CMT on their challenges and concerns during the in-depth discussion with the company representatives:

• Lack of capital

Lack of capital is one of the biggest concerns when it comes to implementing the technologies. According to the adopters, implementing the machines requires a huge fixed cost upfront, especially for large retail chains such as Cold Storage and Fairprice who have to spend millions of dollars for a plan to roll out CMT in multiple stores. For smaller retailers like Far East Orchid and Pink Parlour, the cost of implementing the system can be around 10% of its sales. Besides a heavy initial investment, maintenance cost is also a key concern for the adopters, especially the SMEs. Mr. Benjamin Thorpe, Managing Director of Glory Global Solutions, noted that almost all the customers of Glory Global in Singapore made use of the government grants provided by SPRING and close to none financed the purchase solely using their own capital. He further stressed that such support was key for retailers to continue adopting the solutions.

• Compatibility of CMT and POS systems

This is a major issue faced by an adopter when the company's POS system is unable to communicate with the cash management system. As a result, cashiers have to manually key in the amount for each customer check-out. This increases the possibility of errors as the cashiers may forget to close a particular transaction on CMT, leading to more cash being dispensed to customers. Furthermore, technology providers and retailers alike have expressed that the payments process would be more efficient if there was an end-to-end integration between inventory movement and cash management. Technology providers who participated in the study also acknowledged this issue and mentioned that they have been working with POS providers to address it.

- Integration of CMT and CIT services

The use of CMT certainly changes the process for CIT providers, as instead of handling hard cash, just like what CIT providers have been traditionally doing, they have to deal with the cassettes of cash instead. Furthermore, the CMT system could have been more efficient if it were integrated with cash-in-transit (CIT) services. With an integrated system, companies' CMT can notify CIT providers automatically when it is time for collection, and so double counting of cash at both the store and the CIT office can be eliminated, forming a closed-loop cash handling process. Integrating CMT with CIT can be challenging since different retailers have different cassettes and the CIT process is not entirely standardized.

- Technical issues and system failure

An adopter highlighted that it could have been more effective if the coin recycler model from one of the technology providers could accept all types of coins. Currently, the company still has to handle some types of coins manually.

According to another adopter, several technical issues have occurred since the company piloted the system since the imported technologies had to be redesigned to function in Singapore's environment. However, prompt technical support from the technology provider played a key role in resolving the issue. This also shows that regular maintenance of the machines is important to prevent system failure.

- Training provided to customers

Some adopters implemented models that require customers to insert notes and coins themselves, which may present a challenge in terms of familiarizing customers with the machines. Cashiers will therefore need to assist and instruct customers in using the system and facilitate the check-out process. Overall, the customers have expressed their willingness to use the new technologies when making payment. Specifically, about 60% of the customers surveyed expressed that they are likely to use the CMT the next time they see it.

- Training provided to staff

An adopter has indicated that it could be challenging to convince staff of the benefits of the system at the beginning, as the employees had to change their work routine and adapt to a new procedure. However, close to all companies selected for interviews expressed that their staff are satisfied with the system due to greater efficiency and simplification of tasks. Staff training is important to help the staff adjust to the new cash management process. Fairprice said that they organize one-day workshops together with on-the-job training to ensure that cashiers can adapt to the new process after CMT implementation.

- Greater customization of CMTs

An adopter pointed out that the technologies should be customized to suit the needs of different types of businesses. For example, a company which does not accept coins may still have to purchase a coin recycler as part of the solution package. This issue has been recognized by some technology providers. In fact, Glory has customized its solutions to meet different needs of customers by allowing them to purchase only a note or coin recycler at a discount from the whole package.

3.2.2 *Survey of non-adopters*

Following the discussion on benefits and constraints of existing CMTs encountered by adopters, we switch over to consider the views of non-adopters.

(a) CMTs may not solve problems encountered in the traditional cash management process

Issues with the traditional cash management process can be summarized in 5 categories: (1) long duration in processing payment, (2) inefficiency in topping up changes, (3) lack of manpower to handle a large amount of cash, (4) inaccurate changes given to customers and (5) theft.

The fieldwork survey revealed that the top two issues for retail and F&B stores are inaccuracy in giving changes to customers and lack of productivity while handling cash (which is measured by the amount of time spent on processing payment at point of sales). On

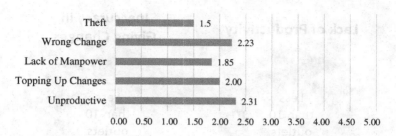

Figure 17:   Mean Score of Traditional Cash Management Issues

Source: Survey of companies who have not adopted CMTs.

a scale of 5, when asked to provide a score for different issues (with 5 being concerning to a great extent), the issue of lack of productivity was given an average score of 2.31 over 5.0, and the issue of inaccurate changes was given 2.23 over 5.0 (Figure 17). Furthermore, these issues become more significant as the number of outlets increases. For example, for companies with less than 10 outlets, about 13% stated that cash-management-related tasks are often carried out in an unproductive manner and the inaccuracy in giving changes was only indicated by 31% of respondents as an issue to some extent. On the other hand, 17% of firms with 10 or more outlets rated the lack of productivity as a prevalent issue and 22% of those confirmed the same for the issue of inaccurate changes (Figure 18).

However, it is important to note that even though inaccuracy in giving changes to customers and lack of productivity are the top ranked issues, the mean score they received on a scale of 5 is still below 2.5, (at 2.23 and 2.31, respectively), which indicates that they are not recognized by companies as significant issues which affect companies' operations to a great extent.

The results of the fieldwork survey are consistent with another study conducted by KPMG which indicates that time and effort required to manage cash payment is the biggest concern (20%) for companies (Figure 19). Similar insights are also obtained from interviews with companies that have adopted CMTs. For instance, IKEA mentioned that their staff often left much later after the store closed at 11 PM due to the daily counting and rec-

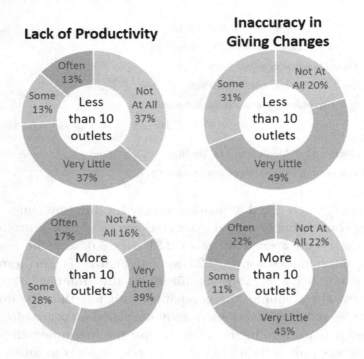

Figure 18: Frequency of Companies Facing Lack of Productivity and Inaccuracy in Giving Change — By Total Number of Outlets

Source: Survey of companies who have not adopted CMTs.

onciliation of cash. Moreover, Mr. Benjamin Thorpe, Managing Director of Glory Global Solutions, noted that the people employed to handle cash are often senior staff who are highly paid professionals, and the rationale behind this is to reduce the risk of employee theft. Hence, managing cash through traditional methods takes up a significant amount of time of a highly paid professional's working hours, resulting in inefficient use of human resources.

CMTs can help to resolve the two most common issues in cash management. In the next section, we will review in detail the awareness and interest of non-adopters toward adopting these technologies.

We asked Businesses: "What challenges do you face with accepting payments?"

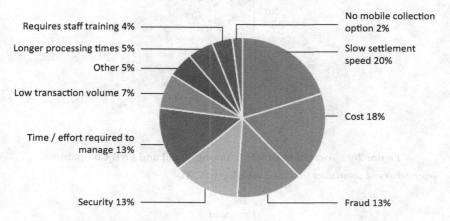

Requires staff training 4%

Longer processing times 5%

Other 5%

Low transaction volume 7%

Time / effort required to manage 13%

Security 13%

No mobile collection option 2%

Slow settlement speed 20%

Cost 18%

Fraud 13%

Figure 19: Challenges Businesses Face with Accepting Payments

Source: KPMG, Singapore Payment Report.

(b) Lack of awareness of existence and capabilities of CMTs.

We have examined non-adopters' awareness of CMTs. As indicated in Figure 20, when asked whether they were aware of the existence of such technologies, about 38% of companies recorded a negative response. While it is encouraging to see that the majority of the companies are aware of the system, there is still a need for CMT providers to inform business operators about their offerings.

In addition, we also examined the interest toward adopting such technologies among non-adopters. The mean score for companies' interest level toward CMTs is relatively low, at 2.12 out of a maximum score of 5 (5 indicates the highest level of interest). Figure 21 provides a breakdown of the level of interest.

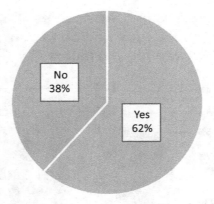

Figure 20:   Awareness of CMT Among Retail and F&B Companies

Source: Survey of companies who have not adopted CMTs.

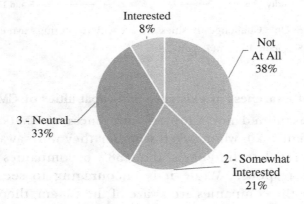

Figure 21:   Level of Interest in Adopting CMTs Among Retail and F&B Companies

Source: Survey of companies who have not adopted CMTs.

(c) Factors hindering adoption of CMTs

Figure 22 provides a breakdown of the key reasons stated by companies with regard to factors hindering their adoption of CMT. Apparently, non-adopters seem the most concerned about the impact of CMTs on customer experience. Besides that, the lack of capital is the second most pressing issue. These observations are further discussed in the following sections.

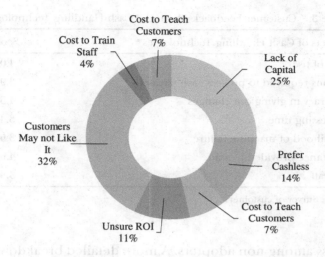

Figure 22: Major Reasons Hindering the Adoption of CMTs

Source: Survey of companies who have not adopted CMTs.

- Wary of negative impact of CMT on customers

In the survey, 16 out of the 26 retailers and F&B operators indicated that they were afraid that their customers might not be satisfied with the new experience CMTs brought about, with more than half of these 16 companies stating this reason as the most pressing concern among all others.

However, this seems to be a concern without much basis, presumably resulting from the lack of understanding of how the technologies work and a general inertia to move from the *status quo*.

Since this issue is related to customer experience, we also draw on information from the customer survey to verify if the non-adopters' concerns are valid. In the customer survey, it was found out that using the technologies generally brought satisfaction to users. About 36% of the customers surveyed had used the cash handling technologies and they provided an overall score of 3.90 over a maximum of 5 to the cash handling machines. This confirms our preceding thesis that the impact on customer experience as a hindrance factor may have emerged due to a lack of

Table 3:　Customer Feedback About the Cash Handling Technologies

Aspects of Cash Handling Technologies*	Score
Ease of use	4.05
Actions required to process cash payment	3.90
Accuracy in giving out changes	4.52
Processing time	3.43
Likelihood of machine failure	3.57
Assistance provided by staff	4.05
Overall	**3.90**

Source: Survey of customers.

awareness among non-adopters. A more detailed breakdown of the customer survey results is illustrated in Table 3.

As presented in the table, users of the cash handling system are most satisfied with the accuracy of change given out (4.52/5.0), as well as the ease of use (4.05/5.0). About 64% of customers who have never used the technologies indicated that they are likely to use it when they see it the next time. These statistics provide encouragement for companies to reassess the potential of implementing cash handling technologies.

- Lack of capital

Lack of capital to install CMT is also an important reason for the limited adoption of CMTs, especially among SMEs. According to interviews with adopters, CMTs can cost up to S$100,000 and adopters may incur thousands of dollars of maintenance fees each year. As a result, SMEs may find it too expensive to fund the entire purchase themselves.

As illustrated in Figure 23, a total of 17 firms cited limited capital availability as the reason behind their non-adoption of CMTs, out of which seven selected this as their first concern and six as their second concern.

- Unable to quantify the cost of current system to enable CMT to be assessed

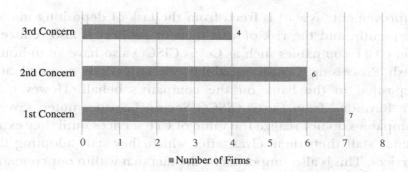

Figure 23: Number of Non-Adopters Mentioning "Lack of Capital" as a Hindrance for Adopting CMTs

Source: Survey of companies who have not adopted CMTs.

Another subtle yet important hindrance factor which was observed during the research is that companies do not see issues in their *status quo*. As mentioned earlier, while companies recognized lack of productivity and inaccuracy in handing changes as problematic to some extent, they gave rather low scores to them and all of the issues received a score of less than 2.5 out of 5 (where 5 indicates the highest level of concern).

Mr. Seeto from Pink Parlour elaborated on this problem: "Most [retailers] think that it is free to manage cash so they do not bother to invest in such a machine." However, this is not the case considering the amount of time employees spend on counting and reconciling cash, transportation cost to deliver the money to the bank and the risk of cash shrinkage, as illustrated earlier in Section 2. According to Mr. Roine Gabrielsson, Senior Vice President and Managing Director of StrongPoint (CashGuard): "Handling cash should not be given so much time, especially in the case of shrinkage or theft. You can spend two hours just to trace back for 5 dollars. These two hours already have cost you more than 5 dollars." Therefore, it is important to recognize the risks companies are exposed to by using the manual cash handling process as well as the costs they entail.

This is also applicable to the company attitudes toward cash-in-transit services. CIT services also serve to enhance productivity improvement, as staff is freed from the task of depositing money frequently, and the risk of staff theft or robbery is also reduced. Some CIT companies such as Certis CISCO also have an in-house Cash Processing Center capability where cash is counted and deposited to the bank on the company's behalf. However, as Mr. Raymond from Certis CISCO Secure Logistics notes, several companies do not realize the value of CIT services until they experience staff theft themselves, after which they start adopting the services. This is also supported by the fact that within our company survey pool, only about 11% of the companies made use of a third-party CIT provider, and majority expressed that a staff member would deposit the cash and that there was no requirement for engaging a CIT provider as banks are often close to the store. However, as emphasized earlier, it is important from a productivity perspective that companies keep in mind the risks they are exposed to and therefore adopt a proactive (rather than reactive) approach in making use of productivity enhancement solutions. Mr. Raymond also shared that not many companies are aware that CIT providers such as Certis CISCO are able to provide end-to-end cash management solutions to handle the tasks of secure cash collections, transporting, counting and crediting of cash for their business. This can help relieve the companies from all those tedious tasks of cash handling, associated cash handling risk and ultimately improve their productivity.

4. Recommendations and Conclusion

4.1 *Adoption issues and recommendations*

We summarize the issues relating to the adoption of CMTs in Table 4 before proceeding to make recommendations to address these issues.

(a) *Recommendations to companies in retail and F&B industry*

(i) Continuously upgrade knowledge and technology know-how
Companies need to be proactive in seeking cash management or payment solutions that suit their needs. The two adopters, Far East

Table 4:   Summary of Issues Regarding Adoption CMTs

Issues	Stakeholders Involved
Mindset Issues:	
— Lack of awareness that manual cash handling is costly — Misperceptions of effects on customer experience by introducing CMT	— Companies — Solution providers — Trade associations and government bodies such as SPRING
Financial Issues:	
— High upfront costs for adopting the technology — Lack of capital	— Companies — Solution providers
Lack of standardization between three players: the existing POS, the cash recycler and the CIT provider	— Solution providers — Trade associations
Efficiency in grants application	Trade associations and government bodies such as SPRING

Source: Case studies and fieldwork survey.

Orchid and Pink Parlour, who were the pioneers among SMEs in adopting CMTs, have been active in attending various conferences and courses on productivity improvement. In order to stay ahead of the competition and to achieve greater efficiency, businesses need to keep themselves updated with different technologies available in the market and be proactive in learning the best practices in the industry.

(ii) Steps for companies to improve productivity in cash management

To help companies improve productivity in cash management, this report will present necessary steps that businesses should adopt. First of all, it is important for businesses to be aware that manual cash handling can be costly. It is found that the lack of awareness of the costs involved in cash management is one of the top hindrances in adoption of CMT. During the first step, businesses need to measure their time and costs of cash handling to understand their existing inefficiencies. The second step is to identify suitable CMTs based on the current

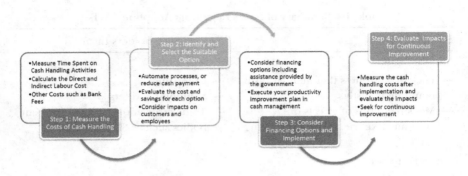

Figure 24:   Steps for Businesses to Improve Productivity in Cash Management

handling costs and business model (this will be elaborated upon in subsequent sections). Since the lack of capital is a major concern among non-adopters, businesses need to be proactive in seeking financing options such as government grants. As for the last step, companies should continue to monitor their costs in cash management and seek continuous improvement. Steps for businesses to improve productivity in cash management are illustrated in Figure 24.

(iii) Different ways to improve productivity in cash handling for companies of different types and sizes
As different companies have different operating models and thereby different cash management needs, there is no one-size-fits-all solution to improve productivity in cash management. There are two main approaches on how businesses can improve productivity in cash management: automating cash handling activities, or reducing cash transactions.

Different methods that companies can use to improve productivity in cash handling are summarized in Table 5.

(b) *Recommendations to cash management technology providers*

(i) Addressing SMEs' concerns of lack of capital
As indicated earlier, the lack of capital is still a concerning issue for SMEs which hinders them from adopting CMTs. If technology providers want to attract more customers from retail and F&B sector,

Table 5: Different Methods to Improve Productivity in Cash Management for Different Types of Companies

Types of Companies	Examples	How to Improve Productivity in Cash Management
With multiple POS and large volume of cash transactions (Figure 25)	Food Courts, Supermarkets, Departmental Stores	• Automate Cash Handling: — Implement a *complete package of CMTs* including front-end, back-end and CIT services • Reduce Cash Transactions: — Offer and *encourage cashless* payment options — Use of E-coupons, gift cards, and prepaid membership cards that offer discounts or rewards to loyal customers.
With single or few POS (Figure 26)	Convenience Stores, Fast Food/Casual Dining, Common Retailers	• Automate Cash Handling: — Consider *front-end* coins and notes recyclers and cash management software • Reduce Cash Transactions: — *Accepting Mobile Payment:* Upgrade POS terminal and encourage cashless payment options — *Use of Mobile Applications:* Offer pre-ordering or checking out using digital payment through mobile applications
Smaller businesses (Figure 27)	Coffee Shops, Neighborhood Shops, Smaller Retailers	• Automate Cash Handling: — Consider automating only one or some of the cash handling activities using *simpler tools such as cash counters* or intelligent cash drawer • Reduce Cash Transactions — *Accepting Mobile Payment:* Consider leveraging on mobile payment technologies, such as free Peer-to-Peer (P2P) transfer applications (e.g. PayLah, Dash, Facebook Messenger) to handle cashless transactions at no costs, while reducing cash transactions — *Use of Mobile Applications:* Consider the use of mobile applications for reservation, pre-ordering and checking-out to encourage customers to pay using digital payment methods

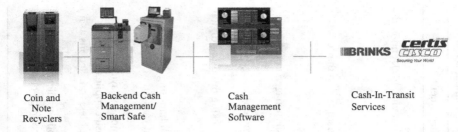

Coin and Note Recyclers   Back-end Cash Management/ Smart Safe   Cash Management Software   Cash-In-Transit Services

Figure 25: Recommendations of CMTs for Companies with Multiple POS and Large Volume of Cash Transactions

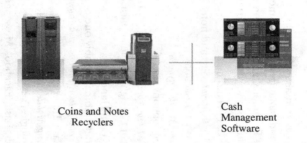

Coins and Notes Recyclers   Cash Management Software

Figure 26: Recommendations of CMTs for Companies with Single POS or Few POS

Intelligent Cash Drawer*   Coins and Notes Counters   Leverage mobile payment technologies such as P2P money transfer applications to reduce cash transactions

Figure 27: Recommendations of CMTs for Small Companies

An intelligent cash drawer knows exactly the amount of cash in the drawer

there should be more offerings that tailor to SMEs. Cheaper and simpler models that are easy to install is one possible solution. Another option is to allow SMEs to rent the machines from technology providers for a specific period of time. This solution has been initialized by StrongPoint (CashGuard) in Singapore when the company agreed to rent out additional cash handling machines to their customers during the peak time of Lunar New Year in 2016.

(ii) Changing marketing tactics to change SMEs' mind-set

In addition to emphasizing CMTs benefits in terms of costs savings, technology providers should also focus on other important issues such as employees' morale and customers' experience while marketing their products. As Mr. Gabrielsson (StrongPoint) explained, "With our system, there is no more so-called "cashier", there will be only "sales assistant" or "promoter". With a nicer occupation title, short working hours, firms would find it easier to retain their staff, as well as cutting recruitment cost." Simultaneously, with shorter cash processing time, more attention will be directed to customers to enhance their shopping experience.

(iii) Network or platform for sharing of information and experience

The lack of standardization between three players — the existing POS providers, the CMT providers and the CIT service providers may lead to various problems in implementing new CMTs, especially for companies that already have a well-established POS and CIT system in place. Thus, creating an association or ecosystem for all the three stakeholders to collectively invest and develop standardized products would help to address these issues. The standardization would be realized more easily if CMT providers could take initiative to lead the process by collaborating with other players such as POS providers and CIT providers. Ultimately, the benefits of standardizing the cash management process will be reaped by all players involved.

(c) *Recommendations to trade associations and government agencies*

One of the priorities of business enterprises is to provide consumers with convenience and confidence when making payments. This objective can be achieved by enabling firms to increase productivity through CMT. When implemented, such technologies can help reduce employees' time spent on handling cash and enable them to focus more on their customers' experience. The accuracy of changes handed to customers or transaction processing time can also be improved, giving consumers greater convenience and satisfaction. While companies may face various challenges in adopting CMTs, trade associations and government agencies may facilitate the adoption process through the following approaches:

(i) Introducing available technologies to companies and helping companies gain technology know-how

Trade associations and government agencies play a critical role in promoting CMTs among companies in the industry. For instance, Far East Orchid, an SME retailer in this study was introduced to CMTs by SPRING, which eventually motivated them to adopt the technologies. It is important to keep SMEs updated with the latest technologies through more outreach activities including seminars and exhibitions on latest technologies and management methods. In addition, publication of case studies illustrating benefits of CMTs will also help to facilitate the adoption process.

(ii) More collaboration with various technology providers

Another issue is that while some companies are aware of the technologies, they are hesitant to adopt them due to their lack of understanding about how CMTs work. Hence, it will be helpful if trade associations and government agencies can collaborate with various technology providers to introduce different technologies available in Singapore to companies and demonstrate the usage of each model. Mr. Benjamin Thorpe, Managing Director of Glory Global Solutions, also emphasized the need for showcasing success stories through road shows and workshops and expressed Glory's willingness to cooperate with different stakeholders to facilitate the adoption of CMTs.

(iii) Acting as a mediator in the standardization process

This recommendation is in relation to the standardization of different systems, including POS, CMT and CIT. As mentioned earlier, while it is necessary for companies to take initiative to collaborate with technology and service providers to standardize the cash management process, trade associations and government agencies can help by acting as a mediator in case there is a conflict of interest between the different players, especially when substantial research and investments are needed to standardize the three systems.

(iv) Increasing the flexibility and efficiency of grant application
The surveyed companies have given feedback that the process for grant application could be tedious and require a lot of paperwork. This may discourage business owners (especially those of small shops/stores) to apply for grants. A retailer also expressed that the ambiguity of the application process has deterred it from applying for the grants. Therefore, it would be more effective if SPRING could make it clear on the websites/publications that adopting CMTs is indeed a candidate for receiving government support, so that companies do not have to get their applications approved on a case-by-case basis.

Furthermore, some technology providers are considering a subscription model which charges companies on a monthly basis while the grant is only limited to purchase of the whole machine. As indicated by one retailer, the grant does not fund companies to develop their own mobile application although mobile payment can help to improve productivity by allowing customers to pay online. Hence, to facilitate more productivity improvement, government agencies should re-evaluate their criteria for grant from time to time to make sure they suit the needs of SMEs.

5. Conclusion

CMTs are able to help businesses achieve not only productivity improvement and cost-savings but also greater customers' and employees' satisfaction. Multiple case studies conducted have proven the effectiveness of the system among retail and F&B companies. However, the two most critical factors that hinder its adoption are high capital commitment upfront and the inertia among enterprises to move away from existing practices.

While CMT is gaining popularity among large retailers, as most local supermarkets have planned to roll out the system in more stores, the adoption is relatively limited among SMEs due to the large capital commitment. To encourage more adoption of CMT, it is important to inform SMEs about the availability of simpler and cheaper CMT models which can be customized to suit their needs.

SMEs also need to understand the cost of their existing cash handling practices through measuring the time and money spent on cash handling activities. Besides implementing CMTs, companies can also be creative in improving productivity by reducing cash usage through cashless payment as demonstrated by cases both local and overseas.

Endnotes

1. Emptying the tills | The Economist (2016). Economist.com. Retrieved 10 September 2016, from http://www.economist.com/news/finance-and-economics/21704807-some-europeans-are-more-attached-notes-and-coins-others-emptying-tills.
2. Europe's disappearing cash: Emptying the tills | The Economist (2016). The Economist. Retrieved 10 September 2016, from http://www.economist.com/news/finance-and-economics/21704807-some-europeans-are-more-attached-notes-and-coins-others-emptying-tills.
3. Singapore Wants to Be Asia's Sweden in Push for Cashless Payment — Bloomberg. (2016). Bloomberg.com. Retrieved 10 September 2016, from http://www.bloomberg.com/news/articles/2016-08-19/singapore-wants-to-be-asia-s-sweden-in-push-for-cashless-payment.
4. Costs of cash versus costs of electronic payment instruments. (2016). CashEssential. Retrieved 10 September 2016, from http://cashessentials.org/cash-is-efficient/costs-of-cash-versus-costs-of-electronic-payment-instruments.
5. *Ibid.*
6. https://www.ncr.com/sites/default/files/white_papers/Cash-Management_strategies_wp.pdf.
7. Cash Shrinkage refers to the difference between the amount of cash collected at POS and the sales recorded.
8. The research team would like to thank the technology providers — Glory and Strong Point — for their support during the course of this

study by providing valuable information on CMT and photographs for demonstration purposes.

9. Cheng, (2016). Trends in Retail Cash Automation: A Market Overview of Retail Cash Handling Technologies. Federal Reserve Bank of San Francisco. Retrieved 7 September 2016, from http://www.frbsf.org/cash/publications/fed-notes/2014/march/retail-cash-automation-technology-trends.

10. CASHINFINITY™ — Smart Cash Management — METRIC Group Ltd. (2016). METRIC Group Ltd. Retrieved 7 September 2016, from http://www.metricgroup.co.uk/solutions-innovations/cashinfinity-smart-cash-management/

11. Planet Retail, (2015). Automated Cash Handling, 2015. Retrieved from https://www.planetretail.net/Reports/ReportDetails?catalogueID=61442.

12. Retail Cash Management — Supermarkets — CashGuard. (2016). Cashguard.com. Retrieved 7 September 2016, from http://www.cashguard.com/Improve-your-business/Retail-Cash-Management/Supermarkets/.

13. Gunnebo, (2014). Closed Cash handling in Retail — Introduction to SafePay™. Presentation.

14. Websites of various technology solutions providers.

15. *Ibid.*: Planet Retail Cash Management Report.

16. The representatives from each company are Mr. Benjamin Thorpe, Managing Director of Glory (Asia Pacific), Mr Roine Gabrielsson, Senior Vice President and Managing Director of StrongPoint, Ms. Karyn Low, Assistant Vice President, Corporate Communications at Certis CISCO, and Mr. Raymond Poh, Senior Manager, Head Operations Division at Certis CISCO Secure Logistics.

17. The research team would like to thank Cold Storage, FairPrice, IKEA, Far East Orchid and Pink Parlour for participating in the study and providing valuable insights on impacts of CMT as well as concerns toward the technologies.

Chapter 9

Adopting Job Redesign Principles to Transform Business Operations and Raise Productivity in the Retail and Food Services Sectors

1. Introduction

In 2014, there were about 189,000 enterprises in Singapore, out of which 99% were categorised as Small and Medium Enterprises (SMEs). Furthermore, seven out of ten Singaporeans are employed by SMEs (Singapore Business Federation, 2016). Productivity has a crucial role in realizing continued sustained growth in Singapore. Less than a decade ago, in 2010, a shift had been made toward making growth productivity-driven, rather than relying on labor and capital inputs. Most sectors have seen noticeable improvements in productivity, with the exception of the retail and Food and Beverage (F&B) sectors which have continued to lag behind. The labor productivity by industry moved into the positive region (0.5% change over corresponding period of previous year) in the first quarter of 2015 for the wholesale and retail trade sector for the first time in over a year. However, growth of labor productivity and value-added per hour worked in the retail sector and the food services sector tend to drop into the negative region more often as compared to other sectors like Financial Services.

The economic environment has changed and evolved to one that is increasingly technological-oriented. There is a perceptible threat that smart machines with artificial intelligence may replace many jobs which are menial, repetitive and low skill intensive. This chapter will examine the current usage of job redesign in the retail and F&B sectors in Singapore. Based on survey and interviews with executives and managers of enterprises, as well as practices and experience in other countries, the chapter will attempt to make recommendations that will assist SMEs in harnessing the strategic benefits of job redesign for enhancing self-esteem and effectiveness of workers.

1.1 *Background*

The productivity levels of the retail and food services sectors lag behind the other service sectors in Singapore. Productivity level in terms of value-add per worker was $44,000 for the retail sector and $26,000 for the food services sector. With the average productivity level for the overall service sector at $97,000, both retail and food services are effectively less than half of the service sector average. In 2015, there were 23,451 retail outlets in Singapore, out of which there are 7260 F&B outlets, according the statistics published in the Yearbook of Statistics (Department of Statistics, 2017).

Small companies are unable to benefit from economies of scale; together with keen competition from inflow of foreign F&B companies and rising popularity of e-commerce, have rendered many local companies struggling to be viable. Those retail and F&B establishments that are heavily reliant on manpower bear the impact of rising cost of labor. The Singapore Productivity Centre was set up to provide productivity expertise and support to SMEs in the two sectors. There are many ways to increase productivity, but the focus of this study will be on the application of job redesign principles. There are different versions of the definition for job redesign, but almost all would convey the idea of "work arrangement", "responsibilities and tasks", and "improved efficiency". Some authors also use "work redesign" to refer to essentially the same core principles.

1.2 *Organization of Chapter*

Following the introduction above, we made a review of existing literature in Section 2. Section 3 describes the methodology and results from the surveys and interviews conducted in the fieldwork. A more detail discussion of the insights on job re-design are highlighted in Section 4. Recommendation for encouraging the adoption of job-redesign among SMEs in Singapore are presented in Section 5. Section 6 concludes the chapter.

2. Literature Review

Numerous job redesign theories and perspectives have emerged over the years. Research on this topic spans from Frederick Winslow Taylor's scientific management introduced in the 19th century, and Frederick Herzberg's two-factor theory published in the mid-20th century (1959), to the 21st century applications of job redesign by writers from various academic backgrounds. This section serves to provide an overview of some of the most widely discussed job design theories.

Management theories mostly discuss job redesign as a method to make work more interesting for employees so that they are intrinsically motivated and become more productive at work (Herzberg *et al.*, 1959; Hackman and Oldman, 1980). The rationale is simple; people work more productively when doing work that interests them. Fried and Ferris's (1987) statistical analysis on existing studies concluded that the five characteristics (task identity, task significance, feedback from job, skill variety, autonomy) identified in Hackman and Oldman's Job Characteristic Model (JCM) are strongly associated with better employee job satisfaction and higher levels of productivity. The Workplace Flexibility Survey conducted in 2013 involving respondents who were in managerial roles or higher reported that their employees were likely to say that their organization's flexibility programs had positive or extremely positive effects on employee engagement, motivation and satisfaction. In that survey, exactly 10% of businesses employed less than 100 full-time employees worldwide and 63% of the organisations employed more than 100 but less than 5,000 full-time employees. A consulting and market research firm, Gallup, reaffirms the connection between active employee engagement and the positive performance outcomes in terms of firm profitability, productivity, and quality of work produced by analyzing 263 research studies of 192 firms in 49 sectors spanning 34 countries (Gallup, 2012).

A portion of the literature available on job redesign examines productivity and profitability issues from an operations management perspective. One of the most prominent and dominant theories is the lean production concept [see Chapter 1 of this volume]. The philosophy originated from Toyota's manufacturing plants in Japan, but has since been applied to service sectors as well, as it started gaining mass popularity and attention in the 1980s (Thor, 2013). For example, the use of handheld portable mobile communications devices to simplify job process is a job redesign project aided by technology undertaken by the Jumbo Group of Restaurants. It resulted in positive outcomes through enhanced business profitability, worker motivation, and overall work morale. Collectively, Jumbo saved about "eight man-hours per day in order taking" by adopting the new system (Lee, 2013). Another key advancement in this area is "telecommute". Merriam-Webster Dictionary defines telecommute as "to work at home by using a computer connection to a company's main office". This is another development in job redesign enabled by rapid advancements in Information and Communication Technologies (ICTs) in the 1990s. The applicability of telecommute may be restricted to office support functions for retail and food services sectors. According to figures reported in the Workplace Flexibility survey, 32% of organizations that formally avail telecommuting work arrangements reported an increased productivity rate. Almost half (47%) of the organisations measured productivity using key perfomance indicators set by line managers and supervisors.

Whether Flexible Work Arrangements (FWAs) introduced through job redesign increase worker productivity is an important question. Several other studies have identified a positive relationship between job redesign and increased productivity (Garg and Rastogi, 2006) although not all of these incorporated FWA. Bloom *et al.* (2006) found a significant positive connection between Work–Life Balance (WLB) practices and Total Factor Productivity (TFP) in a study involving over 700 firms in the manufacturing industry of four countries: US, UK, France and Germany. Part-time work flexibility, time off for family duties, childcare support and the ability to work from home were measures that the authors included in the measurement of WLB (Bloom *et al.*, 2006). However, Bloom *et al.* also forewarned that heightened productivity may not always actualize and cautioned against inferring causality from their statistical findings, since the results simply ascertained a positive association between productivity and WLB. The advice given was for firms to have the mind-set of adopting WLB as a means to improve work environment for the employees.

In a study done by Richman *et al.* (2006), it was found that FWA led to the overall well-being of workers. Apart from being crucial in employee engagement, job design has been recognized as being important for the health of workers (Grzywacz and Dooley, 2003).

The economic impact of job stress from poorly designed jobs cannot be underestimated. According to a paper produced by Sainsbury Centre for Mental Health (2007), reduced productivity at work arising from the inability to concentrate on the job, low motivation, and fatigue accounted for two-thirds of the 26 billion sterling pound costs incurred by employers per year in UK private limited companies. Another study showed that the absence of a service crew due to medical reasons for an 8-h shift costs 233% of the daily wages and benefits of that crew member (Ang *et al.*, 2005). What is inferred from the study is that if expenses incurred from absence were avoided, companies could potentially increase profitability.

Jean Scandura and Lankau (1997) noted that the benefits of implementing workplace flexibility includes reduced stress and absenteeism together with improved job satisfaction and productivity. Other benefits cited in support of off-site work arrangements were more efficient usage of transport and traffic infrastructure in order to soothe congestion during morning and evening rush hours. This leads to environment benefits as well, because through the reduction in carbon dioxide emissions, air quality improves. Better air quality fosters a healthier workforce which directly and indirectly improves work performance.

In 1965, an article by Charles Betts was published in Science News Letter and it discusses how American companies are applying job redesign principles to enable older workers to stay at their jobs and sustain less work-induced injuries. A case study of job redesign undertaken in a shoe manufacturing factory written by Rothberg (1967) found that two months after allocating physically demanding job activities to younger workers, productivity increased by 16%, whereas absenteeism and complaints about the work decreased. The findings resonated with another paper in 2005 which recommends job redesign as a strategy to reduce occurrence of occupational injuries (Dembe *et al.*, 2005).

In Japan, an aging population and the rising cost of labor have prompted the adoption of job redesign in more recent years. Rather than as a motivation theory, some of the current job redesign research aims to solve manpower shortage by making tasks elderly-friendly, thereby enlarging the pool of potential job candidates. Kawakami *et al.* (1998) recommend the redesign of work stations by using principles of physiology and ergonomics to compensate for the decline in assembly task productivity due to deterioration of muscle function occurring in the natural process of biological aging. Kawakami *et al.* (1998) concluded that the weight of an object affects the speed with which the task of assembly is completed. By reducing the weight of objects handled by an elderly worker, the speed at which they work improves, thereby increasing on-the-job productivity.

Canada documented noticeable differences in company performance between those companies that had applied flexible job design and those that have not. Statistics published by the Government of Canada regarding workplace performance indicates that 14.4% of all workplaces included in the survey have applied flexible job design as a high performance work practice (Statistics Canada, 2005). At least 50% of the workplaces that had implemented flexible job design reported improvements in the key performance indicators of productivity, product quality, profitability, and customer satisfaction; with 14.1% more firms that had used flexible job design registering higher profitability compared to firms that did not.

European countries like Switzerland began encouraging businesses to adopt flexi-work as a means of attracting and retaining talent and assisting women with family commitments to stay within the workforce. An often cited rational behind the emphasis on retention is that it costs more to recruit a new employee than to retain an existing one. Different studies yielded vastly different figures, but variables accounted for in the computations of costs incurred from the failure to retain an employees could be broadly classified into two categories. The first category is the loss in productivity due to the reduction in output as the new employee learns on-the-job; and the second category of costs is the logistical costs of arranging for replacement recruits.

Several studies have been undertaken to find out how organisations combine various theories with job redesign and how stakeholders have benefited in terms of productivity, profitability gains and other intangible benefits. The research by Erez (2010) instead explores the significance of cross-cultural differences in the process through which job design is implemented and the extent to which certain job redesign is deemed more beneficial to the individual. The survey in the research was conducted in countries where the psychographics are different from that of Singapore's. According to Hofstede's (1997) original cultural model, there are four dimensions that differentiate national culture. Within the Asian continent, two of the four East Asian Tigers, South Korea (85) and Singapore (8), situate almost on complete opposite ends of the uncertainty avoidance continuum. Depending on which perspective is taken, risk aversion can be interpreted as a positive trait if connotated with words such as prudence, caution, diligence. However, too much uncertainty avoidance stifles creativity, innovation and calculated risk-taking that is neccessary for companies to adopt new ideas and embrace change.

3. Job Redesign in Singapore

3.1 *Methodology*

To assist in our investigation, we gathered information from both primary and secondary sources. In particular, we conducted email inquiry through the use of a prepared questionnaire. In addition, we visited company headquarters and establishments to conduct face-to-face interviews with executives. Queries and or clarifications with respondents were conducted through the phone or in a subsequent round of visits.

The fieldwork done during the month of July 2015 had enabled information from 60 establishments in the Retail and Food Services sectors to be collated and compiled for analysis. As far as possible, businesses under each distinct category of retail are being represented in the survey. The online responses to the survey were administered using Qualtrics, an online survey software provider, whereas manual data entry was used to record information from face-to-face interviews and dialogues with executives of companies.

3.2 *Profile of businesses in the survey*

Table 1 shows the composition of the types of retail and F&B businesses which were included in the survey, categorized by the number of years since establishment and the type of retail business activity performed. The category "Others" includes gift shops, fabric shops, and florists.

A sample of businesses founded and headquartered in Singapore with less than 15 years (71.9%) since establishment forms the bulk of the responses.

Figure 1 indicates that slightly more than 50% of the businesses have less than SGD 5 million in annual sales turnover.

Table 1: Composition of the 60 Businesses Interviewed in the Survey

All figures in percentage (%)	Number of years since established						
Category	<5	5 to 10	11 to 15	16 to 20	21 to 25	>25	Total
Departmental Stores	0	0	0	1	1	1	3
Furniture & Household Equipment	0	0	0	0	0	2	2
Medical Goods & Toiletries	0	0	2	1	0	1	4
Motor Vehicles	0	1	0	0	0	0	1
Optical Goods & Books	0	0	0	0	0	4	4
Recreational Goods	1	0	0	2	0	4	7
Supermarket	0	0	2	0	0	0	2
Telecommunications Apparatus & Computers	2	1	1	0	0	2	6
Watches & Jewellery	2	0	1	1	0	2	6
Wearing Apparel & Footwear	2	1	2	1	1	1	8
Others	1	3	1	1	0	3	9
F&B	2	2	1	2	0	1	8
Total	10	8	10	9	2	21	60

Source: Field survey.

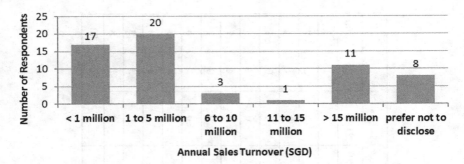

Figure 1:   Size of Annual Sales Turnover

Source: Field survey.

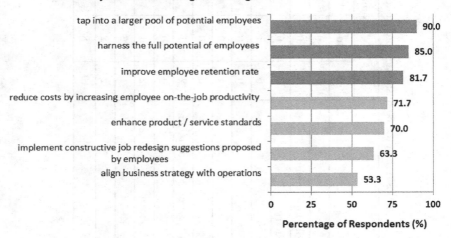

Figure 2:   Businesses' Main Objectives for Pursuing Job Redesign

Source: Field survey.

3.3 *Motives for adopting job redesign*

As Figure 2 shows, the top three objectives for implementing job redesign are (1) to tap into a larger pool of job candidates (90%), (2) to harness the full job capabilities of employees (85%) and (3) to improve employee retention rate (81.7%).

The entrance of international brands and rising labor costs continue to be challenges with which SMEs have to cope. Multinational companies are developing markets in Asia as part of their business expansion strategy. For instance, an American apparel brand has recently opened its first outlet at Vivo City, adding to the competition in the retail market, while a UK-based toy company is expected to launch its flagship store in Singapore shortly. Even without the entrance of these brick and mortar international retail brands, the proliferation of online shopping has become a threat to the viability of retail SMEs in Singapore. An exception of this are consumers that prefer to gather information on price, product specifications, convenient outlet locations from websites operated by retail shops, prior to purchasing in the physical store. Thus, if well managed, online shopping could become a competitive advantage to both retail and F&B alike.

In recent years, local apparel brands such as Osmose have been actively developing their online shopping website in order to expand in markets beyond Singapore borders. As a result, responding to online questions, preparing parcels for shipping, processing refunds for returned goods and more are becoming additional jobs for workers. F&B eateries have been offering catering and door-to-door food delivery services through online websites. This strategy necessitates the redesign of job roles if manpower were to remain limited. On top of this, as competition increases, SMEs have to pro-actively devise strategies to retain talented employees.

To tackle the manpower crunch experienced by SMEs, one possibility is to first analyze the characteristics of those who are having difficulties gaining employment or staying employed; then proceed to redesign jobs that correspond to them. For example, the labor pool can be increased if more discouraged workers decide to re-join the labor force, for example, as back-to-work job seekers. Discouraged workers might have left the labor force due to the inability to find suitable work that matches their skills and capabilities or because they believe that their job search would continue to be futile as employers prefer certain qualities in their workers which they do not have. Instead of being classified as unemployed, discouraged workers are considered economically inactive persons outside the labor force. This is a potential labor source, especially for retail and F&B businesses experiencing labor shortages.

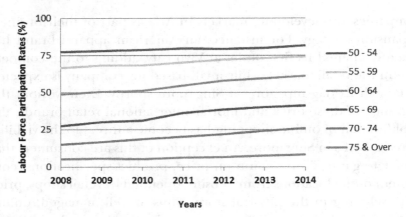

Figure 3: Labor Force Participation Rate in Singapore for People Older Than 50 Years of Age

Source: Department of Statistics, Ministry of Trade & Industry, Republic of Singapore.

According to figures released in July 2015 in the Singapore Yearbook of Statistics, an increasing trend is observed in the labor participation rate for people more than 50 years of age. Figure 3 depicts the trend of employment for older workers in various age groups.

Although the proportion of employees employed by SMEs in the retail and F&B sectors cannot be determined from the figures, the gradual increase observed since 2008 suggests possibilities of a rising acceptance of older workers in the workplace and also more jobs that are redesigned to be older worker-friendly available.

An increase in viability of employment for older workers in the retail and F&B sectors may require a change in the customer perceptions. If patrons expect to be attended to by youthful staff, then in order to achieve sales, employers would have to depend on a younger workforce. In Switzerland and India, workers are typically below 30 years of age, whereas in America, workers are usually below 38 years of age (Bureau of Labour and Statistics, 2014).

There also exists the problem of selecting shop floor staff that match the company's brand image. An apparel shop that is targeted at the youth market segment would find it reasonable to only employ sales and customer service assistants within a certain age group. This inadvertently causes younger workers who are currently being employed as sales assistants in retail sectors and service crew in the F&B sector to perceive their job as having a limited career lifespan. If this sentiment were not managed, most would concurrently be seeking alternative job opportunities elsewhere. This highlights the importance of communicating career progression opportunities during regular performance appraisals to manage employee expectations. Especially for younger and smaller-sized businesses, demonstrating good growth prospects, sustainability of business model and financial stability may be necessary pre-requisites for communicating career progression.

3.4 *Types of job redesign undertaken*

All of the businesses that responded have some form of job redesign being implemented with part-time work arrangements available across the board. Figure 4 illustrates that almost all respondents (95.0%) have applied flexible work hours, while very few have implemented mature worker-centric policies (32.7%).

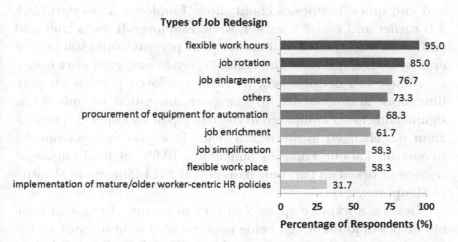

Types of Job Redesign

	Percentage of Respondents (%)
flexible work hours	95.0
job rotation	85.0
job enlargement	76.7
others	73.3
procurement of equipment for automation	68.3
job enrichment	61.7
job simplification	58.3
flexible work place	58.3
implementation of mature/older worker-centric HR policies	31.7

Figure 4: Types of Job Redesign Implemented in the Business Organization
Source: Field survey.

With flexible work hours, an employee can complete the pre-agreed number of work hours within a start and end time of their choosing. This is attractive to employees who have to attend evening classes on some days of the week, or employees who have to provide support to family members diagnosed with certain health conditions. Such an arrangement allows them to take frequent half-day leave to visit treatment centres.

In Australia, an employee who is a parent or has responsibility for the care of a child has the right to request for flexible working arrangements (available options include changes in hours of work, patterns of work, and location of work), subject to certain provisions under the Fair Work Act 2009. Employers who decide to refuse a request must provide 'reasonable grounds' citing reasons for the refusal (Fair Work Act 2009, Sect 65). Other places that have enacted right to request laws relating to flexible work arrangements include the UK, New Zealand, and the State of Vermont in the US.

For employers, one of the more tangible benefits gained through flexible work hours may be in terms of cost savings. It is possible to increase retail or F&B operating hours without incurring additional wage expenses. Instead of having two shop-floor assistants ("Employee A" and "Employee B") working within the same start and end times, businesses could allow "Employee A" to start work 2 h earlier and end 2 h earlier, while Employee B starts later and ends work later. Lunch and dinner peak periods would still be covered by both employees. This is also known as staggered work hours.

Almost two decades ago, in 1998, employed persons on part-time work arrangements in Singapore amounted to only 3.1%, significantly lower compared to the UK, Japan and the US. The situation has changed in the recent years. Based on figures from the Report on Labour Force in Singapore, 10.5% of total employed residents worked on part-time basis in year 2014 (Singapore Ministry of Manpower, 2014).

Flexible workplace appears to remain as one of the least common types of job redesign being implemented in businesses. In the survey, most of the businesses who indicated flexible workplace granted this flexibility only to a few employees. The employees who are on flexible workplace arrangements are often long-serving, valued employees whose work does not require physical presence and whose work performance can be evaluated based on the quality of tangible outputs. The practice of providing this flexibility only to some but not the majority of employees is observed in America too. Based on statistics from the National Study of Employers 2014 conducted by the Families and Work Institute in New York, there are 10 times more employers that allowed some employees to work from home on a regular basis (38%), compared to the percentage of employers that granted it to majority or all of their employees (3%).

3.5 *Challenges encountered with job redesign*

As Figure 5 shows, almost two-thirds (61.7%) of the respondents in the retail and food services sectors cite lack of funds and the lack of an appropriate measure to quantify success as challenges encountered with job redesign. The third most common challenge (60.0%) was convincing stakeholders of the benefits of job redesign.

Although there are several support initiatives meant to enhance SME's bankability, McKinsey estimates that about 44–67% of SMEs still remain unserved or underserved by banks (McKinsey, 2011).

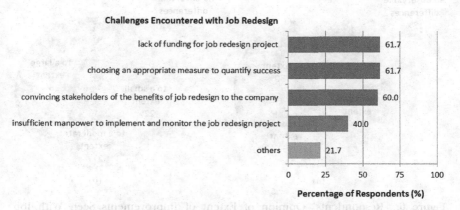

Figure 5: Types of Challenges Businesses Encountered With Job Redesign
Source: Field survey.

Low creditworthiness affects the ability of SMEs to obtain cheap sources of funding. In general, the lower the creditworthiness of borrowers, the higher is the cost of borrowing, where cost of borrowing refers to the loan interest rate. Many SMEs in the retail and food service sectors are young startups without high-quality assets to pledge as collateral that is required by many banks. One loan with exceptions to this condition is offered by the Overseas-Chinese Banking Corporation (OCBC), which launched the Business First Loan in April 2014. The loan provides micro-SMEs with up to S$100,000 in collateral-free debt financing (Overseas Chinese Bank Corporation, 2014). Knowledge of the availability of such financing products may require active search for information.

With regard to choosing an appropriate method to quantify success, Figure 6 shows the proportion of respondents and their opinions of the extent to which improvements were observed in terms of profitability (Fig. 6(a)) and productivity (Fig. 6(b)) after job redesign was implemented. Businesses that reported a gain in profitability to a large extent (30.0%) were 6% less than businesses which noted productivity improvements (36.0%). The proportion

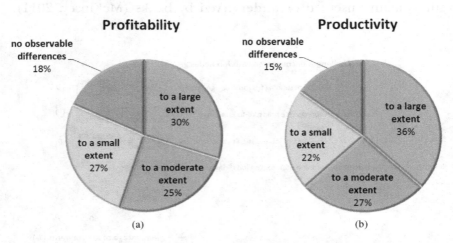

Figure 6: Respondents' Opinion of Extent of Improvements Seen With Job Redesign

Source: Field survey.

of businesses which enjoyed both profitability and productivity gains to a large extent was 21.7%.

From the survey responses tabulated, businesses who have noticed a rise in productivity did not always experience an increase in profitability. It could be that sales did not increase fast enough and capital outlay on machinery and equipment affected the business bottomline.

Capital expenditure to increase productivity might not be producing significant changes in revenue for businesses selling high-value products to a relatively small customer base. Other examples include retailers of goods involving high levels of personal attention during the sales process, for instance, spectacle sellers.

Another reason for a difference between productivity and profitability impact could be the length of time that job redesign initiatives were given to fully register their effects. In some instances, effects may be more apparent with time. Other external factors like threat from new entrants entering the sectors could have affected overall profitability. Singapore ranked second in terms of the number of new retail brands (58) that entered in 2014, according to findings published by CBRE, a global property advisor. The figures in 2014 had doubled compared to the year before (Choo, 2015).

Lastly, the time taken to learn new management techniques and have them incorporated into the business was also cited as one of the challenges encountered.

4. Flexibility & Creative Solutions in Job Redesign

This section comprises insights regarding job redesign that were shared by various retail and F&B businesses during store visits.

4.1 *Nature of business influences importance of job redesign*

The owner of an optometric practice that has a few branches in Singapore commented that the nature of prescribing custom fitted lenses is highly personalized. The job entails explanation and recommendation of suitable optical products, which could have a customer sitting in the shop for up to two hours. From eye examination, to the final step of ensuring the spectacles sits comfortably on the face, almost all of her customers expect end-to-end handling of their prescription spectacles which can cost up to a thousand dollars per pair. They have been using machines that can speed up the process of taking eye prescriptions with considerable accuracy. However, manual eye tests are still being performed to compare the test results, especially if an expensive pair of spectacles using premium lens is made. She laments that technology improves speed and accuracy, but does not always help to save time due to the nature of their business.

Another spectacle chain store says that they have been employing back-to-work employees to do administrative work in order to ease manpower shortage. This was because aspiring young optometry graduates who joined their practice usually leave after a few years, to set up their own practice.

4.2 *Job hours reduced to suit job applicant*

A costume jewellery retailer had advertised for a full-time sales assistant/cashier. However, job applicants who were only available on a part-time basis had applied. Through the interview, he found that a particular job applicant's skills and capabilities were a good match and that he would eventually be available on normal full-time basis. The business owner decided to offer the job as a part-time role in order to have him on board. Since the business scale is small, the business was able to provide more flexibility to employees granted on a case-by-case basis.

Another children's toys retailer had an employee who wanted to resign from the job to further her education at a private university. The employee was concerned that due to the distance between the campus and her work location, she would be late for the evening classes. In order to retain this valuable employee, her job was redesigned which allowed her to leave her workplace an hour earlier on days where she has classes.

4.3 *Job redesigned to improve service standards*

At an F&B outlet, the business decided to adopt semi-automation after receiving several feedbacks of crusty food debris on plates. It was found that one of the workers was suffering from rheumatism and struggled fulfil his task. The business owner decided to acquire a semi-automated dishwasher in order to retain his loyal and hard-working but overworked employee.

His establishment grew from a small family business to one that now has a few outlets across Singapore. Several Asian values have influenced his company culture, such as valuing long term relationships, thus he does not believe in hiring and firing. The time and effort spent on constantly looking for replacement workers for those who leave their jobs is more tedious than investing in automation to simplify job processes. He noted that overworked workers often appeared impatient and sounded harsh, thereby inadvertently offending customers. Now that some of the manual repetitive tasks are automated, the redesigned jobs make his employees happier at their job, which improves the mood at the eatery. The crew can now focus on providing better service experience to customers. This F&B chain in general benefited from increased productivity. Since employees are aware that their company cares about their welfare, they are now more engaged and willing to go the extra mile for their company.

4.4 *Uncovering employee's interest and passion*

A business partner at an apparel shop that currently has nine retail outlets in Singapore and whose business is targeted at young adults says that his company organizes annual Chinese New Year Dinner and Dance for his employees to mingle. He takes the opportunity to engage his staff and tries to get to know them better. Through these activities, he was better able to uncover his employees' passions, aspirations and personalities.

For instance, in addition to being a shop floor sales assistant, an employee subsequently also modeled for the company's fashion collection online as she had experience as a freelance model.

Her job scope was redesigned to become more fulfilling and rewarding because it now incorporates elements of her passion for modeling fashion wear.

He also shared that developing curiosity for learning more about people helps him uncover hidden talents. For instance, he was aware that polytechnics offered specialization for the Diploma in Business Administration course; so he asked one of his employees (who was studying there) which specialisation he took. It turned out that the employee specialized in retail management. Hence, the employee was subsequently given the opportunity to put his window display theories learnt in school into practice at work.

He noted that not all job applicants know the principles of writing a good cover letter and an informative resume. On the other hand, not all job interviewers are professionally trained to elicit meaningful responses from job applicants to gauge their suitability for the job. It may seem like an overly simplistic solution to the long standing problem of finding a suitable candidate for a job, but getting a candidate to talk about personal hobbies, interests and aspirations has an important role to play in that process.

4.5 Job redesign can be inexpensive

A food establishment which was founded in 1984, and in the recent decade grew to become a chain eatery selling local delights, invested in more plates to allow mature workers to wash them at a comfortable pace. The used dishes accumulate during peak hours and can subsequently be washed by mature workers at their own pace during off-peak hours. This job role involves operating the cash register, taking orders, clearing the dining tables and washing dishes. The business owner feels that hiring mature workers and making enhancements to workplace inventory is a win–win situation in the long-run.

Jobs requiring physical strength tend to put mature workers at a disadvantage. On the other hand, in knowledge-based roles involving administrative work, or mentoring, the more mature workforce is able to perform tasks with as much zeal as the younger workforce.

Several business owners responded that most of the mature workers are in good health and have had good education, as they have previously been teachers or have worked in the manufacturing industry. These groups of mature work force are easier to train and were able to take on more important roles.

4.6 *Provide effective cross-training by identifying skills gaps*

Ensuring that each employee is cross-trained to perform more than one job role competently and confidently helps ease the manpower shortage during peak periods. An electronic gadgets retailer keeps a spreadsheet of the skill sets of each team member in order to facilitate job redesign. The skills competency level is self-graded based on the honor system and it ranges from 1 to 3, with 3 being most competent. The file is saved in a shared drive (common platform) together with informal training notes prepared by some of the workers with more initiative and enthusiasm.

He says that this helped him manage limited manpower productively as he systematically knows who is able to perform which tasks. This also facilitates handing over of his role to another manager during regular job rotation between branches.

A simplified example is produced in Table 2. The table indicates that by cross-training Ms Anita and Mr Olando to manage the camera section, this section could better cope with surges in customer traffic. Hence, the manager will incorporate plans for Ms Anita and Mr Olando to train under Mr Xander during off-peak hours.

Table 2:   Monitoring Skills Gap to Provide Required Training

Name of employee/ Activity	Cashier	PC Section	Television Section	Camera Section
Mr Xander	1	3	2	3
Ms Anita	3	0	0	0
Mr Olando	0	3	3	0

Source: Company spreadsheet.

4.7 *Challenging to gain trust from employees and have trust for employees*

One business owner laments that he is not comfortable with delegating downwards as a means to motivate employees through job enrichment as regular customers and suppliers prefer to engage the boss personally. Employees, on the hand, fear that his business may not be sustainable in the long run and are constantly seeking employment opportunities elsewhere, taking days off to go for interviews.

He explains that this skepticism is rational as smaller businesses selling undifferentiated goods are often financially unable to survive economic downturns or unexpected outbreaks of pandemics, like the Asian economic crisis in 1997 and the SARs outbreak in 2003 where several Singapore SMEs were forced to wind down.

He believes that the solution is for these small businesses selling similar products to group together. Adopting a group image should give the impression that the business is large enough to tide through unexpected fluctuations in the performance of the economy.

5. Recommendations

The findings in the earlier section prompted several courses of action. Some of these may seem like minor things, but they have the potential of establishing mutual trust between employer and employee, which will form the foundations for change that is inherent in job redesign. As mutual trust is being established, resistance to change should be lowered. The key recommendations detailed in this section have taken into consideration that many micro enterprises and SMEs do not have a dedicated human resource department.

5.1 *Short-term PROF model*

The PROF method to job redesign is illustrated in Figure 7. It would help if SMEs think of PROF when applying job redesign principles. It is designed to require minimal financial resources.

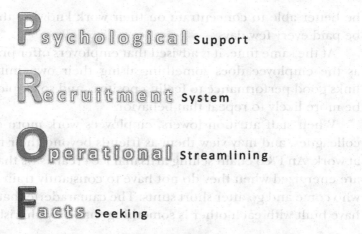

Figure 7: The Short-Term "PROF" Model to Job Redesign

(a) Psychological support (Example: Increasing Informal Verbal Communications and Face-time)

More informal communications is likely to lower the employees' self-defence mechanism and hence may elicit more truthful responses. A line manager or business owner is better able to gain insights into the employees' passions, interests and career aspirations, thereby making suitable changes to the job description to enable better fit. Managers should also note down what the employee has revealed in the conversation and, where possible, follow-up with questions that make the employee feel being cared for.

Allowing employees to directly be involved in job redesign by contributing their ideas, opinions and experience will make them more receptive to the changes being rolled-out. The feel-good factor arises from being asked to participate in management discussions, and this should make employees feel motivated.

In addition, businesses could evaluate if they are financially capable of paying flexi-time and part-time workers more frequently. For instance, instead of twice a month, payment frequency could be increased to twice a week, which is the convention in the construction sector. This can be a form of motivation for workers who should be better able to concentrate on their work knowing that they will be paid every few days.

At the same time, it is advised that employers offer praise as soon as the employee does something using their own initiative. This links good performance to feeling positive, and so employees would be more likely to repeat that behavior.

When staff attrition lowers, employees work more closely with colleagues, and may view them as friends beyond their relationship at work. An F&B chain selling artisanal ice cream says that their staff are energized when they do not have to constantly train newcomers who come and go after short stints. The camaraderie that employees have built with each other is something that they cherish.

(b) Recruitment system (Example: Applying an Applicant-centric Approach)

Not all job redesign efforts involve capital investment on sophisticated technology. A job-seeker-centric approach to the job redesign project can incorporate the effective marketing of job openings that are redesigned with the job-seekers' needs in mind. Similar to the marketing concept of being customer-centric when selling a product or service, in order for companies to effectively "market" its job roles, businesses must understand what the requirements of the job candidates are, and then cater to those unmet needs. Job advertisements should effectively communicate benefits to the applicant, just like an effective product advertisement.

Employers could redesign jobs such that middle-aged people, people from a different discipline, and back-to-work employees can manage. "Back-to-work locals" are defined as Singapore Citizens or Singapore Permanent Residents more than 30 years of age and who were not employed for the past 3 months or more (Singapore Workforce Development Agency, 2014). This group includes the physically challenged, those recently diagnosed with treatable but incurable conditions, those that have work experience but not relevant to retail and food service sectors. This group typically faces difficulties in finding a suitable job.

When the concerns and predicament of these groups of unemployed are unearthed and analyzed, businesses are better able to make adjustments to the job roles to create a better candidate match.

Redesigning jobs by identifying roles that require only a short time to learn allows the company to tap into larger pool of manpower. Recruits can be trained to undertake more important roles as they assimilate into the company and become more familiar with the company operations and office culture. This should encourage workers to apply, particularly those who believe that no company would employ them.

SMEs could find themselves being the party with weaker bargaining power relative to potential job applicants due to the attractive job prospects available at MNCs. Hence, SMEs could consider an applicant-centric approach when advertising jobs.

(c) Operational streamlining (Example: Re-evaluate Job Activities)

Retail and F&B SMEs could approach job redesign by drawing a process flowchart and listing the activities involved in a particular role. This can be done by observation, but would often be more insightful if the employees are involved. Then, it would be essential to objectively evaluate what type of skills and capabilities are required. Furthermore, employers are encouraged to get to know the employee's capabilities better either through informal chats or observation. This will help in planning which activities can be clustered into a new job role. As noted by management guru Drucker (1991), the key in raising productivity is to work smarter by defining the task, what the task seeks to achieve and why do we want to achieve it? Better customer satisfaction, more profits and better manpower deployment are some popular objectives. Lastly, employers can proceed to eliminate the activity that does not add value.

Table 3 illustrates how a business can reduce complexity of a job role and increase effectiveness of available manpower.

By investing in talent development from within, staff attrition should also decrease as employees develop in a business organization that offers opportunities for skills development and career progression.

Table 3:   Steps to Removing Non-Value-Adding Activities for Job Redesigning

1. List activities performed within a specific job role
2. Evaluate activities and only retain activities that value-add
3. Reduce complexity of remaining activities
4. Regroup remaining activities into meaningful clusters that matches worker abilities
5. Redesign workplace if necessary to ensure facilities are in place to support the redesigned job roles.
6. Perform a pilot test on selected employees
7. Monitor and collect feedback: assure employees that honest comments and suggestions will not negatively affect performance appraisal
8. Roll out enterprise-wide and continue to monitor and collect feedback
9. Ensure each employee has a copy of the job role description which lists out their new job responsibilities

Source: Author's compilation.

(d) Facts seeking (Example: Develop Curiosity, Desire Knowledge, Discover Insights)

Amid the struggle to generate revenue and remain profitable, SMEs could endeavor to maintain the drive and curiosity to seek up-to-date information of current best business practices. Availability, accessibility and awareness of places with well-organized informational resources which business decision-makers can access quickly will help busy business owners accomplish this.

(i) **Raise awareness of dedicated YouTube channels:** A picture conveys a thousand words; a video with narration conveys many times more. One of the best ways to learn something new is by watching how others do it. Spring Singapore and Way to Go have many quality video clips on their respective YouTube channels sharing productivity concepts, success stories, etc. Figures 8 and 9 are print-screens of the channel home page.

From recent visits to these channels, however, the number of views and channel subscription observed for each channel suggests

Figure 8: Spring Singapore's Youtube Channel

Source: YouTube, as at 28 July 2015.

Figure 9: Way To Go, Singapore! Youtube Channel

Source: YouTube, as at 28 July 2015.

that enhancements could be made to increase its reach. These could include the following:

- Adding subtitles to make videos accessible to a wider spectrum of audience.
- Including key words in video titles. For example "retail productivity", "F&B productivity", "job redesign", "flexi-hour", "flexi-place" can facilitate quick search

- Creating playlists is an effective way of grouping videos with the same key concepts together. Utilizing keywords will attract the target audience in conjunction with categorization, and viewers can save time from not having to sift for information that is relevant to their business.

  The company sharing the business best practices enjoys intangible benefits such as business goodwill and brand building, which are strong motivators that can drive fellow SMEs to improve productivity.

(ii) **Scheduling events to coincide with non-peak periods:** It is known that retail business tend to peak toward the last quarter of the year. It has significant lows and highs which are cyclical. The seminars, training and workshops could be scheduled during non-peak seasons to accommodate the intended audience.

For example, the business tax filing periods, coincides with the Great Singapore Sale, and Primary and Secondary School holidays. Shopping crowds also usually appear on weekends in Singapore (Singapore Department of Statistics) and local SMEs tend to be short-handed. Due to this predicament, despite knowing that they will benefit from the seminars, many businesses may often choose to forgo the seminar in favour of revenue earning opportunities.

5.2 *Long-term PROFIT model*

Figure 10 illustrates the long-term approach to job redesign. Infrastructure development and technology deployment should be part of the long-term plans as it may require more time and monetary resources to be committed.

This is a motivational model because it has the acronym "PROFIT" as the end result. It answers the question that for-profit SMEs have, of "why must I carry on with job redesign?" The response to this apprehension is that in order to survive today and make profits tomorrow, the move toward productivity is imperative today. When it comes to productivity, there is no choice between "to do" and "not to do", there is only one real option for SMEs, and that is "to do".

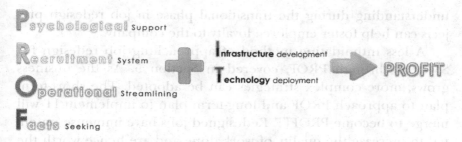

Figure 10: The Long-Term "PROFIT" Model to Job Redesign

6. Conclusion

In this study, the aim was to understand how job redesign can improve the products and services rendered in retail and F&B sectors in Singapore, solve manpower shortage issues and assess how successful businesses have overcome challenges. It is encouraging to note that although all have encountered challenges, none have given up on the initiative.

Job redesign is not a one-off project, nor is it a standalone one. In many cases, there are often other aspects of change that are mixed into the job redesign strategies. One of the key ideas is that in order for job redesign to benefit companies, laying of the foundational work has to be done. From the results of this study, it appears that the most popular form of job redesign is to invest in machinery and technology to automate some aspects of the job. However, some of the strategies covered under recommendations in Section 5 can be implemented without incurring additional costs.

Through job redesign, business in the retail and food service sectors are able to better utilize manpower resources available to them in more productive ways. With redesigned jobs, employees spend time on value-adding activities, attain more job satisfaction and are able to juggle multiple roles in life.

Quality of management has a crucial role in the successful implementation of job redesign initiatives. Emotional support and understanding during the transitional phase in job redesign projects can help foster employee loyalty to the company.

A less intimidating method of approaching job redesign for SMEs is through PROF, covered in Section 5. As the business grows, more complex strategies can be adopted. The short-term plan to approach PROF and long-term plan to implement IT will merge to become PROFIT. Redesigned jobs have immense potential to increase the quality of work done and are hence worth the endeavor.

A limitation of this study was the exclusion of questions pertaining to the extent to which each element of job redesign improved profitability and productivity, which could elucidate whether specific job redesigning strategies worked better for certain categories of retail business. This is an opportunity for further research and does not affect the usefulness of the current study.

Chapter 10

Effectiveness of Loyalty Cards in Improving Business Performance and Productivity: An Appraisal in the Retail and F&B Industry of Singapore

1. Introduction

Loyalty programs are offered by retailers in both retail and F&B contexts in order to develop customer relations and stimulate continued patronage. This is done through discounts, points, gifts or special services such as magazines or a newsletter. With many competitors in the retail industry offering similar products, customer loyalty programs are seen as an important way that business use to differentiate themselves among the competition, and develop long lasting customer relations. In order to better understand what loyalty is meant in this study, a definition is necessary. According to McIlroy and Barnett, loyalty can be described as "customer's commitment to do business with a particular organization, purchasing their goods and services repeatedly, and recommending the services and products to friends and associates" (McIlroy & Barnett, 2000). This will be the definition used by this study in the discussion of customer loyalty.

Studies have shown that it is cheaper to entice long-lasting customers to have more purchases, rather than having to attract new customers to the business. Loyal customers are better customers as they are more profitable to a firm (Dowling & Uncles, 1997). Divett *et al.*, state: "that those customers that demonstrate the greatest level of loyalty toward the product, and service activity, tend to repurchase more, and spend more money" (Divett, Crittenden, & Henderson, 2003). "It has been estimated that attracting a new customer is three to five times more costly than retaining an existing customer" (Jang & Mattila, 2005). As such, loyalty programs can be seen as a cost-effective way to boost profits and make a firm more productive in having to use less resources per unit of profit gained.

Loyalty card programs play an important role in the retail and F&B industry. This is due to the fact that in these industries, competing outlets are in near proximity to each other, especially in Singapore's case. With its small geographical area, Singapore has these retail and F&B outlets located largely in shopping centers, and a competing outlet can be just a short distance away. Thus loyalty card programs can serve as a way to maintain the customer base. With improvements in technology, retailers' usage of instruments to increase customer loyalty has gradually changed from physical collection of stamps for redemption to that of loyalty cards in Singapore. Technological improvement has made it possible for companies to obtain and maintain customized relationships with their customers at a reasonable price (Noordhoff *et al.*, 2004). Loyalty cards have been shown to be an important instrument to increase loyalty in mature markets (Sharp & Sharp, 1997).

However, Singapore can be described as a country that is saturated with loyalty cards in the retail industry. Loyalty cards are seen as necessary to retailers and F&B alike in order to stay competitive, and are seen as a medium of discount rather than a means of developing customer relationship. In fact, Singapore can be considered as "one of the most aggressive discounting societies in the world and is often used as a test bed for loyalty programs that are then rolled out in other countries both in Asia and the West" (Reed, 2012). This begets the question of whether the loyalty cards really make the Singapore consumers loyal customers, or if the cards are mainly left unused, or treated as mere discount programs. This is an important distinction for retailers especially, as large amount of investments are used to develop and maintain these loyalty card programs. This substantially affects the firm's productivity as well, because the profits that the firm can make are lowered should the loyalty card turn out to be a white elephant.

2. Review of Literature on Loyalty Cards and Customers Retention

2.1 *Understanding of loyalty*

In discussing loyalty programs, many definitions have been provided in the literature to better scope the discussion. Leenheer *et al.* bring in the importance of marketing action and consider loyalty programs as an "integrated system of marketing action" (Leenheer *et al.*, 2007). McIlroy and Barnet describe an important facet of loyalty programs where rewards are given for a customer's patronage so that customers would want to have a long-lasting relationship, as customers now receive better value from the company than what they receive from the firm's competitors (McIlroy & Barnett, 2000). Further developing on this point, Dowling and Uncles (1997) claim that loyalty programs must add value to the product or service in order for loyal customers to continue making purchases (Dowling & Uncles, 1997).

An important reason behind loyalty programs is the fact that it is more costly to attract new customers, rather than to get current loyal customers to continue patronizing the same store. This makes developing and maintaining customer loyalty a sustainable competitive advantage in improving a firm's productivity (Dowling & Uncles, 1997). The following conditions are necessary in every loyalty program cited from Ahlström and Wangsell (2014):

1. Customers prefer a more engaged relationship with the products they purchased (Yi & Jeon, 2003).
2. Some of the company's customers show a tendency to be loyal (Yi & Jeon, 2003).

3. There is a profitable group that buys the product/service (Yi & Jeon, 2003).
4. The possibility to reinforce and enhance these customers' loyalty through the loyalty program (Dowling & Uncles, 1997).

As such, it can be seen that not all products and industries are suited for the implementation of a customer loyalty program. Only industries that meet the above conditions and assumptions are able to have a feasible and efficient loyalty program that boosts a company's productivity.

Many past studies have also presented reasons behind the failure of a company's loyalty program. This is an important factor to consider, as such reasons can be used as an effective means to evaluate the current customer loyalty programs in Singapore.

These reasons are presented by Stauss, Schmidt and Schoeler (2005) where customers show frustration at the customer loyalty program and choose not to take part in it. These reasons are:

1. If the customer does not receive the promised reward.
2. If the customer needs to add material and mental cost in order to enjoy the reward.
3. If the customer feels that he or she is treated differently in a negative context compared to other customers.

These reasons are important in evaluation of loyalty programs to check if the programs are achieving their intended objectives of building a close long-term relationship with the customers. If firms fail to consistently evaluate their loyalty program with the available ones in the market, problems in their loyalty programs will never be discovered (Ahlström & Wangsell, 2014).

(a) Behavioral loyalty

Traditionally, behavioral loyalty has been used in literature and surveys to evaluate the effectiveness of customer loyalty programs. Behavioral loyalty is expressed by the actual revisiting of the store and the total budget ratio spent at a single store (De Wulf *et al.*, 2003). Strategies to encourage behavioral loyalty in encouraging repeat purchases is very different from other marketing promotions, such as one-off attempts to reduce prices of goods through sales and campaigns (Sharp & Sharp, 1997). By forming closer relations with customers, it allows the company to have a better understanding of the customers' needs and wants, allowing for the supplying of better service at a lower cost (Sharp & Sharp, 1997). However, purchase behavior does not always provide the accurate loyalty measure, "given that other moderating variables such as social norms (Ajzen & Fishbein, 1980) and situational factors (Smith & Swinjard, 1983) influence a decision to patronize a store" (Noordhoff *et al.*, 2004). A look into attitudinal aspect is necessary to understand and evaluate the entire impact of loyalty card programs.

(b) Attitudinal loyalty

Attitudinal loyalty is defined as "the consumer's predisposition towards a store as a function of psychological processes, [which] includes attitudinal preference and commitment towards the store" (Jacoby & Chestnut, 1978). The attitudinal concept of loyalty captures the emotional and mental attachment of the individual to a store or brand (Noordhoff *et al.*, 2004).

In contrast to behavioral loyalty, attitudinal loyalty focuses on the development of a long-term customer relationship, as compared to just looking at repeat purchases (Bridson *et al.*, 2008). Attitudinal loyalty can be considered as a form of commitment towards a certain brand. Consumers have favorable attitudes or preference toward a particular store or brand. Commitment can thus be used a means of measurement for attitudinal loyalty where committed customers will demonstrate a higher degree of support (Demoulin & Zidda, 2009). Demoulin and Zidda (2009) also show that commitment as a proxy measure of attitudinal loyalty had a greater impact on the loyalty program than the standard behavioral loyalty measures such as repeat purchase behavior (Ahlström & Wangsell, 2014).

In using attitudinal loyalty as a measure, many may consider it as "a mere mediator of marketing instruments that affect behavioral loyalty" (Go'mez *et al.*, 2006). However, its measurement is a prerequisite for understanding how stimuli affect cognitive and affective processes that make customers become or remain loyal in their deeds (Noordhoff *et al.*, 2004). Thus, the measurement of attitudinal loyalty is necessary in this study for the evaluation of loyalty card programs in enhancing productivity of firms in Singapore.

(c) Productivity and loyalty cards

This study deals with analyzing how customer loyalty cards can lead to an increase in firm's productivity. Traditional measures of productivity commonly define it as the ratio of output over input (Stevenson, 2012). However, this is clearly insufficient in the context of loyalty card programs as exemplified by the inadequacy in this measurement from the attitudinal loyalty component.

Loyalty card programs can be considered as a type of marketing effort. As such, marketing productivity can be seen as an effective way of measuring the success of these programs. Traditionally, there has been an implicit belief that marketing efforts do not create any tangible value, and we should cut down on its expenditure as much as possible in order to improve marketing productivity and efficiency (Sheth & Sisodia, 1998). Stevenson, Barnes and Stevenson (1993) suggest that traditional accounting procedures, in the pursuit of uniformity and simplicity, have provided marketing with invalid and inaccurate information. Too often, marketing costs are very easy to calculate and obtain, but the benefits of marketing are usually obscured in sales data. This leads to the upper management being misled about the true costs and benefits of marketing, leading to poor decision-making and strategy formulation (Sheth & Sisodia, 1998).

As such, a revision of marketing productivity in light of the benefits that marketing can bring about is warranted. Thomas (1984) identified two aspects of marketing productivity. These two aspects are the management of the marketing mix and the efficiency of marketing spending. Companies can utilise more than one channel to sell to customers but will also need to be mindful of the costs incurred in creating sales. In simpler terms, "the firm must create the "right" product, set the "right" price for it, distribute it using the "right" distribution channels and the "right" number of outlets, and achieve the "right" level of informational and persuasive communication" (Sheth & Sisodia, 1998).

Applying this to the context of loyalty card programs, we can apply the 8M framework to understand how marketing productivity can be measured (Toh & Thangavelu, 2017: Chapters 2 and 3).

- **Management and Make:** It is important for the firm to identify the right product that is suitable to be promoted with the use of customer loyalty program, and set the "right" price or correct amount of rewards associated to the use of customer loyalty program.
- **Method and Market:** The firm will then have to distribute it using the "right" distribution channels, in terms of thinking of how the loyalty card program should be promoted to the consumers, either through online social media or word of mouth.
- **Message:** In order to achieve the "right" level of informational and persuasive communication, the firm would have to put across how such loyalty card programs are meant to build long-term relationships between consumers and the firms, and not just serve as a means for customers to obtain discounts in the short-term and switch away once such discounts are no longer as attractive as compared to another competitor.

2.2 *Types of rewards*

A classification of the types of rewards that can be obtained from the loyalty card program will serve as an easy means for us to develop the optimal type of loyalty card program that Singapore consumers prefer, and also as a basis for the formulation of the survey questions. This study will use the framework suggested by Ahlström and Wangsell (2014), due to its simplicity and intuitiveness. The following sections are adapted from Ahlström and Wangsell.

Figure 1 gives a clear summary of the categories that the rewards can fall into. The types of rewards are separated pair-wise, and a loyalty card program's rewards can have a combination of the three different pairs.

(a) Direct vs. indirect rewards

Direct rewards are directly connected to the specific product and brand and the value it enhances. Indirect rewards are not directly

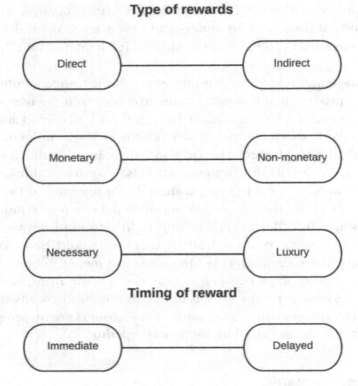

Type of rewards

Direct — Indirect

Monetary — Non-monetary

Necessary — Luxury

Timing of reward

Immediate — Delayed

Figure 1:   Types and Timing of Rewards

Source: Ahlström and Wangsell (2014).

connected to the specific product and brand and it motivates consumers to become loyal through an indirect way (Yi & Jeon, 2003).

A problem with indirect rewards is that it can create a disadvantage for the firm, if the sole reason for the consumers is only to be able to obtain the indirect reward. Once this indirect reward is removed by the firm, the consumers will no longer purchase the product, and hence the consumers are not really loyal to the firm, but only loyal to the indirect reward. For example, in Singapore's context, many supermarkets tie purchases to the collection of stamps, where stamps are given out when spending reaches a certain value. Once sufficient amount of stamps have been collected, they can be exchanged for other products such as pots and pans. Yi and Jeon claim that direct rewards are preferable as well, as customers tend to focus more on the product that they purchase, rather than the products that they don't (indirect rewards) (Yi & Jeon, 2003). Hence direct rewards will create more value for the consumers and can be considered a more efficient way of building customer loyalty.

(b) Monetary vs. non-monetary rewards

Monetary rewards are rewards that allow customers to have cash savings through the use of coupons and cash rebates from purchases. For example, a 5% cash rebate will effectively be a 5% discount on purchases and a 5% monetary reward. In contrast, non-monetary rewards is a value-added service for customers that saves time but not money for the customers (Ahlström & Wangsell, 2014). Non-monetary rewards allow customers to feel special and allow these benefits to be easily recognized by the customers, making such benefits highly effective in retaining customers. For example, in NTUC Fairprice, the pilot project, Scan2Go, implemented in NTUC Bukit Timah, requires customers to sign up for the program and receive a card to use this service. Scan2Go provides customers who have signed up the choice of using a handheld scanner to self-checkout items as they shop, effectively shortening their time at the cashier. If NTUC Fairprice were to extend this service to all branches and tie it down with their NTUC Plus! card, such a value-added service can be seen as a non-monetary reward to consumers of the loyalty card program. The intangibility of non-monetary benefits makes it hard for firms to replicate the same concept, and even miniscule benefits can lead to product differentiation between otherwise very similar products (Mimouni-Chaabane & Volle, 2010).

(c) Necessary vs. luxury rewards

Necessary and luxury rewards are rewards relating to the needs and wants of the customers respectively. Necessary rewards provide customers with necessities that a consumer needs to survive, e.g. food, medical care (Jang & Mattila, 2005). A luxury reward is a reward related to luxury goods, such as expensive wines.

The literature is divided over the consumer preference of necessary or luxury rewards. Some research has shown that necessary rewards are preferred due to them invoking less feelings of guilt as they are necessary for living (Ahlström & Wangsell, 2014). Other research shows that luxury items can result in a greater sense of pleasure. This is especially so, if the effort that is required for the loyalty program is larger; the customer perceives that the reward should correspondingly have a higher value (Kivetz *et al.*, 2004). For example, if the customer were to have to make a larger number of visits to a store, say 50 visits instead of 10 visits, the customer will tend to prefer a luxury reward that have a larger perceived value.

(d) Timing of rewards

Rewards can be immediate or delayed. An immediate reward is one that is given every time a customer visits a store and makes a purchase. A delayed reward is given to a customer after a certain number of visits and/or purchases (Yi & Jeon, 2003). A commonly used delayed reward system is the collection of reward points that can eventually be used to be exchanged for rewards. In a study by Jang and Mattila, 83% of their respondents prefer immediate rewards as compared to a delayed reward point system (Jang & Mattila, 2005). However, the fact is that most companies still make use of point systems in their loyalty reward schemes today.

Two other factors can affect a customer's preference on the timing of rewards, namely the degree of involvement of the customer and perceived value of the reward. Immediate rewards are more effective for low-involvement situations (Rowley, 2007). Delayed rewards are preferred in situations where the perceived value of the reward is higher, as it is more attractive to the customers (Ahlström & Wangsell, 2014).

3. The Loyalty Card Situation in Singapore

The loyalty card situation in the retail market in Singapore is very unique and offers a great opportunity to analyze how the loyalty card system is structured and to analyze how different competitors make use of loyalty card programs as a means of enhancing their competitive advantage.

In the Supermarket industry, for example, as it is a mature industry, it can be said that loyalty cards have become a necessary item that consumers demand, with all supermarkets in Singapore operating with either loyalty cards or some form of points system to encourage repeat purchases.

Fashion boutiques in the retail industry that have sufficient capital are able to afford to have these card programs, such as stores with chain outlets. It also makes more sense to the firms to have loyalty cards, when there are many stores spread out over a large geographical area, as consumers will be more likely to use the cards. The above point applies to the F&B industry as well, with great popularity in the F&B in offering basic loyalty cards to customers to encourage repeat purchases.

Singapore also has a very advanced credit card industry. A common sight in both retail and especially Food & Beverage industry are offers that are tied to payment using credit cards, where consumers can receive credit card bill rebates just by using the cards to pay for their bills at the shopping outlets. Such a marketing strategy can be considered as a wide ranging loyalty card program where banks and credit card firms, namely Visa or MasterCard, tie up with multiple outlets to ensure that their consumer make use of the card from the particular bank.

For example, in the retail industry, DBS Bank Ltd has tied up with Takashimaya Co. Ltd, a Japanese company that operates its department store in Singapore's Orchard Road, to provide 5% voucher rebates for consumer spending at outlets in Takashimaya Department Stores. Other exclusive discount and privileges are also provided through the use of this card.

In the F&B industry, credit cards have also been used extensively to provide promotions with restaurants and dining outlets. There are many different kinds of offers that can be offered, ranging from rebates to 1-for-1 offers. An example of such an advertisement is provided in Figure 3.

Figure 2:   Takashimaya Store Card

Source: DBS (2015).

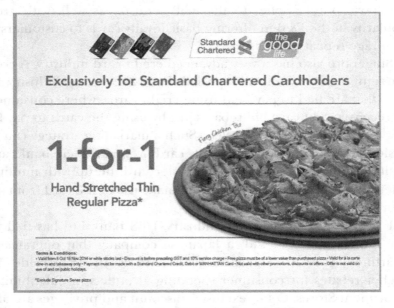

Figure 3:   Credit Card Offers for F&B

Source: Editorial (2014).

In the supermarket industry, there are also tie-ups with the credit card and banking industry to offer unique offers to consumers. This will be presented later in the case study of NTUC Fairprice.

The overview of the loyalty card situation in Singapore will form a good basis for deeper analysis and discussion in later part of the chapter.

3.1 *Types of loyalty cards*

Table 1 has been created based on the suggestions by Berman in the typology of loyalty card programs (Berman, 2006). We adopted his typology, as it reflects to classify the different types of loyalty cards in Singapore. The table has also been modified through the addition of Type 5: Exclusive membership programs. Examples are given in both the retail and F&B industry for the reader to better relate to the situation in Singapore.

There are a total of five types of loyalty programs in this classification. In general, we can observe that the level of sophistication in loyalty card programs in Singapore is quite low, and there is potential in developing loyalty card programs into Type 4 loyalty card programs.

3.2 *Effectiveness of the different type of loyalty cards*

The different types of loyalty card programs presented above have their own advantages and disadvantages. In general, loyalty cards are effective when the right type of firm uses the right card to fulfil their objectives.

The criteria to ensure that loyalty cards are effective are presented by Berman (2006). Type 5 (Exclusive loyalty program) has been included in the table. This criteria presented comes from his understanding of the loyalty card market using examples of firms from many countries that have a very mature loyalty card market. As such, this criteria set is highly suitable for Singapore's market and will allow us to understand and evaluate whether the loyalty card program will be effective in achieving the firm's objective.

Table 1:   Typology of Loyalty Card Programs Adapted from Berman (2006)

Program Type	Characteristics of Program	Example
Type 1: Members receive additional discount at register	• Membership open to all customers • Clerk will swipe discount card if member forgets or does not have card • Each member receives the same discount regardless of purchase history • Firm has no information base on customer name, demographics, or purchase history • There is no targeted communications directed at members	Kopitiam Card
Type 2: Members receive 1 free when they purchase n units	• Membership open to all customers • Firm does not maintain a customer database linking purchases to specific customers	Ichiban Sushi, Watami Restaurant
Type 3: Members receive rebates or points based on cumulative purchases	• Seeks to get members to spend enough to receive qualifying discount	Sephora Card, NTUC, Passion Card.
Type 4: Members receive targeted offers and mailings	• Members are divided into segments based on their purchase history • Requires a comprehensive customer database of customer demographics and purchase history	Foreign supermarkets, e.g. Tesco, Harris Teeter, ShopRite
Type 5: Members attain exclusive membership status through repeated spending	• Members are divided into normal and exclusive members. • Requires members to spend a substantial amount to reach exclusive membership status • Exclusive membership status provides customers with larger discounts and exclusive gifts or vouchers	WingTai card

Source: Berman (2006).

Table 2: Effectiveness of Loyalty Card Program by Types

Type 1 Loyalty Program is most effective when:	• Is small in size.
	• Lacks resources or managerial commitment for a more intensive program.
	• Needs to respond to competitive action quickly.
	• Sees its loyalty program strictly as a defensive measure.
	• Has a low level of expertise in managing a customer database.
	• Does not seek to offer differential rewards to different customers or market segments.
	• Seeks to build traffic by offering sale items to a broad group of customers.
Type 2 Loyalty Program is most effective when:	• Is small in size.
	• Lacks resources or managerial commitment for a more intensive program.
	• Needs to respond to competitive action quickly.
	• Has a low level of expertise in managing a customer database and seeks to shift the database responsibility to consumers.
	• Has a major product that is purchased by a large percentage of its customers that can be used as the basis of the loyalty program.
	• Seeks to reward customer loyalty by offering proportionate discounts to all members.
Type 3 Loyalty Program is most effective when:	• Is medium to large in size.
	• Has sufficient resources and commitment to manage a more comprehensive program.
	• Has sufficient time to plan and implement a loyalty program strategy.
	• Sees its loyalty program as an offensive strategy.
	• Is willing to outsource database and fulfilment responsibilities.
	• Seeks synergy by partnering with other firms offering complementary goods and services.
	• Seeks to attract consumers that have moderate to high levels of involvement to specific products.
	• Seeks to increase purchases by the firm's highly profitable customers through use of tiers and increased points for selected purchases.
	• Needs to offer members a broad range of rewards.

(Continued)

Table 2: (*Continued*)

Type 4 Loyalty Program is most effective when:	• Is large in size. • Offers the highest levels of managerial commitment and resources to its loyalty program. • Has sufficient time to plan and implement a loyalty program strategy. • Sees its loyalty program as an offensive strategy. • Has the ability to manage a data warehouse and data mining or is willing to outsource these functions. • Seeks to attract consumers with high levels of involvement to specific products. • Seeks to offer specialized communications, promotions and rewards to specific groups of consumers based on their purchase history.
Type 5 Loyalty Program is most effective when:	• Is medium to large in size. • Has sufficient resources and commitment to manage a more comprehensive program. • Has sufficient time to plan and implement a loyalty program strategy. • Has sufficient benefits and products that are of sufficient value for customers to achieve a higher program tier.

Source: Berman (2006).

4. Research Methodology and Findings

4.1 *Methodology*

This study will first make use of case studies to understand the loyalty card situation in Singapore better and understand its importance in achieving productivity goals for companies. Case studies are a valuable way of looking at the world around us and asking how or why questions (Yin, 1994). Two case studies will be presented, one from the retail industry and the other from the F&B industry.

The representative firm chosen for the retail industry is NTUC Plus! card. Although NTUC Plus! may seem to be too large for other firms to emulate their program, it is indeed possible to take away lessons from our analysis on their card program to be applied to other Small and Medium Enterprises (SMEs). Furthermore, NTUC Plus! is the only supermarket in Singapore that has their own loyalty card program in Singapore under their own companies' control. This makes it even more essential for us to use NTUC as an example and understand how it is able to implement their card program in the Singapore market.

The representative firm chosen for the F&B industry is the Soup Spoon, largely due to the fact that they are one of the few firms that have innovatively integrated technological solutions to their loyalty card program. The Soup Spoon is also representative of how F&B outlets operate in Singapore, and so it can be seen as a benchmark for SMEs to adopt.

Differences between the two industries will then be presented in order to better aid SMEs to understand the underlying characteristics of each industry and how this will affect their formulation of loyalty card programs. It is important to understand the characteristics of each industry for SMEs to be able to reach their productivity goals through their loyalty card program, and make their loyalty card program a worthwhile investment. Lessons gleaned from the two case studies will be helpful to other SMEs embarking on loyalty cards programs.

Thus far, we have focused on the firm's perspective on the usage of loyalty cards. In this study, we recognize that it is equally important to have the views and suggestions of the consumers using loyalty cards. After all, a loyalty card program aims to increase customer loyalty and develop customer relationship. To this end, a consumer survey was conducted to understand more about the consumer's view of the potential benefits of a loyalty card program, as well as the pitfalls that a company may face from a consumer point of view. The questionnaire was crafted to enable the following issues to be addressed:

- Effectiveness of Current Loyalty Card Programs
- Types of Rewards preferred by consumers
- Problems related to loyalty card programs
- Integration of Technology with Loyalty Cards

In this consumer survey, 184 anonymous participants were surveyed. These participants are residents of Singapore and have a good understanding of how loyalty cards are used in Singapore, and were thus be able to give feedback on the benefits and pitfalls identified by the firm. The survey was conducted using an online questionnaire during the month of July 2015. Respondents in the sample was selected only if they were 18 years or older, as only adults are able to sign up for loyalty cards in Singapore, in order to allow for the survey results to be more representative of the population.

Following the analysis of the problems relating to loyalty card programs, appropriate policies are formulated using the 8M Framework for SMEs to adopt, when they are starting up their loyalty card programs. These policies are crafted to help SMEs in the formulation, goal setting and implementation of their loyalty card program. These policies are presented with clear examples in each case to suggest to potential SMEs how the loyalty card programs can work out using strategies corresponding to Message, Management and Method.

In the method component, companies that can provide technological fixes and improvements to customer loyalty card programs were identified. Indeed, there are companies in Singapore which have the expertise and technology to help the SMEs in loyalty cards initiative. For instance, Taggo.me, a relatively new technology company in

Singapore, hopes to revolutionize the loyalty card industry through the use of the social networking platform, Facebook. It provides merchants with the patented technology to set up a Facebook Fan page that is used as a replacement to the common physical loyalty cards and promotes the merchant's loyalty card program mainly through social media. Taggo.me is funded and supported by Jungle Ventures, Spring Singapore, Streamglobal and National Research Foundation.

4.2 Case studies of companies using loyalty cards program

The two case studies, one for the retail sector and the other for the F&B sector are presented in this section. Case studies are a valuable way of looking at the world around us and asking how or why questions (Yin, 1994). The case study design adopted in this section is that of a holistic single case design. Such a single case design will be useful in revealing special ideas or concepts that a firm has adopted and acts as a point of departure from conventional wisdom and usual unchallenged norms and assumptions.

(a) Case study: Retail

(i) NTUC Plus! LinkPoints

NTUC Plus! was chosen for the following reasons:

- NTUC Plus! card is linked with NTUC Fairprice. NTUC Fairprice is one of the biggest supermarket chain stores in Singapore and has more than 100 outlets spread across the heartlands.
- NTUC Fairprice has a very significant customer base. These customers frequent their local stores weekly or even daily. This allows NTUC Fairprice to be able to easily collect consumer consumption pattern information and use that in their marketing strategies with customer loyalty programs.
- NTUC Plus! is a cooperative and the only national trade union center in Singapore. NTUC represents not just NTUC Fairprice, but holds other social enterprises. These social enterprises are NTUC Choice Homes, NTUC Club, NTUC Enterprise, NTUC FairPrice, NTUC First Campus, NTUC Foodfare, NTUC Health,

NTUC Income, NTUC LearningHub, NTUC Link and NTUC Thrift and Loan (NTUC, 2015). With such a large number of social enterprises, NTUC Plus! Linkpoints can be used in many outlets, other than just where they were obtained from. This allows consumers to easily earn Linkpoints, and spend their Linkpoints.

- NTUC Fairprice has a reputation for implementing innovative solutions in their business strategies. NTUC Fairprice is actively adopting self-service technologies, such as the self-checkout counters at the supermarket. This can complement and support the use of loyalty card programs for a better shopping experience and as conduits for gathering information on product preferences and inventory controls.

- NTUC Fairprice is the only supermarket chain store in Singapore that has its own specific and self-organized loyalty card program. This shows how NTUC Fairprice is a market leader in the field, and leads its competitors in the adoption of innovative technology and marketing strategies.

The following paragraphs will present the different features of NTUC Plus! with an emphasis on the various rewards that it offers and its potential in building a brand web separate from its individual social organizations. This potential arises as a result of the wide ranging umbrella of organizations under NTUC, as well as the existence of an online platform for consumers to access. Other than just its own social organizations, NTUC Plus! also has ties with external companies, such as credit card companies, that serve to further enhance the market value of NTUC Plus! cards.

We would also consider the *Passion Card,* which is the loyalty card used in Giant, NTUC's Fairprice main competitor in the supermarket industry in Singapore. The characteristics of the Passion card will be described briefly, and a comparison of the two loyalty cards will be attempted.

(ii) NTUC Plus! loyalty card

The NTUC Plus! loyalty card is a loyalty scheme that rewards users if they were to spend in participating outlets under National Trade

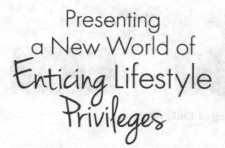

Figure 4: NTUC Plus! Card

Source: Plus card (2015).

Union Congress (NTUC) through the earning of LinkPoints, stored in their individual accounts. Through the use of the NTUC plus! Card (Figure 4) in redeeming rewards, it introduces consumers to not just NTUC Fairprice, which is the largest social organization under NTUC, but the other businesses NTUC holds under its cooperative, as well as other external businesses and organizations. A brand or relationship web, to use the term coined by Rowley, has been built and it further increases the value of the NTUC Plus! brand network. The creation of such a brand web makes marketing effort more efficient and productive, in the sense that less marketing effort is required on the company's side to advertise, and most of the advertising effort is done by the consumers themselves. The brand building of the NTUC Plus! card is discussed in relation to how rewards are earned through the collection of LinkPoints, the collection of rewards, information network online, and collaboration of card with OCBC Bank.

(iii) Collection of LinkPoints

LinkPoints can be collected by presenting the NTUC Plus! loyalty card at participating outlets under NTUC's social organizations. There are also other participating outlets and businesses that are not under NTUC's social organization, but rather under external businesses. A schematic diagram explaining how LinkPoints are earned is presented in Figure 5.

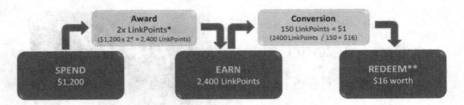

Figure 5:   Earning of LinkPoints

Source: Plus!, Plus Card (2015).

The participating merchants under NTUC Plus! cards are wide ranging and cover categories such as Family Living and Wellness, Travel and Leisure, Property, Transport and Others, Financial Services and Grocery, Food and Shopping (Plus!, Plus Card, 2015). It can be seen that points can be earned by customers that hold the NTUC Plus! card, by meeting everyday needs and carrying out everyday activities, by purchasing daily necessities from the participating merchants under these outlets.

Notably, the only shop that provides Supermarket grocery shopping under the category of Grocery Food and Shopping is NTUC Fairprice. This goes to show how the NTUC Plus! card greatly supports its own organization of NTUC Fairprice. In fact, it can be argued that the NTUC Plus! card may be established to enhance the customer experience of just supermarket shopping from NTUC Fairprice to the everyday life of the consumers by expanding on the various participating merchants. In the survey conducted for this study, an overwhelming 90.7% agreed that the main use of their NTUC Plus! card was for the collection of LinkPoints at NTUC Fairprice rather than for any other purposes (Figure 6).

For example, NTUC Unity provides health care products for consumers and allows consumers to earn LinkPoints from it. This greatly enhances customer loyalty to NTUC outlets through the use of the NTUC Plus! card and makes it an important part of the consumer's everyday life.

Furthermore from a customer data perspective, the earning of LinkPoints through other partner organizations, or its own social organization outside of supermarket shopping through NTUC Fairprice, allows NTUC to expand its customer profiling beyond

Where do you or your parents mostly use NTUC Plus! card?

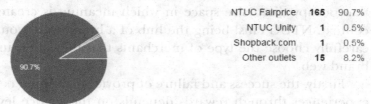

NTUC Fairprice	165	90.7%
NTUC Unity	1	0.5%
Shopback.com	1	0.5%
Other outlets	15	8.2%

Figure 6: Survey Results: Usage of NTUC Plus!

Source: Survey results.

that of just supermarket shopping. For example, a customer earning points through NTUC Unity may give information on the health supplements that a consumer requires.

(iv) Collection of rewards

NTUC Plus! provides a large variety of rewards that customers can choose from. There are four main categories that NTUC club provides, namely, Top Favourites (30% off favourite rewards), uShow (Savour the most popular musicals, plays and movies with LinkPoints!), uBid (The most-anticipated LinkPoints reverse auction. Bid and win a holiday trip and more with just 50 LinkPoints!) and uExperience (Create memorable moments with LinkPoints!) (Plus!, Plus Card, 2015).

By providing such a large range of rewards and lifestyle choices for consumers, NTUC Plus! can be said to stand at the "hub of a wide range of relationship", a phrase used by Rowley in describing how UK's Tesco Clubcard provides similar lifestyle options (Rowley, 2005). NTUC Plus! provides customers with large choice of merchants to choose their rewards from, and at the same time, these merchants are exposed to the customers who claim their rewards with the use of their LinkPoints. This sets up a brand web of NTUC Plus! and its merchants, both under its own social organizations as well as its external organization. This effectively enables NTUC Plus! Card holders to choose the type of rewards and to enjoy both monetary and non-monetary benefits that suit their needs and wants.

Rowley (2005) has stated that "Brands are discursive constructs that occupy discursive space in which meaning is created. In this context, NTUC Plus! being the hub of a brand web, would have to carefully choose the type of merchants that they allow under their brand web.

Firstly, the success and failure of providing customers with great experiences through rewards depends on the service levels of the merchants. Should customers receive bad experiences from the merchants that they redeem their reward from, the NTUC Plus! will subsequently be affected. However, if proper merchant selection is done, NTUC Plus! can build itself successfully as the hub of a brand web, that lives up to the slogan "Do Better, Together".

Secondly, being the hub of the brand web, NTUC Plus! now holds the responsibility of managing the meaning of each corporate brand. Individual brands cannot undermine the value of the brand web; furthermore, monitoring and responding to changes to individual brand positioning is required for the effective management of the brand web.

(v) Online information network

NTUC Plus! has an online portal for customers to login and make better use of the NTUC Plus! card. This develops customer relationship in the sense that customer can access and understand the amount of LinkPoints that they have, and have more information on the NTUC Plus! card and its benefits both online and offline. The brand web is also better represented in the online context, where the customers can easily see the entire web of related merchants easily.

The online portal allows customers to:

- Update customer's personal profile online.
- View customer's LinkPoints transaction history.
- Redeem for attractive items via Plus Online Rewards.
- Request for card replacement and other online card-related services.

Figure 7: NTUC uBid LinkPoint Reward
Source: Plus!, uBid Bid Period (2015).

An interesting way that NTUC Plus! makes use of their LinkPoints other than the usual redemption of online offers is that of uBid. In uBid, customers bid for travel experiences or gadgets using their LinkPoints. The lowest unique bid will win the holiday or gadget stated.

By employing such a unique bidding method, through the online portal, customers start to treat LinkPoints as a dissociated form of reward that is linked to the entire NTUC Plus! brand web rather than the individual outlets that they earned the reward from, most commonly NTUC FairPrice, as established previously (Figure 7).

(vi) Collaboration of NTUC Plus! card with OCBC Bank

As mentioned previously, many loyalty card programs have ties with banks to offer rebates based on the particular banks' credit card. To cater to this demand, NTUC Plus! has also collaborated with OCBC bank to issue NTUC Plus! Card with Visa.

Figure 8: Rebates from NTUC Plus! Visa Card

Source: Plus!, Plus! Visa Card (2015).

Plus! Visa Card members can enjoy a 5% rebate in LinkPoints at NTUC FairPrice, FairPrice Online and Unity. This encourages even greater brand loyalty to NTUC Plus! brand web, as LinkPoints can only be spent at participating outlets in the brand web. Consumers will also take advantage of this offer to earn the 5% rebate by applying for the Visa Card as well.

(vii) Passion Card

Passion Card can be considered the main competitor to the NTUC Plus! Card in terms of the large number of retail outlets it is connected to. However, in contrast to the NTUC Plus! card that is headed by the National Trade Union Congress for the benefits of its own individual organization in building a brand web, the Passion Card is managed by People's Association and its goal is instead to be "just a membership or discount card, it helps to connect members of the public with their community by engaging them via a host of activities by Community Clubs (CCs) and other PA outlets" (EZ Link Co-Brand Passion Card, 2015). This results in a difference in potential that can be achieved by the Passion card in building brand loyalty.

The Passion card is developed as an EZ-Link card and can be used for public transportation in Singapore. In terms of usage in retail stores, there is the TapForMore Rewards Programme that is offered by the Dairy Farm Group in Singapore (TapForMore,

Figure 9: Passion Card

Source: Association (2015).

2015). The Dairy Farm group consists of competing supermarket outlets to NTUC such as Cold Storage, Market Place and Giant. It allows the collection of TapForMore points much like how NTUC Linkpoints are collected.

However, the rewards are much more limited and can be used mainly for instant price-off purchase, attractive vouchers and/or items. The administration of the Passion card under People's Association limits the potential of this loyalty card from being used as a means of developing a brand web like NTUC Plus! to develop customer loyalty. The TapForMore programme can only be considered a subsidiary of the Passion card and has no say over the brands and merchants to be chosen to have discounts under the Passion card. Furthermore, Passion card only presents discounts to these other participating merchants other than the dairy farm group, regardless of purchase. As mentioned earlier, this is similar to a Type 1 Loyalty program and it does not encourage repeat customer purchases as the customer do not stand to gain points from these other merchants not under the TapForMore programme.

Furthermore, there is a lack of an extensive online system to login and check transaction histories on the redemption of collection of points. Points can only be checked by physically entering the unique identification number on the back of the card (TapForMore, 2015). TapForMore points can also be checked physically and will be printed on receipts every time the customer shops at participating outlets under the Dairy Farm Group. This limits the potential of the Passion Card forming an extensive brand web.

As such, it can be seen that the Passion Card lacks some of the features that the NTUC Plus! Card can provide. The NTUC Plus! card is able to provide rewards and information to more merchants, mainly due to its lack of profit incentive. In comparison, the Passion Card lacks the ability of developing a brand web in order to build greater customer loyalty.

(b) Case study: Food Services

(i) The Soup Spoon

In order to have a comparison with the retail industry, The Soup Spoon is selected as the representative firm for the F&B industry in Singapore. This will provide the reader a holistic view and understanding of using loyalty cards in the retail and F&B industry in Singapore.

The Soup Spoon was chosen for the following reasons:

- The Soup Spoon is a relatively large brand in Singapore's F&B industry offering affordable food for Singaporeans. The Soup Spoon is affiliated with other brands namely: The Handburger, Soup Broth Asia, The Grill Knife, The Salad Fork, The Soup Spoon Union.
- The Soup Spoon has many outlets in Singapore that cater to customers in the different geographical regions, and it offers customers the convenience of stores in their local vicinity or in shopping centers. The Soup Spoon has a total of 22 operational outlets as of July 2015, ranging from White sands to Vivocity.
- The Soup Spoon is highly innovative and is one of the few F&B outlets that offers a loyalty card program that is integrated into a mobile application. The Soup Spoon has a mobile application, Souperholic that serves as its loyalty card, and can be used in conjunction with its physical card. The Soup Spoon's website also allows users to access their loyalty cards online.

- The Soup Spoon is also representative of the many F&B dining outlets in Singapore. The Soup Spoon's outlets are located in shopping malls, which is where Singaporeans usually dine in. The existence of multiple outlets as well as the small restaurant size is representative of how F&B outlets usually operate in Singapore.

The following analysis will present the different features of The Soup Spoon's loyalty program, Souperholic, emphasizing on its rewards system, the pricing strategy of its menu, as well as the type of product that Souperholic allows the collection of points from. This analysis will allow us to see how the F&B industry differentiates itself from the retail industry as represented by NTUC Plus!

(ii) Souperholic

Souperholic is a loyalty card program under The Soup Spoon. Souperholic was initially a loyalty card program that made use of a physical card for the collection of points that can be used as discounts of its menu items. The mobile application The Soup Spoon was introduced in 2012 for both Apple and Android phones in their respective application stores. The mobile application is meant to serve as an alternative to the physical loyalty card, should customers forget to bring their loyalty cards with them.

A customer can sign up for Souperholic if the customer first spends $5 at any of The Soup Spoon outlets in Singapore. The customer will receive the loyalty card from the store itself and has an account created. The physical loyalty card is not linked to any customer through this sign up process, as such information is not required from the customer. Instead the customer just receives a card without any name on it, and can use the card for subsequent purchases. This is typical of the F&B industry in Singapore, where customers do not have to provide personal information in order to receive their loyalty cards. This greatly limits a firm's ability to connect with customers and email them with updates and promotions to increase customer loyalty.

To encourage customers to register their cards with their personal information, The Soup Spoon gives customer who registers online free 100 bonus points for their use, once their personal email is verified. Such a move by Souperholic encourages old and new customers to sign up online to receive these bonus points. With customers' personal email, Souperholic can email customers about promotions and offers to increase customer loyalty.

(iii) Collection of points

50 points are awarded to customers for every $5 spent. The points can be collected by either giving the cashier the physical loyalty card, displaying the loyalty card on the mobile application, or by keying in the mobile number registered at the cashier. These methods are shown in Figure 10.

The point collection mentality for customers to try to spend in denominations of $5 can also be used as The Soup Spoon's Pricing Strategy. In Figure 11, we can see that the prices of the soups are not exactly $10 and usually less than $10. This means that customers can only receive 50 points for the soup purchased. This will encourage customers to purchase either a drink along with the soup to top up the total meal value to a value near $10 in order to earn an additional 50 points or to purchase a set meal, which is also near to $10. Thus, we can see that the loyalty program can encourage customers to make additional purchases in order to earn more loyalty points, and this comes from careful deliberation on the prices of the food items on the menu.

(iv) Usage of points

Points can be used by either giving the cashier the physical loyalty card, or by displaying the loyalty card on the mobile application. Every 100 points is considered a dollar off the bill, and if enough points are earned, the entire meal can be offset by the points available in the card. Points can be used on any item on the menu to either partially offset or fully offset the meal. This flexibility in the usage of points will prove to be attractive to customers, as compared to redemption of fixed items on the menu, as it allows customers to have

Figure 10: Different Ways of Collecting Points (top: physical loyalty card; bottom left: mobile application; bottom right: entering mobile number)

Source: Soup Spoon Outlets and App.

a greater option of what to offset and also greater choice of what they can choose to eat in the restaurant.

The Soup Spoon also places an expiry date on the points. This allows The Soup Spoon to reduce its liabilities in the long run and also encourage consumers to finish using their points especially when it is near its expiry date.

(v) Mobile application

The mobile application is a dedicated webpage of the restaurant that consumers can refer and visit easily. It provides customers

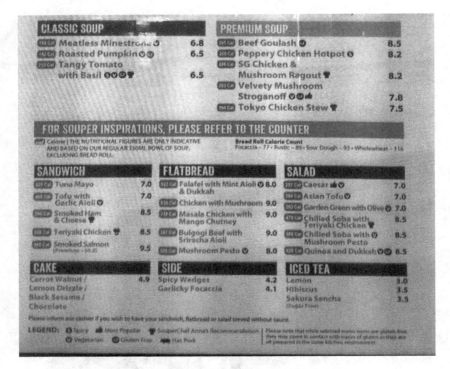

Figure 11:   The Soup Spoon Menu

Source: The Soup Spoon, photograph.

the list of transactions that the customer has done and also allows customers to check the amount of points that they have collected. The mobile application also provides customers with a list of all outlets and a map of outlets for customers to find the nearest outlet near them. The application also provides customers with a list of menu items and also the specials that The Soup Spoon is having.

4.3 *Comparison of the two case studies*

There are substantive similarities in the objectives of having a loyalty cards program despite the difference in nature of businesses. The two companies considered in the case studies make use of point systems to reward their customers. There is also an interest toward the use of technology in their respective loyalty programs, through websites for NTUC Plus! and mobile applications for The Soup Spoon. All these are aimed at building customer loyalty in order to make the marketing efforts of these firms to be more productive.

Perhaps of greater interest are the main differences between the two industries in their ability to develop customer loyalty programs. These main differences result from the nature of these industries and leads to a different kind of customer loyalty card program implemented. The differences can be elucidated from the three perspectives: Share of Wallet, External Partnerships and Product Loyalty.

(a) Share of wallet

Share of wallet refers to the share of purchases in the category, or more simply put, the amount of customer total spending that a particular company captures (Keiningham *et al.*, 2007).

The retail industry is better able to drive better share of wallet. This is simply due to the fact that an enterprise in the retail industry, such as the supermarket, provides a large variety of goods from different companies. Customers visit retail shops often and buy these items in small quantity, allowing the retail industry to capture a larger share of wallet. In contrast, the F&B industry captures a smaller share of wallet. This is due to the fact that customers visit restaurants infrequently, and this makes up a smaller share of wallet.

(b) External partnership

Enterprises in the retail industry are able to have many external partnerships for their loyalty programs as the retail industry provides a large number of goods and services. This larger number of goods and services provides opportunities to cross-sell or up-sell products, for example, in suggesting accessories that are provided by other merchants as rewards that customers can redeem (Berman, 2006).

In contrast, the F&B industry is unable to have as many external partnerships due to the limited number of products that it has, which is just the food that they have in their menu. This limits the redemption of items for restaurants in the F&B industry to only that of the restaurant's own food items in the menu. This limits the potential of the F&B industry in the development of a brand web as well, unless the particular F&B outlet expands its own menu items to offer various types of food under the same brand name that can attract customers. The retail industry (especially supermarkets) is better able to establish such a brand web, due to the larger amount of goods and services it can provide.

(c) Product loyalty

Loyalty card programs in the F&B industry are easier to implement and results are also easier to achieve as compared to the retail industry. This is due to the fact that customers are loyal to the product that the F&B industry produces itself.

For example, a customer who loves drinking soup will be loyal to The Soup Spoon and will take up the loyalty card program as a supplement to his interest in having soup at The Soup Spoon. In this sense, The Soup Spoon is the only outlet that provides such types of soup that is suitable to the customer's liking and preferences. The customer is loyal to The Soup Spoon because he likes the way it is prepared at the Soup Spoon.

However, in the retail industry, such product loyalty is much less prominent. For example, if a customer is shopping for clothes, he will not definitely have to purchase it from a certain brand or outlet. In fact, many may choose to buy from different brands and mix and match these clothes according to the style he likes. The customer is less loyal to the product itself as compared to the F&B industry.

As such, we can see that it will be easier to develop a loyalty card program for the F&B industry as the customers are already loyal to the product itself. In comparison, the retail industry offers largely similar products, and hence the loyalty card program needs to provide sufficient rewards to attract a substantial customer base.

4.4 *Lessons from the two case studies for SMEs*

Lessons learnt from the case studies can be applied to the Small and Medium Enterprises (SME) in the retail and F&B industries. These lessons include:

(a) Brand web — Alliance for SMEs

The main takeaway from the NTUC Plus! case study was the importance of the formation of brand webs. Although this idea is derived from NTUC, which is a rather large cooperative, as compared to the usual smaller-sized SMEs, this idea can easily be applied in the context of SMEs.

SMEs can similarly form such brand webs, in the form of an alliance. The possibility of this will be elaborated in the proposed policies section as exemplified by the Wing Tai Retail Card. Such a brand hub/alliance, can be considered as a production network that combines multiple SMEs dealing with similar products under the same loyalty card program. The purpose of such a brand web moves past merely developing customer loyalty. It can be thought of as a business ecosystem that employs horizontal integration, where companies at the same stage of production are merged together under this brand web. The various SMEs are horizontally integrated. These SMEs become a part of a production network that can reduce costs of advertising and procurement, when they collaborate and advertise together through the same loyalty card program. Such cost reduction can also be shared with consumers. However, such a brand web can dominate and monopolize the market with the hub of the brand web (the main firm organizing the loyalty card program) capturing a large market share. However, this does not rule out the possibility that other firms in the brand web become dominant subsequently. Disruptive innovation in the industries such as technology has increasingly allowed firms to either outsource the development of such brand webs to other companies or to develop their own brand webs much more easily. This is exemplified by the development of the multiple loyalty apps that can be used on mobile phones, such as Perx and Taggo.me. These improvements in technology are very relevant to SMEs, as they provide the ease of the set-up of brand webs, and these will be elaborated later on in the study.

Thus, we can see that the lessons from NTUC Plus!, being the only company that has successfully implemented such an extensive brand web, provides SMEs with a good general direction and increases the sophistication in their current type of loyalty card program.

(b) Customization of loyalty card program for individual SMEs

Drawing lessons from The Soup Spoon, we realize that the main difference in the retail industry and F&B industry is in product loyalty. As such, the development and implementation of loyalty card programs must be customized toward the different needs of each individual industry and their related competitors. SMEs must understand that the policies recommended cannot be considered as one-size-fits-all, and owners must modify these policies based on the needs of their industries. Furthermore, the type of loyalty card program implemented is also important. SMEs must choose the right type of loyalty card and evaluate how the loyalty card has achieved a firm's productivity goals. The following table (Table 3) is presented by Berman in the assessment of a customer loyalty program (Berman, 2006). This table aims to provide questions for SMEs to reflect upon in order to improve their program after implementation and think of possible ways of customising their loyalty card programs, sorted according to the types of loyalty program presented in the literature review.

(c) Advertising — A caveat

Loyalty card programs in Singapore make use of emails provided by consumers to mass-send information on promotions and discounts to customers. In the implementation of loyalty card programs by SMEs, this approach may be the favored form of advertising as it entails minimal costs to send these information, once the emails of the consumers have been obtained through their sign ups.

However, SMEs must realize that such advertising may put off consumers rather than attract them to retail and F&B outlets. As noted by Reed, "A recent report produced by the Chief Marketing Officer Council said that 54% of loyalty program members in a new study say that they feel so inundated by irrelevant messages and impersonal emails that they're ready to unsubscribe from the program and switch brands" (Reed, 2012).

Other key findings from the report by Reed (2012) include:

- Consumers say they've become "promotion-weary". Only 40% say they bother to open loyalty program newsletter emails – emails that they themselves volunteered to receive.

Table 3: Assessing Loyalty Card Programs

	Does the Loyalty Program
Type 1 Program	• Vary special offers to attract a wide proportion of members on a periodic basis? • Require minimum purchases to get special offers (to discourage cherry pickers)? • Change the featured specials to keep the program fresh from a consumer's perspective? • Limit the number of times a consumer can purchase a special to discourage consumers from stocking up? • Monitor related item purchases by consumers?
Type 2 Program	• Compute coupon redemption rates? • Have an expiration date to reduce redemptions by small, infrequent customers? • Consider extending the offer to other goods and services?
Type 3 Program	• Use double or triple points as a means of reducing markdowns for end-of-season merchandise or closeouts? • Base point value on a product's profit margin? • Evaluate partners' contributions in gifts? • Evaluate partners' contributions in ease of accumulating points? • Cross-sell the loyalty program among partners? • Use a closed program to offer points to its most profitable customers? • Develop a differential point structure to reward heavy users? • Enable members to track activity, points, and award shipment through the web? • Use a minimum purchase quantity or a fee to discourage low potential customers from applying? • Drop out unprofitable members or members with low purchase activity over a given time period? • Evaluate reward options based on consumer interest versus difficulty in generating sufficient points? • Allow members to purchase points to facilitate obtaining a reward? • Consider outsourcing the member database, the loyalty program web site and other facets of the loyalty program? • Use loyalty membership usage history data to reduce consumer defections? • Combine free goods and services and rewards with special services (such as special customer support access, invitations to trunk shows, personal shoppers, etc.)?

(*Continued*)

Table 3: *(Continued)*

	Does the Loyalty Program
Type 4 Loyalty Card Program	• Use specialized communications to members based on their purchase history? • Use specialized promotions to members based on their purchase history? • Use specialized rewards to members based on their purchase history? • Have well-defined data mining capability? • Use loyalty membership usage history data to reduce consumer defections? • Use loyalty membership data to determine consumer trends? • Use loyalty membership data to determine advertising effectiveness? • Sell aggregate data to suppliers?
Type 5 Loyalty Card Program	• Use a tiered structure to increase member sales? • Enable members to track activity, points, and award shipment through the web? • Use a minimum purchase quantity or a fee to discourage low potential customers from applying? • Drop out unprofitable members or members with low purchase activity over a given time period? • Use loyalty membership usage history data to reduce consumer defections?

Source: Berman, 2006.

- Almost 20% of consumers say they've never received a personalized communication that factors in their preferences or behavior.
- Nearly three-quarters (73%) say they've received one-size-fits-all promos for products or services they already have.

Rather than increasing brand awareness and consumer loyalty, such mass email communication can even create negative sentiment toward the SMEs themselves. This is definitely the opposite of building brand loyalty for customers. It counteracts the positive effects that loyalty card programs bring about. Instead, advertising should be targeted and customized to the needs of the consumers. Although this may cost higher in terms of managing consumer data and identifying consumer profiles, this may allow customers to have a more positive brand experience toward the SME and the loyalty card program itself.

4.5 *Consumers' response to loyalty cards program*

Loyalty cards have been in use and owned by many Singaporeans. In our survey, 73.2% of our respondents own at least one loyalty card (Figure 12).

This shows that loyalty cards have been around for a substantial amount of time, and firms are definitely able to reap the benefits of these loyalty card programs, which can include benefits other than its main goal of customer loyalty. At the same time, some loyalty card programs may have failed to achieve their target goal of customer loyalty and high retention effect. In the following sections, the potential benefits that loyalty card programs can offer and the potential pitfalls that loyalty card programs have are summarized. These benefits and pitfalls are supported by the consumer survey conducted, whenever possible.

(a) **Access to consumer information and consumer trends**

Type 3 or Type 4 loyalty card programs allow for collection of information on consumers' consumption patterns as well as data on items purchased in each transaction. Firms can make use of this information to profile their customers and provide specific offers to specific

How many loyalty cards do you own in the retail industry (eg. supermarkets and fashion industry?)

0	**49**	26.8%
1	**52**	28.4%
2	**34**	18.6%
3	**12**	6.6%
More than 3	**36**	19.7%

Figure 12:   Survey Results — Number of Loyalty Cards Owned

Source: Survey Results

Will you be willing to provide personal information to facilitate the planning of specific rewards based on your consumption?

Yes	**88**	47.8%
No	**96**	52.2%

Figure 13:   Survey Results — Personal Information

Source: Survey results.

group of customers. This information can also be used for "inventory management, pricing, and promotional planning" (Berman, 2006) where the individual customers need not be identified.

In the consumer survey of this study, 52.2% of respondents indicated that they are willing to provide personal information in order to better facilitate the planning of rewards and communication to the customers from the firm (Figure 13). This indicates the possibility of making use of consumer information and profiling in the Singapore loyalty card market to improve the efficiency and productivity in marketing effort. However, 52.2% indicates a roughly neutral stand toward providing personal information, and firms may need to step up their efforts in promising customers that customer privacy measures will not be breached through data leaks.

Even if customers are unwilling to provide specific customer data and have privacy concerns toward being profiled, the agglomeration of data from loyalty cards that can be anonymous will allow for better inventory management, pricing and promotional planning. This allows a firm to be more productive in reducing wastage on ordering too much and hence incurring unnecessary additional costs, and it also provides a firm with data on implementing the optimal pricing strategy. The firm is now able to find the "right" price for the product, and distribute using the "right" distributional channels, by having sufficient inventory for the product when necessary, based on consumption trends recorded.

(b) Increasing demand in slow seasons

A loyalty program can boost demand in slow seasons, if more rewards or offers are given for the purchase of the same quantity of goods. For example, if we were to look at the case study of NTUC Plus!, more LinkPoints can be given for the purchase of certain goods that are facing low demand. Changing consumer behavior through the use of providing more rewards is currently being done by NTUC Plus! For example, in its recent promotions, a customer can earn two times more Linkpoints if they were to shop at its own participating merchant, EverBest. Indeed, in the consumer's survey of this study, 63.6% of the respondents indicated that they are likely to purchase items that reward them with more LinkPoints (Figure 14).

Assume that you hold a loyalty card that provides you with reward points. Will you purchase more of a particular item, if purchasing such a particular item gives you 2 times more reward points

Yes **117** 63.6%
No **67** 36.4%

Figure 14: Survey Results — Increasing Demand in Slow Seasons
Source: Survey results.

Such promotions are targeted and should make a firm much more productive and reduce wastage (Berman, 2006). Furthermore, through the loyalty card program, the data collected can be monitored to identify which types of promotions have been successful, and hence more efficient allocation of promotion budgets can be effected. In this regard, there are two ways in which the firm can make more optimal decisions. Firstly, the firms are able to decide on the "right" goods to carry out such promotions for, with these goods being selected as there is a high inventory of them. Secondly, the firms are able to achieve the "right" level of informational and persuasive communication by understanding what kinds of promotional methods will work by working through the statistics obtained regarding the increase in sales after a promotional period.

(c) Lower Advertising Costs

With consumer information obtained through consumers signing up for the program, firms can now make use of emails collected to advertise their new products at a very low cost.

For example, Sephora sends customers advertisements regarding their new products and states explicitly in the emails that these new cosmetic products are available at a special price for members only (Figure 15). This encourages customers to visit their stores to check out these new products that will only be exclusively offered to them at a discounted price for a promotional period. Furthermore, Sephora also makes use of emails to offer free samples to their members, where members have to buy a certain product in order to receive these free samples. Such samples encourage members to makes additional trips and purchases in Sephora as well.

(d) Exposure to merchants that provide rewards

In the NTUC Plus! loyalty program, there are many other merchants that provide rewards to customers in the redemption of loyalty card rewards. In order to better use their hard-earned points, customers choose to spend time and effort looking through the list of merchants to find out the reward that best suits them. This exposes the customers to the merchants that provide rewards to customers.

Figure 15: Sephora Email Advertisement, (top: free sample, bottom: special offers for members)

Source: Author's compilation.

Furthermore, it establishes the brand web built up by the loyalty card program and establishes the loyalty card as the hub of the brand web.

In consumers' survey of this study, 53.8% of respondents agreed that through the browsing of the rewards they were exposed to merchants that they have not heard of before, and 85.3% agreed that they will be willing to try out their products outside of using reward points if the experience they had with the merchant was good (Figure 16). These results suggest that it is important to further improve on the exposure towards merchants, but once a good experience has been perceived by customers, it will allow these merchants to have a greater increase in sales.

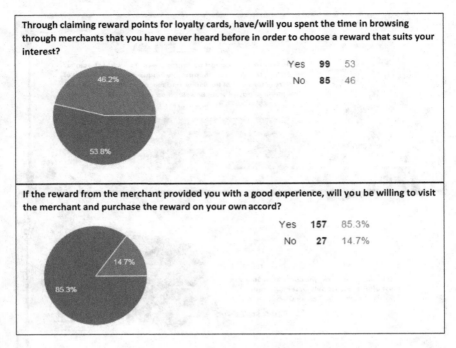

Figure 16:   Survey Results — Merchant Exposure

Source: Survey results.

4.6 *Potential pitfalls of loyalty card programs*

In this section, we consider the pitfalls of loyalty card programs. These pitfalls are summarized from the interview with NTUC Plus! and also from literature written by Stone *et al.* (2003) and Berman (2006).

(a) Market saturation

In mature markets, firms competing often offer loyalty programs with similar rewards, requirements and benefits. In such a competitive environment, firms are expected to have a loyalty card program and reward their customers. Firms are unable to withdraw their loyalty program and terminate it, fearing the possibility of losing market share to competitors, but at the same time, are unable to secure a long-term competitive advantage over other firms due to the high costs of maintaining the loyalty card program, or the ease of copying of the loyalty card program (Berman, 2006).

However, this does not seem to be the situation in Singapore right now. In the retail industry, the most established loyalty card program is the card program by NTUC Plus!, as noted in the case study. Furthermore, supermarkets such as Sheng Siong, (a relatively new entrant in Singapore's supermarket industry) have started loyalty card programs only recently.

As noted in the case study, other supermarkets under the Dairy Group, such as Giant and Cold Storage do not have an established loyalty card program as comprehensive as that of NTUC Plus! As such, the retail industry in Singapore does not have a very saturated market as compared to other countries.

(b) Low consumer commitment

There may be low levels of consumer commitment to a particular loyalty card if there is no specific difference between the loyalty programs as perceived by the consumers. Consumers can easily join multiple loyalty programs and switch loyalty between multiple programs in order to derive benefits from all programs. This defeats the purpose of loyalty card programs, which is to build customer loyalty.

In Singapore's context, consumers may own multiple loyalty cards and are not loyal to a specific customer loyalty program. In our survey, a proxy of this measure is through the frequency a customer uses their loyalty cards. Furthermore 67.4% of the respondents indicate that they never or only sometimes use their loyalty cards (Figure 17).

To make the point stronger, 53.3% of respondents indicate that the main reason for not using their loyalty card is the fact that they do not frequent the same store usually (Figure 18).

This further substantiates the point that the current loyalty program may be insufficient in building customer loyalty.

One conjecture is that the low consumers' commitment to loyalty card is due to the consumers' dislike of technological feature embedded in the loyalty card, or the lack of sophistication in the cards to meet the needs of the consumers.

How often do you use your loyalty cards?

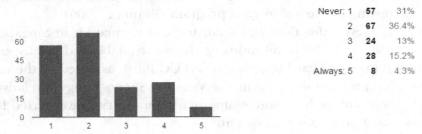

Never: 1	**57**	31%
2	**67**	36.4%
3	**24**	13%
4	**28**	15.2%
Always: 5	**8**	4.3%

Figure 17: Survey Results — Frequency of Loyalty Card Usage

Source: Survey results.

What are the reasons why you do not use your loyalty cards?

Too cumbersome to bring around	**48**	26.7%
The rewards are worth too little	**58**	32.2%
The rewards take too long to accumulate	**70**	38.9%
I do not frequent the same store usually	**96**	53.3%
I do not have loyalty cards	**42**	23.3%
Other	**7**	3.9%

Figure 18: Survey Results — Reasons for Not Using Loyalty Cards

Source: Survey results.

Our survey results have also confirmed that customers are willing to try out these new technologies as a replacement to the current loyalty card. Our respondents were asked to rank, on a 5-Level Likert scale, the likelihood that they will try out such technologies on a mobile phone. A mean of 3.614 is obtained, showing great promise in the adoption of these technologies (Figure 19).

(c) Drawing lessons from consumers' survey results for SMEs

As mentioned earlier, the top reason for consumers is that customers do not patronise the same store regularly. More than half of the respondents (53.3%) pick that as the reason for not using their loyalty cards. This is especially important for SMEs, as they do not have many outlets located across Singapore, further exacerbating this problem of limited usage of the loyalty cards.

Integration of cards into a smartphone will encourage me to use loyalty cards more

Strongly Disagree: 1	**5**	2.7%
2	**23**	12.5%
3	**41**	22.3%
4	**84**	45.7%
Strongly Agree: 5	**31**	16.8%

Figure 19: Survey Results — Integrating Loyalty Cards with Technology
Source: Survey results.

As such, to make loyalty cards more effective, the main solution proposed by this study is the formation of a brand web with multiple SMEs in this brand web itself. This brand web is similar to how NTUC Plus! has organized their loyalty card program and will be further discussed in the Proposed Policies section.

The second reason why consumers do not use their loyalty card often is the fact that the rewards take too long to accumulate. This is especially significant for the SMEs in the F&B industry. Often, F&B industries require consumers to visit a store multiple times to collect stamps to exchange for rewards. For example in Ichiban Sushi, stamps are collected from the store for every $20 spent. Upon reaching certain amount of stamps, side dishes from special menus can be redeemed or a cash voucher can be redeemed.

Such a loyalty card system takes too long to get the reward, and customers prefer a more immediate reward. Perhaps a more preferred way of organizing loyalty card programs is that adopted by The Soup Spoon where rewards can be redeemed any time, in the form of rebates of their meals. This let customers feel that the loyalty card program is worthwhile and encourages them to revisit the stores. SMEs in the F&B industry must understand that customers do not frequent their store often as there simply are too many alternatives in the F&B industry, and thus rewards cannot take too long to accumulate. If rewards take too long to accumulate, customers may not appreciate much about the loyalty card program.

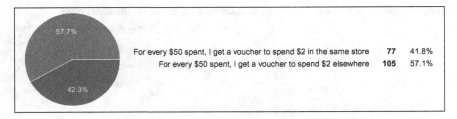

Figure 20: Survey Result — Direct/Indirect Rewards

Source: Survey results.

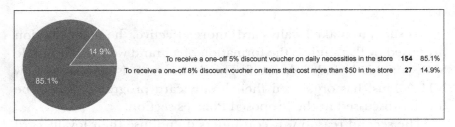

Figure 21: Survey Results — Necessities/Luxury

Source: Survey results.

Results from the survey support the analysis and observation alluded to above. Figure 20 shows that 58% of respondents prefer incentive rewards that can be used in-store and elsewhere. Figure 21 shows that more customers prefer vouchers that can be used for procurement of necessities rather than for luxury items and non-essentials. Immediate rewards or redemption of benefits are appreciated by a large majority (93%) of the consumers when participating in a loyalty card program, as shown in Figure 22.

(d) Customer privacy issues

One other benefit of the loyalty card program is the ability of the system to track the purchase habits and experience of customers, thereby making more targeted market and effective promotion feasible. It can also help consumers to have better dining and purchasing experience when enterprises can possibly structure their services to their needs.

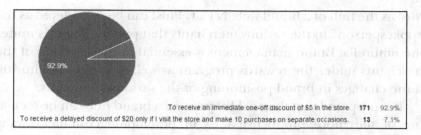

Figure 22: Survey Results — Immediate/Delayed Reward

Source: Survey results.

With the development of such huge databases of customer profiles comes the issue of customer privacy. Measures must be taken to prevent any loss of customer confidentiality and infringement on the customer privacy. Lapses in data security can have serious consequences for the patronage and revenue streams of the companies.

5. Policy Recommendations

Based on the analysis and findings of surveys in the previous section, this section focuses on proposing policies and use of technologies to maximize the benefits to be gained from the implementation of loyalty card programs and minimize the pitfalls that are associated with such programs. The 8M Framework (Toh and Thangavelu, 2017, Chapter 3) will be used as a basis in policy proposals and discussion. In particular, three of the 8Ms, namely, Message, Management and Method, will be highlighted.

(a) Message

In considering the Message component of the 8Ms, this study proposes that the firms that are implementing customer loyalty programs should consider the message that they are delivering to the customers of the loyalty program.

Branding and external communication are essential in maintaining the effectiveness of a customer loyalty program. In our analysis of NTUC Plus! case study, it is reckoned that by positioning the NTUC

Plus! as the hub of a brand web, NTUC Plus! can be considered as the "spokesperson" to the various merchants that provide rewards under one umbrella. Brand management is essential in the selection of the merchants under the rewards program as well as in the monitoring of the changes in brand positioning of the various merchants.

It is proposed that the establishment of a brand hub can be seen as one of the more productive ways in developing customer loyalty through loyalty cards. It also delivers a clear message to the customers about the loyalty card program and its vision through the merchants of the brand web. For example, in the NTUC Plus! case, its vision of "Do Better, Together" is clearly established, in that customers now get greater value in having high-quality merchants to redeem their rewards from. This develops customer loyalty, as customers get the message that by earning points through this loyalty program, they can get access to better merchants and a large variety of merchants (together).

The establishment of a brand web is definitely not simple. This study asserts that the following two conditions must be met in the formation of an effective brand web:

1. The organization must be large enough and must have established sufficient connections and relationships with a large variety of merchants in order to form a brand web.
2. The organization must have the technical expertise in order to establish an online network to connect these organizations.

In Singapore, an example of an upcoming loyalty card brand web in the retail industry is the wt+ card under Wing Tai Retail. It is a brand web that consists of multiple fashion boutiques in the retail industry. The wt+ card allows members to earn points when spending at participating outlets, and the points earned can be used to offset future purchases. The participating outlets are from the fashion retail industry. They include Dorothy Perkins, G2000, Topman, and Topshop, leading fashion outlets with multiple chain stores that Singapore consumers frequent (Wing Tai Retail, 2015).

Wing Tai retail has the potential to set up a brand web and be a prime mover of the brand web. Wing Tai Retail fulfils the two criteria stated above. Firstly, Wing Tai Retail has a total of 13 outlets under them, and has been established for a sufficient long period of time, hence establishing its brand. Wing Tai Retail will be able to attract more merchants to be under its brand web with its reputation. Moving forward, Wing Tai has to invest resources in developing its online platform to better establish its brand web. Currently, members are able to login to the Wing Tai Retail website to check their points and redeem vouchers and monitor transactions. However, this is insufficient in establishing a brand web. Promotions related to the participating merchants should be established, and even more innovative rewards such as the uBid system under NTUC Plus! can also be considered in further enhancing Wing Tai's brand web. A clear message cannot be seen from Wing Tai's choice of merchants, and this can be detrimental to the development of customer loyalty to the Wing Tai Card.

As alluded in earlier section of the study, the retail industry experiences a lower level of loyalty compared to the F&B sector in the use of loyalty cards. One of the main reason is that the spectrum of services offered in the retail for repurchase is lower than that of the other sector. By establishing a brand hub, there is a larger variety of products that is covered by the loyalty card program. If several related brands are connected through a brand hub, the products offered by this brand hub will be more unique in the eyes of the customers. The awareness and success of the loyalty card program is given a boost.

(b) Management

In considering the management component of the 8M framework, this study proposes the importance of managing an internal data warehouse with data mining capacity as well as having a strong evaluation and surveillance system to monitor the loyalty program.

(i) *Managing an internal data warehouse*

Data and information regarding consumer purchasing can be recorded with the use of a loyalty card. Each loyalty card has its own unique identification card that is tagged to each member, and at the Point of Sales (POS) terminal at check-out, purchases made by customers using this loyalty card can be tracked (Worthington & Fear, 2009).

There is an opportunity in gathering such consumer data with the loyalty card programs in Singapore. Unfortunately, this data has not been used in the form of targeted advertising in Singapore. NTUC Fairprice has only been sending mass emails to customers without targeting specific consumer groups. The Soup Spoon, on the other hand, is only on the uptake of linking loyalty cards to their owners, by encouraging customers to register for their card online and receiving 100 bonus points from doing so. A study conducted by Wansink (2003) found that the best loyalty programs collected information on "product usage, purchasing habits, and attitudes — and used this information to tailor products to the specific needs of consumers. The best loyalty programs were also found to use enrolment forms to capture demographic, usage frequency, and preference-related data" (Berman, 2006; Wansink, 2003).

Similarly, Singapore's loyalty programs can be more productive in the management of these internal data and build customer loyalty through business data analytics applied to the consumer data collected. There has indeed been a move towards the collection of such consumer data with the introduction of loyalty mobile applications. Several companies like Perx, Taggo.me and Poket have already advertised their expertise in this areas.

(ii) *Surveillance and improvement of loyalty card programs*

Companies with loyalty card programs should also take an active role in evaluating the success or failure of the loyalty programs implemented. Management should make use of appropriate measurement analytics to evaluate the efficacies of loyal programs. With the setting up of brand webs, simply using sales as a performance measure is insufficient. For example, "American Express (Amex) cardholders earn points through charging purchases with the Amex card that can be used for a variety of awards. To evaluate the success of the loyalty program, Amex has used such metrics as increased customer retention, increased purchases, and lower acquisition costs for new customers" (Berman, 2006). The metrics developed by each customer loyalty program will be different, depending on the management vision of what the customer loyalty program should deliver. What is important is for management to understand that sales is not a sufficient measure of the success or failure of loyalty programs. It can merely be one of the measures employed by management.

(c) Method

The last type of policy suggestion is related to the Method of the 8Ms. As technology develops, companies in the retail sector will experience new production possibilities. Similarly, in the loyalty card market, new technologies exist that can improve on the current loyalty card system. Two recent technologies worth mentioning are *Perx*, a loyalty card using mobile app, and Taggo.me, a Facebook-based loyalty card.

Perx is a mobile application available on both Android and Apple devices. The main concept behind *Perx* is that it is an application that stores all loyalty card-related information. Using Global Positioning System (GPS), *Perx* is able to locate participating outlets nearby and inform customers about the offers that these retailers have. Points are stored in the form of stamps, and upon collecting a certain amount of stamps, a reward can be obtained from the retailer.

Another interesting feature of *Perx* is its ability to form groups in order to gain stamps. For example, if a customer were to join a group, a reward is redeemable if the entire group earns a certain amount of stamps. It is the total number of stamps earned in the group that allows the group to be eligible for rewards. Together with the ease of locating participating outlets in the vicinity using GPS, *Perx* allows for a further enhancement in the formation of brand webs as in the case study on NTUC Plus!

Taggo.me is yet another technological method that can be used to implement customer loyalty card programs. Taggo.me makes use of Facebook's Page function to keep track of purchases by customers and also regarding customer's identity. Customer joins the fan club by scanning a QR code in the company advertisement brochure. The cashier will then ask for the customer's mobile number to verify the customer's credentials in order for the customer to earn the discount.

The limitation of the current Taggo.me is that there is no point or reward system for customers to earn points. This limits Taggo.me to a Type 1 loyalty card program and does not encourage customers to have repeat behavior. Customers are only able to get one-off discounts, and this will not encourage customers to come back again. However, Taggo.me provides firms more opportunities to gather information on the customers, through linking the loyalty card program to their Facebook account. This allows for companies to be able to employ the management strategy of the 8Ms and allow for the expansion of their data warehouse to better align their offers to the consumers. Furthermore, through the use of Facebook, the loyalty card program is automatically marketed to friends of the customers. This makes the firm be more productive in their marketing efforts in advertising the loyalty card program, through sign ups.

In fact, enterprises should not hold back in the introduction of loyalty cards that incorporate new technologies. The consumers' survey conducted in this study has indicated that consumers are not averse to the introduction of new technologies.

6. Conclusion

This study has reviewed the previous literature on loyalty schemes in the retail and F&B industry. Through a literature review, this study has identified the different types of rewards that are available to loyalty card programs. A discussion on loyalty was also conducted, and it was concluded that both behavioral and attitudinal loyalty were important in the development of a loyalty card program.

The loyalty card situation in Singapore was then evaluated, and a classification on the 5 types of loyalty program was recommended, namely Type 1: Members receive additional discount at register; Type 2: Members receive 1 free when they purchase n units; Type 3: Members receive rebates or points based on cumulative purchases; Type 4: Members receive targeted offers and mailings; Type 5: Members attain exclusive membership status through repeated spending.

Two case studies of loyalty card programs, the NTUC Plus! Card and the Soup Spoon Card, were made in this study. The NTUC Plus! loyalty card program was shown to exhibit sufficient features to qualify as the hub of a brand web and through this build customer loyalty in a relatively successful manner. The Soup Spoon card was presented as a representative example of loyalty card program in the F&B sector. The key takeaway from the comparison of the two case studies is the importance of loyalty to the product itself.

The potential benefits and pitfalls of loyalty card program were then evaluated, with supporting evidence provided from a consumer survey conducted. The main benefits that can be obtained from a loyalty card program is the exposure to merchants that provide rewards, access to consumer information and increasing demand during slow seasons. The potential pitfalls of loyalty card program are market saturation, low consumer commitment and data privacy issues.

Policies were then proposed with the use of 8M as a framework for evaluation and analysis. Using the Message component of the 8M Framework, the idea of a brand hub is proposed in the development of a customer loyalty program. Small enterprises with limited resources and scale of operation but selling similar products can seriously consider getting together to form an alliance for the purpose of launching a brand web via loyalty card program. This will enable the benefits of the brand web currently enjoyed by big retailers to be replicated for smaller enterprises. Management is also recommended to maintain consumer data and also critically evaluate the success of loyalty programs with multiple measures. Lastly, technological improvements through the use of smartphones were also presented as Methods by which companies can choose to deliver their customer loyalty programs. As such, we have seen that it is highly possible that these policies can be applied to SMEs in both the Retail and F&B sectors.

Concluding Remarks

It is hoped that this book has provided business owners and other stakeholders with useful information about tools available to enhance productivity. Due to the wide-ranging nature of topics discussed as well as their relevance in the 8M Framework context, it is desired that a wide variety of SMEs will have something to learn and takeaway.

Throughout the chapters, there are few key observations which can be made, about the key stakeholders involved in the productivity improvement process.

Certainly, *business owners* are becoming more cognizant that the commercial environment is becoming increasingly competitive, and that it is important to transform business operations in order to remain competitive. Some of the SMEs have also made themselves the role model in terms of implementation of new technologies and are showing the path to other SMEs, who may feel more confident after reading the success stories of other enterprises.

Furthermore, *customers* are also increasingly willing to accept these productivity-enhancing tools. Customers have certainly instilled more trust in online systems and payments in recent years, giving retailers a better opportunity to reach out to customers. Furthermore, with the growing acceptance of the shared economy, and increased emphasis on "the experience" rather than "ownership", it is expected that resources would be allocated more efficiently and sustainably. In particular, it is expected that areas like M-commerce and Shared Services would grow exponentially, on account of this trend.

Finally, *employees* also play a very important role in the development of a productive ecosystem. Employees are exposed to several training programs in order to keep them up-to-date with industry developments. Employees (especially the younger employees) are appreciating on-the-job training to implement productivity tools, as it improves their profile, and also makes them more employable.

Therefore, keeping in mind that the entrepreneurs, customers and employees are the key stakeholders in productivity improvement success, it is clear that in comparison to the past, all three of them have recognized the need to implement tools, and also have something to gain from the implementation.

However at the same time, there are a few major challenges, which enterprises face, and these are consistent throughout the case studies presented. These are in particular, the (i) Lack of awareness (or sometimes, correct awareness) about productivity-enhancing technology and practices among business owners. (ii) Issues in hiring and retaining a committed workforce, especially in the Food Services Sector. (iii) Lack of feasible economies of scale to implement productivity enhancing tools. (iv) Technology anxiety among the mature population, which poses challenges for businesses especially with the aging demographic profile in Singapore.

The lack of awareness issue is persistent in several chapters. Whether it is Lean Management, SSTs, RFID or 3D printing, business owners and employees are not aware of the existence of such technologies, or are sometimes misinformed about their usage and benefits. This causes a two-pronged issue. First, the lack of awareness makes it difficult to convince business owners to adopt these technologies, as they do not understand the benefits that they bring along. It is possible that several of these business owners also fit into a mature age segment, and hence they may have their own technology anxiety when it comes to implementation. Second, since employees are also not much aware about these technologies, owners also feel that the training of employees entails additional costs, and therefore they altogether decide against the implementation of the technology or practice.

The second key issue identified is with relation to the manpower of the business. Especially, for the Food Services sector, several SMEs have been identified to be highly dependent on part-time staff members, who are often students simply looking for avenues to earn cash during vacation periods. It is natural that when a considerable portion of the workforce is there just on a temporary basis, business owners would find little value in trying to train this workforce about productivity enhancement. Hence, the focus is simply to get the day's operations done, rather than to bring about any major overhaul to the strategy of the business.

Finally, several business owners have noted that while they are eager to include technologies in their operations, they feel that their business size does not warrant the inclusion of technologies. This was true for a wide range of tools, from RFID to loyalty card programs. This is because some efforts to increase productivity are too expensive and are in mismatch with the actual sales generation of the firm. While a lot of productivity improvement tools can be shared by multiple businesses, thereby easing the cost aspect, several business owners are not open to sharing tools with other companies, due to the fear of encroachment of privacy and exclusivity. In order to be able to afford and economically use productivity-enhancing tools, it is important that businesses view the effort as an industry-wide effort rather than looking at their own firm in isolation.

The final key problem identified is the process of educating the mature population about productivity-enhancing tools and assisting them to reduce their technology anxiety. It is important to note that the mature individual could be an employee or a customer. Mature employees see little value in trying to unlearn and relearn new processes, and hence they often shun away from them. Thus, it is important that the business carefully designs jobs, such that complex jobs are not assigned to mature workers, and that they are able to obtain assistance to use these technologies, whenever they desire.

In order to cope and survive in this challenging econo–techno environment and constraining demographic situation, it is essential for firms to create a workspace which smartly integrates both technology and mature employees, and businesses certainly should not choose one over the other. Furthermore, even when the mature individual is a customer, it would be prudent for businesses to offer timely help to the customer and assist them in using the technology. For example, as illustrated in the chapter, customers above the age of 50 have shown a willingness to engage in m-commerce, provided that there is someone to assist them. Therefore, it is hoped that over the years, with exposure to and assistance with using technologies, the mature segment would also be accept these technologies as part of their life.

Following the fact that the issues are now more focused on the knowledge about tools and practices, the recommendations suggested are also in congruence to that. Moving over from financial support, it is suggested that the government play a role in educating business owners and employees alike about the existence and working of new technologies. It was shown in many case studies that when interviewees were informed about the technologies, they showed keen interest in adopting them. Also, several chapters have emphasized the need to appropriately promote the information and training sessions that are being held. Business owners are at times neither aware of the technology, and nor are they aware of grants available to implement it. Therefore, it is essential to not just hold sessions but also encourage business owners and attend these and learn from them. In this way, the aim should be focused on assisting companies and creating industry leaders who would then be an inspiration to other SMEs who would also aspire to be as successful as the leaders. This would work hand-in-hand with the financial support that the government is providing already and will inform business owners as to how to best utilize the support provided.

In addition, a lot of the recommendations given also focus on the importance of collaboration and partnerships between SMEs in order to achieve productivity. SMEs, due to their size, are unable to carry out several projects as they do not provide SMEs the economies of scale. However, if several SMEs in the same industry were to collaborate together, then many of the investments that were previously considered costly would now make more sense for SMEs to adopt from a productivity perspective. Collaboration also enables the creation of a viable talent pool that is trained in technologies, thereby reducing the burden of training when they hire new employees. It is also expected that collaboration would help to set industry standards, especially for emerging industries, where the lack of standardization across the industry was seen as a challenge in implementation (for example, in the case of RFID or 3D Printing).

In terms of further research scope, it is true that most of the case studies covered are of enterprises that carry out business-to-consumer transactions. There may be several enterprises that carry out business-to-business transactions, and there exist several tools that enhance their productivity, apart from those mentioned in the book. Those tools could be explored in another book. Furthermore, it is expected that the technologies mentioned in the book will be constantly updated and replaced by other technologies. Hence the technologies mentioned here are by no means the end, and businesses would have to constantly look out for new technologies and keep upgrading themselves.

References

Abbott, S. (2004). "RFID: How far, how fast: the rest of the world." *Deloitte Touche Tohmatsu.* Available at: http://rfid.ctu.edu.tw/8_lab/RFID_reference/1/HowFarHowFast_final.pdf [Accessed on 14 December 2016].

Ahlström, S. and Wangsell, N. (2014). The impact of club card on store loyalty — An empirical study of a Swedish grocery retailer.

Ajzen, I. (1991) "The theory of planned behavior." *Organizational Behavior and Human Decision Processes*, 50, pp. 179–211.

Ajzen, I. and Fishbein, M. (1980). *Understanding Attitudes and Predicting Social Behavior.* Prentice-Hall.

Amit (2015). *Probably the Best Payments System in the World has Little or No Mobile to it. Let's Talk Payments.* Available at: https://letstalkpayments.com/mobile-payments-lost-in-this-contactless-eutopian-environment-hong-kong-octopus/ [Accessed 7 September 2016].

Anckar, B. and D'Incau, D. (2002). "Value-added services in mobile commerce: An analytical framework and empirical findings from a national consumer survey. HICSS." In *Proceedings of the 35th Annual Hawaii International Conference on System Sciences.* IEEE, pp. 1444–1453.

Ang, S., Quazi, Hesan A., Tay, C., and Khim, K. (2005). "Studies on the impact of work-life initiatives on employee and firm performance." Available at: http://www.mom.gov.sg/~/media/mom/documents/employment-practices/studies-on-the-impact-of-work-life-initiatives-on-employee-and-firm-performance.pdf.

Ang, V. (2015). Let it roll. *Asiaone Business.* Available at: http://business. asiaone.com/sme-central/news/let-it-roll.

Anitsal, I. and Paige, R.C. (2006). "An exploratory study on consumer perceptions of service quality in technology-based self-service." *Services Marketing Quarterly*, 27(3), pp. 53–67.

Arfmann, D. and Federico, G.T.B. (2014). "The value of lean in the service sector: A critique of theory & practice." *International Journal of Business and Social Science*, 5(2), pp. 18–24.

Arnfield, R. (2014). "Supermarket self-checkout technology approaching tipping point?" *Kiosk Marketplace.* Available at: http://www. kioskmarketplace.com/articles/supermarket-self-checkout-technology-approaching-tipping-point/.

Asif, Z. and Munir M. (2005). "Integrating the supply chain with RFID: A technical and business analysis." *Communications of the Association for Information Systems*, 15(24), pp. 393–426.

Association, P. (2015). *Register For Passion Card.* Available at onePA Bringing People Together. Available at: https://one.pa.gov.sg/CRMSPortal/ CRMSPortal.portal%3F_nfpb%3Dtrue%26_st%3D%26_ windowLabel%3DCRMSPortal_1%26_urlType%3Drender%26wlpCR MSPortal_1_action%3DETMMshipRegister%26_pageLabel% 3DCRMSPortal_page_1%26idProduct%3D792874.

Attaran, M. (2012). Critical success factors and challenges of implementing RFID in supply chain management. *Journal of Supply Chain and Operations Management*, 10(1), pp. 144–167.

Automated Cash Handling (2016). *Wikipedia.* Available at: https://en.wiki-pedia.org/wiki/Automated_cash_handling [Accessed 7 September 2016].

Bake, B. (n.d.). Butter&Bake About Us. *Butter&Bake.* Available at: http:// www.butterandbake.com.sg/our-story.

Balasubramanian, S., Peterson, R. A., and Jarvenpaa, S. L. (2002). "Exploring the implications of M-commerce for markets and marketing." *Journal of the Academy of Marketing Science*, 30(4), pp. 348–361.

Bashir, M.S. and Albarbarawi, S.A.H. (2011). "Factors influencing the adoption of self-service technologies (SSTs)." *University UMEA*, pp. 1–37.

Bátiz-Lazo, B. and Wood, D. (2001). "Management of core capabilities in Mexican and European banks." *International Journal of Bank Marketing*, 19(2), pp. 89–100.

Bell, S. (2005). *Lean Enterprise Systems: Using IT for Continuous Improvement.* Wiley, Hoboken, NJ.

Bergeron, B. P. (2003). *Essentials of Shared Services.* John Wiley & Sons, Hoboken, NJ.

Berman, B. (2006). "Developing an effective customer loyalty program." *California Review Management,* 49(1), pp. 123–148.

Betts, C.A. (1965). "New plans for older workers." *The Science News-Letter,* 87(19). Available at: http://www.jstor.org/stable/3948679.

Bhattacharya, M., Chu, C. H., and Mullen, T. (2007). RFID implementation in retail industry: Current status, issues, and challenges. In *Proceedings of 38th Annual Meeting of the Decision Sciences Institute,* Phoenix, AZ, pp. 2171–2176.

Bicheno, J. (2008). *The Lean Toolbox for Service Systems.* PICSIE Books, Buckingham.

Bitner, M., Ostrom, A., and Meuter, N. (2002). "Implementing successful self-service technologies." *Academy of Management Executive,* 16(4), pp. 96–109.

Blogtkz (2013). SMEs ponder beyond carrots, sticks. *Singapore Towkay Zone.* Available at: http://www.towkayzone.com.sg/entries/23-SMEs-ponder-beyond-carrots-sticks#.VcCyJ-EYNcE.

Bloom, N., Krestchmer T., and John Van R. (2006). "Work-life balance, management practices and productivity." *Oxford Review of Economic Policy,* 22(4). Available at: http://web.stanford.edu/~nbloom/OXREP_BLOOMVANREENEN.pdf.

Bloomberg (2008). "Howard Schultz's memo." Available at http://www.bloomberg.com/bw/stories/2008-01-07/howard-schultzs-memobusinessweek-business-news-stock-market-and-financial-advice.

Bloomberg Business (2014). *Wal-Mart CEO Says Retailer May Consider Buying 3-D Printer Maker.* Available at: http://www.bloomberg.com/news/articles/2014-05-28/wal-mart-ceo-says-retailer-may-consider-buying-3-d-printer-maker [Accessed 28 July 2015].

Bonaccorsi, A., Carmignani, G., and Zammori, F. (2011). "Service value stream management (SVSM): Developing lean thinking in the service industry." *Journal of Service Science and Management,* 4(4), pp. 428–439.

Boon, R. (2016). Rise of Apple Pay drives DBS to push for a cashless Singapore. *The Straits Times.* Available at: http://www.straitstimes.com/business/banking/rise-of-apple-pay-drives-dbs-to-push-for-a-cashless-singapore [Accessed 7 September 2016].

Boyer, K. and Verma, R. (2010). *Operations and Supply Chain Management for the 21st Century.* South-Western, Mason, OH.

Brennan, D. and Gortz, K. (2008). *The Philosophy and Practice of Coaching: Insights and Issues for a New Era.* Jossey-Bass, SanFrancisco, CA.

Bridson, K., Evans, J., and Hickman, M. (2008). "Assessing the relationship between loyalty program attributes, store satisfaction and store loyalty." *Journal of Retailing and Consumer Services,* 15(5), pp. 364–374.

Brynjolfsson, E., Hu, Y. J., and Rahman, M. S. (2013). "Competing in the age of omnichannel retailing." *MIT Sloan Management Review,* 54(4), pp. 23–29.

Brynjolfsson, E., Hu, Y., and Smith, M. D. (2003). "Consumer surplus in the digital economy: Estimating the value of increased product variety at online booksellers." *Management Science,* 49(11), pp. 1580–1596.

Bureau of Labour and Statistics (2014). *Age.* Available at: https://www.bls. gov/cps/demographics.htm#age [Accessed on 19 December 2016].

Burke, C. Stewart, K., and Macdonald, I. (2012). *Systems Leadership: Creating Positive Organisations.* Ashgate, Burlington, VT.

Burning Platform (2012). *Bricks & Mortar Retailing Crumbling.* Available at: https://www.theburningplatform.com/2012/12/15/bricks-mortar-retailing-crumbling/ [Accessed on 13 December 2016].

Business Dictionary (n.d.). "What is service management? definition and meaning." Available at http://www.businessdictionary.com/definition/service-management.html [Accessed on 13 December 2016].

Byrnes, J. (2003). "Who will profit from Auto-ID?", In *Harvard Business School (HBS),* Online. Available at: http://hbswk.hbs.edu/item. jhtml?id=3651&t=dispatch [Accessed on 14 December 2016].

Cagape, E. (2012). *HK cab drivers say 'no thanks' to Octopus payment — Asian Correspondent.* Asiancorrespondent.com. Available at: https://asiancorrespondent.com/2012/03/hong-kong-taxi-octopus-payment/ [Accessed 7 September 2016].

Case, G. (2014). "Age and the retail worker." *Online Career Tips.* Available at: http://onlinecareertips.com/2014/09/age-and-the-retail-worker/.

Cash Drawer (2016). Tellermate.com. Available at: http://www.tellermate. com/en-gb/products/t-ice [Accessd 7 September 2016].

CashGuard (2016). *CashGuard — White Paper.* Cashguard.com. Available at: http://www.cashguard.com/Improve-your-business/cash-management-whitepaper/ [Accessed 7 September 2016].

CASHINFINITY™ — Smart Cash Management — Glory (2016). Available at: http://www.cashinfinity.net/ [Accessed 16 November 2016].

CASHINFINITY™ (Glory) (2016). Cashinfinity.net. Available at: http:// www.cashinfinity.net/ [Accessed 7 September 2016].

Chang, H., Lee, J., and Tseng, M. (2008). "The influence of service recovery on perceived justice under different involvement level-an evidence of retail industry." *Contemporary Management Research*, 4(1), pp. 57–82.

Charantimath (2006). *Total Quality Management*. Dorling Kindersley (India), New Delhi India.

Chau, P.Y. (1996). "An empirical assessment of a modified technology acceptance model." *Journal of Management Information Systems*, 13(2), pp. 185–204.

Chen, C. C., Crandall, R. E., and Yu, Y. C. (2005). "Barriers to RFID adoption." In *Proceedings of the 10th Annual Conference of Asia-Pacific Decision Sciences Institute*. Available at https://www.researchgate.net/publication/267976468_Barriers_to_RFID_Adoption [Accessed on 14 December 2016].

Chen, Y.-H. (2015). "Competitiveness, strategy, and productivity." PhD International College Ming-Chuan University.

Cheng, E. (2016). *Trends in Retail Cash Automation: A Market Overview of Retail Cash Handling Technologies*. Federal Reserve Bank of San Francisco. Available at: http://www.frbsf.org/cash/publications/fed-notes/2014/march/retail-cash-automation-technology-trends [Accessed 7 September 2016].

Cho, H. and Fiorita, S.S. (2010). "Self-service technology in retailing. The case of retail kiosks. *Symphonya. Emerging Issues in Management*, 1, pp. 43–56.

Choo, F. (2015). "Singapore is second hottest global city for entrance of new retail brands". *The Straits Times*. Available at: http://www.straitstimes.com/business/singapore-is-second-hottest-global-city-for-entrance-of-new-retail-brands.

Chua, A. (2010). Bengawan Solo. *Singapore Infopedia*. Available at: http://eresources.nlb.gov.sg/infopedia/articles/SIP_1682_2010-07-01.html.

CNN News (2013). *Obama's speech highlights rise of 3D printing*. Available at: http://edition.cnn.com/2013/02/13/tech/innovation/obama-3d-printing/ [Accessed 28 July 2015].

Collins, K. and Muthusamy, S. (2007). "Applying the Toyota production system to a healthcare organization: A case study on a rural community healthcare provider." *The Quality Management Journal*, 14(4), pp. 41–52.

Contactless Payments Growing, but Cash Still King: Analysts (2016). *Channel NewsAsia*. Available at: http://www.channelnewsasia.com/news/singapore/contactless-payments/1857214.html [Accessed 7 September 2016].

Costs of Cash versus Costs of Electronic Payment Instruments (2016). *CashEssential.* Available at: http://cashessentials.org/cash-is-efficient/costs-of-cash-versus-costs-of-electronic-payment-instruments [Accessed 10 September 2016].

Coursaris, C. and Hassanein, K. (2002). "Understanding M-commerce: A consumer-centric model." *Quarterly Journal of Electronic Commerce*, 3, pp. 247–272.

Credit and Charge Card Statistics (2016). Data.gov.sg. Available at: https://data.gov.sg/dataset/credit-and-charge-card-statistics?view_id=a2daba98-5c68-422c-b101-626d74c93e24&resource_id=aae7f304-f003-4c82-83e2-c0c05590f061 [Accessed 7 September 2016].

Cronin, J.J. and Taylor, S.A. (1992). "Measuring service quality: A re-examination and extension." *Journal of Marketing*, 56(3), pp. 55–68.

Curran, J., Meuter, M., and Surprenant, C. (2003). "Intentions to use self-service technologies: A confluence of multiple attitudes." *Journal of Service Research*, 5(3), pp. 209–224.

D.C. Twist. (2005). "The impact of radio frequency identification on supply chain facilities." *Journal of Facility Management*, 3(3), pp. 226–239.

Dabholkar, P.A., Bobbitt, L.M., and Lee, E.J. (2003). "Understanding consumer motivation and behavior related to self-scanning in retailing: Implications for strategy and research on technology-based self-service." *International Journal of Service Industry Management*, 14(1), pp. 59–95.

Dahlgaard, J. J. and Ostergaard, P. (2000). "TQM and lean thinking in higher education." *The Best on Quality*, 11(15), pp. 203–266.

Damrath, F. (2012). "Increasing competitiveness of service companies: Developing conceptual models for implementing Lean Management in service companies." *Politecnica di Milano*, Madrid, Spain.

Davis, F.D. (1989). "Perceived usefulness, perceived ease of use and user acceptance of information technology." *MIS Quarterly*, 13(3), pp. 319–339.

Davison, J. and Smith, S. E. (2005). *Retail RFID Stirs Process Change and Improves Product Availability.* Gartner, Stamford, CT.

DBS. (10 July, 2015). *DBS Takashimaya Visa Card.* Available at: DBS: http://www.dbs.com.sg/personal/cards/credit-cards/dbs-takashimaya-visa-platinum-card.

De Wulf, K., Odekerken-Schröder, G., De Canniere, M., and Van Oppen, C. (2003). "Assessing the impact of a retailer's relationship efforts on consumers: Aattitudes and behavior." *Journal of Retailing and Consumer Services*, 10(2), pp. 95–108.

Dembe, A.E., Erickson, J.B., Delbos, R.G., and Banks, S.M. (2005). *Occupational and Environmental Medicine*, 62(9), pp. 588–597. Available at: http://www.jstor.org.libproxy1.nus.edu.sg/stable/27732586.

Demoulin, N. and Zidda, P. (2009). "Drivers of customers' adoption and adoption timing of a new loyalty card in the grocery retail market." *Journal of Retailing*, 85(3), pp. 391–405.

Department of Statistics Singapore (2017). Services Survey Series: Food & Beverage Services.

Department of Statistics, Ministry of Trade & Industry, Republic of Singapore (2015). *Yearbook of Statistics 2015*. Available at: http://www.singstat.gov.sg/docs/default-source/default-document-library/publications/publications_and_papers/reference/yearbook_2015/yos2015.pdf.

Diamond, J., Diamond, E., and Litt, S. (2015). *Fashion Retailing: A Multi-Channel Approach*. Bloomsbury Publishing, London.

Ding, X., Iijima, J., and Ho, S. (2004). "Unique features of mobile commerce." *Journal of Electronic Science and Technology of China*, 2(3), pp. 206–210.

Divett, M., Crittenden, N., and Henderson, R. (2003). "Actively influencing consumer loyalty." *Journal of Consumer Marketing*, 20(2), pp. 109–126.

Dorman, A. J. (2013). "Omni-channel retail and the new age consumer: An empirical analysis of direct-to-consumer channel interaction in the retail industry." *CMC Senior Theses*. Paper 590. Available at: http://scholarship.claremont.edu/cmc_theses/590 [Accessed 13 December 2016].

Dowling, G. and Uncles, M. (1997). "Do customer loyalty programmes really Work." *Sloan Management Review, Summer*, pp. 71–82.

Drucker, P.F. (1991). "The new productivity challenge." *Harvard Business Review*. Available at: https://hbr.org/1991/11/the-new-productivity-challenge.

Economic Development Board, Singapore (2015). *3D Printing's Revolutionary Potential*. Available at: https://www.edb.gov.sg/content/edb/en/news-and-events/news/singapore-business-news/Feature/3d-printings-revolutionary-potential.html [Accessed 27 July 2015].

Economic Development Board, Singapore (2015). *UL opens S$8 Million Global Additive Manufacturing Centre of Excellence in Singapore*. Available at: https://www.edb.gov.sg/content/edb/en/news-and-events/news/2015-news/ul-opens-8-million-singapore-dollar-global-additive-manufacturing-centre-of-excellence-in-singapore.html [Accessed 28 July 2015].

Economists Incorporated (2014). *Retailer Payment Systems: Relative Merits of Cash and Payment Cards.*

Editorial, G. (2014). *Standard Chartered Deals.* Available at Great Singapore Deals. Available at: http://www.greatdeals.com.sg/2014/11/03/1-for-1-regular-pizza-hut-stanchart-cards-november-2014/.

Einav, L., Levin, J., Popov, I., and Sundaresan, N. (2014). "Growth, adoption, and use of mobile E-commerce." *The American Economic Review*, 104(5), pp. 489–494.

Emiliani, M. L. (2005). "Using Kaizen to improve the graduate business school degree program." *Quality Assurance in Education*, 13(1), pp. 37–52.

Emptying the Tills (2016). *The Economist.* Economist.com. Available at: http://www.economist.com/news/finance-and-economics/21704807-some-europeans-are-more-attached-notes-and-coins-others-emptying-tills [Accessed 10 September 2016].

EnterpriseOne (2014). "SMEs looking at restructuring their businesses: SME survey." Available at: https://www.enterpriseone.gov.sg/en/News/2014/October/141023%20SMEs%20Looking%20At%20Restructuring%20Their%20Business%20SME%20Survey.aspx.

Erez, M. (2010). "Culture and job design." *Journal of Organization Behavior*, 31, pp. 389–400. doi: 10.1002/job.651.

Euromonitor International (2014). Consumer Foodservice in Singapore. Available at: http://www.euromonitor.com/consumer-foodservice-in-singapore/report.

Euromonitor International (2015). *Consumer Payments 2015: Trends, Developments and Prospects.* Available at: http://www.euromonitor.com/consumer-payments-2015-trends-developments-and-prospects/report.

Euromonitor International (2015). *Financial Cards and Payments in Singapore.*

Europe's Disappearing Cash: Emptying the Tills (2016). *The Economist.* Available at: http://www.economist.com/news/finance-and-economics/21704807-some-europeans-are-more-attached-notes-and-coins-others-emptying-tills [Accessed 10 September 2016].

EZ Link Co-Brand Passion Card (2015). Available at: EZ Link: http://ezlink.com.sg/co-brand-cards/passion-card.

F&B Market (n.d.). F&B Market News. *F&B Market*. Available at: www.fnb-market.com/news/

Fair Work Act (2009, Austl). Available at: https://www.comlaw.gov.au/Details/C2009A00028.

Families and Work Institute (2014). *2014 National Study of Employers: Including the Talents of Employees with Disabilities*. Available at: http://worknow1.com/wp-content/uploads/2015/01/4J05-Study_of_Employers.pdf.

Fast Retailing (2012). Annual Report 2012. Available at: http://www.fastretailing.com/eng/ir/library/pdf/ar2012_en_n.pdf [Accessed on 14 December 2016].

Fickel, L. (2000). "Power to the people." *CFO Magazine*. Available at: http://www.cio.com.au/article/80235/customer_self-service_power_people/ [Accessed on 9 December].

Financial Times (2014). *Regulatory concerns hold back 3D printing on safety*. Available at: http://www.ft.com/intl/cms/s/2/bfab071c-6abc-11e4-a038-00144feabdc0.html#axzz3jPAmbfyT [Accessed 21 August 2015].

Fishbein, M. and Ajzen, I. (1975). *Belief, Attitude, Intention and Behavior: An Introduction to Theory and Behavior*. Addison-Wesley, Reading, MA.

Forbes, Tech (2013). *The 3D Printing Revolution You Have Not Heard About*. Available at: http://www.forbes.com/sites/rakeshsharma/2013/07/08/the-3d-printing-revolution-you-have-not-heard-about/ [Accessed 13 July 2015].

Forbes, Tech (2015). *2015 Roundup of 3D Printing Market Forecasts and Estimates*. Available at: http://www.forbes.com/sites/louis-columbus/2015/03/31/2015-roundup-of-3d-printing-market-forecasts-and-estimates/ [Accessed 25 July 2015].

Fortune News (2015). *Why Fords is partnering with a hot 3D printing startup*. Available at: http://fortune.com/2015/06/23/ford-hot-startup-3d-printing/ [Accessed 1 August 2015].

Fox News (2015). *Proposed regulations could keep 3D printed gun blueprints offline for good*. Available at: http://www.foxnews.com/tech/2015/07/01/proposed-regulation-could-keep-3d-printed-gun-blueprints-offline-for-good/ [Accessed 20 August 2015].

Fox, Z. (2013). *The 15 Countries With the Highest Smartphone Pentration*. Available at: http://mashable.com/2013/08/27/global-smartphone-penetration/ [Accessed on 13 December 2016].

Fried, Y. and Ferris, G.R. (1987). "The validity of the job characteristics model: A review and meta-analysis." *Personnel Psychology*, 40, pp. 287–322.

Available at: http://www.researchgate.net/publication/227890804_
The_validity_of_the_Job_Characteristics_Model_a_review_and_
metaanalysis.

Frolick and Chen (2004). "Assessing M-commerce opportunities."
Information Systems Management, 21(2), pp. 53–61. doi: 10.1201/1078/4
4118.21.2.20040301/80422.8.

Fulk, J., Steinfield, C. W., Power, J.G., and Schmitz, J. (1987). "A social
information processing model of media use in organizations.'
Communication Research, 14(5), pp. 529–552.

Gallup, I. (2012). "Gallup Q12® Meta-Analysis Report." Available at:
http://www.gallup.com/services/191489/q12-meta-analysis-report-
2016.aspx [Accessed 19 December 2016].

Garg, P. and Rastogi, R. (2006). "New model for job design: Motivating
employees' performance." *Journal of Management Development,* 25(6),
pp. 572–587.

Gartner (2014). *Will Hasbro and 3D Systems Jump-start the Consumer 3D
Printing Market?* Available at: http://blogs.gartner.com/pete-
basiliere/2014/02/14/will-hasbro-and-3d-systems-jump-start-the-
consumer-3d-printing-market/ [Accessed 13 July 2015].

Gartner (2015). Gartner Says Medical Applications Are Leading
Advancement in 3D Printing. Available at: http://www.gartner.com/
newsroom/id/3117917 [Accessed 10 December, 2016].

GembaAcademy (2009). Online Lean and Six Sigma Training Videos |
Gemba Academy. Available at: https://www.gembaacademy.com/
school-of-lean/5s-workplace-productivity/5s-overview [Accessed on 13
December 2016].

Gilliam, D., Taylor-Jones, S., and Costanza, J. R. (2005). *The Quantum Leap:
Next Generation: The Manufacturing Strategy for Business.* J. Ross Pub.,
Boca Raton, FL.

Go'mez, B. G., Arranz, A. G., and Cilla'n, J. S. (2006). "The role of loyalty
programs in behavioral and affective loyalty." *Journal of Consumer
Marketing,* 23(7), pp. 387–396.

Goy, P. (2015). Sharing the SG50 Birthday Cake. *Asiaone.* Available at: http://
news.asiaone.com/news/singapore/sharing-sg50-birthday-cake.

Greenwood, T., Bradford, M., and Green, B. (2002). "Becoming a lean
enterprise: A tale of two firms." *Strategic Finance,* 84(5), pp. 32–39.

Grimes, W. (2004). "When the cashier is you." *New York Times,* New York.
Available at: http://www.nytimes.com/2004/04/07/dining/just-
browsing-when-the-cashier- is you.html?pagewanted=print&src=pm.

Grönroos, C. (2001). "The perceived service quality concept — A mistake?" *Managing Service Quality: An International Journal*, 11(3), pp. 150–152.

Groß, M. (2015). "Mobile shopping: A classification framework and literature review". *International Journal of Retail & Distribution Management*, 43(3), pp. 221–241.

Gruen, T., Corsten, D. and Bharadwaj, S. (2005). "Retail out-of-stocks: A worldwide examination of extent, causes and consumer responses." Available at: www.ecr-academics.org/pdf_uploads/50_GruenCorsten Bharadwaj2002.pdf.

Grzywacz, J.G. and Dooley, D. (2003). "Good jobs to bad jobs": Replicated evidence of an employment continuum from two large surveys." *Social Science & Medicine*, 56, pp. 1749–1760. ISSN 0277–9536. Available at: http://www.sciencedirect.com/science/article/pii/S0277953602001703?np=y.

Gunnebo (2014). *Closed Cash handling in Retail — Introduction to SafePay™*. Presentation.

Gutierrez, A. (2012). "Changing clothes. Changing conventional wisdom. Change the world." Available at http://arturoarturo.com/uniqlo/#_ftn22 [Accessed on 13 December 2016].

Hackman, J.R. and Oldham, G.R. (1980). *Work Redesign*. Addison-Wesley, Mass.

Hall, M. (2004)."Forget Wal-Mart." *ComputerWorld*, 38(51), p. 38. Available at: https://books.google.com.sg/books?id=80O15hD_6DgC&pg=PA3 8&lpg=PA38&dq=computerworld 2004 top three technology risks&sou rce=bl&ots=a8xmALVMw6&sig=M_g51_6CU1eL_4jIxFC8f7jKRaU&hl =en&sa=X&ved=0ahUKEwi68MuUp-fQAhVLKY8KHcouDhcQ6AEIGj AA#v=onepage&q=computerworld 2004 top three technology risks &f=false [Accessed on 9 December 2016].

Hamano, M. (2010). "RFID implementation in Japan." Available at http://www.gs1jp.org/pdf/rfid.pdf [Accessed on 27 August 2015].

Handfield, R. (2011). "What is supply chain management?" Available at: http://scm.ncsu.edu/scm-articles/article/what-is-supply-chain-management [Accessed on 14 December 2016].

Hanna, J. (2007). "HBS article: Bringing 'Lean' principles to service industries." Available at http://hbswk.hbs.edu/item/bringing-lean-principles-to-service-industries [Accessed at 14 December 2016].

Hendricks, H. (2002). "'Self' respect". *Entrepreneur Magazine*, July 2002. Available at: https://www.entrepreneur.com/article/52734 [Accessed on 9 December].

Henry, J. and Jillian, D.F. (2007). "Putting it right: Service failure and customer loyalty in UK banks." *International Journal of Bank Marketing*, 25(3), pp. 161–172.

Herzberg, F., Mausner, B., and Synderman, B.B. (1959). "The motivation to work." *In Work and the Nature of Man*. Mentor Book, New York, pp. 91–111.

Hofstede, G. (1991). *Cultures and Organizations: Software of the Mind.* McGraw-Hill, London.

Holzer, M. and Isaacs, H. L. (2002). "Building effective shared service partnerships." *International Review of Public Administration*, 7(1), pp. 53–64.

Hsieh, C.T. (2005). "Implementing self-service technology to gain competitive advantage." *Communications of the IIMA*, 5(1), pp. 77–83.

Huber, N., Michael, K., and McCathie, L. (2007). "Barriers to RFID adoption in the supply chain." *2007 1st Annual RFID Eurasia, Istanbul*, pp. 1–6.

HV, V., Istace, F., and Kamal, R. (2016). *Insights from McKinsey's Asia-Pacific Payments Map.*

IBM (2008). "Shrink and self-checkout: Trends, technology and tips." Self-Checkout Solutions. Available at: ftp://ftp.software.ibm.com/software/retail/marketing/pdf/sco/RTE03002-USEN-00.pdf.

IMDA Singapore (2012). *Statistics on Telecom Services for 2012 (Jul — Dec)* Available at: http://www.ida.gov.sg/Infocomm-Landscape/Facts-and-Figures/Telecommunications/Statistics-on-Telecom-Services/Statistics-on-Telecom-Services-for-2012-Jul-Dec.

Industry Leading Cash Counting Technology (2016). Cashmaster.com. Available at: http://www.cashmaster.com/en-us/ [Accessed 7 September 2016].

International Labour Organization (ILO) (2011). "A changing world: Adapting to an ageing population in the workplace." Available at: http://www.ilo.org/global/publications/magazines-and-journals/world-of-work-magazine/articles/WCMS_170533/lang--en/index.htm.

Internet Retailer (n.d.). *U.S. Retail M-commerce Sales Via Smartphones & Tablets 2014–2018*. Available at: https://www.internetretailer.com/trends/mobile-commerce/us-retail-m-commerce-sales-via-smartphones-tablets/ [Accessed on 13 December 2016].

Intrasys (2014). "Leading retail apparel Paul Frank Singapore implements RFID for Inventory." Available at: https://www.intrasys.com.sg/RFIDSolution/CaseStudies/RFID-Paul-Frank [Accessed on 27 August 2015].

Investopedia (2015). "Inventory management." Available at: http://www. investopedia.com/terms/i/inventory-management.asp?version=v1 [Accessed on 14 December 2016].

Islam, M. A., Khan, M. A., Ramayah, T., and Hossain, M. M. (2011). "The adoption of mobile commerce service among employed mobile phone users in Bangladesh: Self-efficacy as a moderator." *International Business Research*, 4(2), p. 80.

Jacoby, J. and Chestnut, R. (1978). *Brand Loyalty: Measurement and Management*. John Wiley & Sons, New York.

Jang, D. and Mattila, A. (2005). "An examination of restaurant loyalty programs: What kinds of." *International Journal of Contemporary Hospitality*, 17(5), pp. 402–408.

Jessica, L. (2013). *Eateries Serving Up Lean, Mean Model of Productivity. The Straits Times.* Available at: http://justice4workerssingapore.blogspot. sg/2013/02/eateries-serving-up-lean-mean-model-of.html.

Jianwen, L. (2013). These CEOs Wash Your Dirty Dishes. *The New Paper.* Available at: http://www2.tnp.sg/content/these-ceos-wash-your-dirty-dishes.

Jones, D. and Mitchell, A. (2006). "Lean thinking for the NHS." NHS Confederation, London. Available at: http://www.nhsconfed.org/~/ media/Confederation/Files/Publications/Documents/Lean%20thinking%20for%20the%20NHS.pdf [Accessed on 14 December 2016].

Jones, P., Clarke-Hill, C., Hillier, D., Shears, P., and Comfort, D. (2004a) "Radio frequency identification in retailing and privacy and public policy issues." *Management Research News* 27(8/9), pp. 46–56.

Juban, R. L. and Wyld, D. C. (2004). "Would you like chips with that?: Consumer perspectives of RFID." *Management Research News*, 27(11/12), pp. 29–44.

Kang, Y. and Gershwin, S.B. (2005). "Information inaccuracy and inventory systems: Stock loss and stockout." *IIE Trans*, 37(9), pp. 843–859.

Kara, A. and Orel, F.D. (2007). "Supermarket self-checkout service quality, customer satisfaction, and loyalty: Empirical evidence from an emerging market." *Journal of Retailing and Consumer Services*, 21(2), pp. 118–129.

Kärkkäinen, M. and Holmström, J. (2002). "Wireless product identification: Enabler for handling efficiency, customization and information sharing." *Supply Chain Management: An International Journal*, 7(4), pp. 242–252.

Kawakami, M., Inoue, F., Ohkubo, T., and Ueno, T. (1998). "Job redesign needs for aged workers." *International Journal of Occupational Safety And Ergonomics*

1998, 4(3), pp. 471–483. Available at: http://www.ciop.pl/CIOPPortalWAR/file/72469/2013121293727&R1998-V4-N4-str471-483.pdf.

Kearney, A. T. (2004). A.T. Kearney's 2004 Offshore Location Attractiveness Index: Making Offshore Decisions. Available at: https://www.atkearney.com/documents/10192/509907/Making_offshore_s.pdf/a3dc6fae-0ef9-44fc-8a29-29e2911f7786.

Kearney, A. T. (2007). Shared Services in Government 2. Available at: https://newsroom.cisco.com/dlls/2007/eKits/AT_Kearney_Report_070307.pdf.

Keeping it Simple (2014). DBS SME Banking. Available at: https://www.dbs.com.sg/sme/businessclass/articles/innovation-and-technology/keeping-it-simple-char-grill.page

Keiningham, T. L., Cooil, B., Aksoy, L., Andreassen, T. W., and Weiner, J. (2007). "The value of different customer satisfaction and loyalty metrics in predicting customer retention, recommendation, and share-of-wallet." *Managing Service Quality*, 17(4), pp. 361–384.

Keith, A. *et al.* (2002). "Focus on the supply chain: Applying auto-ID within the distribution center." *IBM Business Consulting Services, Auto-ID Center, Massachusetts Institute of Technology*. Available at: http://cocoa.ethz.ch/downloads/2014/06/None_IBM-AUTOID-BC-003.pdf [Accessed on 14 December 2016].

Kiba-Janiak, M. (2014). "The use of mobile phones by customers in retail stores: A case of Poland." *Economics & Sociology*, 7(1), pp. 116–130.

Kim, C. S. (1995). Hawker entrepreneurs who ride on food-court boom. *The Sunday Times*.

Kim, S. and Garrison, G. (2010). "Understanding users' behaviors regarding supply chain technology: Determinants impacting the adoption and implementation of RFID technology in South Korea." *International Journal of Information Management*, 30(5), pp. 388–398.

Kiosk Marketplace (2012). "Convenience is key in Walmart's plans to deploy more NCR Self-service checkouts." Kiosk Marketplace. Available at: <http://www.kioskmarketplace.com/news/convenience-is-key-in-walmarts-plans-to-deploy-more-ncr-Self-service checkouts/>.

Kivetz, R., Netzer, O., and Srinivasan, V. (2004). "Extending compromise effect models to complex buying situations and other context effects." *Journal of Marketing Research*, 41(3), pp. 262–268.

Kopitiam (2015). *Kopitiam Card*. Available at: Kopitiam True Singapore Taste. Available at: http://www.kopitiam.biz/kopitiam-card/.

KPMG (2016). *Singapore Payments Roadmap Report.* Available at: http://www. mas.gov.sg/~/media/MAS/News%20and%20Publications/Press%20 Releases/Singapore%20Payments%20Roadmap%20Report%20%20 August%202016.pdf.

Kurohi, R. (2015). Delays Hit Local Creator of 3D Printer. *The Straits Times.* Available at: http://www.straitstimes.com/singapore/delays-hit-local-creator-of-3d-printer [Accessed 11 December, 2016].

Kwan, J., Nadeau, M., and Steitz, J. (2015). Digital wallets in the U.S.: Minding the consumer adoption curve. *Mckinsey On Payments,* 8(22).

Laksania (2014). About Laksania. *Laksania.* Available at: http://www.lak-sania.com/socialenterprise.html.

Laudon, K. and Traver, C. (2013). *E-Commerce 2014.* Prentice Hall, Upper Saddle River, N.J.

Lean Enterprise Research Centre (2015). "The five principles of lean thinking." Available at http://www.leanenterprise.org.uk/what-is-lean-thinking/what-is-lean-thinking-and-key-lean-thinking-principles.html [Accessed on 13 December 2016].

Lee, A. (2015). *Lacklustre response to cashless payment at hawker centres.* TODAYonline. Available at: http://www.todayonline.com/singapore/ sluggish-take-rate-cashless-payments-hawker-centres?page=1 [Accessed 7 September 2016].

Lee, E-J., Lee, L., and Schumann, D.W. (2002). "The influence of communication source and mode on consumer adoption of technological innovations." *Journal of Consumer Affairs,* 36(1), pp. 1–27.

Lee, H. and Özer, Ö. (2007). "Unlocking the value of RFID." *Production and operations management,* 16(1), pp. 40–64.

Lee, H.J., Fairhurst, A.E., and Lee, M.Y. (2009). "The importance of self-service kiosks in developing consumers' retail patronage intentions." *Managing Service Quality,* 19(6), 687–701.

Lee, M. (2013). "Smart work." *SME Magazine,* July/August Issue. Available at: http://www.kpmg.com/sg/en/pressroom/pages/mc20130704. aspx.

Lee, T. (2012). *Singapore's m-commerce market jumps seven-fold to US$259M in one year.* Available at: https://www.techinasia.com/singapores-mobile-commerce-market-in-2011-jumps-seven-fold-to-us259m-from-previous-year/.

Lee, Y. E. and Benbasat, I. (2003). "Interface design for mobile commerce." *Communications of the ACM,* 46(12), 48–52. doi:10.1145/953460.953487.

Leenheer, J., Van Heerde, H., Bijmolt, T., and Smidts, A. (2007). "Do loyalty programs really enhance behavioral loyalty? An empirical analysis accounting for self-selecting members." *International Journal of Research in Marketing*, 24(1), pp. 31–47.

Leknes, J. and Munkvold, B. E. (2006). "The role of knowledge management in ERP implementation: A case study in Aker Kvaerner." *Proceedings of the 14th European Conference on Information Systems (ECIS 2006)*, Göteborg, Sweden, June 12–14.

Leung, K. and Antypas, J. (2001). "Improving returns on m-commerce investments." *Journal of Business Strategy*, 22(5), 12–13.

Lim, C. and Yi, Q. (2014). "Mobile commerce application: Exploration of the emergence of mobile commerce applications within retailers in Singapore, and the implications it has on shoppers' behavior." University of Sterling.

Locher, D. (2011). *Value Stream Mapping for Lean Development: A How-To Guide for Streamlining Time to Market*. Taylor & Francis, Boca Raton.

Loh, T. (2012). "Paypal and the M-commerce market in Singapore." *The Business Times*.

Lukic, R. (2012). "The effects of application of lean concept in retail." *Economia. Seria Management*, 15(1), pp. 88–98.

Mahatanankoon, P., Wen, H. J., and Lim, B. (2005). "Consumer-based m-commerce: Exploring consumer perception of mobile applications." *Computer Standards & Interfaces*, 27(4), pp. 347–357.

Manjur, R. (2014). "How mobile is contributing to showrooming." Available at: http://www.marketing-interactive.com/mobile-contributing-showrooming/ [Accessed on 14 December 2014].

Manley, M. (2012). *Store Closing: The Death of Brick and Mortar Retail — Work of the World*. Available at: http://workoftheworld.com/store-closing-the-death-of-brick-and-mortar-retail/ [Accessed 13 December 2016].

Mann, D. (2015). *Creating a Lean Culture: Tools to Sustain Lean Conversions*, Third Edition. CRC Press, Taylor and Francis Group, Boca Raton.

Manyika, J., Chui, M., Bughin, J., Dobbs, R., Bisson, P., and Marrs, A. (n.d.). Disruptive technologies: Advances that will transform life, business, and the global economy. Available at: http://www.mckinsey.com/business-functions/digital-mckinsey/our-insights/disruptive-technologies [Accessed 10 December 2016].

Mapletree Industrials (2012). MIT Express. Popular Food Businesses Chose Ka Foodlink as their *New Central Kitchen*. Available at: http://

www.mapletreeindustrialtrust.com/Customer-Solutions/Newsletter/
MIT%20Express%20-%20December%202012/Section-2.aspx.

Marzocchi, G.L. and Zammit, A. (2006). "Self-scanning technologies in retail: Determinants of adoption." *The Service Industries Journal*, 26(6), pp. 651–669.

MAS Monthly Statistical Bulletin — I.1 Money Supply (DBU) (2016). Secure.mas.gov.sg. Available at: https://secure.mas.gov.sg/msb-xml/Report.aspx?tableSetID=I&tableID=I.1 [Accessed 7 September 2016].

Mathieson, Kieren. (1991) "Predicting user intentions: Comparing the technology acceptance model with the theory of planned behavior." *Information Systems Review.* 2(3), pp. 173-191.

Matta, V. and Moberg, C. (2006) "The development of a research agenda for RFID adoption and effectiveness in supply chains." *Issues in Information Systems*, 7(2), pp. 246–251.

McClenahan (2005) "Wal-Mart's Big Gamble." *Industry Week*. Available at http://www.industryweek.com/companies-amp-executives/wal-marts-big-gamble [Accessed on 14 December 2016]

McDonald, M. (2012). *Market Segmentation: How to Do It and How to Profit from It.* Wiley, Hoboken, NJ.

McIlroy, A. and Barnett, S. (2000). "Building customer relationships: Do discount cards work?" *Managing Service Quality* , 10(6), pp. 347–355.

McKinsey & Company (2015). *Global Payments 2015: A Healthy Industry Confronts Disruption.*

McLaney, E.J. and Atrill, P. (2010). *Accounting: An Introduction.* Financial Times/Prentice Hall, New York.

Menon, R. (2016). *A Smart Financial Centre.* Mas.gov.sg. Available at: http://www.mas.gov.sg/news-and-publications/speeches-and-monetary-policy-statements/speeches/2015/a-smart-financial-centre.aspx [Accessed 7 September 2016].

Mesure, S. (2003). "Loyalty card costs tesco pounds 1b in profits — But is worth every penny." *The Independent*, pp. 24.

Meuter, M., Ostrom, A., Bitner, M., and Roundtree, R. (2003). "The influence of technology anxiety on consumer use and experiences with self-service technologies." *Journal of Business Research*, 56(11), pp. 899–906.

Meuter, M.L., Ostrom, A.L., Roundtree R.I., and Bitner M.J. (2000). "Self-service technologies: Understanding customer satisfaction with technology based service encounters." *American Marketing Association*, 64(3), pp. 50–64.

Meuter, M.L., Ostrom, A.L., Roundtree, R.I., and Bitner, M. (2000). "Self-service technologies: Understanding customer satisfaction with technology-based service encounters. *Journal of Marketing*, 64(3), pp. 50–64.

Michael, K. and McCathie, L. (2005) "The pros and cons of RFID in supply chain management." In *International Conference on Mobile Business, ICMB 2005*. IEEE, pp. 623–629.

Michel, S. (2001). "Analyzing service failures and recoveries: A process approach." *International Journal of Service Industry Management*, 12(1), pp. 20–33.

Mimouni-Chaabane, A. and Volle, P. (2010). "Perceived benefits of loyalty programs: Scale development and implications for relational strategies." *Journal of Business Research*, 63(1), pp. 32–37.

Min, C. Y. (2014). Big F&B Players Turn To Automation. *The Straits Times*. Available at: http://www.stjobs.sg/career-resources/others/big-fandb-players-turn-to-automation/a/152295.

Ministry of Manpower (2014). Manpower Resource Guide for Food & Beverage Industry.

Ministry of Manpower, Singapore (2014). "Labour force in Singapore, 2014: Employment table(s)." Available at: http://stats.mom.gov.sg/Pages/Labour-Force-in-Singapore-2014-Employment.aspx.

Ministry of Manpower. (2015). *Labour Market First Quarter: 2015*. Manpower Research and Statistics Department, Singapore.

Ministry of Manpower. (n.d.). Additional Measures to Moderate Demand for Foreign Manpower. Available at: http://www.mom.gov.sg/~/media/mom/documents/announcements/faq-measures-to-moderate-demand.pdf?la=en.

Ministry of National Development, Singapore (2014). *Opening Remarks by SMS Lee at the Launch of NTU Additive Manufacturing Centre*. Available at: http://app. mnd.gov.sg/Newsroom/NewsPage.aspx?ID=5359&category=Speech [Accessed 28 July 2015].

Ministry of Trade and Industry (2014) "Drivers of labour productivity growth trends in Singapore". Available at: http://www.mti.gov.sg/ResearchRoom/SiteAssets/Pages/Economic-Survey-of-Singapore-2014/FA_AES2014.pdf [Accessed on 3 August 2015].

Ministry of Trade and Industry (2015). Economics Review Committee: Subcommittee on Domestic Enterprises.

Ministry of Trade and Industry (n.d.). Food and Beverage Work Group Report (Singapore). Available at: https://www.mti.gov.sg/researchroom/

documents/app. mti.gov.sg/data/pages/507/doc/erc_dom_mainreport_part%203.3a.pdf.

Ministry of Trade and Industry, Singapore (2014). *Economic Survey of Singapore Second Quarter 2014*. Available at: http://www.mti.gov.sg/ResearchRoom/SiteAssets/Pages/Economic-Survey-of-Singapore-Second-Quarter-2014/BA_2Q14.pdf.

MIT Technology Review (2014). *How to Build 3-D Printing*. Available at: http://www.technologyreview.com/news/530721/how-to-build-3-d-printing/ [Accessed 13 July 2015].

Moriarty, R. T. and Moran, U. (1990). "Managing hybrid marketing systems." *Harvard Business Review*. Available at: https://hbr.org/1990/11/managing-hybrid-marketing-systems [Accessed on 13 December 2015].

Morris, M.G. and Venkatesh, V. (2000) "Age differences in technology adoption decisions: Implications for a changing workforce." *Personnel Psychology*, 53, pp. 375–403.

Mort, G. S. and Drennan, J. (2005). "Marketing M-services: Establishing a usage benefit typology related to mobile user characteristics." *The Journal of Database Marketing & Customer Strategy Management*, 12(4), pp. 327–341.

Mukherjee, P. N. (2010). *Total Quality Management*. PHI Learning, New Delhi.

Murphy, S. (2007). "Kiosks 411." *Chain Store Age*, 83(1), p. 68.

Nakata, C. and Zhu, Z. (2003). "Self-service technology failure: Understanding the customer perspective." Power-point Presentation. February 14, 2003. Available at: http://www.uic.edu/cba/crim/CrimNewsFiles/Colloquia/.

Narsing, A. (2011). "RFID and supply chain management: An assessment of its economic, technical, and productive viability in global operations." *Journal of Applied Business Research (JABR)*, 21(2). pp. 75–80.

Natalie, J.S. and Williams, B. (2010). *Lean For Dummies*. Wiley, Hoboken, NJ.

National Productivity Council (2015). Supermarket retailer adopts manpower-saving solutions to improve efficiency and raise productivity.

NCS (2014). "Solutions for Urbanised Future Volume 2". Available at: http://www.ncs.com.sg/c/document_library/get_file?p_l_id=14001&folderId=649059&name=DLFE-10901.pdf [Available at 27 August 2015].

New York Magazine (2013). "Uniqlons." Available at: http://nymag.com/fashion/features/65898/index1.html [Accessed on 14 December 2016].

Ngai, E. W. and Gunasekaran, A. (2009). "RFID adoption: issues and challenges." *International journal of enterprise information systems*, 5(1), pp. 1.

No More Shouts of 'Bill, Please' as F&B Outlets Go Cashless (2016). *TODAYonline.* Available at: http://www.todayonline.com/business/no-more-shouts-bill-please-fb-outlets-go-cashless [Accessed 10 September 2016].

Noordhoff, C., Pauwels, P., and Odekerken-Schröder. (2004). "The effect of customer card programs: A comparative study in Singapore and The Netherlands." *International Journal of Service Industry Management,* 15(4), pp. 351–364.

Noren, E. (2013). *The Non-Traditional Retail Business Model.* Available at: http://www.digitalbusinessmodelguru.com/ [Accessed on 13 December 2015].

NTUC (2015). NTUC Social Enterprises. Available at: NTUC: http://www.ntuc.org.sg/wps/portal/up2/home/aboutntuc/organisationdirectory/ntucsocialenterprises/!ut/p/a1/jZLRboIwFIZfRS-43DiFQuGSI ApuCgpO5YaUUkwTBQNoMp9-xW3JFjNn707zna__yamaqhs1re-hZ7Ggn6oru-zo1MyPSA2_sawDGyINgZs0NY_oaYR0ksJUA_HEc-K9_raa_kXC1QBCYpvNi-SECG.

Nunes, J. C. and Dréze, X. (2006). "Your loyalty program is betraying you." *Harvard Business Review,* 84(4), pp. 124–131.

Oakland, J.S. (2014). *Total Quality Management and Operational Excellence: Text with Cases.* Routledge, New York.

Octopus (2016). *Company Profile,* 1st edition. Available at: http://www.octopus.com.hk/web09_include/_document/en/company_profile.pdf.

One Maker Group (xxxx). *The prototyping-Lab.* Available at: http://onemakergroup.sg/the-prototyping-lab/ [Accessed 28 July 2015].

Ong, L.I. (2010). "Can self-service technologies work in the hotel industry in Singapore? A conceptual framework for adopting self service technology." UNLV Theses, Dissertations, Professional Papers, and Capstone. Available at: http://digitalscholarship.unlv.edu/cgi/viewcontent.cgi?article=1695&context=thesesdissertations [Accessed on 9 December].

Online retailers and festive season hiccups — IT-Online (2014). Available at: http://it-online.co.za/2014/12/05/online-retailers-festive-season-hiccups/ [Accessed on 12 December 2014].

Overseas-Chinese Banking Corporation Limited, OCBC Bank (2015). "The first loan to give your business a head-start." *Business First Loan.* Available at: http://www.ocbc.com.sg/business-banking/loans/micro-loan.html.

Paul, D., Thomas, P., and Cadle, J. (2012). *The Human Touch: Personal Skills for Professional Success.*British Computer Society, London.

Paypal (2011). *Online and Mobile Shopping Insights* (Rep.).

Perx (2015). Perx-Mobile Loyalty Cards. Available at: Google Play Store: https://play.google.com/store/apps/details?id=com.getperx.perx&hl=en.

Planet Retail (2015). Automated Cash Handling, 2015. Available at: https://www.planetretail.net/Reports/ReportDetails?catalogueID=61442.

Plus!, N (2015). NTUC Mission and Vision. Available at: NTUC Plus!: http://plus.com.sg/vision-mission.

Plus!, N (2015). Plus Card. Available at: Plus!: https://plus.com.sg/plus-cards/plus.

Plus!, N (2015). Plus! Visa Credit Card. Available at: NTUC Plus!: http://plus.com.sg/pluscards/plusvisa-credit.

Plus!, N (2015). Promotions. Available at: Plus!: https://plus.com.sg/whatsnew/walk-style-everbest.

Plus!, N (2015). uBid Bid Period. Available at: NTUC Plus!: http://plus.com.sg/may-2015/bid-period.

Poket (2015). Available at: http://poket.com/.

3D Print.com (2014). *3D Printhuset to Open Denmark's Largest Printing Store in Downtown Copenhagen.* Available at: http://3dprint.com/16326/3d-printhuset-denmark/ [Accessed 18 May 2015].

3D Printing Industry (2014). *MakerBot 3D Printers Make Their Way into 50 Staples Store.* Available at: http://3dprintingindustry.com/2014/11/25/makerbot-3d-printers-50-staples-stores/ [Accessed 18 May 2015].

3D Printing Industry (2014). *One Year On and ITALYmaker Is Making Milan's Future.* Available at: http://3dprintingindustry.com/2014/12/10/italy-maker-3d-printing-milan/ [Accessed 18 May 2015].

3D Printing Industry (2015). *Amazon Sets Out to Conquer Entire 3D printing Industry with New Patent Application.* Available at: http://3dprintingindustry.com/2015/02/25/amazon-sets-out-to-conquer-entire-3d-printing-industry-with-new-patent-application/ [Accessed 18 May 2015].

3D Printing Industry (2015). *Argos Takes 3D Printed Designer Jewelry to the Masses.* Available at: http://3dprintingindustry.com/2015/03/18/argos-digital-forming-taking-3d-printed-designer-jewelry-masses/ [Accessed 18 May 2015].

3D Printing Industry (n.d.). 3D Printing History: *The Free Beginner's Guide — 3D Printing Industry.* Available at: http://3dprintingindustry.com/3d-printing-basics-free-beginners-guide/history/ [Accessed 13 July 2015].

Productivity-led Growth is Key to Sustaining Business Competitiveness (2013). *MTI Singapore*. Available at: https://www.mti.gov.sg/NewsRoom/Pages/Productivity-led-Growth-is-Key-to-Sustaining-Business-Competitiveness.aspx.

Protek (n.d.). Dishwashing Machines Catalogue. *Protek Dishwashing Machines*. Protek, Singapore.

Quinn, B., Cooke, R., and Kris, A. (2000). *Shared Services: Mining for Corporate Gold*. Financial Times Prentice Hall, Harlow, England.

Quirk, R.E. and Borrello, S.J., (2005) "RFID: Rapid deployment and regulatory challenges." *Venable LLP White Paper*. Available at: /www.venable.com/ publications.cfmS.

Räisänen, R. (2013). Agility in International Fast Fashion Retailing. Turku School of Economics (Master's Thesis).

Raza, N., Bradshaw, V., and Hague, M. (1999) "Applications of RFID technology." *IEE Colloquium on RFID Technology*, pp. 1–5.

Redman, T., Snape, E., Wass, J., and Hamilton, P. (2007). Evaluating the Human Resource Shared Services Model: Evidence from the NHS. *International Journal of Human Resource Management*, 18, pp. 1486–1506.

Reed, C. (2012). Is there any loyalty in Singapore? *Singapore Business Review*. Available at: http://sbr.com.sg/financial-services/commentary/there-any-loyalty-in-singapore.

Reinartz, W., Dellaert, B., Krafft, M., Kumar, V., and Varadarajan, R. (2011). "Retailing innovations in a globalizing retail market environment." *Journal of Retailing*, 87(S1), pp. S53–S66.

Retail Cash Management — Supermarkets (2016). Cashguard.com. Available at: http://www.cashguard.com/Improve-your-business/Retail-Cash-Management/Supermarkets/ [Accessed 7 September 2016].

Retail Systems (2005). "In the fast lane." Available at: the Factiva database.

RFID Solutions (n.d.). Available at: http://www.impinj.com/resources/about-rfid/how-do-rfid-systems-work/ [Accessed on 9 December 2016].

Richman, A., Johnson, A., and Buxbaum, L. (2006). *Workplace Flexibility for Low Wage Workers*. Available at: http://www.cvworkingfamilies.org/system/files/lowerwageflexreviewreport.pdf.

Rick, O. (2015). *How Apple killed the digital wallet*. Available at: http://www.mobilepaymentstoday.com/blogs/how-apple-killed-the-digital-wallet/ [Accessed on 9 January 2015].

Rigby, D. (2011). "The future of shopping." *Harvard Business Review*, 89(12), pp. 65–76.

Roberti, M. (2003). "RFID (radio frequency identification) technology news & features". *RFID Journal*. Available at: https://www.rfidjournal.com/purchase-access?type=Article&id=1792&r=/articles/view?1792 [Accessed on 3 August 2015].

Roberti, M., 2003. RFID: the cost of being smart. *CIO Insight 1 (30)*, September 1. Available at: /www.cioinsight.com/previous/issues_/S.

Rogers, E.M. (1962). *Diffusion of Innovations*. The Free Press, New York.

Roman, D. and Chanjaroen, C. (2016). *Singapore Wants to Be Asia's Sweden in Push for Cashless Payment — Bloomberg*. Bloomberg.com. Available at: http://www.bloomberg.com/news/articles/2016-08-19/singapore-wants-to-be-asia-s-sweden-in-push-for-cashless-payment [Accessed 7 September 2016].

Ross, K. (2013). "Lean is even more important in services than manufacturing." Available at http://www.industryweek.com/blog/lean-even-more-important-services-manufacturing [Accessed 14 December 2016].

Rothberg, H.J. (1967). "Job redesign for older workers: Case studies." *Monthly Labor Review*, 90(1), pp. 47–51. Available at: http://www.jstor.org.libproxy1.nus.edu.sg/stable/41836648.

Rother, M. and Shook, J. (2007). *Learning to See: Value Stream Mapping to Add Value and Eliminate Muda*. Lean Enterprise Institute, Brookline, MA.

Route to productivity Paradise (2012). *Asiaone News*. Available at: http://news.asiaone.com/News/Latest+News/Singapore/Story/A1Story20120229-330849.html.

Rowley, J. (2005). "Building brand webs Customer relationship management through the Tesco Clubcard loyalty scheme." *International Journal of Retail & Distribution Management*, 33(3), pp. 194–206.

Rowley, J. (2007). "Reconceptualising the strategic role of loyalty schemes." *Journal of Consumer Marketing*, 246), pp. 366–374.

Russell, R. and Taylor, B. (2006). *Competitiveness, Strategy and Productivity*. John Wiley & Sons.

Sabry, H. (2010). "Six rules for an effective Kanban system." Available at: http://www.processexcellencenetwork.com/lean-six-sigma-business-transformation/articles/what-is-kanban [Accessed on 14 December 2016]

Sainsbury Centre for Mental Health (2007). "Mental health at work: Developing the business case." Policy paper 8. Sainsbury Centre for Mental Health, London.

Sakae Holdings (2013). *Milestones.* Sakae Holdings. Available at: http://www.sakaeholdings.com/milestones.html.

Scandura, T.A. and Lankau, M.J. (1997). "Relationships of gender, family responsibility and flexible work hours to organizational commitment and job satisfaction." *Journal of Organisational Behavior,* 18, pp. 377–391. Available at: http://www.researchgate.net/publication/229646291_Relationships_of_gender_family_responsibility_and_flexible_work_hours_to_organizational_commitment_and_job_satisfaction.

Schulman, D.S., Dunleavy, J.R., Harmer, M.J., and Lusk, J.S. (1999). *Shared Services, Adding Value to Business Units.* Wiley, Toronto.

Sedera, D. and Dey, S. (2007). Everyone is different! exploring the issues and problems with ERP enabled shared service initiatives. *Proceedings Americas Conference on Information Systems 2007,* KeyStone, Colarado.

Seideman, T. (2003). "The race for RFID." *The Journal of Commerce,* 4(48), pp. 16–18.

Select Group (2010). *Select Group Milestone/History.* Available at: http://select.com.sg/selectgroup/milestone.htm.

Selection of Variables/Time Period (2016). Tablebuilder.singstat.gov.sg. Available at: http://www.tablebuilder.singstat.gov.sg/publicfacing/createDataTable.action?refId=1907 [Accessed 9 September 2016].

Seng, L. C. (xxxx). Study on the Adoption Rate of RFID Technology in Warehouse in JB.

Sephora (2015). The Sephora Card Program. Available at: Sephora: http://loyalty.sephora-sea.com/sea_avantage.

Shah, B. (1998). "Shared Services, is it for you?" *Industrial Management September/October,* 40(5), pp. 4–9.

Sharp, B. and Sharp, A. (1997). "Loyalty programs and their impact on repeat-purchase loyalty patterns." *International Journal of Research in Marketing,* 14(5), pp. 473–486.

Sheng Siong (2015). Sheng Siong FAQ. Available at: Sheng Siong: http://www.shengsiong.com.sg/pages/FAQ.html.

Sheth, J. N. and Sisodia, R. S. (1998). "Marketing productivity: Issues and analysis." *Journal of Business Research,* 55, pp. 349–362.

Shih, D. H., Chiu, Y. W., Chang, S. I., and Yen, D. C. (2009). "An empirical study of factors affecting RFID's adoption in Taiwan." *Technological Advancement in Developed and Developing Countries: Discoveries in Global Information Management: Discoveries in Global Information Management.* 16(2), p. 58.

Siau, K., Lim, E. P., and Shen, Z. (2001). "Mobile commerce: Promises, challenges and research agenda." *Journal of Database Management* (JDM), 12(3), 4–13.

Singapore Business Federation (2016). *SME Committee: Recommendations for Budget 2016*. Available at: https://www.sbf.org.sg/images/pdf/2016/ SME_Committee_Budget_2016_Recommendations.pdf.

Singapore Press Holdings Ltd. (2014). "SMEs remake themselves amid cost pressures." *The Business Times*. Available at: http://www.businesstimes. com.sg/sme/smes-remake-themselves-amid-cost-pressures-0.

Singapore Wants to Be Asia's Sweden in Push for Cashless Payment (2016). Bloomberg.com. Available at: http://www.bloomberg.com/news/ articles/2016-08-19/singapore-wants-to-be-asia-s-sweden-in-push-for-cashless-payment [Accessed 10 September 2016].

Singapore Workforce Development Agency (2013). "Update in definition of SMEs applicable to eligibility for enhanced training support for SMEs scheme and follow-up action by companies." Available at: https://www.skillsconnect.gov.sg/web/guest/update_SME_definition.

Singh, M. (2013). "Retailers, F&B bosses fearing the worst in foreign-worker curbs." Available at: http://news.asiaone.com/print/News/ AsiaOne+News/Business/Story/A1Story20130227-404988.html [Accessed on 3 August 2015].

Singh, N. (2003). "Emerging technologies to support supply chain management." *Communications of the ACM*, 46(9), pp. 243–247.

Singh, V. (2015). Singapore's Productivity Drive: Entering the Second Half. Available at http://www.britcham.org.sg/static-pages/o48-feature-singa-pores-productivity-drive-entering-second-half [Accessed on 3 August 2015].

Smith, R. and Swinjard, W. (1983). "Attitude behavior consistency: The impact of product trial versus advertising." *Journal of Marketing Research*, 20(3), pp. 257–267.

SMU (2010). "Lean thinking: A case for 'rubber band' organizations." Available at: https://www.smu.edu.sg/perspectives/2012/06/26/lean-thinking-case-rubber-band-organisations [Accessed on 14 December 2016].

Social Enterprise (n.d.). Hong Chi Association. Available at: http://www. hongchi.org.hk/en_service_adult.asp?id=9.

SPRING (2011). *Singapore Food Services Productivity Improvement Plans*. SPRING news.

SPRING (2015). *F&B Capability Solution*. SPRING Singapore. Available at: http://www.spring.gov.sg/Developing-Industries/FBS/FBS-programmes/ Pages/f-b-productivity-capability-solutions.aspx.

Spring Singapore (2014). "Developing industries." Available at: http:// www.spring.gov.sg/Developing-Industries/Pages/developing-indus- tries-overview.aspx.

Spring Singapore (2014). "Fact sheet in new SME definition." Available at: http://www.spring.gov.sg/NewsEvents/PR/Documents/Fact_Sheet_ on_New_SME_Definition.pdf.

Stanoevska-Slabeva, K. (2003). "Towards a reference model for m-com- merce applications." In *ECIS 2002 Proceedings*, Paper 159.

Statistics Canada (2005). "Table 3.2: Use of innovative work practices, 2005." *Workplace and Employee Survey Compendium*. Available at: http:// www.statcan.gc.ca/pub/71-585-x/2008001/table/table3p2-eng.htm.

Statistics Canada (2005). "Table 3.3: High-performance work practices and workplace performance, 2005." *Workplace and Employee Survey Compendium*. Available at: http://www.statcan.gc.ca/pub/71-585-x/ 2008001/table/table3p3-eng.htm.

Stauss, B., Schmidt, M., and Schoeler, A. (2005). "Customer frustration in loyalty programs." *International Journal of Service Industry Management*, 16(3), 229–252.

Stevenson, T. H., Barnes, F. C., and Stevenson, S. A. (1993). "Activity-based costing: An emerging tool for industrial marketing decision makers." *Journal of Business & Industrial Marketing*, 8(2), pp. 40–52.

Stevenson, W. J. (2012). *Operations Management*. McGraw-Hill/Irwin, New York.

Stone, M., Bearman, D., Butscher, S. A., Gilbert, D., and Crick, P. (2003). The Effect of retail customer loyalty schemes-detailed measurement or transforming marketing?" *Journal of Targeting, Measurement & Analysis for Marketing*, 12(3), pp. 305–318.

Strueker, J. and Gille, D. (2008). The SME Way of Adopting RFID Technology: Empirical Findings from a German Cross-Sectoral Study. In *ECIS*, pp. 1094–1105.

Swank, C. K. (2003). "The lean service machine." *Harvard Business Review*, 81, pp. 123–129.

Taggo.me (2015). How it Works. Available at: Taggo.me: http://taggo.me/ help/#demo.

Tajima, M. (2007). "Strategic value of RFID in supply chain management." *Journal of purchasing and Supply Management*, 13(4), pp. 261–273.

TapForMore (2015). TapForMore. Available at: https://tapformore.com.sg/.

TechinAsia (2013). *Tech in Asia — Connecting Asia's startup ecosystem*. Available at: https://www.techinasia.com/2014-breakout-year-mobile- commerce-southeast-asia [Accessed on 13 December 2016].

Tensator (2013). "Tensator survey reveals shoppers self-service frustration." Available at: http://blog.tensator.com/uk/post/2013/10/15/Tensator-survey-reveals-shoppers-self-service- frustration.aspx.

Teo, C. (2010). Available at: Entree Kibbles: http://cavinteo.blogspot.sg/2010/04/men-ichi-kyoto-ramen-since-my-last.html.

Teo, E. (2012). "Business feeling the pinch from rising rents." *The Straits Times.* Available at: http://www.stproperty.sg/articles-property/singapore-property-news/businesses-feeling-the-pinch-from-rising-rents/a/48494 [Accessed on 19 July].

Tepsich, C. (2010). "Process improvements in after sales quality management — Lean principles implementation in a service context." Politecnico di Milano, Master's Thesis.

Teresko, J. (2003), "Winning with wireless". *Industry Week*, 252(6), pp. 60–66. [Accessed on 12 October 2004].

Tetteh, E.G. and Uzochukwu, B.M. (2015). *Lean Six Sigma Approaches in Manufacturing, Services, and Production.* Business Science Reference, an imprint of IGI Global, Hershey.

Thangavelu, S. M., Toh, M. H., and Woon, K. C. (n.d.). Analysis of Singapore's productivity performance and proposal for 8M framework to raise productivity growth in the retail and F&B sectors.

The Business Times (2011). *Jack's Recipe for Success: Value, Quality and Service.*

The Business Times (2013). "Addressing the F&B manpower crunch." Available at: http://www.stjobs.sg/career-resources/hr-updates/addressing-the-fandb-manpower-crunch/a/116469 [Accessed 31 July 2014].

The Next Web (2014). *Survey Shows 60% Of Chinese Online Shoppers Made Purchases On Mobile.* Available at: http://thenextweb.com/asia/2014/02/26/mastercard-survey-finds-that-nearly-60-of-chinese-online-shoppers-made-purchases-via-smartphones/ [Accessed on 13 December 2016].

The Standards, Productivity and Innovation Board Singapore (2014). "Industry background and statistics." Available at: http://www.spring.gov.sg/Industry/FBS/Pages/industry-background-statistics.aspx [Accessed on 19 July 2014].

Thiesse, F., Staake, T., Schmitt, P., and Fleisch, E. (2011). "The rise of the "next-generation bar code": An international RFID adoption study." *Supply Chain Management: An International Journal*, 16(5), pp. 328–345.

Thom, I. (2006). "Challenges in today's U.S. supermarket industry." *Microsoft Retail and Hospitality*, 2.

Thomas, M. J. (1984). "The meaning of marketing productivity analysis." *Marketing Intelligence & Planning*, 2(2), pp. 13–28.

Thor, S. (2013). "The evolution of quality management: Tracing historical influences of lean six sigma." Available at: http://www.scottthor. com/wp-content/uploads/2013/05/The-Evolution-of-Quality-Management-Tracing-Historical-Influences-of-Lean-Six-Sigma-Scott-Thor.pdf.

Thrasher, J. (2013). Active RFID vs. Passive RFID: What's the Difference? Available at: http://blog.atlasrfidstore.com/active-rfid-vs-passive-rfid [Accessed on 3 August 2015].

Tidel Engineering L.P. (2016). *Enhancing Profitability Through a Cash Management System*. Available at: https://www.tidel.com/pdf/whitepapers/EnhancingProfitabilityThroughaCashManagementSolution.pdf.

Today (2015). 36% jump in workers undergoing training at e2i. Available at: http://www.channelnewsasia.com/news/singapore/36-jump-in-workers/1955190.html [Accessed on 3 August 2015].

Today Online (2014). Teaming Up for Productivity. *Today Online*. Available at: http://m.todayonline.com/business/teaming-productivity.

Today Online, Singapore (2014). *Shape your imagination: Singapore warms up to 3D printing*. Available at: http://www.todayonline.com/business/shape-your-imagination-singapore-warms-3d-printing [Accessed 3 July 2015].

Toh, C. Y. (2013). Robo-cooks take some heat off kitchen staff crunch at TungLok. *The Straits Times*. Available at: http://www.straitstimes.com/singapore/robo-cooks-take-some-heat-off-kitchen-staff-crunch-at-tunglok?page=4.

Toh, M. H. and Thangavelu, S. (2014). *Construction and Measurement of Productivity Performance Based on 8Ms — Application to Retail and F&B Sectors*.

Toh, M. H. and Thangavelu, S. (2017). *Productivity in Retail and Food Services Sectors: Contemporary Issues*. World Scientific Publishing, Singapore.

U.S. Bureau of Labor Statistics (2012). *Current Population Survey, 2012*. Available at: http://www.bls.gov/cps/cpsaat18b.htm.

U.S. Global Development Lab (2016). *Making the Journey from Cash to Electronic Payments: A Toolkit for USAID Implementing Partners and Development Organizations*. Presentation.

University of California, Santa Cruz (2015). "ITS service management: Key elements." Available at: http://its.ucsc.edu/itsm/servicemgmt.html [Accessed on 14 December 2016].

Van Baal, S. and Dach, C. (2005). "Free riding and customer retention across retailers' channels." *Journal of Interactive Marketing*, 19(2), pp. 75–85.

Varshney, U. and Vetter, R. (2002). "Mobile commerce: framework, applications and networking support." *Mobile networks and Applications*, 7(3), pp. 185–198.

Veijalainen, J., Terziyan, V., and Tirri, H. (2006). "Transaction management for m-commerce at a mobile terminal." *Electronic Commerce Research and Applications*, 5(3), pp. 229–245.

Velasquez, I. (2014). *Mobile Retail is Asia's Hottest Business Trend — TechView Asia*. Available at: http://www.techviewasia.com/mobile-retails-asias-hottest-business-trend [Accessed on 14 December 2014].

Vijayan, J. and Brewin, B. (2003). "Wal-Mart Backs RFID technology." Available at: http://www.computerworld.com/article/2570642/enterprise-resource-planning/wal-mart-backs-rfid-technology.html. [Accessed 14 December 2016].

Vowels, S. A. (2006). "A strategic case for RFID: An examination of Wal-Mart and its supply chain." In *Proceedings of the 2006 Southern Association for Information Systems Conference*, pp. 148–152.

Wall Street Journal (2009). "Latest Starbucks buzzword: Lean." Available at: http://search.proquest.com.libproxy1.nus.edu.sg/docview/399122722?pq-origsite=summon [Accessed on 14 December 2016].

Wallace (2011). "The value of shared services." *Healthcare Financial Management*, 65(7), pp. 58–62.

Walsh, P. and McGregor-Lowndes, M., and Newton, C. (2006). Shared Services: Lessons from the Public and Private Sectors for the Nonprofit Sector. *CPNS Working Paper No 34*. QLD, Brisbane.

Wang, Y. M., Wang, Y. S., and Yang, Y. F. (2010). Understanding the determinants of RFID adoption in the manufacturing industry. *Technological Forecasting and Social Change*, 77(5), pp. 803–815.

Wansink, B. (2003). "Developing a cost-effective brand loyalty program." *Journal of Advertising Research*, 43(3), pp. 301–309.

Weizhen, T. (2014). Old brands, new strategies. *Today Online*. Available at: http://www.todayonline.com/singapore/old-brands-new-strategies.

Wing Tai Retail (2015). Wing Tai Retail. Available at: https://wingtairetail.com.sg/.

Womack and Jones, D.T. (2005). *Lean Solutions: How companies and customers can create wealth together*. Simon & Schuster, London.

Womack, J. P. and Jones, D. T. (1996). *Lean Thinking: Banish Waste and Create Wealth in Your Corporation*. Simon & Schuster, New York.

WorldatWork (2013). *Survey on Workplace Flexibility 2013*. Available at: http://www.worldatwork.org/adimLink?id=73898.

Worthington, S. and Fear, J. (2009). "The hidden side of loyalty card programs." *The Australian Centre For Retail Studies*.

Wu, N. C., Nystrom, M. A., Lin, T. R., and Yu, H. C. (2006). "Challenges to global RFID adoption." *Technovation*, 26(12), pp. 1317–1323.

Xue, J.Y. (2014). "Consumer attitudes towards self-service take time to change." *Today Newspaper*. Availbale at: http://www.todayonline.com/singapore/consumer-attitudes-towards-self-service-take-time-change [Accessed on 9 December].

Yi, Y. and Jeon, H. (2003). "Effects of loyalty programs on value perception, program loyalty, and brand loyalty." *Journal of the Academy of Marketing Science*, 31(3), 229–240.

Yin, R. (1994). *Case Study Research*. Thousand Oaks, CA, Sage.

Zaleski, A. (2015). MakerBot lays off 20% of its staff—again. *Fortune*. Available at: http://fortune.com/2015/10/08/makerbot-lays-off-20-percent-of-staff-again/ [Accessed 11 December 2016].

Zebra Technologies (2004). Zebra's RFID Readiness Guide: Complying with RFID Tagging Mandates, p. 3.

八達通買餸你 *buy* 唔 *buy*. (2012). *Apple Daily* 蘋果日報. Available at: http://hk.apple.nextmedia.com/news/art/20120103/15947517 [Accessed 7 September 2016].

專家批八達通發展落後. (2016). *Paper.wenweipo.com*. Available at: http://paper.wenweipo.com/2016/05/23/FI1605230023.htm [Accessed on 7 September 2016].

雲籌網略: 八達通見證香港大停滯. (2015). *Apple Daily* 蘋果日報. Available at: http://hk.apple.nextmedia.com/financeestate/art/20150531/19166314 [Accessed 7 September 2016].

Printed in the United States
By Bookmasters

Printed in the United States
By Bookmasters